A Concise Encyclopedia of

WILD FLOWERS

A Concise Encyclopedia of
WILD FLOWERS

Illustrated by

JOHN E. SOWERBY

*with an introduction, descriptive text and key to
the natural orders by*
C. PIERPOINT JOHNSON

Wordsworth Editions

This edition published 1989 by Wordsworth Editions Ltd,
8b East Street, Ware, Hertfordshire.

Copyright © Wordsworth Editions Ltd 1989.

ISBN 1-85326-924-7

Printed and bound in Spain by Gráficas Estella SA.

INTRODUCTION.

It is not the object of the present work to teach the science of Botany, or even to furnish a treatise upon the natural history and classification of the flowering plants of the British Islands. The first, like all other branches of natural knowledge, is an abstruse and complicated study, to which there is no 'royal road,' and the pursuit of which, however pleasing, involves the diligent perusal of many volumes, with close and unremitting attention to that Great One whose pages lie ever open before us: the last, though a less comprehensive subject, would demand far more space for its elucidation than can be accorded to it here. Intended merely as a volume of reference for the field-botanist, the country resident or summer rambler, when works of more pretension are not at hand, our book can comprise little more descriptive matter than is absolutely necessary, with the assistance of the plates, to identify each plant. Those who are desirous of acquiring an intimate knowledge of the structure and affinities of the vegetable kingdom we must refer to the compendious treatises of Lindley, Balfour and others; while the student of the British Flora will find detailed descriptions of each species, and most of the information that has been accumulated on the subject, in the 'English Botany' and other works to which references are given. But as this book may probably fall into the hands of many who, while they have no previous acquaintance with botanical science and little leisure or inclination for its study, are yet desirous of learning the names of the flowers they meet with in their walks, it may be advisable to add a few lines explanatory of the general structure of flowering plants, which, with the Glossary of terms, will probably enable any educated person, however unscientific, to understand the descriptions given in the body of the work.

The vegetable kingdom is naturally divided into two great sections, the plants of which, while exhibiting for the most part considerable differences in internal structure, are more remarkably distinguished by the mode in which they propagate their kind. Those of one division possess no distinct flowers or seeds in which the germ of the future plant is enveloped, but multiply by means of minute cellular bodies called spores. Those of the other have distinct floral organs and produce seeds properly so called. The former section, called by botanists Cryptogamia, includes Ferns, Mosses, Lichens, Seaweeds and Fungi, with some other vegetables not comprised under these designations; the latter, the Phanerogamia or Flowering Plants, to the British species of which our present book alone refers.

A plant, in this, its more highly developed form, usually consists of four distinct parts, which, while they are all modifications of the same organic type, consisting of cells and vessels variously arranged, have yet very different offices assigned them in the œconomy of Nature. They are the root, stem, leaves, and flower.

The *root* is the organ by which the plant absorbs nutriment from the soil; it generally consists of a number of branches, whence various small fibres spring and penetrate into the surrounding earth in search of the nourishment, principally absorbed by their tender extremities. Where this form prevails, the root is said to be *fibrous*. In some cases, however, the vessels of the root form a thickened mass, from which the absorbent fibres diverge, and to which various names are given according to its shape and proportions; the most common varieties being the *tap-root*, where it descends in a tapering form into the ground, as in the Radish and Parsnip, and the *tuber*, in which it forms several more or less irregular, rounded masses, as in the Orchis and Potato. In the latter vegetable, however, the tuber is considered by botanists to be a modification of the stem, and not a root in the strict sense of the word. The same is the case with the leafy *bulbs* of the Lily and Onion, and the *corm* or solid bulb of the Crocus, and some other subterranean portions of plants to which the name of root is applied in common language. In this work the word is used in its popular meaning.

The *stem* is that portion of the plant which, rising from the root, supports the leaves and flowers. In some plants it is wanting, being represented only by the thickened rim or apex of the root from which the leaves and flower-stalks proceed, as in the Dandelion; in other instances it creeps along the ground, as in the Iris, when it is called a *rhizome*. The stem is in all cases formed of the vessels that descend from the leaves and flowers to the root, and in which the sap circulates, and the various juices and secretions of the plant are elaborated. In some plants it dies down every year, fresh stems rising to supply its place the following season; the plant is then termed *herbaceous*. In other vegetables it becomes a permanent portion of the plant, the leaf-buds continuing to send down their fibres through it as long as growth lasts, and thus producing the substance we call wood; the plant is then a tree or shrub. Whether the stem be herbaceous or permanent, the buds which produce the leaves and branches are formed at certain points on its surface called *nodes*, where a change of direction takes place in the fibres; the space between being termed an *internode* or *joint*.

The manner in which the fibres descend from the buds through the stem differs in different classes of vegetables, and two of these modes require a short notice, as a most important division of the flowering plants is partly founded upon them. If we examine the stem of a Palm when cut transversely, we shall find it presents a dotted appearance, as in Fig. 1,[*] the dots being sections of the vessels descending from the leaves, in their way to the root. There is no distinct bark, the stem being covered by a mere rind or cuticle; and the wood itself is the same throughout, the fibres being only rather closer together towards the outer portion. Stems of this class are called *endogenous*, or inward-growing. If we take a section of the branch of an Oak, or any of our forest trees, we find a very different arrangement. The wood presents a series of concentric circles surrounding a central column of pith, from which numerous rays diverge towards the bark, as in Fig. 2. In stems of this kind the fibres or bud-rootlets descend each year on the outside of the previously formed wood, between the latter and the bark, and thus each circle represents the annual growth of the stem. The bark is distinct and highly organized, consisting of an inner portion, formed of vessels descending from the leaves and carrying off their secretions, and an outer mass made up of the growth of previous years, filled up with cellular tissue. Stems presenting this aspect are termed *exogenous*, or outward-growing. These forms characterize the two great families or classes into which the flowering plants are divided, named from the circumstance Endogens and Exogens. The endogenous plants of this country have nearly all annual stems, and most of the exogenous ones being likewise herbaceous, it is not always easy for the unpractised observer to distinguish the difference in their internal structure; but there are other peculiarities by which they are more readily recognized, as will be presently noticed.

The *leaves* are the breathing organs of the plant, and, like the lungs of an animal, they are formed of a number of vessels

The figure nos. here refer to the illustrations on page xlx, following the Table of Genera.

ramifying in every direction, by which the sap is brought into contact with the air. These vessels are arranged in two sets; the upper one, in exogenous plants, communicating with the vessels of the wood, and the lower with those of the bark. The nutriment taken up by the root passes through the upper series to the upper surface of the leaves, and after undergoing the necessary chemical changes, returns by the lower through the bark to the root, depositing various secretions by the way. The spaces between the vessels are filled up with cellular matter, in which numerous minute pores establish communication between the fluid in the vessels and the air; they are chiefly on the under surface in most plants.

In exogenous plants the principal fibres or veins of the leaf branch off from a central vein or midrib, distributing themselves in numerous net-like ramifications over the whole leaf, as in Fig. 3. In plants with endogenous stems, on the other hand, they are usually arranged in a parallel series, diverging from the stalk and uniting again at the apex of the leaf, being connected during their course only by minute cross-veins at right angles to the others, as in Fig. 4. The leaves are generally supported on a stalk called a *petiole*, but are sometimes stalkless, or, to speak technically, *sessile*. At or near the base of the petiole two or more leaf-like appendages are often found, to which the name of *stipules* is given. The angle between the leaf and the stem is called the *axil*, and is the place where the bud of the ensuing growth is developed. In some few plants the buds drop off, and falling on the earth become bulbs, and thus propagate the plant, as in the Tiger Lily; a bulb is, in fact, only an underground bud.

Leaves are either *simple*, or composed of a number of leaflets arranged upon the same stalk, when they are styled *compound*. Simple leaves are either *entire*, or variously cut and divided; but their forms are far too numerous to admit of mention here, and for the explanation of the technical terms by which botanists have been compelled to distinguish the diversified figures of these important organs we must refer the reader to the Glossary. Leaves in the axils of which flower-buds are developed are called *bracts*; they are frequently of different form to the other leaves of the plant, and are sometimes *membranaceous* or scale-like.

The leaves of most woody plants in this country drop from the stem in the autumn, or are *deciduous*; and though the Holly, Pine, and some other trees and shrubs retain their old leaves until the new ones are formed in the ensuing spring, and are consequently *evergreen*, all our trees change their leaves at some period of the year.

Leaves are arranged in various ways upon the stem; but generally they are *alternate*, or situated singly at each node, on alternate sides of the stem, or in a spiral manner,—a mode of growth to which there appears to be a general tendency in plants, probably the result of the two movements of lateral and longitudinal growth proceeding at the same time at right angles to each other, in accordance with a well-known mechanical law. In many plants the leaves are *opposite*, or arranged in pairs on opposite sides of the stem; and in some they are in *whorls*, a number being situated in a circle round each node. The leaves of climbing plants are often furnished with elongated appendages called *tendrils*, by which they cling to the stems or other objects near them; the petioles in other cases twine in a similar manner, as in the Clematis of our hedges.

These organs are all employed in preserving the life of the vegetable and fulfilling the various functions of its existence. Their form and appearance are often of great importance in botanical classification, particularly in distinguishing species, but must be considered of secondary value, as regards systematic arrangement, to those organs of reproduction forming the most conspicuous feature of the flowering plants, and upon the characters of which the arrangement and classification of this portion of the vegetable kingdom chiefly depend.

A flower, in its most perfect form, consists of an outer envelope composed of several leaf-like divisions called the *calyx*, an inner series of similar leaves called the *corolla*, and a number of small bodies situated within these denominated *stamens* and *pistils*. The usual arrangement of these parts may be seen in Fig. 5. The outer series of leaves, forming the calyx, are termed *sepals*; they are usually green. The leaves of the inner series, or corolla, are called *petals*, and, being generally highly coloured, form the most conspicuous part of the flower; in our figure they are of the same number as the sepals and alternate with them, but in many flowers several series of petals are developed. The calyx is sometimes coloured like the corolla, and can then only be distinguished from the latter by its position, as in Lilies and most other endogenous flowers; the floral leaves are then collectively styled a *perianth*. Where only one series of floral leaves is present, it is considered as a calyx, whether coloured or not. Sometimes the calyx is *deciduous*, that is, it falls off before the flower opens, as in the Poppy tribe, aad in some plants both calyx and corolla are wanting. The sepals are occasionally united at their base into a tube, and the same is frequently the case with the petals, as in the Foxglove, Primrose, and many other flowers. The calyx is frequently reduced to a mere rim, as in some of the Umbelliferæ; while in the Compositæ, the order to which the Dandelion and Thistle belong, it is represented only by a circle of hairs or scales beneath the corolla, and is then denominated a *pappus*. In the Grasses there is no regular calyx or corolla, these envelopes being represented by two series of scale-like bracts, the outer of which are called *glumes*, the inner *paleæ*. Sometimes, as in the Calla and the wild Arum of our hedges, the floral organs are enclosed in one large bract, which receives the name of a *spathe*.

The petals are usually equal in number to the sepals, or some multiple of that number, and such flowers are called by botanists *symmetrical*; when the contrary is the case the flower is said to be *unsymmetrical.* The petals are often very different in form and size, and the flower then becomes *irregular,* as in the Snapdragon, Foxglove, and Monkshood. One peculiar form of irregular flower prevalent in the Leguminosæ or Pea tribe is known as *papilionaceous,* from a fancied resemblance of the petals to a butterfly with its wings expanded. The upper of the five petals, usually larger than the rest, termed the *vexillum,* is somewhat curved backwards; the two lateral ones are called *alæ* or wings; while the two lower, which are united slightly by their margins, are styled the *carina,* or keel.

Attached to the petals, or between them and the stamens, are sometimes found small processes of various form, to which the name of *nectaries* is usually given.

The stamens are arranged within the petals, in one or more whorls. They consist generally of a long slender column or *filament* bearing a small body at the apex called the *anther,* which contains the *pollen* or powdery matter by which the seed is fertilized. This anther is usually two-celled, but sometimes one-celled, and the manner in which the cells open to discharge their pollen is often a most important character in distinguishing plants. The stamens are sometimes united by their filaments into a column with the pistil, or into several groups, and in some plants the anthers are similarly connected. The anther is the only essential part of the stamen, the filament being often wanting.

The pistil is the body through which the fertilization of the seed takes place. There is sometimes only one, and sometimes many; they always occupy the centre of the flower. A pistil generally consists of a club-shaped or variously divided process called the *stigma,* supported on a column termed the *style,* by which it communicates with the *ovary* or embryo seed-vessel at its base; the style, however, is often absent.

Like all other parts of the flower, the ovary is formed of modified leaves variously arranged. Sometimes it consists of one leaf with the margins united so as to form a vessel in which the seeds are contained,—these latter, called in their immature state the *ovules*, being attached to the adherent margins of the folded leaf (Fig. 6). The vessel thus formed is denominated a carpel; the line of adhesion is termed the *ventral suture*, that opposite to it, representing the midrib of the leaf, the *dorsal suture*. In many flowers two or more carpels are united, the edges of each carpel-leaf being curved inwards, forming divisions more or less complete, called *dissepiments* (Fig. 7). In every case the ovules are attached to the ovary by means of a substance called the *placenta*, formed partly of a prolongation of the vessels of the leaf, partly of cellular tissue connected with that of the pistil; by the former they receive their nourishment, while through the latter their fertilization is accomplished. When these placentas all meet in the centre, forming with the dissepiments a perfect division between the carpels, the ovary becomes, of course, two- or many-celled; the united placentas are then said to be *central* or *axile* (Fig. 8). When they form by their junction a distinct column in the middle of the cavity, they are styled *free* and *central* (Fig. 9); when they appear as mere projections from the sides of the vessel, they are called *parietal*, as in the Poppy (Fig. 10). The ovules are attached to the placenta by means of a small appendage of that organ, to which the name of *funiculus* is given.

The ovary is sometimes adherent to the tubular portion of the calyx, so as to appear below the teeth or sepals of the latter; it is then termed *inferior*, the calyx being *superior* (Fig. 11). When free in the middle of the flower, it is called *superior*, the calyx becoming *inferior* (Fig. 12).

In the Coniferæ or Fir tribe and a few other plants there is no ovary,—the ovules being produced without any covering, in the axils of the modified bracts or leaves which form the *cone*, or covered only by those leaves converted into a fleshy substance as in the so-called berries of the Juniper and Yew.

In some plants the ovaries and the stamens are contained in

distinct flowers, then termed *unisexual*. They are either upon the same plant, or *monœcious*, or upon different plants, when they are styled *diœcious*.

The manner in which the fertilization of the ovules takes place is still involved in much obscurity. It is, however, certain that the contact of the pollen with the stigma is necessary for its accomplishment; and this end is attained by Nature in various ways. In some instances the filaments of the stamens are endowed with a peculiar irritability, which causes them, when touched by insects or otherwise, to bend towards the stigma and discharge the contents of the anthers; this is the case with the flowers of the Barberry. In the Stinging Nettle the filaments are curved spirally within the calyx, and, when the latter expands, spring up suddenly and scatter the fertilizing grains over the adjacent pistils. In many plants the elastic coat of the anther itself performs a similar office, and the liberated pollen floats in clouds and becomes deposited upon the stigmas; in Pine woods, during the flowering season, the air is frequently filled with the minute yellow grains of pollen thus discharged. That of monœcious and diœcious plants is often conveyed to the pistils by the bees and flies attracted by the honey in the flowers, and whose bodies are usually furnished with hairs, to which the grains readily adhere. The pollen-grains, however, conveyed to the stigma, are retained upon that organ by means of a viscid fluid secreted upon its surface, and, after remaining there a short time, send forth tubes, which, piercing the substance of the pistil and penetrating into the ovary, impregnate the ovules therein contained.

The numerous hybrids of some flowers so abundantly raised by the florist are produced by the contact of the pollen with the stigmas of distinct species of the same genus. Similar varieties are not uncommon in Nature; but they rarely produce seed, and consequently these abnormal forms never become permanent.

The ovary, when matured, becomes the *fruit* of the plant, and either discharges its perfected ovules through openings made in the vessel, or drops to the ground and decays, allowing the seeds to germinate. The mode of opening, technically called *dehiscence,* is often an important characteristic; non-opening seed-vessels are said to be *indehiscent.*

There is a great variety of form and structure in the fruit of plants; but we can here notice only some of the more frequent kinds. A dry fruit dehiscing by valvular openings or pores is termed a *capsule,* as in the Poppy and Foxglove. A *siliqua* is a capsule opening by two valves and leaving the seeds attached to a membranous frame or *replum* formed by the placentas in the centre, as in the Wall-flower and other Cruciferæ; when short and thick, it is called by some writers a *silicula.* A *legume* or pod is a fruit formed of one carpel bearing a row of seeds along the united margins of the leaf, and opening by both sutures, as in the Pea and Broom; the term pod, however, is often given to the siliqua of Cruciferæ and to other fruits which resemble the legume externally. A *follicle* is a pod opening only by the ventral suture, or that along which the seeds are attached, as in the Larkspur; it is usually produced in flowers bearing several pistils, two or more follicles constituting the fruit. Among the indehiscent varieties may be mentioned the *achænium,* a one-seeded carpel with a separable covering, generally, like the follicle, found several together, as in the Buttercup; the *nut,* a hard one-celled fruit, containing a single seed; the *drupe,* a fleshy fruit enclosing a nut-like seed-vessel, as in the Cherry; the *berry,* in which the seeds are imbedded in a pulpy mass, as in the Hawthorn fruit; and the *pome* or apple, where the adherent calyx forms, with the outer covering of the ovary, a succulent body in which are cells containing the seeds.

The *seed* consists of the *embryo* or young plant, surrounded usually by a quantity of matter stored up for its nutriment, called *albumen,* and enclosed in a *testa* or cuticle. The albumen is of various consistence,—*farinaceous,* as in Wheat; *fleshy,* as in the

Hazel-nut; or *horny*, as in the Date and Coffee. Sometimes it is not present, the testa then enclosing the embryo alone, and the seed is said to be *exalbuminous*, as in the Bean and Almond. The embryo is formed of a *radicle* and *plumule*, the rudiments respectively of the root and stem of the future plant, and the *cotyledons*, which eventually become its first or *seed-leaves*. In Exogens these cotyledons are generally two in number; but in a few instances several are situated in a whorl around the plumule. In Endogens there is only one present; and the plumule, usually hidden by it while in the seed, rises, after germination, from a small slit at its base. These two great divisions of the flowering plants have, from this circumstance, been also termed Di-cotyledons and Mono-cotyledons. The embryo being frequently very minute, it is often difficult to distinguish its nature until after germination; its two principal forms may be better understood by reference to the Plate. Fig. 13 represents a Bean with its testa and one of the cotyledons removed, showing the other with the small plumule and radicle at its base. Fig. 14 is the young plant after germination has taken place: the testa is thrown off; the cotyledons have expanded; and the radicle is extended downwards into the ground. Fig. 15 is a section of a grain of Wheat, a monocotyledonous seed, with the embryo lying on one side of the farinaceous albumen, which here forms the principal contents of the testa. In fig. 16 the grain has germinated; and the single, long, pointed cotyledon is rising, the plumule emerging from the slit at its base, while the radicle is extending in the contrary direction. The form and position of the embryo, however, vary very much in both monocotyledonous and dicotyledonous plants, and afford to the systematic botanist a most valuable point of distinction between different families. At that part of the seed where it is attached to the funiculus, a small scar is always found, called the *hilum*,—while at some point of its surface a pore exists, termed the *foramen* or *micropyle*, the opening through which the radicle is eventually protruded. The position of the foramen or of the radicle, with regard to the hilum, is the most important feature of the embryo. When the radicle is directed to the extremity of the seed opposite the hilum, the embryo is said to be *antitropal*; when it is next the hilum, it is termed *orthotropal*; when the embryo lies across the seed with its radicle towards one side, it is *heterotropal*; when so curved that both extremities are pointed towards the hilum, it becomes *amphitropal*. The cotyledons are variously arranged in the seed, being often curiously folded and twisted; they are sometimes leaf-like, and in some instances thick and fleshy. In a very few exogenous plants the cotyledons are wanting or are not distinguishable from the plumule. These characters of the embryo, being generally discernible only by the aid of a lens and distinguished with difficulty by the unpractised eye, have been little employed in the present work.

The floral organs above described are all placed upon the more or less expanded apex of the flower-stalk, denominated the *disk, receptacle,* or *thalamus*. In many flowers the sepals, petals, stamens, and pistils are all situated immediately upon the receptacle, forming so many distinct concentric whorls; but in some a different arrangement prevails,—a circumstance of which botanists have availed themselves in classification. Where the stamens are placed directly upon the disk, beneath the pistil, they are called *hypogynous*; where they are attached to the calyx, around the pistil, *perigynous*; when placed apparently upon the ovary, they are said to be *epigynous*. It frequently happens that the filaments of the stamens in hypogynous flowers are attached to the petals, while in epigynous ones the calyx and ovary are often so united that the stamens appear to be in connexion with both organs.

The manner in which the flower-buds open, technically called their *æstivation,* is a feature of some importance in distinguishing tribes of plants. The petals are sometimes so folded that their margins just meet—the æstivation is then *valvate*; in some flowers they overlap each other like tiles—it is then *imbricate*; in other instances they are doubled inwards at the edges, or *induplicate*; while in many they are *twisted* or *contorted*.

The arrangement of the flowers upon the stem likewise requires notice. They are frequently situated singly at the apex of a stalk or *peduncle* rising from the root, or are *solitary*. In most plants, however, the stem is variously divided into small branches bearing the flowers. When a number of flowers are placed along a stalk without foot-stalks or *pedicels*, it is called a *spike* (Fig. 17). A drooping spike, containing stamens or pistils only, and dropping from the branch when withered, is termed an *amentum* or *catkin*. When the flowers of the spike are each supported by a foot-stalk, it becomes a *raceme* (Fig. 18). When the raceme is branched it is a *panicle* (Fig. 19). When the outer branches of the raceme or panicle are so elongated that the flowers are brought nearly to the same level with the inner ones, it is a *corymb* (Fig. 20). When the branches of the corymb terminate in a flower and then produce lateral stalks, as in the elder, it is styled a *cyme* (Fig. 21). When the flowers are arranged upon stalks branching from the apex of the stem, an umbel is formed, which, like the corymb, may be either *simple* or *compound* as the flowers stand singly upon the branches of the umbel or are supported upon secondary umbels rising from the extremities of the latter (Figs. 22 and 23). Sometimes the flowers are arranged in a close head or *capitulum* without pedicels, being situated upon a common disk or receptacle, as in the Dandelion and other Compositæ. The flowers are in this case surrounded by a whorl of leaves like a calyx, to which the name of *involucrum* is given, a term applied to any whorl of leaves or bracts situated upon the flower-stalk. In the compound umbel there is usually a general involucrum beneath the primary umbel, while each secondary umbel has one of its own, to which the term *involucel* is applied.

All the parts of the flower must be regarded as modifications of the leaf. The sepals and petals are nothing more than leaves somewhat altered in form and colour; the stamens are leaves, of which the petioles are represented by the filaments, while the expanded portion, being turned inwards upon the midrib, becomes the anther; the carpels of the pistil are likewise leaves variously modified. This interesting fact, long since surmised by Goethe, has been long verified by accurate observation; and some of its results are of importance even to the non-scientific observer of flowers. Occasionally portions of the corolla are found developed as green leaves,—a monstrosity frequently occurring in the garden Tulip. The flowers called *double* are produced by a similar metamorphosis, the leaves that are usually developed as stamens and pistils assuming the petaloid form; hence perfectly double flowers are incapable of maturing seed.

The duration of plants is variable in different species; but the general process of growth is the same in all. The seed, lying upon the ground, germinates under the influence of heat and moisture; the radicle is elongated, and, penetrating the soil, pushes forth fibres which draw up nutriment for the support of the growing plant; the plumule rises, bearing with it the cotyledons, which acquire the green colour of leaves, and are soon succeeded by the true leaves. At some period of its growth the leaves are developed in forms more or less modified, and become no longer organs of respiration and transpiration, but assume the characters of floral envelopes and of stamens and pistils, through the mutual action of which the seed is produced.

Some plants spring up from the seed and bear flowers and fruit within a single season, dying when the process is completed—or are *annual*. Others produce no flowers the first year, but store up during that period of growth the nutriment which is absorbed in the production of seed in the following summer, when they die; these are called *biennial*. When the plant survives for an indefinite period it becomes *perennial*, either throwing up stems from the root each year, which die down after bearing flowers, or producing a permanent, more or less woody trunk. In exogenous trees, vegetation is chiefly carried on through the inner bark and young wood, the heart-wood and outer bark retaining little vitality, as may be often seen in the case of hollow trees, which, though the trunk and principal branches are reduced to a mere shell, the interior having wholly decayed, still continue to put forth leaves and flowers for many successive years.

All the organs of plants consist of cells of various form and arrangement, either connected in masses, forming what is called *cellular tissue*, or elongated and joined together end to end so as to present a tubular appearance. *Woody fibre* is made up of a number of such tubular cells, united by their overlapping extremities. These cells are all originally membranous; and communication is established between the liquids contained within them by the peculiar process of exudation called endosmose. During growth, however, the walls of the cells are thickened by the gradual deposition of earthy and other substances from the liquid, and are sometimes converted in this manner into a solid mass. Growth is the formation of new cells, either by a process of subdivision and extension of those previously existing, or from the development of a minute body called a nucleus, which, formed in the cell-fluid, is afterwards extended through the membrane and becomes a cell itself. In each cell, during growth, a fluid is constantly circulating with more or less rapidity, holding in suspension various matters which are eventually deposited within it. One of the most important of these organic matters is the *chlorophyll* or colouring-substance of the plant, usually of a green tint. Light is necessary for its production; and consequently, when plants are grown in the dark, they become *etiolated* or blanched. Starch, gum, and sugar form the principal other substances floating in the cell-fluid; they are present in all plants during growth. Besides these, various resinous and oily secretions are elaborated in certain cells of the plant, principally in those containing that portion of the fluid which has been exposed through the medium of the leaves to the action of the atmosphere.

These elaborated matters and the cellular substance itself are all formed of oxygen, hydrogen, carbon, and nitrogen, combined in various proportions. Carbon, the most abundant element in the solid parts of all vegetables, is derived chiefly, if not entirely, from the small quantity of carbonic acid existing in the air; nitrogen, which only enters into the composition of a few vegetable products, is obtained from the nitrates and ammoniacal salts present in the soil; while the two other elements are probably due to the decomposition of a portion of the water taken up by the root, the superfluous oxygen being exhaled by the leaves during the day. Thus plants form a necessary part of the great cycle of Nature, absorbing those gaseous particles produced by the respiration of animals and the decay of organic matter, and restoring to the air, in a purified state, that principle which is necessary to the support of all animate being.

Water forms a considerable portion of growing vegetables, and is necessary to their existence. It is chiefly drawn up by the fibres of the root, though some plants doubtless absorb much from the atmosphere. Being required in very varying proportion by different species, the amount present in the soil has a great influence upon its vegetation. Some plants will only grow entirely submersed, others flourish in the stagnant bog or peat-moss, some require the moist but well-drained hill-side, and a few are found in the most arid localities, where occasional dews form the only source of moisture.

In addition to these elementary components, vegetables always contain a considerable quantity of various other substances of inorganic origin. Potash and soda are the most prevalent of these; they are present in all plants, the former alkali existing in by far the greater proportion in most inland species, while an abundance of the latter is characteristic of those growing near the sea, being derived from the salt spray continually drifting over them. Such plants have generally a greenish-white or *glaucous* hue; they seldom flourish far from the shore, and when growing inland the soda usually existing in their tissues is replaced by potash. Silica is always present in more or less quantity, and is particularly abundant in the cuticle of Grasses and Horsetails. Lime is also found in most species; and its presence in the soil seems necessary to some, as may be seen in the peculiar vegetation of our chalk-downs and limestone hills; indeed the growth of plants is so intimately connected with the composition of the soil, that a botanist can generally detect the prominent mineralogical features of a country through which he is travelling by the aspect of its vegetation.

There is no department of botanical study more interesting than that which traces the relation of plants to the nature of their *habitats*, or places of natural growth. Mountain, bog, woodland, sea-cliff, wet meadow, and upland pasture have all their characteristic vegetation; and even the hillocks of drifting sand, that line some parts of our storm-beaten coast, have a flora peculiar to themselves, or rarely found elsewhere. Difference of soil or situation will even produce great changes in the appearance of plants of the same species, sometimes to an extent that renders them difficult of recognition by the unpractised observer. Those usually inhabiting marshy localities, when growing on dry ground become smaller and more rigid, while the native of the hills, when transferred to the lowland, acquires a more succulent and luxuriant habit; the plants of the clay and loam often present a very different appearance to those of the same kind growing upon chalk or sand. In determining species, allowance must always be made for these accidental variations from the typical form; the points in which deviation most frequently occurs are, in the size of the plant, the form and dimensions of the leaves, the colour of the flower, and the degree of development of hairs, prickles, and other appendages of the cuticle.

Besides these differences occasioned by accidental circumstances of growth, all plants are apt to exhibit permanent variations from the general form, due to the operation of more obscure causes, giving rise to what are termed *varieties*. These varieties are, in perennial plants, capable of propagation by subdivision of the root, or from slips or cuttings; but their seed usually reproduces the normal form, though it is yet a doubtful and disputed point whether they may not in some instances be permanently propagated by seed: they often diverge so greatly from the typical plant, that they are apt to be regarded by the ordinary observer as distinct, and even our most experienced botanists are sometimes unable to decide upon their real character.

Among our native plants, the groups of Roses, Brambles, and Willows are remarkable instances of this obscurity regarding specific distinctions. Of upwards of seventy Willows figured and described in the present work, certainly not more than fourteen or fifteen can be satisfactorily distinguished as species. The twenty-four Roses are probably varieties of not more than five distinct plants; and the species of Rubus, which have been multiplied by some writers to a far greater extent than in this book, are perhaps referable to four specific types. The confusion naturally existing between species and varieties has been unfortunately greatly increased, by the anxiety of the students of local floras to extend the apparent field of their labours by the addition of new species,—an object more easily attained in a well-explored country by the subdivision of well-known groups, than by the discovery of really new plants, and a habit the more to be deplored, as it tends to destroy that simplicity of arrangement which is the only object of classification.

Whether *species* have any definite limits in Nature, is a question foreign to the scope of the present work. As the term is applied in Botany, it may be generally defined as an assemblage of plants possessing a certain similarity in all essential points of structure, capable of being permanently propagated by *seed*, and which may therefore be supposed to have descended from a single individual.

Species are perhaps the only truly natural divisions of plants; but naturalists, for convenience of reference and description, have been compelled to arrange them in more or less artificial groups or families. Certain plants possessing a great resemblance to each other in structure are formed into *genera*; these are collected into larger groups called *orders*, and the orders into *subclasses* and *classes*. All these divisions are dependent upon some general similarity in the structure of the plants composing them, usually in that of the flower and seed, those organs being less liable to variation than others. Linnæus, the founder of modern systematic Natural History, adopted the number and position of the stamens and pistils as the basis of his classification of the flowering plants, forming the names of most of his classes by affixing the word *andria*, the synonym of stamen, to the Greek numeral expressing the number of those organs present in the flower: thus plants, the flowers of which contained but one stamen, were called Monandria; those having two, Diandria. The orders or subdivisions of these were formed in a similar way by adding the word *gynia*, adopted as synonymous with pistil, to the numeral. Other divisions he made dependent upon the connexion of the filaments or anthers, and the monœcious or diœcious character of the plant. We have not space to enter into the details of his system, and have only made allusion to it because it has been adopted in the 'English Botany' and some other works of reference still in use. Its simplicity rendered it of easy application by the unscientific; but it had the great disadvantage of bringing together plants of widely different affinities into the same artificial section, owing to some coincidence in the development of a single organ, while it separated others evidently closely connected; it is therefore no longer used by naturalists, and the mode of classification adopted by Jussieu and De-Candolle, variously modified by other botanists, has been substituted.

By this system, plants are grouped into classes and orders according to certain structural characters, more or less definite, and of a similar nature to those upon which the primary divisions of genera and species are made. The plants thus connected by structure are usually found to possess a resemblance in general appearance or *habit*, and not unfrequently in properties; so that the term *natural*, commonly applied to this mode of arrangement, is, in a relative sense, not altogether inapplicable.

Flowering plants, by this plan of classification, are primarily divided into *Exogens* and *Endogens*,—a distinction founded upon peculiarities of the stem and seed which have been already explained. Exogens are grouped into four subclasses, according to the relative position of the parts of the flower. The first subclass, called *Thalamiflorœ*, contains those groups of plants which have the petals distinct and the stamens hypogynous, or inserted beneath the pistil upon the thalamus or receptacle. The second, *Calyciflorœ*, consists of those having the stamens perigynous or epigynous, or placed upon the calyx or the ovary. The third, *Corollifloræ*, includes those with the petals united, and the stamens either hypogynous or joined to the petals. The fourth, *Monochlamydeœ*, is formed of those exogenous plants having only one floral envelope, and of those having neither calyx nor corolla.

The Endogens have been variously divided by botanists; but they present at least two well-marked sections—those possessing a perianth, or floral envelope, more or less perfect, Florideæ, and those whose flowers are enclosed only in scaly bracts or glumes, Glumiferæ, a division including the two great families of Grasses and Carexes. Some botanists separate certain Endogens with net-veined leaves and wood of a peculiar structure into a third group, Dictyogenæ; these latter appear to form a connecting link between Exogens and Endogens.

These subclasses are divided into *Natural Orders*, composed of certain *genera*, or assemblages of species which bear a general resemblance in essential characters. Some of these orders are well-defined natural groups whose affinities are undoubted, like the great families of Compositæ and Cruciferæ; others are more or less artificial, and appear to pass into each other by almost insensible gradations; their limits are variously defined by different botanists, and are often made dependent upon obscure structural peculiarities only appreciable by an advanced student of the science. The Flora of this country is too limited to require reference to the minute and complex details of botanical classification, upon which the general arrangement of the Vegetable Kingdom has been founded; and the characters given in the accompanying Table of Orders and Genera must be regarded as applicable only to British plants,—it being intended merely as a Key or Index to enable the reader to refer any wild plant to the Natural Order under which it is figured and described in this work. The British Flowering Plants are here arranged in the order stated below,—with few exceptions, that usually adopted by British botanists.

EXOGENS.

THALAMIFLORÆ.

1. Ranunculaceæ.
2. Berberidaceæ.
3. Nymphæaceæ.
4. Papaveraceæ.
5. Fumariaceæ.
6. Cruciferæ.
7. Resedaceæ.
8. Cistaceæ.
9. Violaceæ.
10. Droseraceæ.
11. Polygalaceæ.
12. Frankeniaceæ.
13. Caryophyllaceæ.
14. Linaceæ.
15. Malvaceæ.
16. Tiliaceæ.
17. Hypericaceæ.
18. Aceraceæ.
19. Geraniaceæ.
20. Balsaminaceæ.
21. Oxalidaceæ.
22. Staphyleaceæ.

CALYCIFLORÆ.

23. Celastraceæ.
24. Rhamnaceæ.
25. Leguminosæ.
26. Rosaceæ.
27. Onagraceæ.
28. Haloragaceæ.
29. Lythraceæ.
30. Tamaricaceæ.
31. Cucurbitaceæ.
32. Portulaceæ.
33. Illecebraceæ.
34. Crassulaceæ.
35. Grossulariaceæ.
36. Saxifragaceæ.
37. Umbelliferæ.
38. Araliaceæ.
39. Cornaceæ.
40. Loranthaceæ.
41. Caprifoliaceæ.
42. Rubiaceæ.
43. Valerianaceæ.
44. Dipsaceæ.
45. Compositæ.
46. Campanulaceæ.
47. Lobeliaceæ.
48. Vacciniaceæ.

COROLLIFLORÆ.

49. Ericaceæ.
50. Pyrolaceæ.
51. Monotropaceæ.
52. Aquifoliaceæ.
53. Oleaceæ.
54. Apocynaceæ.
55. Gentianaceæ.

56. Polemoniaceæ.
57. Convolvulaceæ.
58. Boraginaceæ.
59. Solanaceæ.
60. Orobanchaceæ.
61. Scrophulariaceæ.

62. Labiatæ.
63. Verbenaceæ.
64. Lentibulariaceæ.
65. Primulaceæ.
66. Plumbaginaceæ.
67. Plantaginaceæ.

MONOCHLAMYDEÆ.

68. Amaranthaceæ.
69. Chenopodiaceæ.
70. Scleranthaceæ.
71. Polygonaceæ.
72. Thymelaceæ.
73. Santalaceæ.
74. Aristolochiaceæ.

75. Empetraceæ.
76. Euphorbiaceæ.
77. Callitrichaceæ.
78. Ceratophyllaceæ.
79. Urticaceæ.
80. Ulmaceæ.

81. Elæagnaceæ.
82. Myricaceæ.
83. Betulaceæ.
84. Salicaceæ.
85. Cupuliferæ.
86. Coniferæ.

ENDOGENS.

DICTYOGENÆ.

87. Dioscoreaceæ.   88. Trilliaceæ.

FLORIDEÆ.

89. Hydrocharidaceæ.
90. Orchidaceæ.
91. Iridaceæ.
92. Amaryllidaceæ.
93. Liliaceæ.
94. Melanthaceæ.

95. Restiaceæ.
96. Juncaceæ.
97. Butomaceæ.
98. Alismaceæ.
99. Juncaginaceæ.

100. Typhaceæ.
101. Araceæ.
102. Orontiaceæ.
103. Pistiaceæ.
104. Naiadaceæ.

GLUMIFERÆ.

105. Cyperaceæ.   106. Gramineæ.

Plants being arranged under the Natural System according to general characters only, some genera of certain orders will be found to possess the structural form of a different subclass to that in which the order is placed. For instance, though most Leguminosæ have petals and stamens arranged in the manner characteristic of the subclass Calycifloræ, some exotic plants of that order have no floral envelope, and would therefore be referred to Monochlamydeæ by the inexperienced student, while a few British species having hypogynous stamens would seem to be naturally placed in the Thalamifloral division. To avoid the confusion thus arising, a more artificial arrangement, like that adopted in the accompanying Key, becomes necessary, to enable the unscientific student to discover the order to which any plant he may meet with in the fields is to be referred. The characters given, referring only to the plants of the order or genus indigenous to this country, are as simple as possible, and will probably enable the reader to find readily the description and figure of any native plant in the work.

The space allotted to the descriptive portion of our book is so small, that it has been impossible to give in many instances one sufficient, alone, for the perfect identification of the plant; and the aim has been rather to add those characteristics not clearly shown in the figure, and which are most easily recognized, than those by which the species is accurately determined by the botanist: in many cases three or four lines would have been necessary to give such characters as would enable the student to determine the species without the aid of the figure, when one line of description only could be admitted; the descriptions must therefore be considered only subordinate to the plates. The normal habitat of each plant is given, together with the general height above the ground, its duration, time of flowering, and the colour of the flower; the height and colour are, however, in most cases very variable. The fraction at the end of the description denotes the scale upon which the flower is drawn in the plate—usually one-half or two-thirds the natural size: the size of the flower, however, is likewise subject to much variation; where no scale is made, the figure is the natural size. The works to which references are made, are the 1st edition of the 'English Botany,' by Sowerby and Smith; the 2nd edition of the same work by Sowerby and Johnson; the 7th edition of Hooker and Arnott's 'British Flora;' the 4th edition of Babington's 'Manual of British Botany;' and Lindley's 'Synopsis of the British Flora.'

KEY TO THE NATURAL ORDERS.

EXOGENS.

Stem with distinct *wood, pith,* and *bark.*
Leaves net-veined.
Embryo with 2 or more cotyledons.
Parts of the flower generally 2, 4, or 5, or their multiples—rarely
    3 or its multiples.

Petals distinct.   Stamens hypogynous.

* Stamens 12, or more.

1. RANUNCULACEÆ.   Ovary of 1 or more distinct carpels.
3. NYMPHÆACEÆ.   Aquatic plants.   Petals passing into stamens towards the centre.   Ovary many-celled.
4. PAPAVERACEÆ.   Herbs.   Ovary of 2 or more carpels, 1-celled, with parietal placentas.   Sepals falling when the flower opens.
8. CISTACEÆ.   Small shrubs.   Ovary of several carpels, 1-celled.   Sepals permanent.
17. HYPERICACEÆ.   Herbs or shrubs.   Ovary many-celled.   Leaves opposite, dotted. Stamens united into several groups.
15. MALVACEÆ.   Herbs or shrubs.   Ovary many-celled.   Stamens united into a column.
16. TILIACEÆ.   Trees.   Ovary many-celled, 1-celled when in fruit.   Stamens distinct.
7. RESEDACEÆ.   Herbs.   Ovary 1-celled, opening at the top.   Flowers irregular.

** Stamens under 12, filaments distinct.
† *Flowers regular.*

6. CRUCIFERÆ.   Herbs.   Petals 4.   Stamens 4 long and 2 short.
10. DROSERACEÆ.   Herbs with entire radical leaves covered with glandular hairs.
2. BERBERIDACEÆ.   Herbs or shrubs.   Stamens all opposite the petals.   Ovary 1-celled.   Anthers opening by recurved valves.
13. CARYOPHYLLACEÆ.   Herbs with jointed stems and opposite leaves.   Placenta free and central.
12. FRANKENIACEÆ.   Herbs.   Stamens alternate with the petals.   Sepals united. Placentas parietal.
18. ACERACEÆ.   Trees.   Fruit 2-winged.   Ovary 2-lobed, 2-celled.
22. STAPHYLEACEÆ.   A shrub.   Fruit bladder-like.
19. GERANIACEÆ.   Carpels 5, surrounding a long beak.

†† *Flowers irregular.*

9. VIOLACEÆ.   Stamens 5.   Ovary 1-celled, opening by 3 valves.
20. BALSAMINACEÆ.   Stamens 5.   Ovary 5-celled.

*** Stamens under 12, filaments more or less connected at the base.
† *Flowers regular.*

14. LINACEÆ.   Stamens 4 or 5.   Carpels 1- or 2-seeded, without a beak.
19. GERANIACEÆ.   Stamens 10.   Carpels 5, surrounding a long beak.   Style 1.
21. OXALIDACEÆ.   Stamens 10.   Styles 5.

†† *Flowers irregular.*

5. FUMARIACEÆ. Stamens 6, in 2 bundles. Fruit 1-celled.
11. POLYGALACEÆ. Stamens 8, in 2 bundles. Fruit 2-celled.
25. LEGUMINOSÆ. Stamens 10. Flowers papilionaceous. Fruit a legume.
7. RESEDACEÆ. Stamens 10 or more. Fruit 1-celled, opening at the top.

Petals distinct. Stamens perigynous or epigynous.

25. LEGUMINOSÆ. Corolla papilionaceous.
26. ROSACEÆ. Corolla regular. Stamens numerous. Carpels more or less distinct. Leaves with stipules.

* Ovary superior or half-inferior.

† *Carpels several.*

34. CRASSULACEÆ. Carpels 2 or more, distinct. Leaves without stipules.

†† *Ovary solitary, 1-celled.*

32. PORTULACEÆ. Sepals 2. Placenta central. Leaves without stipules.
33. ILLECEBRACEÆ. Sepals 5. Placenta central with several seeds, or fruit 1-seeded.
17. HYPERICACEÆ (Parnassia). Sepals 5. Placentas 4, parietal. Seeds many.
30. TAMARICACEÆ. A shrub. Placentas 3, parietal. Stigmas 3, feathery.

††† *Ovary solitary, 2- or more-celled.*

36. SAXIFRAGACEÆ. Herbs. Stamens twice as many as the petals. Styles 2, diverging. Seeds numerous.
24. RHAMNACEÆ. Shrubs. Stamens equal in number to the petals, and opposite to them. Fruit a berry.
23. CELASTRACEÆ. A shrub. Stamens alternating with the petals. Fruit a capsule.
29. LYTHRACEÆ. Herbs. Calyx valvate in æstivation. Style 1.
50. PYROLACEÆ. Herbs. Calyx imbricated in æstivation. Style 1.

** Ovary inferior.

† *Ovary 1-celled.*

35. GROSSULARIACEÆ. Ovary 1-celled. Fruit a berry. Sepals and petals 4–5. Stamens 4–5, alternate with the petals.

†† *Ovary 2- or more-celled.*

27. ONAGRACEÆ. Stamens 2, 4, or 8. Style 1. Leaves opposite or alternate. Petals twisted in æstivation.
28. HALORAGACEÆ. Aquatic herbs. Flowers monœcious. Leaves whorled.
39. CORNACEÆ. Petals 4, valvate in æstivation. Stamens 4, alternating with the petals. Leaves opposite.
38. ARALIACEÆ. An evergreen creeping shrub. Petals 5, valvate in æstivation.
37. UMBELLIFERÆ. Herbs. Flowers in umbels. Petals 5. Stamens 5. Fruit splitting into 2 dry 1-seeded carpels. Leaves alternate.

Petals united.

* Ovary inferior or half-inferior.

† *Flowers sessile, in close heads upon a disk within an involucrum (capitate).*

45. COMPOSITÆ. Stamens 5; anthers united into a tube.
44. DIPSACEÆ. Stamens 4; anthers separate.

†† *Flowers not capitate.*

31. CUCURBITACEÆ. A climbing herb. Flowers diœcious. Ovules several in each cell.

§ *Ovary with 1 seed-bearing cell ; ovule solitary.*

40. LORANTHACEÆ. A parasitic evergreen shrub.
43. VALERIANACEÆ. Style thread-like, bearing a trifid stigma.
41. CAPRIFOLIACEÆ. Stigmas sessile.

§§ *Ovary with 2 or more seed-bearing cells.*

48. VACCINIACEÆ. Small shrubs. Stamens free from the corolla. Leaves alternate.
41. CAPRIFOLIACEÆ. Shrubs. Stamens upon the corolla. Leaves opposite.
38. ARALIACEÆ (Adoxa). An herb. Styles 4 or 5. Stamens united in pairs.
42. RUBIACEÆ. Herbs. Leaves whorled, or opposite with leafy stipules between. Stamens upon the corolla. Styles 1 or 2.
46. CAMPANULACEÆ. Herbs. Corolla regular. Stamens free from the corolla. Style 1.
47. LOBELIACEÆ. Herbs. Corolla irregular. Style 1.

** *Ovary superior. Flowers irregular.*

60. OROBANCHACEÆ. Plant leafless, scaly.
62. LABIATÆ. Ovary in 4 distinct lobes.
61. SCROPHULARIACEÆ. Ovary undivided. Stamens 5.

† *Ovary undivided. Stamens 2.*

64. LENTIBULARIACEÆ. Corolla spurred at the base.
61. SCROPHULARIACEÆ (Veronica). Corolla not spurred.

†† *Ovary undivided. Stamens 2 long and 2 short.*

63. VERBENACEÆ. Cells of the ovary 2 or 4, single-seeded.
61. SCROPHULARIACEÆ. Cells of the ovary 2, with 2 or more seeds in each.

††† *Stamens 8, in 2 groups.*

11. POLYGALACEÆ. Stamens connected with the petals.

*** *Ovary superior. Flowers regular, or nearly so.*
† *Stamens free from the corolla.*

49. ERICACEÆ. Small shrubs. Petals quite united. Style 1.
50. PYROLACEÆ. Herbs. Petals but slightly united. Style 1. Stamens 10.
67. PLANTAGINACEÆ. Herbs. Flowers monœcious. Style 1. Stamens 4.
34. CRASSULACEÆ. Styles several.

†† *Stamens 2, upon the corolla.*

53. OLEACEÆ. Trees or shrubs.
61. SCROPHULARIACEÆ (Veronica). Herbs. Petals slightly irregular.

††† *Stamens 4, upon the corolla.*

52. AQUIFOLIACEÆ. An evergreen tree or shrub.
61. SCROPHULARIACEÆ (Limosella). An herb. Leaves radical. Capsule 1-celled. Calyx 5-cleft.
67. PLANTAGINACEÆ. Herbs. Capsule 2- or 4-celled. Calyx 4-cleft. Leaves all radical.
65. PRIMULACEÆ (Centunculus). An herb. Leaves alternate. Calyx 4-cleft. Capsule 1-celled.
55. GENTIANACEÆ. Herbs. Leaves opposite.

†††† *Stamens 5 or more, upon the corolla.*

54. APOCYNACEÆ. Ovaries 2. Style 1.
58. BORAGINACEÆ. Ovary 4-lobed. Style 1.
52. AQUIFOLIACEÆ. Fruit a succulent berry. Stigmas sessile.
59. SOLANACEÆ. Fruit a succulent berry, 2-celled. Style 1.

65. PRIMULACEÆ. Stamens opposite the petals. Fruit dry, 1-celled. Style 1.
66. PLUMBAGINACEÆ. Fruit dry, 1-celled. Seed 1. Styles 5.
57. CONVOLVULACEÆ. Stamens alternate with the petals. Fruit dry, 1- or 2-celled. Seeds few. Style 1.
55. GENTIANACEÆ. Stamens alternate with the petals. Fruit dry, 1- or 2-celled, many-seeded. Leaves opposite.
59. SOLANACEÆ. Stamens alternate with the petals. Fruit dry, 2-celled, or nearly 4-celled, many-seeded. Leaves alternate.
56. POLEMONIACEÆ. Fruit dry, 3-celled.
51. MONOTROPACEÆ. Fruit dry, 4- or 5-celled. Plant scaly, leafless.

Floral envelope (*calyx*) single or wanting.

A. Barren and fertile flowers in catkins.

82. MYRICACEÆ. Monœcious or diœcious. Fruit a succulent drupe.
83. BETULACEÆ. Fruit dry. Monœcious.
84. SALICACEÆ. Fruit dry. Diœcious.

B. Barren flowers only, in catkins.

81. ELEAGNACEÆ. Ovary superior. Diœcious.
85. CUPULIFERÆ. Ovary inferior. Monœcious.
86. CONIFERÆ. Seed in cones, or surrounded by a fleshy involucrum. Leaves linear, needle-like.

C. Flowers not in catkins.

40. LORANTHACEÆ. An evergreen parasitic shrub.
76. EUPHORBIACEÆ. Flowers in terminal clusters, surrounded by bracts. Ovary stalked, with 3 one-seeded cells. Juice milky.

* Ovary inferior.
† *Cells many-seeded.*

36. SAXIFRAGACEÆ. Stamens 8–10. Styles 2.
27. ONAGRACEÆ. Stamens 4. Style 1.
74. ARISTOLOCHIACEÆ. Stamens 6–12.

†† *Cells 1-seeded.*

28. HALORAGACEÆ. Leaves whorled. Aquatic.
73. SANTALACEÆ. Leaves alternate. Terrestrial.

** Ovaries several, superior.

1. RANUNCULACEÆ. Stamens hypogynous.
26. ROSACEÆ. Stamens perigynous.

*** Ovary 1, superior, with 2 or more cells.
† *Monœcious or diœcious.*

76. EUPHORBIACEÆ. Terrestrial. Fruit capsular, of 2 or 3 one-seeded cells.
75. EMPETRACEÆ. Terrestrial. Fruit fleshy. Stamens 3.
77. CALLITRICHACEÆ. Aquatic plants. Fruit of 4 one-seeded carpels.

†† *Flowers perfect.*

80. ULMACEÆ. Trees. Stamens 5. Fruit dry, winged.
24. RHAMNACEÆ. Shrubs. Stamens 4 or 5. Fruit a berry.
53. OLEACEÆ. Trees. Stamens 2.
29. LYTHRACEÆ. Herbs.

**** Ovary 1, superior, 1-celled.
† *Calyx coloured and petal-like.*

65. PRIMULACEÆ. Leaves without stipules. Stamens 5.

72. THYMELEACEÆ. Leaves without stipules. Stamens 8.
71. POLYGONACEÆ. Leaves with stipules sheathing the stem.

†† *Calyx not petal-like. Leaves with stipules.*

71. POLYGONACEÆ. Stipules sheathing the stem.
26. ROSACEÆ. Stipules attached to the petiole.
79. URTICACEÆ. Stipules deciduous.

††† *Calyx not petal-like. Leaves without stipules.*

§ *Terrestrial herbs.*

70. SCLERANTHACEÆ. Calyx contracted round the fruit.
68. AMARANTHACEÆ. Calyx free. Stamens hypogynous. Fruit opening transversely.
69. CHENOPODIACEÆ. Calyx free. Stamens perigynous. Fruit indehiscent.

§§ *Aquatic plants.*

78. CERATOPHYLLACEÆ. Stamens 12 or more.
28. HALORAGACEÆ. Stamens 1–8.

ENDOGENS.

Stem without distinct *wood* and *bark*.
Leaves usually with parallel veins.
Embryo with 1 cotyledon.
Parts of the flower usually 3 or its multiples.

Leaves with netted veins.

87. DIOSCOREACEÆ. A climbing herb. Leaves alternate.
88. TRILLIACEÆ. An herb. Leaves in a terminal whorl.
98. ALISMACEÆ. Leaves radical.

Leaves with parallel veins.

* Flowers with distinct calyx and corolla.

98. ALISMACEÆ. Ovaries several, superior.
89. HYDROCHARIDACEÆ. Ovary 1, inferior. Diœcious.
90. ORCHIDACEÆ. Ovary 1, inferior. Stamens and pistil united.

** Flowers enclosed in a perianth.

† *Ovary inferior.*

90. ORCHIDACEÆ. Flowers irregular. Stamens and pistil united, obscure.
91. IRIDACEÆ. Flowers regular. Stamens 3.
92. AMARYLLIDACEÆ. Flowers regular. Stamens 6.

†† *Ovary superior. Perianth petal-like.*

93. LILIACEÆ. Stamens 6. Anthers opening inwards. Style entire.
94. MELANTHACEÆ. Stamens 6. Anthers opening outwards. Style divided into 3.
96. JUNCACEÆ (Narthecium). Stamens 6. Perianth becoming dry and scale-like when withered, persistent.
97. BUTOMACEÆ. Stamens 9. Flowers in an umbel.
95. RESTIACEÆ. Flowers in a compact scaly head, monœcious.

††† *Ovary superior. Perianth dry and scale-like.*

96. JUNCACEÆ. Fruit a capsule. Flowers in panicles or clusters, with a bract beneath.
102. ORONTIACEÆ. Fruit a berry. Flowers arranged in a spike, springing from the leaf.
100. TYPHACEÆ. Flowers in globular heads. Monœcious.

*** Perianth inconspicuous.

99. JUNCAGINACEÆ. Sepals herbaceous. Marsh plants.
104. NAIADACEÆ. Sepals scale-like. Plants aquatic, submerged or floating.
93. LILIACEÆ (Ruscus). An evergreen shrub with spiny leaves.

**** Flowers enclosed in a spathe or membranous sheath.

101. ARACEÆ. Flowers in a spike or spadix, monœcious. Herbs.
103. PISTIACEÆ. Small stemless floating plants. Flowers on the margin of the leaf.
104. NAIADACEÆ. Submerged or floating. Flowers axillary.

***** Flowers without any covering.

104. NAIADACEÆ. Aquatic, submerged. Flowers in a slit in the grass-like leaf.
100. TYPHACEÆ. Marsh plants. Flowers on a spike. Monœcious.

Flowers enclosed in *glumes* or scales, one above another.

106. GRAMINEÆ. Stems jointed. Anthers attached by the middle.
105. CYPERACEÆ. Stems not jointed. Anthers attached by the base.

TABLE OF GENERA.

Order I. RANUNCULACEÆ.

1. CLEMATIS. A climber with opposite leaves. Petals none. Sepals white. Carpels 1-seeded.

* Herbs. Carpels 1-seeded.

2. THALICTRUM. Involucrum none. Petals none. Stamens longer than the sepals.
3. ANEMONE. Involucrum of 3 leaves, somewhat beneath the flower. Petals none. Sepals petaloid, coloured.
4. ADONIS. Petals 5–10, without a scale at the base.
5. MYOSURUS. Carpels very numerous, in a long column. Sepals with a spur at the base. Petals very small.
6. RANUNCULUS. Petals with a scale at the base. Sepals not spurred at the base. Carpels in a globular or oblong head.

** Carpels with several seeds.

7. CALTHA. Petals none. Sepals yellow and petaloid.
8. TROLLIUS. Petals small, flat, linear. Sepals yellow, very concave.
9. HELLEBORUS. Petals very small, tubular. Sepals green.
10. AQUILEGIA. Sepals flat, coloured, deciduous. Petals 5, each with a long spur at the base.
11. DELPHINIUM. Sepals 5, coloured; upper one with a spur at the base. Petals 4, connected, forming a spur.
12. ACONITUM. Sepals 5, coloured; upper one hood-shaped. Petals small, irregular.
13. ACTÆA. Stamens placed upon a glandular disk. Carpels solitary, berry-like. Petals 4. Calyx deciduous, petaloid.
14. PÆONIA. Stamens upon a glandular disk. Calyx green, persistent. Carpels several.

Order II. BERBERIDACEÆ.

1. BERBERIS. A bush. Stamens 6.
2. EPIMEDIUM. Herbaceous. Stamens 4.

Order III. NYMPHÆACEÆ.

1. NYMPHÆA. Calyx greenish without, of 4 sepals. Petals and stamens placed upon the base of the ovary.
2. NUPHAR. Calyx yellow, of 5 sepals. Petals and stamens placed upon the receptacle.

Order IV. PAPAVERACEÆ.

1. PAPAVER. Fruit nearly globular or oblong. Stigma rayed, sessile.
2. MECONOPSIS. Fruit oblong. Stigma rayed, with a short style.
3. GLAUCIUM. Fruit linear. Flowers large, red or purple.
4. CHELIDONIUM. Fruit linear. Flowers small, yellow.

Order V. FUMARIACEÆ.

1. FUMARIA. Fruit a roundish nut, 1-seeded.
2. CORYDALIS. Fruit elongated, many-seeded, 2-valved.

Order VI. CRUCIFERÆ.

* Fruit a short pod (*Silicula*).

1. CAKILE. Pod angular, compressed, formed of 2 joints; the upper one deciduous. Joints 1-seeded, the lower sometimes barren. Indehiscent.
2. CRAMBE. Pod formed of 2 joints; upper joint globose, deciduous, 1-seeded; lower one abortive, like a short footstalk. Indehiscent.
3. CORONOPUS. Pod of 2 cells, placed side by side; cells 1-seeded, indehiscent. Leaves pinnatifid.
4. ISATIS. Pod linear-oblong, smooth, 1-celled, 1-seeded, laterally compressed; the valves keeled, at length separating.
5. VELLA. Pod elliptical, terminating in a flat winged style, twice the length of the valves.
6. THLASPI. Pod laterally compressed, emarginate, with the valves winged at the back; cells 2–8-seeded. Petals entire.
7. CAPSELLA. Pod laterally compressed, obcordate, wedge-shaped at the base; valves sharply keeled; cells many-seeded. Petals entire.
8. HUTCHINSIA. Pod elliptical, entire; valves keeled at the back; cells 2-seeded. Petals entire.
9. TEESDALIA. Pod oval, depressed, indented at the apex; valves keeled; cells 2-seeded. Calyx deciduous. Petals entire, unequal. Stamens with a scale at the base.
10. IBERIS. Pod much depressed, emarginate; valves winged; cells 1-seeded. Two outer petals largest.
11. LEPIDIUM. Pod ovate or cordate; valves keeled; cells 1-seeded. Petals equal.
12. COCHLEARIA. Pod globular or ovate, turgid; cells many-seeded; style persistent. Petals entire.
13. SUBULARIA. Aquatic, with awl-shaped leaves. Pod oval; style deciduous; cells 4-seeded.
14. DRABA. Pod oval or oblong, entire, sometimes twisted; valves flat or slightly convex. Seeds numerous in each cell.
15. CAMELINA. Pods inflated, subovate, on long stalks; cells many-seeded. Flowers yellow.
16. KONIGA. Pod subovate; valves nearly flat; cells 1-seeded. Leaves entire.
17. ALYSSUM. Pod compressed, indented at the apex; valves convex in the middle, flat at the edges; cells usually 2-seeded. Petals notched.

** Fruit an elongated pod (*Siliqua*).

18. DENTARIA. Pods flat, linear, tapering; valves without ribs. Seed-stalks broad. Style filiform. Seeds ovate, not bordered, in one row.

19. CARDAMINE. Pod flat, linear; valves flat, ribless. Style short, or absent. Seed-stalks slender. Seeds ovate, not bordered.
20. ARABIS. Pod linear, compressed; valves with 1 rib, or many longitudinal veins. Stigma sessile. Seeds in 1 row. Calyx erect.
21. TURRITIS. Pod linear, 2-edged; valves with a prominent rib. Seeds in 2 rows. Calyx lax.
22. BARBAREA. Pod linear, 4-angled; valves keeled, concave, not pointed. Seeds in 1 row. Calyx erect.
23. NASTURTIUM. Pod nearly cylindrical, oblong or linear, without veins or keel. Seeds in 2 irregular rows. Calyx spreading.
24. SISYMBRIUM. Pod linear, rounded or angular; valves concave. Calyx equal. Seeds in 1 row.
25. ERYSIMUM. Pod linear, 4-angled; valves prominently keeled. Style very short. Seeds in 1 row. Calyx erect, equal at the base.
26. CHEIRANTHUS. Pod linear, compressed, or 2-edged, with an elevated rib on each valve. Stigma upon a style, 2-lobed. Calyx erect, 2 opposite sepals saccate at the base.
27. MATTHIOLA. Pod rounded or compressed. Stigma sessile, lobes erect. Calyx erect, 2 opposite sepals saccate at the base. Longer filaments dilated.
28. HESPERIS. Pod 4-angled or compressed. Stigmas 2, erect, nearly sessile. Seeds somewhat triangular. Calyx erect, 2 opposite sepals saccate at the base.
29. BRASSICA. Pod rounded or angular, with a conical beak. Calyx erect.
30. SINAPIS. Pod rounded or angular, with a conical beak. Calyx spreading.
31. RAPHANUS. Pod without valves, separating into several joints.

Order VII. RESEDACEÆ.

1. RESEDA. The only British genus.

Order VIII. CISTACEÆ.

1. HELIANTHEMUM. The only British genus.

Order IX. VIOLACEÆ.

1. VIOLA. The only British genus.

Order X. DROSERACEÆ.

1. DROSERA. The only British genus.

Order XI. POLYGALACEÆ.

1. POLYGALA. The only British genus.

Order XII. FRANKENIACEÆ.

1. FRANKENIA. The only British genus.

Order XIII. CARYOPHYLLACEÆ.

1. ELATINE. Sepals distinct. Capsule completely 3- or 4-celled, opening by 4 valves. Stem creeping.

* Calyx tubular. Stamens 10.

2. DIANTHUS. Calyx with bracts beneath.
3. SAPONARIA. Calyx without bracts, rounded. Styles 2.
4. CUCUBALUS. Capsule fleshy, berry-like.
5. SILENE. Capsule dry, opening at the apex. Styles 3 or 4.
6. LYCHNIS. Capsule opening at the apex. Styles 5. Petals with a scale at the base.

7. AGROSTEMMA. Capsule opening at the apex. Styles 5. Petals without appendage. Calyx-teeth long and linear.

** Sepals distinct.

8. BUFFONIA. Sepals 4. Petals 4. Stamens 4. Capsule opening by 2 valves.
9. SAGINA. Styles as many as the sepals, and opposite to them, 4–5. Capsule opening by an equal number of valves. Petals minute.
10. MŒNCHIA. Sepals 4. Petals 4, entire. Stamens 4. Styles 3. Capsule opening by 8 valves or teeth.
11. HOLOSTEUM. Sepals 5. Petals 5, indented at the end. Capsule opening at the apex with 6 teeth. Styles 3.
12. SPERGULA. Sepals 5. Petals 5. Styles 5, alternating with the sepals.
13. STELLARIA. Sepals 5. Petals 5, bifid. Styles 3. Capsule opening by 6 valves or teeth.
14. ARENARIA. Sepals 5. Petals 5, entire. Styles 3 or 5, and opposite the sepals.
15. CERASTIUM. Sepals 5. Petals 5, bifid. Capsule opening with 10 teeth. Styles 3–5.
16. CHERLERIA. Sepals 5. Petals very minute or wanting. Styles 3. Capsule opening by 3 valves.

Order XIV. LINACEÆ.

1. LINUM. Petals and stamens 5.
2. RADIOLA. Petals and stamens 4.

Order XV. MALVACEÆ.

1. LAVATERA. Involucrum 3-cleft.
2. MALVA. Involucrum of 3 distinct bracts.
3. ALTHÆA. Involucrum 6–9-cleft.

Order XVI. TILIACEÆ.

1. TILIA. The only British genus.

Order XVII. HYPERICACEÆ.

1. HYPERICUM. Stamens many, united into 3 or 4 groups at the base. Flowers yellow.
2. PARNASSIA. Stamens 5, perigynous, with 5 fringed nectaries between. Flowers white.

Order XVIII. ACERACEÆ.

1. ACER. The only British genus.

Order XIX. GERANIACEÆ.

1. GERANIUM. Fruit with a long recurved awn.
2. ERODIUM. Fruit with a long spiral awn.

Order XX. BALSAMINACEÆ.

1. IMPATIENS. The only British genus.

Order XXI. OXALIDACEÆ.

1. OXALIS. The only British genus.

Order XXII. STAPHYLEACEÆ.

1. STAPHYLEA. The only British genus.

Order XXIII. CELASTRACEÆ.

1. EUONYMUS. The only British genus.

Order XXIV. RHAMNACEÆ.

1. RHAMNUS. The only British genus.

Order XXV. LEGUMINOSÆ.

* Stamens all united by their filaments.

1. ULEX. All the branches spinous. Leaves minute. Calyx with 2 bracts at the base. Sepals nearly as long as the corolla. Standard bifid.
2. GENISTA. Flowering branches not spinous. Calyx without bracts, much shorter than the corolla, 3-cleft. Standard entire.
3. CYTISUS. Calyx much shorter than the corolla, without bracts, 2-lipped, the lower lip with 3 teeth. Standard large, ovate. Pod flat.
4. ONONIS. Calyx much shorter than the corolla, 5-cleft. Leaves simple or ternate.
5. ANTHYLLIS. Calyx much shorter than the corolla, 5-cleft. Leaves pinnate.

** One stamen distinct, the rest united.

6. MEDICAGO. Pod sickle-shaped, or spirally curved. Leaves ternate.
7. MELILOTUS. Pod nearly straight. Calyx-teeth 5, nearly equal. Keel blunt. Leaves ternate. Petals deciduous.
8. TRIFOLIUM. Pod nearly straight. Calyx-teeth 5, unequal. Petals slightly connected, persistent; keel blunt. Leaves ternate.
9. LOTUS. Pod nearly straight. Calyx-teeth nearly equal. Keel with a narrow point. Leaves ternate.
10. OXYTROPIS. Pod nearly 2-celled. Keel with a narrow point. Leaves pinnate.
11. ASTRAGALUS. Pod nearly 2-celled. Keel obtuse. Leaves pinnate.
12. ORNITHOPUS. Pod compressed, curved, jointed. Leaves pinnate.
13. HIPPOCREPIS. Pod compressed, formed of crescent-shaped joints. Leaves pinnate.
14. ONOBRYCHIS. Pod 1-seeded, toothed on the lower margin. Leaves pinnate.
15. VICIA. Pod 1-celled, many-seeded. Style filiform, hairy beneath the stigma. Leaves pinnate, with tendrils.
16. ERVUM. Pod 1-celled, with several seeds. Stigma downy all over. Leaves pinnate, with tendrils.
17. LATHYRUS. Pod 1-celled, many-seeded. Style flat, dilated upwards, downy in front. Leaves pinnate or simple, sometimes with tendrils.
18. PISUM. Pod 1-celled, many-seeded. Style compressed, keeled, somewhat triangular, downy above. Leaves pinnate, with tendrils.
19. OROBUS. Pod 1-celled. Style flat, downy on the upper side. Leaves pinnate, without tendrils.

Order XXVI. ROSACEÆ.

1. PRUNUS. Fruit a drupe. Ovary superior, of 1 carpel. Calyx deciduous.
2. SPIRÆA. Fruit formed of several follicles, arranged in a ring upon the calyx-tube.
3. DRYAS. Carpels with a feather-like awn. Disk flat.
4. GEUM. Carpels with a feather-like jointed awn. Disk elongated.
5. RUBUS. Fruit formed of a number of drupes, in a simple calyx.
6. FRAGARIA. Fruit formed of carpels on a fleshy receptacle, falling when ripe. Calyx double.
7. COMARUM. Carpels on a spongy persistent receptacle. Calyx double. Petals smaller than the calyx.

8. POTENTILLA. Carpels on a dry flat disk. Calyx double. Petals 5, larger than the calyx.
9. TORMENTILLA. Carpels on a dry flat disk. Calyx double. Petals 4, larger than the calyx.
10. SIBBALDIA. Carpels on the bottom of the calyx. Calyx double. Petals 5, minute.
11. AGRIMONIA. Carpels 2, enclosed within the calyx-tube. Petals 5. Calyx single.
12. ALCHEMILLA. Carpels 1 or 2, within the calyx-tube. Petals none. Calyx double.
13. SANGUISORBA. Carpels 1 or 2, within the calyx-tube. Petals none. Calyx single, with bracts below. Stamens 4.
14. POTERIUM. Carpels 1 or 2, within the calyx-tube. Petals none. Calyx single. Stamens numerous.
15. ROSA. Fruit formed of small nuts, within the fleshy calyx-tube.

Fruit a pome.

16. MESPILUS. Calyx-teeth large and leafy. Petals large. Disk nearly as broad as the fruit.
17. CRATÆGUS. Calyx-teeth small. Petals large. Carpels bony.
18. COTONEASTER. Calyx-teeth small. Petals small, erect.
19. PYRUS. Calyx-teeth small. Petals large. Carpels cartilaginous. Disk of fruit small.

Order XXVII. ONAGRACEÆ.

1. EPILOBIUM. Calyx 4-cleft. Stamens 8.
2. ŒNOTHERA. Calyx tubular below. Stamens 8.
3. ISNARDIA. Calyx 4-cleft. Stamens 4.
4. CIRCÆA. Calyx 2-cleft, deciduous. Stamens 2.

Order XXVIII. HALORAGACEÆ.

1. HIPPURIS. Stigma 1.
2. MYRIOPHYLLUM. Stigmas 4.

Order XXIX. LYTHRACEÆ.

1. LYTHRUM. Calyx tubular, cylindrical. Style filiform.
2. PEPLIS. Calyx bell-shaped. Style very short.

Order XXX. TAMARICACEÆ.

1. TAMARIX. The only British genus.

Order XXXI. CUCURBITACEÆ.

1. BRYONIA. The only British genus.

Order XXXII. PORTULACEÆ.

1. MONTIA. The only British genus.

Order XXXIII. ILLECEBRACEÆ.

1. CORRIGIOLA. Fruit 1-seeded, indehiscent. Petals oblong. Leaves alternate.
2. HERNIARIA. Fruit 1-seeded, indehiscent. Petals filiform. Leaves opposite.
3. ILLECEBRUM. Fruit 1-seeded, opening in 5 valves. Leaves opposite.
4. POLYCARPON. Fruit with several seeds, 3-valved.

Order XXXIV. CRASSULACEÆ.

1. TILLÆA. Petals distinct, 3 or 4. Stamens alternating with the petals.
2. COTYLEDON. Petals united into a tube.

3. SEMPERVIVUM. Petals distinct, about 12.
4. RHODIOLA. Plant dioecious.
5. SEDUM. Petals distinct, 4–6.

Order XXXV. GROSSULARIACEÆ.

1. RIBES. The only British genus.

Order XXXVI. SAXIFRAGACEÆ.

1. SAXIFRAGA. Petals 5. Ovary 2-celled.
2. CHRYSOSPLENIUM. Petals none. Ovary 1-celled.

Order XXXVII. UMBELLIFERÆ.

1. HYDROCOTYLE. Leaves peltate. Flowers nearly sessile.

* Umbels simple, or partly so. Fruit ovate, without ridges.

2. SANICULA. Fruit covered with hooked prickles.
3. ERYNGIUM. Fruit covered with scales. Leaves prickly.

** Umbels compound.

† *Fruit laterally compressed, with 5 ridges.*

4. CICUTA. Involucrum wanting, or of few leaves. Involucels many-leaved. Calyx 5-toothed. Petals with an inflexed point. Fruit double; carpels with 5 nearly flat equal ridges, with single vittæ between.
5. APIUM. Involucrum and involucels wanting. Calyx-teeth wanting. Petals with an involute point. Fruit roundish, contracted laterally; carpels with 5 filiform ridges, with vittæ between.
6. PETROSELINUM. Involucrum few-leaved. Involucels many-leaved. Petals with a long inflexed lobe. Fruit contracted laterally; carpels with 5 equal ridges, with vittæ between.
7. TRINIA. Flowers dioecious. (The only dioecious genus.)
8. HELOSCIADIUM. Involucel many-leaved. Calyx of 5 teeth, or obsolete. Petals ovate, pointed. Fruit ovate or oblong; carpels 5-ribbed, with single vittæ between.
9. SISON. Involucrum few-leaved. Calyx-teeth wanting. Petals obcordate, with an incurved point. Fruit ovate, with short clavate vittæ between the ridges.
10. ÆGOPODIUM. Involucrum wanting. Calyx-teeth wanting. Petals with an inflexed point. Carpels without vittæ.
11. CARUM. Calyx-teeth wanting. Petals obovate, with a narrow inflexed point. Fruit oblong. Vittæ single between the ribs.
12. BUNIUM. Involucrum wanting. Involucel few-leaved. Petals obovate, with a broad inflexed point. Fruit linear-oblong. Vittæ 2 or 3 between the obtuse ribs.
13. PIMPINELLA. Involucrum and involucels wanting. Calyx-teeth wanting. Petals obovate, with an inflexed point. Fruit ovate. Vittæ 3 or more together.
14. SIUM. Calyx-teeth 5, or wanting. Petals obcordate, with an inflexed point. Fruit laterally compressed or contracted, crowned by the depressed base of the styles. Vittæ 3 or more together.
15. BUPLEURUM. Calyx obsolete. Petals roundish, with a broad reflexed point. Fruit laterally compressed. Leaves simple.

†† *Fruit rounded, with 5 ridges.*

16. ŒNANTHE. Calyx 5-toothed. Petals obcordate, with an inflexed point. Fruit tapering, crowned by the straight styles. Vittæ single. Ridges blunt.
17. ÆTHUSA. Involucrum wanting. Involucel 3-leaved, pendulous. Calyx obsolete. Petals obcordate, with an inflexed point. Fruit roundish-ovate. Ridges acute. Vittæ single.

18. Fœniculum. Calyx obsolete. Petals roundish, with a broad inflexed lobe. Fruit oblong. Vittæ single.

19. Seseli. Calyx 5-toothed. Petals obcordate, with a reflexed point. Fruit oval or oblong. Ridges thick, elevated. Vittæ single.

20. Ligusticum. Calyx 5-toothed or obsolete. Petals obcordate, with an inflexed point. Fruit elliptical. Ridges sharp. Vittæ many together. Leaves biternate.

21. Silaus. Involucrum few-leaved. Involucel many-leaved. Petals obovate, with an inflexed lobe. Ridges sharp, with many vittæ between. Leaves pinnatifid.

22. Meum. Involucrum few-leaved. Involucel many-leaved. Petals elliptical, incurved at the point. Ridges acute. Vittæ many.

23. Crithmum. Involucrum and involucel many-leaved. Petals elliptical, entire, involute. Ridges sharp. Vittæ many. Plant succulent.

††† *Fruit dorsally compressed, with a wing on each side.*

24. Angelica. Involucrum deciduous. Involucel many-leaved. Three middle ridges elevated; two lateral spreading into a double wing on each side the fruit.

25. Peucedanum. Calyx 5-toothed or obsolete. Petals obovate or obcordate, with an inflexed point. Fruit flattened at the back, with a thin dilated margin. Vittæ single.

26. Pastinaca. Involucrum wanting. Calyx nearly obsolete. Petals roundish, entire, involute, pointed. Fruit much compressed, with a dilated margin. Ridges very slender. Vittæ linear, single.

27. Heracleum. Fruit dorsally compressed, with a broad flat margin. Vittæ short.

28. Tordylium. Involucrum and involucel many-leaved. Wings of fruit waved or crenated.

†††† *Fruit prickly. Carpels with secondary ridges between the others.*

29. Daucus. Fruit compressed dorsally. Carpels with 5 bristly ridges, and 4 secondary ones with prickles. Seed plane in front.

30. Caucalis. Fruit laterally compressed. Ridges prickly. Vittæ beneath the secondary ridges.

31. Torilis. Fruit laterally compressed. Secondary ridges hidden beneath the prickles.

††††† *Fruit compressed at the side, elongated, with primary ridges only.*

32. Scandix. Calyx obsolete. Petals obovate, with an inflexed point. Fruit with a very long beak. Carpels with 5 obtuse ridges. Vittæ none.

33. Anthriscus. Calyx obsolete. Petals obcordate, with a short inflexed point. Fruit beaked; beak only with ridges. Vittæ none.

34. Chærophyllum. Calyx obsolete. Petals obcordate, with an inflexed point. Fruit not beaked. Carpels with 5 obtuse ridges. Vittæ single.

35. Myrrhis. Calyx obsolete. Petals obcordate, with an inflexed point. Fruit not beaked. Ridges 5, sharp. Vittæ none.

36. Echinophora. Fruit ovate, included in the receptacle, with a projecting beak.

37. Conium. Carpels with 5 prominent, equal, crenated ridges. Vittæ none.

38. Physospermum. Calyx 5-toothed. Carpels with 5 equal filiform ridges. Vittæ single.

39. Smyrnium. Calyx obsolete. Petals lanceolate, with a long inflexed point. Fruit double. Three dorsal ridges prominent and sharp. Vittæ many.

†††††† *Fruit globular.*

40. Coriandrum. Calyx 5-toothed. Petals obcordate, with an inflexed point; the outer radiant and bifid. Fruit globular, the carpels scarcely separating. Secondary ridges prominent, primary nearly obsolete.

Order XXXVIII. ARALIACEÆ.

1. ADOXA. An herbaceous plant.
2. HEDERA. An evergreen climbing shrub.

Order XXXIX. CORNACEÆ.

1. CORNUS. The only British genus.

Order XL. LORANTHACEÆ.

1. VISCUM. The only British genus.

Order XLI. CAPRIFOLIACEÆ.

1. SAMBUCUS. Stigmas sessile. Corolla rotate. Leaves pinnate.
2. VIBURNUM. Stigmas sessile. Corolla bell-shaped. Leaves simple.
3. LONICERA. Stigma on a filiform style. Stamens 5.
4. LINNÆA. Stigma on a filiform style. Stamens 4.

Order XLII. RUBIACEÆ.

1. RUBIA. Corolla rotate. Fruit succulent.
2. GALIUM. Corolla rotate. Fruit dry.
3. SHERARDIA. Corolla funnel-shaped. Fruit crowned with the calyx.
4. ASPERULA. Corolla funnel-shaped. Fruit not crowned with the calyx.

Order XLIII. VALERIANACEÆ.

1. CENTRANTHUS. Stamen 1.
2. VALERIANA. Stamens 3. Fruit 1-celled.
3. FEDIA. Stamens 3. Fruit 3-celled.

Order XLIV. DIPSACEÆ.

1. DIPSACUS. Receptacle with spinous scales.
2. SCABIOSA. Receptacle scaly or hairy.

Order XLV. COMPOSITÆ.

* Florets all perfect.

† *Corollas all ligulate.*

1. TRAGOPOGON. Involucrum simple. Fruit longitudinally striated. Pappus feathery, stalked.
2. HELMINTHIA. Involucrum double. Fruit transversely striated. Pappus feathery, stalked.
3. PICRIS. Involucrum double. Fruit transversely striated. Pappus feathery, sessile.
4. SONCHUS. Involucrum of 2 or 3 rows of imbricated scales, oblong, swelling at the base. Fruit longitudinally striated. Pappus sessile, hair-like.
5. LACTUCA. Involucrum cylindrical, imbricated, the scales membranous at the margin. Pappus simple, stalked.
6. PRENANTHES. Involucrum cylindrical, the principal scales equal, with small ones below. Florets few. Pappus simple, sessile.
7. LEONTODON. Involucrum imbricated, with flaccid scales, the outer ones reflexed. Pappus simple, stalked.
8. APARGIA. Involucrum imbricated; inner scales equal, outer smaller. Receptacle punctured. Pappus feathery, sessile.

9. THRINCIA. Pappus of the outer series scaly (otherwise as Apargia).

10. HIERACIUM. Involucrum imbricated, with linear-oblong scales, ovate. Receptacle punctured. Pappus simple, sessile.

11. CREPIS. Involucrum swollen at the base, surrounded by deciduous scales. Pappus simple, sessile.

12. BORKHAUSIA. Involucrum oval, with deciduous scales at the base, ribbed when in fruit. Pappus nearly simple, stalked.

13. HYPOCHŒRIS. Involucrum oblong, imbricated. Receptacle chaffy. Pappus feathery.

14. LAPSANA. Involucrum with small scales at the base; the inner ones equal, linear-lanceolate. Pappus wanting.

15. CICHORIUM. Involucrum of 8 united scales, with 5 smaller at the base. Pappus sessile, scaly, shorter than the fruit.

†† *Corollas all tubular.*

16. ARCTIUM. Involucrum globose, the scales terminating in a hook. Pappus simple, short, persistent.

17. SERRATULA. Diœcious. Involucrum oblong; scales acute, unarmed. Pappus persistent, the hairs rigid, in 3 or 4 rows.

18. SAUSSUREA. Involucrum oblong, scales unarmed. Anthers bristly below. Pappus sessile, in 2 rows.

19. CARDUUS. Involucrum swollen; the scales simple, spine-pointed. Receptacle hairy. Pappus deciduous, hair-like, united into a ring at the base.

20. SILYBUM. Filaments of stamens united (otherwise as Carduus).

21. CNICUS. Pappus feathery (otherwise as Carduus).

22. ONOPORDUM. Involucrum swollen; the scales spreading, spine-pointed. Receptacle honeycombed.

23. CARLINA. Involucrum swollen; the outer scales leaf-like, sinuous, very spiny; the inner ones long and linear, coloured. Pappus feathery.

24. BIDENS. Involucrum double; the outer scales leafy, spreading. Outer florets sometimes ligulate. Receptacle chaffy. Pappus of 2–5, rough, persistent awns.

25. EUPATORIUM. Involucrum oblong. Florets few. Receptacle naked. Pappus feathery.

26. CHRYSOCOMA. Involucrum hemispherical. Pappus hairy. Style scarcely longer than the florets.

27. DIOTIS. Involucrum hemispherical. Receptacle convex, chaffy, the scales not fringed. Pappus wanting. Fruit with 2 ear-like processes.

** Florets of the centre perfect, those of the circumference with pistils only.

† *Outer florets not ligulate.*

28. TANACETUM. Involucrum hemispherical. Receptacle naked. Florets all tubular; those of the margin 3-cleft, sometimes wanting, the rest 5-cleft. Pappus obscure.

29. ARTEMISIA. Involucrum ovate or rounded. Receptacle naked or hairy. Florets all tubular; those of the margin slender, entire. Pappus wanting.

30. ANTENNARIA. Involucrum imbricated; the scales membranous. Receptacle naked. Florets of the margin awl-shaped. Pappus rough or feathery. Flowers diœcious.

31. GNAPHALIUM. Flowers perfect (otherwise as Antennaria).

32. CORYZA. Involucrum roundish, imbricated. Florets all tubular; those of the circumference 3-toothed. Pappus hairy, rough.

†† *Florets of the margin ligulate, those of the disk tubular.*

33. ERIGERON. Involucrum imbricated; scales linear, acute, very numerous.

34. TUSSILAGO. Involucrum simple; scales linear, membranous on the margin. Florets of the margin ray-like, numerous, linear, long; those of the disk few.

35. PETASITES. Flower-heads in a dense oval spike; outer florets not ray-like.
36. SENECIO. Involucrum scales linear, with smaller ones at the base, brown at
      the points. Outer florets ray-like (sometimes very slightly). Pappus simple,
      hair-like.
37. ASTER. Involucrum imbricated, scales linear. Outer florets ray-like, nume-
      rous, blue or purplish.
38. SOLIDAGO. Involucrum closely imbricated. Florets of margin few, ray-like,
      yellow.
39. INULA. Involucrum imbricated; scales leaf-like, spreading. Flower-heads
      large, terminal; outer florets ray-like. Pappus simple.
40. PULICARIA. Involucrum hemispherical, closely imbricated, with narrow scales.
      Pappus double. Outer florets more or less ray-like.
41. LIMBARDA. Involucrum imbricated, with linear scales. Pappus simple. An-
      thers with bristles at the base. Leaves succulent.
42. CINERARIA. Involucrum simple; scales many, equal, upright. Pappus simple,
      hair-like. Outer florets ray-like.
43. DORONICUM. Involucrum double, the scales longer than the disk. Pappus of
      the outer florets wanting. Outer florets ray-like. Heads very large.
44. BELLIS. Involucrum hemispherical, simple. Receptacle conical. Pappus
      wanting. Outer florets ray-like, white or pinkish. Leaves entire.
45. CHRYSANTHEMUM. Involucrum hemispherical, imbricated; scales membranous
      on the margin. Pappus wanting. Outer florets white or yellow, ray-like.
      Leaves pinnatifid or jagged.
46. PYRETHRUM. Fruit crowned with a membranous border. Otherwise as
      Chrysanthemum.
47. MATRICARIA. Involucrum hemispherical, imbricated; scales obtuse, with a
      membranous border. Pappus wanting. Outer florets ray-like, white. Re-
      ceptacle naked, nearly cylindrical.
48. ANTHEMIS. Involucrum hemispherical, imbricated; scales membranous at the
      border. Outer florets ray-like. Receptacle chaffy.
49. ACHILLEA. Involucrum ovate, imbricated. Receptacle narrow, plain, chaffy.
      Pappus wanting. Outer florets few, ray-like. Heads in corymbs.

*** Outer florets with neither stamens nor pistils; the rest with both. Florets all
tubular.
50. CENTAUREA. Outer florets funnel-shaped, much longer than the rest.

**** Heads monœcious.
51. XANTHIUM. Fertile involucrum prickly, 2-flowered.

Order XLVI. CAMPANULACEÆ.

1. CAMPANULA. Corolla bell-shaped.
2. PHYTEUMA. Corolla rotate. Anthers distinct.
3. JASIONE. Corolla rotate. Anthers adhering at the base.

Order XLVII. LOBELIACEÆ.

1. LOBELIA. The only British genus.

Order XLVIII. VACCINIACEÆ.

1. VACCINIUM. Segments of corolla short, nearly erect.
2. OXYCOCCUS. Segments of corolla long, reflexed.

Order XLIX. ERICACEÆ.

1. ERICA. Fruit dry. Calyx simple. Corolla persistent.
2. CALLUNA. Fruit dry. Calyx double. Corolla persistent.

3. MENZIESIA. Fruit dry. Corolla deciduous. Stamens 8–10. Capsule-valves opening at the margins of the carpels.
4. AZALEA. Fruit dry. Corolla deciduous. Stamens 5.
5. ANDROMEDA. Fruit dry. Corolla deciduous. Stamens 10. Capsule-valves opening down the middle of the carpels.
6. ARBUTUS. Fruit a many-seeded berry.
7. ARCTOSTAPHYLOS. Fruit a 1-seeded berry.

Order L. PYROLACEÆ.

1. PYROLA. The only British genus.

Order LI. MONOTROPACEÆ.

1. MONOTROPA. The only British genus.

Order LII. AQUIFOLIACEÆ.

1. ILEX. The only British genus.

Order LIII. OLEACEÆ.

1. LIGUSTRUM. A shrub. Fruit a succulent berry.
2. FRAXINUS. Trees. Fruit winged, dry.

Order LIV. APOCYNACEÆ.

1. VINCA. The only British genus.

Order LV. GENTIANACEÆ.

1. EXACUM. An herb. Corolla funnel-shaped. Calyx 4-cleft. Style deciduous.
2. ERYTHRÆA. Herbs. Corolla funnel-shaped. Calyx 5-cleft. Style deciduous.
3. GENTIANA. Herbs. Corolla funnel- or salver-shaped. Style persistent.
4. CHLORA. Herbs. Corolla rotate. Style deciduous.
5. MENYANTHES. A bog-plant. Leaves ternate.
6. VILLARSIA. A floating plant. Leaves heart-shaped.
7. SWERTIA. An herb. Corolla rotate. Style persistent.

Order LVI. POLEMONIACEÆ.

1. POLEMONIUM. The only British genus.

Order LVII. CONVOLVULACEÆ.

1. CONVOLVULUS. Leafy twining herbs.
2. CUSCUTA. Leafless, twining, parasitic plants.

Order LVIII. BORAGINACEÆ.

* Nuts upon a disk below the style, their base flat.

1. ECHIUM. Corolla irregular, nearly bell-shaped. Filaments long.
2. PULMONARIA. Corolla regular, funnel-shaped. Throat naked. Leaves rough.
3. LITHOSPERMUM. Corolla regular, funnel-shaped; its throat naked. Leaves rough. Or throat of corolla with 5 small projections; leaves smooth and glaucous.
4. MYOSOTIS. Throat of corolla closed with scales. Corolla salver-shaped.

** Nuts upon a disk below the style, indented at their base.

5. ANCHUSA. Corolla funnel-shaped; tube straight.

6. LYCOPSIS. Corolla-tube slightly bent.
7. SYMPHYTUM. Corolla cylindrical, bell-shaped, straight.
8. BORAGO. Corolla rotate. Filaments bifid.

*** Nuts attached to the base of the style.

9. ASPERUGO. Calyx with unequal valves.
10. CYNOGLOSSUM. Calyx equally divided.

Order LIX. SOLANACEÆ.

1. DATURA. Fruit a prickly 4-valved capsule.
2. HYOSCYAMUS. Fruit dry, opening with a transverse lid.
3. ATROPA. Fruit a berry. Anthers distant.
4. SOLANUM. Fruit a berry. Anthers close together.

Order LX. OROBANCHACEÆ.

1. OROBANCHE. Corolla 4- or 5-cleft, the base persistent.
2. LATHRÆA. Corolla 2-lipped, deciduous.

Order LXI. SCROPHULARIACEÆ.

1. VERONICA. Stamens 2.

* Stamens 4, calyx 4-cleft.

2. BARTSIA. Upper lip of corolla entire, not flattened laterally.
3. EUPHRASIA. Upper lip of corolla bifid, not flattened.
4. RHINANTHUS. Upper lip of corolla laterally compressed. Calyx inflated.
5. MELAMPYRUM. Upper lip of corolla laterally compressed. Calyx not inflated.

** Stamens 4, calyx 5-cleft.

6. PEDICULARIS. Calyx inflated. Corolla 2-lipped; upper lip compressed laterally.
7. SCROPHULARIA. Corolla nearly globular.
8. DIGITALIS. Corolla bell-shaped, unequal. Capsule 2-celled.
9. ANTIRRHINUM. Corolla-mouth closed by the lips meeting, with a rounded projection at the base.
10. LINARIA. Corolla-mouth closed by the lips meeting, with a spur at the base.
11. LIMOSELLA. Corolla bell-shaped, equal. Capsule 1-celled.
12. SIBTHORPIA. Corolla rotate, regular. Capsule 2-celled.

*** Stamens 5.

13. VERBASCUM. Corolla rotate, petals unequal.

Order LXII LABIATÆ.

* Stamens 2.

1. LYCOPUS. Corolla nearly equal. Calyx with 5 segments.
2. SALVIA. Corolla lipped. Calyx 2-lipped.

** Stamens 4, nearly equal.

3. MENTHA. Corolla 4-cleft, nearly regular.
4. THYMUS. Corolla 2-lipped. Flowers in whorls.
5. ORIGANUM. Corolla 2-lipped. Flowers panicled.

*** Stamens 4, 2 longer than the others.

† *Upper lip of corolla very short.*

6. TEUCRIUM. Stamens projecting beyond the upper lip. Upper lip cleft.
7. AJUGA. Stamens projecting beyond the upper lip. Upper lip nearly entire.

†† *Upper lip of corolla longer than the stamens. Calyx 5-toothed. Stamens longer than the tube.*

8. BALLOTA. Calyx salver-shaped, 10-ribbed. Upper lip erect, concave. Lower stamens longest.
9. LEONURUS. Calyx tubular, nearly as long as the corolla. Lower stamens longest.
10. GALEOPSIS. Calyx bell-shaped. Middle lobe of lower lip the largest. Upper lip vaulted. Lower stamens longest.
11. GALEOBDOLON. Calyx bell-shaped. Lobes of lower lip nearly equal. Upper lip incurved. Lower stamens longest.
12. LAMIUM. Calyx bell-shaped. Upper lip erect; 2 lateral lobes of lower lip very small, middle bifid. Lower stamens longest.
13. BETONICA. Calyx ovate, with 5 awned teeth.
14. STACHYS. Calyx bell-shaped. Sides of the lower lip reflexed, middle lobe nearly entire. Lower stamens longest.
15. NEPETA. Upper stamens longest. Middle lobe of lower lip crenated.
16. GLECHOMA. Upper stamens longest. Middle lobe of lower lip indented.

††† *Calyx 10-toothed. Stamens shorter than the tube.*

17. MARRUBIUM. Lower stamens longest. Plant very woolly.

†††† *Calyx 2-lipped.*

18. ACINOS. Upper lip of corolla straight. Flowers in whorls. Stamens diverging.
19. CALAMINTHA. Upper lip of corolla straight. Flowers in lateral cymes. Stamens diverging.
20. CLINOPODIUM. Upper lip of corolla straight. Flowers in whorls, with linear bracts beneath. Stamens diverging.
21. MELITTIS. Calyx bell-shaped, open in fruit. Anthers approaching in pairs.
22. PRUNELLA. Calyx ovate, closed when in fruit; upper lip 3-toothed, lower bifid.
23. SCUTELLARIA. Calyx ovate, closed when in fruit, its lips entire.

Order LXIII. VERBENACEÆ.

1. VERBENA. The only British genus.

Order LXIV. LENTIBULARIACEÆ.

1. PINGUICULA. Bog-plants with entire leaves.
2. UTRICULARIA. Water-plants. Leaves in numerous linear segments.

Order LXV. PRIMULACEÆ.

1. HOTTONIA. A water-plant. Leaves pectinated.
2. PRIMULA. Calyx tubular. Corolla-limb spreading, tube including the stamens.
3. CYCLAMEN. Calyx tubular. Corolla reflexed.
4. GLAUX. Calyx tubular, coloured. Corolla none.
5. TRIENTALIS. Calyx 7-cleft.
6. LYSIMACHIA. Calyx 5-cleft. Capsule with 5 or 2 valves.
7. ANAGALLIS. Calyx 5-cleft. Capsule opening transversely.
8. CENTUNCULUS. Calyx 4-cleft.
9. SAMOLUS. Calyx 5-cleft. Capsule opening with reflexed teeth, half inferior.

Order LXVI. PLUMBAGINACEÆ.

1. ARMERIA. Flowers in a close head.
2. STATICE. Flowers in panicles.

Order LXVII. PLANTAGINACEÆ.

1. PLANTAGO. Stamens upon the corolla.
2. LITTORELLA. Stamens hypogynous.

Order LXVIII. AMARANTHACEÆ.

1. AMARANTHUS. The only British genus.

Order LXIX. CHENOPODIACEÆ.

1. BETA. Stamens 5, on a fleshy ring. Ovary adhering to the calyx.
2. CHENOPODIUM. Stamens 5, on the receptacle. Ovary free.
3. ATRIPLEX. Stamens 5. Flowers monœcious, of different forms.
4. SALICORNIA. Stems jointed, succulent, leafless. Stamens 1 or 2. Calyx entire, fleshy.
5. SALSOLA. Stamens 5, from an hypogynous ring. Calyx 5-parted.

Order LXX. SCLERANTHACEÆ.

1. SCLERANTHUS. The only British genus.

Order LXXI. POLYGONACEÆ.

1. POLYGONUM. Sepals 5.
2. RUMEX. Sepals 6. Styles 3.
3. OXYRIA. Sepals 4. Styles 2.

Order LXXII. THYMELACEÆ.

1. DAPHNE. The only British genus.

Order LXXIII. SANTALACEÆ.

1. THESIUM. The only British genus.

Order LXXIV. ARISTOLOCHIACEÆ.

1. ARISTOLOCHIA. Anthers 6, sessile on the style. A climbing plant.
2. ASARUM. Stamens 12. A low herb.

Order LXXV. EMPETRACEÆ.

1. EMPETRUM. The only British genus.

Order LXXVI. EUPHORBIACEÆ.

1. MERCURIALIS. Calyx 3-parted. Diœcious or monœcious.
2. EUPHORBIA. Flowers in monœcious heads, surrounded by bracts. Ovary stalked.
3. BUXUS. An evergreen shrub. Stamens 4. Monœcious.

Order LXXVII. CALLITRICHACEÆ.

1. CALLITRICHE. The only British genus.

Order LXXVIII. CERATOPHYLLACEÆ.

1. CERATOPHYLLUM. The only British genus.

Order LXXIX. URTICACEÆ.

1. URTICA. Flowers monœcious or diœcious, in racemes.

2. PARIETARIA. Flowers in axillary clusters, surrounded by an involucrum.
3. HUMULUS. A climber. Diœcious. Fertile flowers in an oval catkin.

Order LXXX. ULMACEÆ.

1. ULMUS. The only British genus.

Order LXXXI. ELEAGNACEÆ.

1. HIPPOPHAË. The only British genus.

Order LXXXII. MYRICACEÆ.

1. MYRICA. The only British genus.

Order LXXXIII. BETULACEÆ.

1. BETULA. Stamens 8–12.
2. ALNUS. Stamens 4.

Order LXXXIV. SALICACEÆ.

1. SALIX. Scales of catkins entire. Stamens 1–5.
2. POPULUS. Scales jagged. Stamens 4–30.

Order LXXXV. CUPULIFERÆ.

1. FAGUS. Barren flowers in a globular catkin. Fertile flowers within a prickly
   involucrum. Stigmas 3.
2. CASTANEA. Barren flowers in a cylindrical catkin. Fertile flowers in a 4-lobed
   involucrum. Stigmas 6.
3. QUERCUS. Barren catkin lax, long. Nut surrounded by the cup-like involucrum.
4. CORYLUS. Barren catkin long, cylindrical. Nut covered by a coriaceous involucrum.
5. CARPINUS. Barren catkin long, lax. Involucrum of 2 leaf-like scales.

Order LXXXVI. CONIFERÆ.

1. PINUS. A tree. Fertile flowers in a cone.
2. JUNIPERUS. A bush. Fruit berry-like.
3. TAXUS. A tree. Seed enveloped in a cup-like fleshy receptacle.

Order LXXXVII. DIOSCOREACEÆ.

1. TAMUS. The only British genus.

Order LXXXVIII. TRILLIACEÆ.

1. PARIS. The only British genus.

Order LXXXIX. HYDROCHARIDACEÆ.

1. ANACHARIS. Leaves whorled. Plant submersed.
2. HYDROCHARIS. Leaves floating, kidney-shaped.
3. STRATIOTES. Leaves submerged, sword-shaped, with marginal prickles.

Order XC. ORCHIDACEÆ.

* Anther cohering to the face of the stigma.

1. ORCHIS. Lip with a spur. Glands of the stalks of the pollen-masses in a pouch.

2. GYMNADENIA. Lip with a spur. Glands of the pollen-masses naked.
3. HABENARIA. Lip with a spur. Perianth hooded. Anther-cells diverging at the base.
4. ACERAS. Lip without a spur. Perianth helmet-shaped. Segment of the lip linear.
5. HERMINIUM. Lip without a spur. Perianth bell-shaped.
6. OPHRYS. Lip without a spur. Perianth spreading. Lip lobed.

** Anther on the back of the column, attached by its base.

7. GOODYERA. Two lateral sepals spreading. Lip free from the column, entire at the apex.
8. NEOTTIA. Two lateral sepals erect. Lip embracing the column.
9. LISTERA. Lip linear or oblong, 2-lobed at the end.
10. EPIPACTIS. Lip free from the column, contracted in the middle.

*** Anther 1, terminal, free.

11. MALAXIS. Perianth spreading. Lip superior.
12. LIPARIS. Perianth spreading. Lip inferior.
13. CORALLORHIZA. Perianth converging.

**** Anthers 2.

14. CYPRIPEDIUM. Lip very large, inflated.

Order XCI. IRIDACEÆ.

1. IRIS. Stigmas petaloid, covering the stamens.
2. TRICHONEMA. Stigmas 3, bifid; lobes slender.
3. CROCUS. Stigmas 3-cleft; lobes widening towards the apex.

Order XCII. AMARYLLIDACEÆ.

1. NARCISSUS. Perianth spreading, with a bell-shaped nectary within.
2. GALANTHUS. Perianth bell-shaped; 3 inner sepals smaller, erect.
3. LEUCOJUM. Perianth bell-shaped. Sepals all equal.

Order XCIII. LILIACEÆ.

* Fruit a berry.

1. ASPARAGUS. Leaves soft, setaceous.
2. RUSCUS. A small diœcious shrub. Leaves spiny.
3. CONVALLARIA. Herbs. Leaves broad.

** Fruit dry and capsular. Stalks not leafy.

4. HYACINTHUS. Perianth tubular below; segments reflexed.
5. MUSCARI. Perianth tubular, nearly globose, contracted at the mouth.
6. ALLIUM. Flowers in umbels, with a spathe beneath. Sepals distinct.
7. SCILLA. Flowers in racemes. Perianth deciduous. Sepals distinct.
8. ORNITHOGALUM. Flowers in racemes. Perianth persistent. Sepals distinct.

*** Fruit dry. Stalks leafy.

9. GAGEA. Style erect. Flowers yellow, in umbels.
10. ANTHERICUM. Style erect. Flowers white or pink, solitary or very few.
11. TULIPA. Style absent. Flowers solitary.
12. FRITILLARIA. Style 3-cleft at the apex. Flowers solitary, drooping, large.
13. LILIUM. Sepals reflexed. Style undivided. Flowers in panicles.

Order XCIV. MELANTHACEÆ.

1. COLCHICUM.   Perianth funnel-shaped ; tube very long.
2. TOFIELDIA.   Perianth 6-parted.   Styles short.

Order XCV. RESTIACEÆ.

1. ERIOCAULON.   The only British genus.

Order XCVI. JUNCACEÆ.

1. NARTHECIUM.   Perianth yellow, petal-like.
2. JUNCUS.   Perianth scale-like.   Capsule 3-celled.
3. LUZULA.   Perianth scale-like.   Capsule 1-celled.

Order XCVII. BUTOMACEÆ.

1. BUTOMUS.   The only British genus.

Order XCVIII. ALISMACEÆ.

1. ACTINOCARPUS.   Stamens 6.   Carpels 2-seeded.
2. ALISMA.   Stamens 6.   Carpels 1-seeded.
3. SAGITTARIA.   Flowers monœcious.   Stamens many.   Leaves sagittate.

Order XCIX. JUNCAGINACEÆ.

1. TRIGLOCHIN.   Ovary 1.
2. SCHEUCHZERIA.   Ovaries 3.

Order C. TYPHACEÆ.

1. TYPHA.   Flowers in a long spike (spadix).
2. SPARGANIUM.   Flowers in globular heads.

Order CI. ARACEÆ.

1. ARUM.   The only British genus.

Order CII. ORONTIACEÆ.

1. ACORUS.   The only British genus.

Order CIII. PISTIACEÆ.

1. LEMNA.   The only British genus.

Order CIV. NAIADACEÆ.

1. POTAMOGETON.   Perianth of 4 sepals.   Carpels 4, sessile.
2. RUPPIA.   Perianth wanting.   Carpels 4, on long stalks.
3. ZANNICHELLIA.   Flowers axillary, in a membranous bract.
4. ZOSTERA.   Flowers in a slit in the grass-like leaf.

Order CV. CYPERACEÆ.

1. CYPERUS.   Spikelets many-flowered, 2-ranked, nearly all fertile.
2. SCHŒNUS.   Spikelets 2–4-flowered, 2-ranked.   Lower glumes empty.   Style deciduous.

* Glumes imbricated.

3. CLADIUM. Glumes 5 or 6. Bristles none. Nut crowned with the conical base of the style.

4. RHYNCHOSPORA. Glumes 5 or 6. Bristles several. Nut crowned with the dilated base of the style.

5. ELEOCHARIS. Spikelets solitary, terminal. Bristles 4–12. Base of style persistent.

6. ELEOGITON. Spikelets solitary, terminal. Bristles none. Style deciduous.

7. SCIRPUS. Spikelets in umbels. Bristles about 6.

8. ERIOPHORUM. Bristles silky, very long when in seed.

9. ELYNA. Flowers monœcious, in aggregated spikelets.

10. CAREX. Flowers monœcious, in imbricated spikes.

Order CVI. GRAMINEÆ.

1. ANTHOXANTHUM. Panicle spike-like. Glumes unequal, containing 3 florets; the middle one perfect, with 2 stamens, the outer imperfect.

2. NARDUS. Flowers in one-sided spikes. Glumes wanting. Paleæ 2, the outer one with a long point. Style 1.

3. ALOPECURUS. Flowers in cylindrical spikes. Glumes 2, 1-flowered. Palea 1, awned at the base.

4. PHALARIS. Flowers panicled, or in ovate spikes. Glumes 2, 1-flowered, keeled, longer than the paleæ. Paleæ 4, the inner pair investing the seed.

5. AMMOPHILA. Panicle spike-like. Glumes 2, keeled. Paleæ 2, with hairs at the base, one awned.

6. PHLEUM. Flowers in cylindrical spikes. Glumes 2, equal, sharp, 1-flowered. Paleæ 2, awnless, within the glumes, loosely coating the seed.

7. LAGURUS. Flower in an ovate hairy spike. Glumes 2, 1-flowered, fringed. Paleæ 2; outer one with an awn and 2 bristles.

8. MILIUM. Panicle loose. Glumes 2, pointed, longer than the floret. Paleæ 2, awnless, coating the seed.

9. GASTRIDIUM. Panicle contracted. Glumes 2, acute, swollen at the base, longer than the floret. Paleæ 2, investing the seed; outer one awned.

10. STIPA. Panicle erect. Outer palea with a very long feather-like awn, coating the seed.

11. POLYPOGON. Glumes 2, notched at the end, with a long straight awn. Paleæ unequal; outer one awned.

12. CALAMAGROSTIS. Panicle loose, spreading. Glumes 2, unequal, acute, 1-flowered. Paleæ surrounded by long silky hairs.

13. AGROSTIS. Panicle more or less spreading. Glumes 2, unequal, 1-flowered. Paleæ 2, unequal, membranous. Seed free.

14. CATABROSA. Panicle spreading. Glumes 2, obtuse, 2–3-flowered. Paleæ truncated, awnless. Seed free.

15. AIRA. Flowers panicled. Glumes 2, pointed, with 2 perfect florets. Paleæ membranous; outer one awned at the base. Seed free.

16. MELICA. Flowers panicled. Glumes 2, with 2 perfect florets, and 1 or 2 rudimentary ones between. Paleæ coating the seed.

17. HOLCUS. Panicle lax. Glumes 2, 2-flowered; upper floret imperfect, awned; lower perfect, awnless. Seed coated by the paleæ.

18. ARRHENATHERUM. Panicle lax. Glumes 2, 2-flowered; upper floret perfect, with a short bristle; lower imperfect, with a long awn. Seed coated by the paleæ.

19. HIEROCHLOE. Flowers panicled. Glumes 2, 3-flowered; the inner floret with 2 stamens; the outer ones barren, with 3 stamens.

20. KŒLERIA. Panicles spike-like. Glumes 2, longer than the florets, unequal. Paleæ awnless. (Otherwise as Aira.)

21. SESLERIA. Panicle ovate, spike-like. Glumes 3-flowered, pointed. Paleæ 2, the outer pointed, the inner cloven. Styles united. Seed free.

22. PANICUM. Panicle close. Glumes 2, unequal, 2-flowered, 1 floret imperfect. Seed coated with the paleæ.

23. SETARIA. Panicle spike-like, bristly. Spikelets surrounded by bristles at the base. (Otherwise as Panicum.)

24. POA. Panicle usually loose. Spikelets rounded at the base. Glumes 2, pointed, with many florets. Paleæ 2, ovate, awnless. Seed free.

25. TRIODIA. Panicle close. Glumes 2, many-flowered. Paleæ 2, broad; the outer one with 3 teeth. Seed free.

26. BRIZA. Panicle very lax. Glumes 2, many-flowered, swollen. Paleæ 2, awnless, obtuse; the outer one swollen. Seed depressed, attached to the paleæ.

27. DACTYLIS. Spikelets crowded, leaning one way. Glumes 2, unequal; the larger one keeled, many-flowered. Paleæ pointed.

28. CYNOSURUS. Panicle one-sided, spike-like, or short, with few spikelets. Spikelets in pairs, one fertile and one abortive. Glumes 2, with several florets.

29. FESTUCA. Flowers panicled. Glumes 2, pointed, unequal. Spikelets many-flowered, rather cylindrical. Paleæ 2; the outer awned, the inner downy. Seed free.

30. BROMUS. Panicle loose. Spikelets oblong. Glumes 2, with many florets. Paleæ 2; the outer awned beneath the cloven apex, the inner bristly. Seed attached to one palea.

31. AVENA. Flowers panicled. Glumes membranous, with several florets. Outer palea coating the seed, with a bent awn at the back.

32. ARUNDO. Panicle loose and spreading. Glumes 2, with 5 florets, with long silky hairs at the base.

33. ELYMUS. Flowers spiked, in 2 rows, several together. Glumes 2, both on one side, with several florets.

34. HORDEUM. Flowers spiked, in 2 rows, 3 together. Glumes 2, both on one side, with 1 floret. Seed attached to the paleæ. Glumes and palea both awned.

35. TRITICUM. Flowers spiked, in 2 rows, their sides towards the stalk. Glumes 2, with several florets. Inner palea bifid.

36. BRACHYPODIUM. Flowers spiked, in 2 rows, their sides towards the stalk, nearly cylindrical. Glumes 2, unequal, many-flowered. Paleæ 2, awned. Seed loose.

37. LOLIUM. Flowers spiked, in 2 rows. Glume 1, fronting the stalk, many-flowered.

38. LEPTURUS. Flowers in an awl-shaped spike. Glumes 2, united below. Florets imbedded in the stalk.

39. KNAPPIA. Flowers spiked, in 2 rows. Glumes 2, obtuse, 1-flowered. Paleæ 2, very hairy.

40. SPARTINA. Flowers spiked, in 2 rows, on one side of the stalk. Glumes 2, compressed. Paleæ 2, compressed. Styles united. Seed free.

41. CYNODON. Spikes linear, 3-5 together on the top of the stalk. Seed coated by the paleæ.

42. DIGITARIA. Flowers spiked, in pairs, on one side of the flattened stalk. Spikes several together on the top of the stalk. Seed coated by the paleæ.

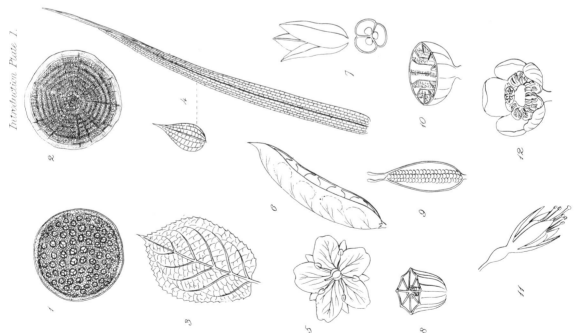

J.E. Sowerby, Fecit.

Order I. RANUNCULACEÆ.

Genus 1. Clematis.

C. Vitalba. *Traveller's Joy.* **Fig. 1.**
A climbing plant, with pinnate leaves. Fruit feathered with long silvery plume. Hedges on chalky soil. Perenn. June and July. White. ($\frac{1}{2}$) *E. B. 1. 612. E. B. 2. 776. H. & Arn. 4. Bab. 3. Lind. 8.*

Genus 2. Thalictrum.

T. alpinum. *Alpine Meadow Rue.* **Fig. 2.**
Stem nearly leafless, simple. Fl. drooping, in simple racemes. Moist fissures of rocks in alpine districts. 6 in. Perenn. July. Pale yellow. ($\frac{1}{2}$) *E. B. 1. 262. E. B. 2. 772. H. & Arn. 5. Bab. 3. Lind. 8.*

T. minus. *Lesser Meadow Rue.* **Fig. 3.**
Leaves 2- or 3-pinnate, glaucous on both sides. Stem zigzag, branched. Fl. drooping. Limestone pastures and the sea-coast. 1 ft. Perenn. July. Purplish, stamens yellow. ($\frac{1}{2}$) *E. B. 1. 11. E. B. 2. 773. H. & Arn. 5. Bab. 3. Lind. 9.*

T. majus. *Great Meadow Rue.* **Fig. 4.**
Leaves tripinnate, glaucous beneath. Fl. drooping, on branched stem. Northern hill-pastures. 1 to 2 ft. Perenn. July. Greenish-yellow. ($\frac{1}{2}$) *E. B. 1. 611. E. B. 2. 774. H. & Arn. 5. Bab. 4. Lind. 9.*

T. flavum. *Common Meadow Rue.* **Fig. 5.**
Stem erect, leafy. Leaves bipinnate. Fl. erect, in compact panicles. Moist meadows; common. Plant acrid. 2 to 3 ft. Perenn. July. Yellow. ($\frac{3}{4}$) *E. B. 1. 367. E. B. 2. 775. H. & Arn. 5. Bab. 4. Lind. 9.*

Genus 3. Anemone.

A. Pulsatilla. *Pasque Flower.* **Fig. 6.**
Leaves bipinnate, with linear lobes. Involucrum with linear segments. Plant hairy. Fl. solitary. Petals 6. Fruit with feathery awns. Chalky pastures. 9 in. Perenn. May. Purple. ($\frac{1}{2}$) *E. B. 1. 51. E. B. 2. 777. H. & Arn. 6. Bab. 4. Lind. 9.*

A. nemorosa. *Wind Flower. Wood Anemone.* **Fig. 7.**
Flowers solitary, with involucrum of 3, stalked, deeply-cut leaves. Petals 6. Woods and thickets. 6 to 8 in. Perenn. April. White, purplish underneath. ($\frac{1}{2}$) *E. B. 1. 355. E. B. 2. 778. H. & Arn. 6. Bab. 4. Lind. 9.*

A. apennina. *Blue Anemone.* **Fig. 8**
.Petals numerous. Leaves triternate. Involucrum of 3 deeply-cut ternate leaves. Woods; a doubtful native. 6 in. Perenn. April. Blue. ($\frac{1}{2}$) *E. B. 1. 1062. E. B. 2. 780. H. & Arn. 6. Bab. 4. Lind. 9.*

A. ranunculoides. *Yellow Anemone.* **Fig. 9.**
Involucrum of 3–5 deeply-cut leaves. Fl. solitary or in pairs. Petals 5 or 6. Woods in Kent and Herts; a doubtful native. 6 in. Perenn. April. Yellow. ($\frac{1}{2}$) *E. B. 1. 1484. E. B. 2. 779. H. & Arn. 6. Bab. 5. Lind. 10.*

Genus 4. Adonis.

A. autumnalis. *Pheasant's Eye.* **Fig. 10.**
Stem branched. Petals 8 generally. Seed-vessels forming an ovate head. Corn-fields. 10 in. Ann. May–Sept. Scarlet. ($\frac{1}{2}$) *E. B. 1. 308. E. B. 2. 781. H. & Arn. 6. Bab. 5. Lind. 9.*

Genus 5. Myosurus.

M. minimus. *Mouse-tail.* **Fig. 11.**
Calyx of 5 sepals elongated at the base. Seed-vessels arranged on a long columnar receptacle. Leaves long and narrow. Fields and waste places. 6 in. Ann. May. Greenish. ($\frac{1}{2}$) *E. B.* 1. 435. *E. B.* 2. 461. *H. & Arn.* 7. *Bab.* 5. *Lind.* 10.

Genus 6. Ranunculus.

R. aquatilis. *Water Crowfoot.* **Fig. 12.**
Lower leaves under water, hair-like; upper ones floating, 3-lobed, sometimes wanting. Ponds, ditches and slow streams. Perenn. May. White. ($\frac{1}{2}$) *E. B.* 1. 101. *E. B.* 2. 795. *H. & Arn.* 7. *Bab.* 6. *Lind.* 12.

R. pantothrix. *Small Water Crowfoot.* **Fig. 13.**
All the leaves hair-like and submersed. Petals little larger than calyx. Ditches. Perenn. May–Aug. White. ($\frac{1}{2}$) *H. & Arn.* 7.? *Bab.* 7.? *Lind.* 12.

R. hederaceus. *Ivy-leaved Crowfoot.* **Fig. 14.**
Stem creeping. Leaves glossy, roundish, slightly 3–5-lobed, all floating or spreading. Wet places and shallow pools. Perenn. June–Sept. White. ($\frac{1}{2}$) *E.B.* 1. 2003. *E.B.* 2. 796. *H. & Arn.* 8. *Bab.* 8. *Lind.* 11.

R. Lingua. *Great Spearwort.* **Fig. 15.**
Leaves lanceolate, serrated. Stem erect, many-flowered. Ditches; not common. 2 to 3 ft. Perenn. July. Bright yellow. ($\frac{1}{2}$) *E. B.* 1. 100. *E. B.* 2. 782. *H. & Arn.* 9. *Bab.* 9. *Lind.* 10.

R. ophioglossifolius. *Adder's-tongue Spearwort.* **Fig. 16.**
Lower leaves oval heart-shaped, serrated, with very long foot-stalks. Stem erect, many-flowered. Marshes, Jersey. 2 ft. Perenn. June. Yellow. ($\frac{1}{2}$) *E. B. Supp.* 2833. *H. & Arn.* 9. *Bab.* 9.

R. Flammula. *Lesser Spearwort.* **Fig. 17.**
Lower leaves ovato-lanceolate, serrated, with long foot-stalks. Stem reclining. Ditches and wet places; common. 1 to 2 ft. Perenn. June–Sept. Yellow. ($\frac{1}{2}$) *E. B.* 1. 387. *E. B.* 2. 783. *H. & Arn.* 9. *Bab.* 9. *Lind.* 10.

R. gramineus. *Grass-leaved Crowfoot.* **Fig. 18.**
All the leaves linear-lanceolate, not serrated. Stem erect, with few flowers. Dry alpine pastures. 1 ft. Perenn. June. Yellow. ($\frac{1}{2}$) *E. B.* 1. 2306. *E. B.* 2. 784. *H. & Arn.* 10. *Bab.* 9. *Lind.* 10.

R. Ficaria. *Small Celandine. Pilewort.* **Fig. 19.**
Leaves heart-shaped. Flowers solitary, with many petals. Roots consisting of clustered tubers. Hedge-banks and shady places; common. 4 to 6 in. Perenn. March and April. Yellow. ($\frac{1}{2}$) *E. B.* 1. 584. *E. B.* 2. 785. *H. & Arn.* 10. *Bab.* 10. *Lind.* 10.

R. alpestris. *Alpine Crowfoot.* **Fig. 20.**
Lower leaves in 3 deep, lobed segments. Stem-leaf lanceolate. Flowers solitary. Moist places on mountains; rare. Acrid. 6 in. Perenn. May. White. ($\frac{1}{2}$) *E. B.* 1. 2390. *E. B.* 2. 786. *H. & Arn.* 9. *Bab.* 9. *Lind.* 10.

Fig. 1. to 20.

J. E. Sowerby, Fecit.

R. AURICOMUS. *Wood Crowfoot. Goldilocks.* Fig. 21.
Leaves 3-parted, with deeply-cut lobes. Stem erect, slender, many-flowered. Petals with a pore at the base. Dry woods. 1 ft. Perenn. April–June. Yellow. ($\frac{1}{2}$) *E. B.* 1. 624. *E. B.* 2. 788. *H. & Arn.* 10. *Bab.* 10. *Lind.* 10.

R. SCELERATUS. *Celery-leaved Crowfoot.* Fig. 22.
Lower leaves palmate, with 3 slightly lobed segments, shining; stem ones fingered in 3 lobes. Fruit forming a cylindrical head. Watery places; common. Acrid. 1 to 2 ft. Ann. June–Sept. ($\frac{1}{2}$) *E. B.* 1. 681. *E. B.* 2. 787. *H. & Arn.* 10. *Bab.* 8. *Lind.* 11.

R. ACRIS. *Buttercup.* Fig. 23.
Stem erect, hairy, round. Calyx spreading. Petals with a small scale at the base. Very common in meadows and pastures. Acrid. 1 ft. Perenn. June. Yellow. ($\frac{1}{2}$) *E. B.* 1. 652. *E. B.* 2. 789. *H. & Arn.* 10. *Bab.* 10. *Lind.* 11.

R. REPENS. *Creeping Buttercup.* Fig. 24.
Shoots creeping. Flower-stalks furrowed. Calyx spreading. Pastures; common. 10–12 in. Perenn. June–Sept. Yellow. ($\frac{1}{2}$) *E. B.* 1. 516. *E. B.* 2. 790. *H. & Arm.* 10. *Bab.* 10. *Lind.* 11.

R. BULBOSUS. *Bulbous Buttercup.* Fig. 25.
Root bulbous. Flower-stalks furrowed, hairy. Calyx reflexed. Pastures; common. 1 ft. Perenn. May. Yellow. ($\frac{1}{2}$) *E. B.* 1. 515. *E. B.* 2. 791. *H. & Arn.* 10. *Bab.* 10. *Lind.* 11.

R. HIRSUTUS. *Hairy Buttercup.* Fig. 26.
Root fibrous. Calyx reflexed. Plant hairy. Fruit tuberculated. Moist meadows. 4 to 18 in. Ann. June–Oct. ($\frac{1}{2}$) *E. B.* 1. 1504. *E. B.* 2. 792. *H. & Arn.* 11. *Bab.* 10. *Lind.* 11.

R. ARVENSIS. *Corn Crowfoot.* Fig. 27.
Leaves with narrow lanceolate segments. Stem much branched. Fruit prickly. Corn-fields. Acrid. 1 ft. Ann. June. ($\frac{1}{2}$) *E. B.* 1. 135. *E. B.* 2. 793. *H. & Arn.* 11. *Bab.* 11. *Lind.* 11.

R. PARVIFLORUS. *Small-flowered Crowfoot.* Fig. 28.
Stem prostrate. Leaves roundish, 3-lobed. Hairy. Calyx as long as the petals. Corn-fields. Ann. June–Sept. Yellow. ($\frac{1}{2}$) *E. B.* 1. 120. *E. B.* 2. 794. *H. & Arn.* 11. *Bab.* 11. *Lind.* 11.

Genus 7. CALTHA.

C. PALUSTRIS. *Marsh Marigold.* Fig. 29.
Stem erect. Lower leaves large, rounded heart-shaped, deep glossy green. Marshes and river-sides. Acrid. 1–1½ ft. Perenn. May. Bright yellow. ($\frac{1}{2}$) *E. B.* 1. 506. *E. B.* 2. 798. *H. & Arn.* 11. *Bab.* 11. *Lind.* 12.

C. RADICANS. *Creeping Marsh Marigold.* Fig. 30.
Stem reclining. Leaves triangular. Scotch Mountains. Perhaps a variety of the preceding species. 6 in. Perenn. May and June. Yellow. ($\frac{1}{2}$) *E. B.* 1. 2175. *E. B.* 2. 799. *H. & Arn.* 11. *Bab.* 11. *Lind.* 12.

Fig. 21. to 40.

J. E. Sowerby, Fecit.

Genus 8. TROLLIUS.

T. EUROPÆUS. *Globe Flower.* **Fig. 31.**
Leaves divided into 5 deep segments, cut and serrated. Sepals and petals converging. Hill-pastures. 2 ft. Perenn. June. Bright yellow. ($\frac{1}{2}$) *E.B.* 1. 28. *E.B.* 2. 797. *H.&Arn.* 12. *Bab.* 11. *Lind.* 12.

Genus 9. HELLEBORUS.

H. VIRIDIS. *Green Hellebore.* **Fig. 32.**
Stem few-flowered. Leaves dark green, digitate. Calyx spreading. Woods on chalk. Violently cathartic. 1 ft. Perenn. April. Green. ($\frac{1}{2}$) *E. B.* 1. 200. *E. B.* 2. 800. *H. & Arn.* 12. *Bab.* 12. *Lind.* 12.

H. FŒTIDUS. *Stinking Hellebore. Bear's-foot.* **Fig. 33.**
Stem many-flowered. Calyx converging. Leaves pedate. Woods. Violently cathartic. 1 ft. Perenn. Jan.–April. Green tipped with purple. ($\frac{1}{2}$) *E. B.* 1. 613. *E. B.* 2. 801. *H. & Arn.* 12. *Bab.* 12. *Lind.* 13.

Genus 10. AQUILEGIA.

A. VULGARIS. *Columbine.* **Fig. 34.**
Leaves 2-ternate, lobed. Spur of petals incurved. Woods and pastures. 18 in. Perenn. June. Purple or rose colour. ($\frac{1}{2}$) *E. B.* 1. 297. *E. B.* 2. 770. *H. & Arn.* 12. *Bab.* 12. *Lind.* 13.

Genus 11. DELPHINIUM.

D. CONSOLIDA. *Larkspur.* **Fig. 35.**
Stem erect, with straggling branches. Leaves sessile, in many linear segments. Fields. Acrid. 2 ft. Ann. July. Blue or pink. ($\frac{1}{2}$) *E. B.* 1. 1839. *E. B.* 2. 769. *H. & Arn.* 13. *Bab.* 12. *Lind.* 13.

Genus 12. ACONITUM.

A. NAPELLUS. *Monkshood. Wolfsbane.* **Fig. 36.**
Lateral petals hairy inside. Leaves deeply 5-cleft, the lobes deeply cut. River-sides; rare. Poisonous. 3–4 ft. Perenn. June. Blue. ($\frac{1}{2}$) *E. B. Supp.* 2730. *E. B.* 2. 769*. *H. &Arn.* 13. *Bab.* 12. *Lind.* 13.

Genus 13. ACTÆA.

A. SPICATA. *Herb Christopher. Bane-berry.* **Fig. 37.**
Raceme erect, elongated. Petals as long as stamens. Mountain woods; rare. Poisonous. 2 ft. Perenn. June. White; berries black. ($\frac{1}{2}$) *E.B.* 1. 918. *E.B.* 2. 746. *H. & Arn.* 13. *Bab.* 12. *Lind.* 14.

Genus 14. PÆONIA.

P. CORALLINA. *Pæony.* **Fig. 38.**
Leaves bi-ternate, smooth; segments undivided. Steep Holmes in the Severn. 2 ft. Perenn. June. Crimson. ($\frac{1}{3}$) *E. B.* 1. 1513. *E. B.* 2. 768. *H. & Arn.* 14. *Bab.* 13. *Lind.* 14.

ORDER II. BERBERIDACEÆ.

Genus 1. BERBERIS.

B. VULGARIS. *Barberry.* **Fig. 39.**
A shrub. Flowers in pendulous racemes. Spines 3-cleft. Hedges. Berries acid. 4–10 ft. June. Yellow; berries red. ($\frac{1}{2}$) *E. B.* 1. 49. *E. B.* 2. 462. *H. & Arn.* 14. *Bab.* 13. *Lind.* 14.

Genus 2. EPIMEDIUM.

E. ALPINUM. *Barren-wort.* **Fig. 40.**
No root-leaves. Leaf on stem solitary, 2-ternate, leaflets pointed, heart-shaped. Mountain woods; rare. 8–10 in. Perenn. April. Red. ($\frac{1}{2}$) *E. B.* 1. 438. *E. B.* 2. 226. *H. & Arn.* 14. *Bab.* 13. *Lind.* 15.

5

Order III. NYMPHÆACEÆ.
Genus 1. Nymphæa.

N. alba. *White Water Lily.*   **Fig. 41.**
Leaves heart-shaped. Rays of stigma 16, curved upward. Clear water. Perenn. June and July. White; stigma yellow. ($\frac{1}{3}$) *E. B.* 1. 160. *E. B.* 2. 765. *H. & Arn.* 15. *Bab.* 14. *Lind.* 15.

Genus 2. Nuphar.

N. lutea. *Yellow Water Lily.*   **Fig. 42.**
Leaves heart-shaped, lobes meeting. Border of stigma entire. Slow streams. Perenn. July. Yellow. ($\frac{1}{2}$) *E. B.* 1. 159. *E. B.* 2. 766. *H. & Arn.* 15. *Bab.* 14. *Lind.* 15.

N. pumila. *Small Yellow Water Lily.*   **Fig. 43.**
Lobes of leaves rather distant. Stigma toothed on margin. Highland lakes. Perenn. July. Yellow; stigma green. ($\frac{1}{2}$) *E. B.* 1. 2292. *E. B.* 2. 767. *H. & Arn.* 16. *Bab.* 14. *Lind.* 15.

Order IV. PAPAVERACEÆ.
Genus 1. Papaver.

P. Argemone. *Prickly-headed Poppy.*   **Fig. 44.**
Capsule club-shaped, ribbed, bristly. Corn-fields and waste ground. Narcotic. 1½ ft. Ann. June. Pale scarlet, black at base. ($\frac{1}{2}$) *E. B.* 1. 643. *E. B.* 2. 752. *H. & Arn.* 17. *Bab.* 15. *Lind.* 16.

P. hybridum. *Rough-headed Poppy.*   **Fig. 45.**
Capsule nearly globular, furrowed, bristly. Chalky fields. Narcotic. 1½ ft. Ann. July. Crimson, often black at base. ($\frac{1}{2}$) *E. B.* 1. 43. *E. B.* 2. 753. *H. & Arn.* 17. *Bab.* 15. *Lind.* 16.

P. dubium. *Long-headed Poppy.*   **Fig. 46.**
Capsule smooth, oblong. Flower-stalk covered with closely pressed hairs. Corn-fields. Narcotic. 2 ft. Ann. July. Pale scarlet. ($\frac{1}{3}$) *E. B.* 1. 644. *E. B.* 2. 754. *H. & Arn.* 17. *Bab.* 15. *Lind.* 17.

P. Rhœas. *Corn Poppy.*   **Fig. 47.**
Capsule smooth, nearly globular. Hairs on flower-stalk spreading. Corn-fields. Narcotic. 2 ft. Ann. June and July. Deep scarlet, often black at base. ($\frac{1}{3}$) *E. B.* 1. 645. *E. B.* 2. 755. *H. & Arn.* 17. *Bab.* 15. *Lind.* 17.

P. somniferum. *White Poppy.*   **Fig. 48.**
Capsule nearly globular. Leaves unequally divided, glaucous. Waste places. Narcotic. 3 ft. Ann. July. White or purplish, purple at base. ($\frac{1}{3}$) *E. B.* 1. 2145. *E. B.* 2. 756. *H. & Arn.* 17. *Bab.* 15. *Lind.* 17.

P. nudicaule. *Naked-stalked Yellow Poppy.*   **Fig. 49.**
Capsule oblong-ovate, rough. Flower-stems long. Plant covered with tawny hairs. Rocks and hills on the north-west coast of Ireland. 1 ft. Perenn. July. Pale yellow. ($\frac{1}{2}$) *E. B. Supp.* 2681. *E. B.* 2. 753*. *Lind.* 17.

Genus 2. Meconopsis.

M. cambrica. *Welsh Poppy.*   **Fig. 50.**
Capsule smooth, elongated. Humid, rocky places. 1 ft. Perenn. July and Aug. Orange-yellow. ($\frac{1}{2}$) *E. B.* 1. 66. *E. B.* 2. 751. *H. & Arn.* 17. *Bab.* 15. *Lind.* 17.

Genus 3. GLAUCIUM.

G. LUTEUM. *Horned Poppy.* **Fig. 51.**
Stem smooth. Stem-leaves wavy. Pods very long, curved. Plant glaucous. Sea-coast. 1–3 ft. Biennial. June–Aug. Bright yellow. ($\frac{1}{3}$) *E. B.* 1. 8. *E. B.* 2. 748. *H. & Arn.* 18. *Bab.* 16. *Lind.* 17.

G. PHŒNICEUM. *Scarlet Horned Poppy.* **Fig. 52.**
Stem hairy. Stem-leaves pinnatifid, cut. Sandy shores. A doubtful native. 2 ft. Ann. June and July. Scarlet. ($\frac{1}{2}$) *E. B.* 1. 1433. *E. B.* 2. 749. *H. & Arn.* 18. *Bab.* 16. *Lind.* 18.

G. VIOLACEUM. *Violet Horned Poppy.* **Fig. 53.**
Stem slightly hairy. Leaves 3-pinnatifid, with linear segments. A doubtful native. 2 ft. Ann. May. Purple, red at the base. ($\frac{1}{2}$) *E. B.* 1. 201. *E. B.* 2. 750. *H. & Arn.* 18. *Bab.* 16. *Lind.* 18.

Genus 4. CHELIDONIUM.

C. MAJUS. *Celandine.* **Fig. 54.**
Flowers in umbels. Plant slightly hairy. Juice yellow, acrid. Waste ground and thickets. 2 ft. Perenn. May and June. Yellow. ($\frac{1}{2}$) *E. B.* 1. 1581. *E. B.* 2. 747. *H. & Arn.* 18. *Bab.* 16. *Lind.* 18.

ORDER V. FUMARIACEÆ.

Genus 1. FUMARIA.

F. CAPREOLATA. *Rampant Fumitory.* **Fig. 55.**
Stem climbing. Petioles twining. Calyx-leaves longer than fruit. Corn-fields. 1½–3 ft. Ann. May–Aug. Pale purple. ($\frac{1}{2}$) *E. B.* 1. 943. *E. B.* 2. 987. *H. & Arn.* 19. *Bab.* 17. *Lind.* 19.

F. OFFICINALIS. *Common Fumitory.* **Fig. 56.**
Stem spreading. Leaves glaucous. Calyx not longer than fruit. Fields and road-sides. 1 ft. Ann, May–Aug. Purple. ($\frac{1}{2}$) *E. B.* 1. 589. *E. B.* 2. 986. *H. & Arn.* 19. *Bab.* 17. *Lind.* 19.

F. PARVIFLORA. *Small-flowered Fumitory.* **Fig. 57.**
Stem spreading. Calyx minute. Fruit pointed. Chalky fields. 1 ft. Ann. Aug. and Sept. Purple. ($\frac{1}{2}$) *E. B.* 1. 590. *E. B.* 2. 988. *H. & Arn.* 19. *Bab.* 17. *Lind.* 19.

Genus 2. CORYDALIS.

C. SOLIDA. *Bulbous Corydalis.* **Fig. 58.**
Root a tuber. Stem erect, simple. Bracts large, palmate. A doubtful native. 9 in. Perenn. April. Purple. ($\frac{1}{2}$) *E. B.* 1. 1471. *E. B.* 2. 983. *H. & Arn.* 20. *Bab.* 16. *Lind.* 19.

C. LUTEA. *Yellow Corydalis.* **Fig. 59.**
Root fibrous. Stem erect. Bracts minute. Old walls; rare. 6 in. Perenn. May and June. Yellow. ($\frac{1}{2}$) *E. B.* 1. 588. *E. B.* 2. 984. *H. & Arn.* 20. *Bab.* 17. *Lind.* 19.

C. CLAVICULATA. *Climbing Corydalis.* **Fig. 60.**
Stem climbing, branched. Bracts minute. Foot-stalks with tendrils. Bushy places. 1 to 4 ft. Ann. June. Nearly white. ($\frac{1}{2}$) *E. B.* 1. 103. *E. B.* 2. 985. *H. & Arn.* 20. *Bab.* 17. *Lind.* 19.

Fig. 41. to 60.

J.E.Sowerby, Fecit.

Order VI. CRUCIFERÆ.
Genus 1. Cakile.

C. maritima. *Sea Rocket.* **Fig. 61.**
Leaves succulent, pinnatifid. Joints of fruit smooth, 2-edged. Sandy coasts. 9 in. Ann. June–Sept. Purple or white. ($\frac{3}{4}$) *E. B.* 1. 231. *E. B.* 2. 891. *H. & Arn.* 34. *Bab.* 34. *Lind.* 28.

Genus 2. Crambe.

C. maritima. *Sea Kale.* **Fig. 62.**
Leaves roundish, glaucous, waved, toothed, very smooth. Sandy coasts. Young shoots edible. 2 ft. Perenn. June. White. ($\frac{1}{2}$) *E. B.* 1. 924. *E. B.* 2. 892. *H. & Arn.* 43. *Bab.* 34. *Lind.* 34.

Genus 3. Coronopus.

C. Ruellii. *Wart Cress. Swine's Cress.* **Fig. 63.**
Stem prostrate, smooth. Fruit undivided. Waste ground, abundant. 1 to 3 in. Ann. June–Sept. White. *E. B.* 1. 1660. *E. B.* 2. 893. *H. & Arn.* 39. *Bab.* 33. *Lind.* 30.

C. didyma. *Small Wart Cress.* **Fig. 64.**
Stem procumbent, hairy. Fruit cloven. Waste ground near the sea. 1 to 2 in. Ann. July. White. *E. B.* 1. 248. *E. B.* 2. 894. *H. & Arn.* 39. *Bab.* 33. *Lind.* 31.

Genus 4. Isatis.

I. tinctoria. *Woad.* **Fig. 65.**
Upper leaves sagittate; lower ones oblong, crenated. Fruit oblong, smooth. Fields; rare. Yields a blue dye. 3 ft. Bienn. July. Yellow. ($\frac{1}{2}$) *E. B.* 1. 97. *E. B.* 2. 895. *H. & Arn.* 39. *Bab.* 33. *Lind.* 32.

Genus 5. Vella.

V. annua. *Cress Rocket.* **Fig. 66.**
Fruit pendulous, with a flat dilated style. Fields; a doubtful native. 9 in. Ann. July. Pinkish white. ($\frac{1}{2}$) *E. B.* 1. 1442. *E. B.* 2. 896. *H. & Arn.* 43. *Bab.* 30. *Lind.* 33.

Genus 6. Thlaspi.

T. arvense. *Penny Cress.* **Fig. 67.**
Leaves arrow-shaped. Fruit nearly flat, with broad wings. Fields; not common. 1 ft. Ann. July. White. ($\frac{1}{2}$) *E. B.* 1. 1659. *E. B.* 2. 897. *H. & Arn.* 32. *Bab.* 30. *Lind.* 27.

T. perfoliatum. *Perfoliate Penny Cress.* **Fig. 68.**
Stem-leaves heart-shaped, clasping at the base. Fruit inversely heart-shaped. Style very short. Limestone pastures; rare. 6 in. Ann. May. White. ($\frac{1}{2}$) *E. B.* 1. 2345. *E. B.* 2. 898. *H. & Arn.* 32. *Bab.* 30. *Lind.* 27.

T. alpestre. *Alpine Penny Cress.* **Fig. 69.**
Stem-leaves arrow-shaped; root-leaves ovate. Fruit with a prominent style. Limestone mountains. 6 in. Perenn. July. ($\frac{1}{2}$) *E. B.* 1. 81. *E. B.* 2. 899. *H. & Arn.* 32. *Bab.* 31. *Lind.* 28.

Genus 7. Capsella.

C. Bursa-Pastoris. *Shepherd's Purse.* **Fig. 70.**
Fruit laterally compressed, without wings. Leaves generally pinnatifid, sometimes entire. A common weed. 3 to 18 in. Ann. Throughout the year. White. ($\frac{1}{2}$) *E. B.* 1. 1485. *E. B.* 2. 900. *H. & Arn.* 37. *Bab.* 33. *Lind.* 31.

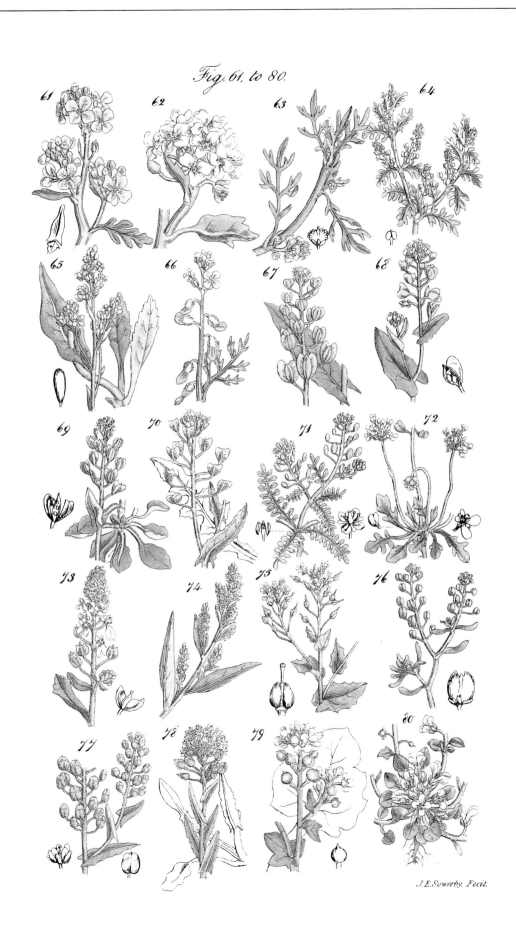

Fig. 61. to 80.

J.E.Sowerby, Fecit.

Genus 8. HUTCHINSIA.

H. PETRÆA. *Rock Hutchinsia.* Fig. 71·
Leaves pinnate, lobes entire. Petals the length of the calyx. Limestone rocks. 3 in. Ann. March. White. ($\frac{1}{2}$) *E. B.* 111. *E. B.* 2. 901. *H. & Arn.* 33. *Bab.* 31. *Lind.* 28.

Genus 9. TEESDALIA.

T. NUDICAULIS. *Teesdalia.* Fig. 72
Petals unequal. Leaves spreading on the ground. Stamens with a petal-like appendage at base. Sandy places. 2 to 4 in. Ann. June. White. ($\frac{1}{2}$) *E. B.* 1. 327. *E. B.* 2. 902. *H. & Arn.* 33. *Bab.* 31. *Lind.* 28.

Genus 10. IBERIS.

I. AMARA. *Bitter Candy Tuft.* Fig. 73.
Leaves lanceolate, somewhat toothed. Chalky-fields. 6 to 10 in. Ann. July. White. ($\frac{1}{2}$) *E. B.* 1. 52. *E. B.* 2. 903. *H. & Arn.* 33. *Bab.* 31. *Lind.* 28.

Genus 11. LEPIDIUM.

L. LATIFOLIUM. *Broad-leaved Pepper Wort.* Fig. 74.
Leaves ovato-lanceolate, serrated. Fruit oval. Salt marshes. Acrid. 2 ft. Perenn. July. White. ($\frac{1}{2}$) *E. B.* 1. 182. *E. B.* 2. 904. *H. & Arn.* 37. *Bab.* 32. *Lind.* 31.

L. DRABA. *Whitlow Pepper Wort.* Fig. 75.
Leaves oblong, clasping the stem. Fruit heart-shaped, with the style the same length. Doubtful native. 1 ft. Perenn. June. White. ($\frac{1}{2}$) *E. B. Supp.* 2683. *E. B.* 2. 907*. *H. & Arn.* 38. *Bab.* 32.

L. RUDERALE. *Narrow-leaved Pepper Wort.* Fig. 76.
Lower leaves pinnatifid, upper ones entire. Flowers without petals. Fruit notched. 1 ft. Ann. June. ($\frac{1}{2}$) *E. B.* 1. 1595. *E. B.* 2. 905. *H. & Arn.* 37. *Bab.* 32. *Lind.* 31.

L. CAMPESTRE. *Common Pepper Wort.* Fig. 77.
Stem-leaves arrow-shaped. Fruit rough, winged at upper part; style short. Fields; common. 1 ft. Ann. July. White. ($\frac{1}{2}$) *E. B.* 1. 1385. *E. B.* 2. 906. *H. & Arn.* 38. *Bab.* 32. *Lind.* 31.

L. SMITHII. *Smooth-fruited Pepper Wort.* Fig. 78.
Stem-leaves arrow-shaped. Fruit smooth, winged; style prominent. Fields. 8 in. Perenn. June. White. ($\frac{1}{2}$) *E. B.* 1. 1803. *E. B.* 2. 907. *H. & Arn.* 38. *Bab.* 32. *Lind.* 31.

Genus 12. COCHLEARIA.

C. OFFICINALIS. *Scurvy Grass.* Fig. 79.
Root-leaves roundish, nearly entire. Fruit globose. Sea-coast; common. 4 in.–1 ft. Ann. May. White. ($\frac{1}{2}$) *E. B.* 1. 551. *E. B.* 2. 908. *H. & Arn.* 29. *Bab.* 29. *Lind.* 27.

C. GRŒNLANDICA. *Greenland Scurvy Grass.* Fig. 80.
Leaves heart-shaped or kidney-shaped. Fruit globose. 6 in. Ann. June and July. White or purplish. ($\frac{1}{2}$) *E. B.* 1. 2403. *E. B.* 2. 909. *H. & Arn.* 29. *Bab.* 29. *Lind.* 27.

C. ANGLICA. *English Scurvy Grass.*   Fig. 81.
Root-leaves heart-shaped or ovate. Fruit elliptical, reticulated with
veins. Muddy sea-shores. 6 in. Ann. May and June. White ($\frac{1}{2}$)
E. B. 1. 552. *E. B.* 2. 910. *H. & Arn.* 29. *Bab.* 29. *Lind.* 27.

C. DANICA. *Danish Scurvy Grass.*   Fig. 82.
Leaves all triangular. Fruit elliptical, reticulated with veins. Sea-
coast and salt marshes. 4 in. Ann. May and June. White.
E. B. 1. 696. *E. B.* 2. 911. *H. & Arn.* 29. *Bab.* 29. *Lind.* 27.

C. ARMORACIA. *Horse-radish.*   Fig. 83.
Root-leaves large, oblong, wrinkled, on long foot-stalks. Fruit
oblong. Waste places; a doubtful native. Root pungent, used as a
condiment. 2–3 ft. Perenn. June. White. ($\frac{1}{2}$) *E. B.* 1. 2323.
E. B. 2. 912. *H. & Arn.* 29. *Bab.* 30. *Lind.* 27.

Genus 13. SUBULARIA.

S. AQUATICA. *Awl-Wort.*   Fig. 84.
Leaves few, awl-shaped, springing from the root. Alpine lakes, in
shallow water. 4 in. Ann. July. White. ($\frac{2}{3}$) *E. B.* 1. 732.
E. B. 2. 913. *H. & Arn.* 36. *Bab.* 33. *Lind.* 319.

Genus 14. DRABA.

D. VERNA. *Whitlow Grass.*   Fig. 85.
Leaves lanceolate, hairy, toothed. Petals deeply notched. Walls
and dry banks. 3 in. Ann. March. White. ($\frac{2}{3}$) *E. B.* 1. 586.
E. B. 2. 914. *H. & Arn.* 30. *Bab.* 29. *Lind.* 26.

D. AIZOIDES. *Yellow Draba.*   Fig. 86.
Leaves tufted, rigid, hairy. Petals slightly notched. Plant growing
in moss-like tufts. Pennard Castle, Glamorganshire. 2 in. Perenn.
April. Bright yellow. *E. B.* 1. 1271. *E. B.* 2. 915. *H. & Arn.* 31.
Bab. 28. *Lind.* 26.

D. RUPESTRIS. *Rock Draba.*   Fig. 87.
Leaves in tufts, lanceolate, slightly toothed, hairy. Petals entire.
Highland Mountains. 2 in. Perenn. May and June. White.
E. B. 1. 1338. *E. B.* 2. 916. *H. & Arn.* 31. *Bab.* 28. *Lind.* 26.

D. INCANA. *Twisted-podded Draba.*   Fig. 88.
Stem-leaves deeply toothed, root-ones often entire. Pods twisted.
Plant covered with white hairs. Limestone rocks. 2 in.–1 ft. Bienn.
May. White. ($\frac{2}{3}$) *E. B.* 1. 388. *E. B.* 2. 917. *H. & Arn.* 31.
Bab. 28. *Lind.* 26.

D. MURALIS. *Broad-leaved Draba.*   Fig. 89.
Leaves heart-shaped, toothed, hairy. Limestone rocks. 6 in.–1 ft.
Ann. April and May. White. ($\frac{2}{3}$) *E. B.* 1. 912. *E. B.* 2. 918.
H. & Arn. 31. *Bab.* 29. *Lind.* 26.

Genus 15. CAMELINA.

C. SATIVA. *Gold of Pleasure.*   Fig. 90.
Leaves sagittate. Fruit obovate, rounded. Cultivated ground,
scarcely wild. Cultivated for the oil contained in the seeds. 3 ft.
Ann. July. Yellow. ($\frac{1}{2}$) *E. B.* 1. 1254. *E. B.* 2. 920. *H. & Arn.*
36. *Bab.* 30. *Lind.* 30.

Genus 16. KONIGA.

K. MARITIMA. *Sweet Alyssum.* **Fig. 91.**
Leaves alternate, linear-lanceolate, hoary. Stem woody below.
Sea-coast, scarcely wild. 1 ft. Perenn. July–Sept. White. ($\frac{1}{2}$)
E. B. 1. 1729. *E. B.* 2. 919. *H. & Arn.* 30. *Bab.* 28. *Lind* 26.

Genus 17. ALYSSUM.

A. CALYCINUM. *Calycine Alyssum. Madwort.* **Fig. 92.**
Leaves linear-lanceolate. Stems several, erect. Hairy. Calyx
persistent. Sea-coast in Scotland. 4–6 in. Ann. June. Yellow.
($\frac{1}{2}$) *E. B. Supp.* 2583. *Bab.* 28.

Genus 18. DENTARIA.

D. BULBIFERA. *Coral-root.* **Fig. 93.**
Lower leaves pinnate, upper ones simple with bulbs at the base,
by which the plant is propagated. Woods. 2 ft. Perenn. May.
Purple. ($\frac{1}{2}$) *E. B.* 1. 309. *E. B.* 2. 921. *H. & Arn.* 26. *Bab.* 24.
Lind. 25.

Genus 19. CARDAMINE.

C. AMARA. *Bitter-Cress.* **Fig. 94.**
Leaves without stipules, pinnate; leaflets of the lower ones roundish
and entire, those of the upper toothed. Hairy. Wet meadows.
6 in.–1 ft. Perenn. May. Yellowish white, anthers purple. ($\frac{1}{2}$)
E. B. 1. 1000. *E. B.* 2. 926. *H. & Arn.* 27. *Bab.* 24. *Lind.* 25.

C. PRATENSIS. *Lady's Smock.* **Fig. 95.**
Leaves pinnated; upper leaflets narrow, entire; lower ones roundish,
toothed. Smooth. Meadows. 1 ft. Perenn. May. Lilac, anthers
yellow. ($\frac{1}{2}$) *E. B.* 1. 776. *E. B.* 2. 925. *H. & Arn.* 27. *Bab.* 24.
Lind. 25.

C. IMPATIENS. *Narrow-leaved Bitter-Cress.* **Fig. 96.**
Leaves pinnate, with stipules. Petals linear, often wanting. Moist
rocks. 1 ft. Ann. May and June. White. ($\frac{1}{2}$) *E. B.* 1. 80.
E. B. 2. 923. *H. & Arn.* 27. *Bab.* 24. *Lind.* 25.

C. HIRSUTA. *Hairy Bitter-Cress.* **Fig. 97.**
Leaves pinnate, without stipules; leaflets roundish, notched. Hairy.
Moist places in fields. 4 in.–1 ft. Ann. March–June. White. ($\frac{1}{2}$)
E. B. 1. 492. *E. B.* 2. 924. *H. & Arn.* 27. *Bab.* 24. *Lind.* 25.

C. BELLIDIFOLIA. *Daisy-leaved Lady's Smock.* **Fig. 98.**
Leaves simple, ovate, on rather long foot-stalks. Doubtful native.
2 in. Perenn. July–Sept. White. ($\frac{2}{3}$) *E. B.* 1. 2355. *E. B.*
2. 922. *Lind.* 25.

Genus 20. ARABIS.

A. STRIATA. *Bristol Rock-Cress.* **Fig. 99.**
Leaves toothed, purplish beneath. Petals erect. Hairy. Rocks
near Bristol. 6 in. Perenn. March. White. ($\frac{2}{3}$) *E. B.* 1. 614.
E. B. 2. 927. *H. & Arn.* 25. *Bab.* 23. *Lind.* 24.

A. PETRÆA. *Rock-Cress.* **Fig. 100.**
Root-leaves toothed. Petals spreading. ... st rocks in Wales and
Scotland. 4 in. Perenn. June and July. Lilac. ($\frac{2}{3}$) *E. B.* 1. 469.
E. B. 2. 928. *H. & Arn.* 25. *Bab.* 23. *Lind.* 24.

Fig. 81. to 100.

1. Aug.ᵗ 1858.

J. E. Sowerby, Fecit.

A. CILIATA. *Fringed Rock-Cress.* **Fig. 101.**
Leaves oval, toothed, fringed with hairs. Sea-cliffs ; rare. 4 in.
Bienn. July. White. ($\frac{2}{3}$) *E. B.* 1. 1746. *E. B.* 2. 929. *H. &*
Arn. 26. *Bab.* 23. *Lind.* 24.

A. HIRSUTA. *Hairy Wall-Cress.* **Fig. 102.**
Leaves toothed. Pods straight. Hairy. Flower-stem without bracts.
Rocks and walls. 1 ft. Bienn. June. White. ($\frac{2}{3}$) *E. B.* 1. 587.
E. B. 2. 930. *H. & Arn.* 26. *Bab.* 23. *Lind.* 24.

A. TURRITA. *Tower Wall-Cress.* **Fig. 103.**
Leaves toothed, stem clasping. Stem with leaf-like bracts below the
flower-stalks. ·Pods recurved. Walls. 1 ft. Bienn. May. Pale
yellow. ($\frac{2}{3}$) *E. B.* 1. 178. *E. B.* 2. 931. *H. & Arn.* 26. *Bab.* 23.
Lind. 24.

Genus 21. TURRITIS.

T. GLABRA. *Tower Mustard.* **Fig. 104.**
Root-leaves toothed, hairy ; stem-leaves smooth, entire, stem-clasping.
Glaucous. Dry banks and road-sides. 1–3 ft. Ann. May and June.
Pale yellow. ($\frac{2}{3}$) *E. B.* 1. 777. *E. B.* 2. 932. *H. & Arn.* 25.
Bab. 23. *Lind.* 24.

Genus 22. BARBAREA.

B. VULGARIS. *Winter-Cress. Yellow Rocket.* **Fig. 105.**
Lower leaves lyrate, the terminal lobe rounded. Hedge-banks and
waste ground; common. 1–3 ft. Perenn. May–Sept. Bright
yellow. ($\frac{1}{2}$) *E. B.* 1. 443. *E. B.* 2. 933. *H. & Arn.* 24. *Bab.* 22.
Lind. 23.

B. PRÆCOX. *Early Winter Cress.* **Fig. 106.**
Lower leaves lyrate ; upper ones deeply pinnatifid. Waste ground.
Used as salad. 1–2 ft. Perenn. April–Oct. Yellow. ($\frac{1}{2}$) *E. B.*
1. 1129. *E. B.* 2. 934. *H. & Arn.* 25. *Bab.* 22. *Lind.* 23.

Genus 23. NASTURTIUM.

N. OFFICINALE. *Water-Cress.* **Fig. 107.**
Leaves pinnate ; leaflets ovate, waved on the margin, the terminal one
larger than the rest and rounded. Clear water; common. Used
as salad. 6–9 in. Perenn. July. White. ($\frac{1}{2}$) *E. B.* 1. 855.
E. B. 2. 935. *H. & Arn.* 28. *Bab.* 22. *Lind.* 23.

N. SYLVESTRE. *Creeping-Cress.* **Fig. 108.**
Root creeping. Leaves pinnate ; leaflets lanceolate, cut. Upper
leaves entire, linear. Wet places. 6 in. Perenn. July–Sept. Bright
yellow. ($\frac{1}{2}$) *E. B.* 1. 2324. *E. B.* 2. 936. *H. & Arn.* 28. *Bab.* 22.
Lind. 23.

N. TERRESTRE. *Marsh-Cress.* **Fig. 109.**
Leaves pinnatifid. Root tapering. Petals not longer than the
calyx. Wet places. 6–10 in. Ann. June–Sept. Pale yellow. ($\frac{1}{2}$)
E. B. 1. 1747. *E. B.* 2. 937. *H. & Arn.* 28. *Bab.* 22. *Lind.* 23.

N. AMPHIBIUM. *Amphibious Marsh-Cress.* **Fig. 110.**
Root fibrous. Leaves oblong, pinnatifid or serrated. Ditches and
wet places. 2–3 ft. Perenn. June–Aug. Yellow. ($\frac{1}{2}$) *E. B.* 1. 1840.
E. B. 2. 938. *H. & Arn.* 28. *Bab.* 30. *Lind.* 23.

Fig. 101. to 120.

1. Aug. 1858.

J. E. Sowerby. Fecit.

Genus 24. Sisymbrium.

S. officinale. *Hedge Mustard.* **Fig. 111.**
Leaves lyrate, hairy. Pods short, pressed against the stalk. Common on waste ground and hedge-banks. 2 ft. Ann. June–Aug. Yellow. ($\frac{1}{2}$) *E. B.* 1. 735. *E. B.* 2. 939. *H. & Arn.* 34. *Bab.* 24. *Lind.* 29.

S. Iris. *London Rocket.* **Fig. 112.**
Leaves pinnatifid. Pods long, erect. Walls near London. 1–2 ft. Ann. July and Aug. Yellow. ($\frac{1}{2}$) *E. B.* 1. 1631. *E. B.* 2. 940. *H. & Arn.* 35. *Bab.* 25. *Lind.* 29.

S. Sophia. *Flix-weed.* **Fig. 113.**
Leaves bipinnate, with linear lobes. Waste places. 2 ft. Ann. July and Aug. Pale yellow. ($\frac{1}{2}$) *E. B.* 1. 963. *E. B.* 2. 941. *H. & Arn.* 35. *Bab.* 25. *Lind.* 29.

S. Thalianum. *Thale-Cress.* **Fig. 114.**
Leaves oblong, toothed; lower ones in a tuft. Common on walls. 2–8 in. Ann. April and May. White. ($\frac{1}{2}$) *E. B.* 1. 901. *E. B.* 2. 942. *H. & Arn.* 35. *Bab.* 25. *Lind.* 24.

Genus 25. Erysimum.

E. cheiranthoides. *Treacle-Mustard. Worm-seed.* **Fig. 115.**
Leaves lanceolate. Waste places and fields. Acrid. 1–2 ft. Bienn. May–Nov. Yellow. ($\frac{1}{2}$) *E. B.* 1. 942. *E. B.* 2. 943. *H. & Arn.* 36. *Bab.* 26. *Lind.* 30.

E. Alliaria. *Hedge-Garlic.* **Fig. 116.**
Leaves heart-shaped, with foot-stalks. Hedge-banks and waste places; very common. Plant smells like garlic. 2–3 ft. Bienn. May. White. ($\frac{1}{2}$) *E. B.* 1. 796. *E. B.* 2. 944. *H. & Arn.* 35. *Bab.* 26. *Lind.* 29.

E. orientale. *Hare's-ear Mustard.* **Fig. 117.**
Leaves oblong heart-shaped, stem-clasping. Glaucous. Fields. 1–2 ft. Ann. June. Yellowish white. ($\frac{1}{2}$) *E. B.* 1. 1804. *E. B.* 2. 945. *H. & Arn.* 36. *Bab.* 26. *Lind.* 30.

Genus 26. Cheiranthus.

C. Cheiri. *Wall-flower.* **Fig. 118.**
Stem shrubby, branches angular. Leaves lanceolate. Pods linear. Walls. 1–1$\frac{1}{2}$ ft. Bienn. usually. April. Orange-yellow. ($\frac{1}{2}$) *E. B.* 1. 934. *E. B.* 2. 946. *H. & Arn.* 24. *Bab.* 21. *Lind.* 22.

Genus 27. Matthiola.

M. incana. *Hoary Stock.* **Fig. 119.**
Stem shrubby. Leaves lanceolate, entire, hoary. Sea-cliffs in the south of England. 1–2 ft. Bienn. May–July. Purple. ($\frac{1}{2}$) *E. B.* 1. 1935. *E. B.* 2. 947. *H. & Arn.* 24. *Bab.* 21. *Lind.* 22.

M. sinuata. *Great Sea-Stock.* **Fig. 120.**
Stem herbaceous, spreading. Leaves downy, waved. Sandy sea-shores. 2 ft. Bienn. May–Aug. Purple. ($\frac{1}{2}$) *E. B.* 1. 462. *E. B.* 2. 948. *H. & Arn.* 24. *Bab.* 21. *Lind.* 22.

Genus 28. HESPERIS.

H. MATRONALIS. *Dame's Violet.* **Fig. 121.**
Stem erect. Leaves ovate-lanceolate, toothed. Moist hilly pastures and waste places. 2–3 ft. Perenn. May and June. Rose-colour. ($\frac{1}{2}$) *E. B.* 1. 731. *E. B.* 2. 949. *H. & Arn.* 34. *Bab.* 25. *Lind.* 29.

Genus 29. BRASSICA.

B. NAPUS. *Wild Rape.* **Fig. 122.**
Root fusiform. Lower leaves lyrate, toothed; upper ones lanceolate, stem-clasping. Smooth. Waste ground. Cultivated for its oily seeds. 1–2 ft. Bienn. May and June. Bright yellow. ($\frac{1}{2}$) *E. B.* 1. 2146. *E. B.* 2. 950. *H. & Arn.* 40. *Bab.* 26. *Lind.* 32.

B. RAPA. *Wild Turnip.* **Fig. 123.**
Root orbicular, fleshy. Root-leaves lyrate, rough; stem-ones nearly entire, smooth. Fields and waste places. Cultivated for its edible root. 1–2 ft. Bienn. April and May. Bright yellow. ($\frac{1}{2}$) *E. B.* 1. 2176. *E. B.* 2. 951. *H. & Arn.* 40. *Bab.* 26. *Lind.* 32.

B. OLERACEA. *Cabbage.* **Fig. 124.**
Root cylindrical, fleshy. Leaves large, partly lyrate, waved and lobed, glaucous, smooth. Sea-cliffs. Cultivated as an esculent. 6 in.– 2 ft. Bienn. June. Lemon-yellow. ($\frac{1}{2}$) *E. B.* 1. 637. *E. B.* 2. 952. *H. & Arn.* 40. *Bab.* 26. *Lind.* 32.

B. MONENSIS. *Isle of Man Cabbage.* **Fig. 125.**
Leaves glaucous, deeply pinnatifid, unequally toothed. Sandy sea-shores in the Isle of Man and elsewhere. Eaten by cattle. 6 in.–1 ft. Perenn. June and July. Yellow. ($\frac{1}{2}$) *E. B.* 1. 962. *E. B.* 2. 953. *H. & Arn.* 41. *Bab.* 27. *Lind.* 32.

B. CHEIRANTHUS. *Wall-flower Cabbage.* **Fig. 126.**
Root woody. All the leaves deeply pinnatifid, hairy. Perhaps a variety of the preceding. Sandy shores, Jersey. Perenn.? July. Deep yellow. ($\frac{1}{2}$) *E. B. Supp.* 2821. *Bab.* 27. *Lind.* 320.

B. CAMPESTRIS. *Field Cabbage. Colza. Swedish Turnip.* **Fig. 127.**
Root tapering. Root-leaves lyrate, rough; those of the stem entire or partly pinnatifid, stem-clasping. River-sides and cultivated ground. Varieties cultivated for their oily seeds and edible roots. 1–2 ft. Ann. June–Aug. Yellow. ($\frac{1}{2}$) *E. B.* 1. 2243. *E. B.* 2. 954. *H. & Arn.* 40. *Bab.* 26. *Lind.* 32.

Genus 30. SINAPIS.

S. ARVENSIS. *Charlock. Wild Mustard.* **Fig. 128.**
Leaves toothed, partly lyrate. Pods with many angles, rugged, longer than their beak. A common weed. 1–2 ft. Ann. May and June. Yellow. ($\frac{1}{2}$) *E. B.* 1. 1748. *E. B.* 2. 953. *H. & Arn.* 41. *Bab.* 27. *Lind.* 33.

S. ALBA. *White Mustard.* **Fig. 129.**
Leaves pinnatifid. Pods bristly, rugged, spreading, shorter than the beak. Waste ground. 1 ft. Ann. July. Yellow. ($\frac{1}{2}$) *E. B.* 1. 1677. *E. B.* 2. 956. *H. & Arn.* 42. *Bab.* 27. *Lind.* 33.

S. NIGRA. *Black Mustard.* **Fig. 130.**
Lower leaves lyrate, rough; upper ones linear-lanceolate. Beak of pod very short. Pungent seeds used as a condiment. 3–4 ft. Ann. June. Yellow. ($\frac{1}{2}$) *E. B.* 1. 969. *E. B.* 2. 957. *H. & Arn.* 41. *Bab.* 27. *Lind.* 33.

S. INCANA. **Fig. 131.**
Leaves lyrate, rough; stem-ones linear-lanceolate. Pods closely pressed to the stem, very short, with beak nearly as long. Sandy shores. Jersey. 2–3 ft. Ann. July. Yellow. ($\frac{1}{2}$) *E. B. Supp.* 2843. *H. & Arn.* 41. *Bab.* 27.

S. TENUIFOLIA. *Wall Rocket.* **Fig. 132.**
Stem smooth. Leaves pinnatifid. Foot-stalks spreading. Seeds in two rows. Walls. 1–1$\frac{1}{2}$ ft. Perenn. July–Sept. Yellow. ($\frac{1}{2}$) *E. B.* 1. 525. *E. B.* 2. 958. *H. & Arn.* 27. *Bab.* 42. *Lind.* 33.

S. MURALIS. *Sand Rocket.* **Fig. 133.**
Stem hairy, spreading. Leaves toothed or lyrate. Foot-stalks spreading. Seeds in two rows. Sandy shores. 1 ft. Ann. Aug. Yellow. ($\frac{1}{2}$) *E. B.* 1. 1090. *E. B.* 2. 959. *H. & Arn.* 42. *Bab.* 28. *Lind.* 33.

Genus 31. RAPHANUS.

R. RAPHANISTRUM. *Wild Radish.* **Fig. 134.**
Lower leaves lyrate. Pods jointed, striated. Petals deeply veined. A common weed. Variety cultivated for its edible root. 1$\frac{1}{2}$ ft. Ann. July. Yellow or white with purple veins. ($\frac{1}{2}$) *E. B.* 1. 856. *E. B.* 2. 960. *H. & Arn.* 43. *Bab.* 34. *Lind.* 34.

R. MARITIMUS. **Fig. 135.**
Lower leaves unequally lyrate. Pods jointed, deeply furrowed. Sea-coast. 3 ft. Bienn. May and June. Yellow. ($\frac{1}{2}$) *E. B.* 1. 1643. *E. B.* 2. 961. *H. & Arn.* 43. *Bab.* 34. *Lind.* 34.

ORDER VII. RESEDACEÆ.

Genus 1. RESEDA.

R. LUTEOLA. *Weld.* **Fig. 136.**
Leaves all lanceolate, entire. Calyx with 4 segments. Waste ground. Yields a yellow dye. 2–3 ft. Ann. July and Aug. Greenish yellow. ($\frac{1}{2}$) *E. B.* 1. 320. *E. B.* 2. 685. *H. & Arn.* 44. *Bab.* 35. *Lind.* 219.

R. LUTEA. *Wild Mignonette.* **Fig. 137.**
Leaves deeply 3-cleft or pinnatifid. Calyx with 6 segments. Chalky hills. 2–3 ft. Ann. July and Aug. Yellow. ($\frac{1}{2}$) *E. B.* 1. 321. *E. B.* 2. 686. *H. & Arn.* 44. *Bab.* 34. *Lind.* 219.

R. FRUTICULOSA. *Shrubby Mignonette.* **Fig. 138.**
Shrubby. Leaves all pinnatifid, glaucous. Calyx with 5 segments. Petals trifid. Hedge-banks. 1 ft. Perenn. June. Nearly white. ($\frac{1}{2}$) *E. B. Supp.* 2628. *E. B.* 2. 686. *H. & Arn.* 44. *Bab.* 35. *Lind.* 333.

ORDER VIII. CISTACEÆ.

Genus 1. HELIANTHEMUM.

H. CANUM. *Hoary Rock-Rose.* **Fig. 139.**
Shrubby. Leaves without stipules, opposite, hoary beneath. Alpine rocks. 3–4 in. Perenn. May and June. Bright yellow. ($\frac{2}{3}$) *E. B.* 1. 396. *E. B.* 2. 757. *H. & Arn.* 45. *Bab.* 35. *Lind.* 36.

H. GUTTATUM. *Spotted Annual Rock-Rose.* **Fig. 140.**
Herbaceous. Leaves without stipules. Sandy pastures; rare. 6 in. Ann. June and July. Yellow, with purple spot at base. ($\frac{1}{2}$) *E. B.* 1. 544. *E. B.* 2. 758. *H. & Arn.* 45. *Bab.* 35. *Lind.* 37.

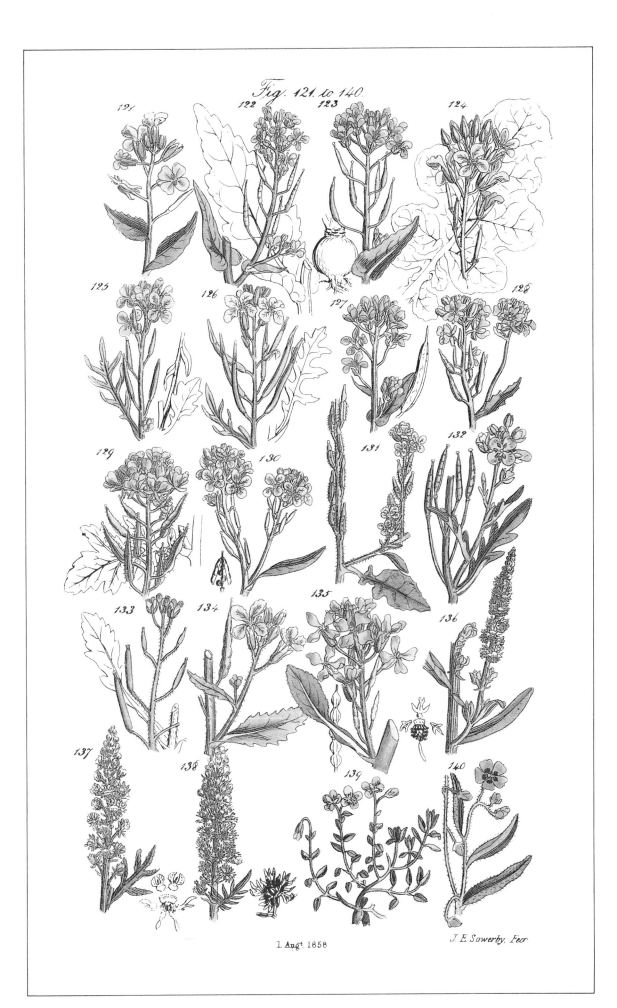

Fig. 121. to 140.

1 Augt. 1858

J. E. Sowerby, Fecit.

H. LEDIFOLIUM. *Ledum-leaved Rock-Rose.* **Fig. 141.**
Leaves with stipules. Petals shorter than the calyx. Sandy places; rare. 6 in. Ann. July. Pale yellow. ($\frac{1}{2}$) *E. B.* 1. 2414. *E. B.* 2. 759. *H. & Arn.* 45. *Bab.* 36. *Lind.* 37.

H. VULGARE. *Rock-Rose. Sun-Cistus.* **Fig. 142.**
Shrubby, procumbent. Leaves with stipules. Petals large. Common on chalk or limestone pastures. 6 in. Perenn. July and Aug. Bright yellow. ($\frac{1}{2}$) *E. B.* 1. 1321. *E. B.* 2. 760. *H. & Arn.* 45. *Bab.* 36. *Lind.* 37.

H. SURREJANUM. *Dotted Sun-Cistus.* **Fig. 143.**
Shrubby, procumbent. Leaves with stipules, dotted beneath. Petals small. Chalky pastures. 6 in. Perenn. July. Yellow. ($\frac{2}{3}$) *E. B.* 1. 2207. *E. B.* 2. 761. *H. & Arn.* 46. *Bab.* 36. *Lind.* 37.

H. POLIFOLIUM. *White Sun-Cistus.* **Fig. 144.**
Shrubby, procumbent. Leaves with stipules. Petals large. Rocky hills near the sea; rare. 6 in. Perenn. July. White. ($\frac{1}{2}$) *E. B.* 1. 1322. *E. B.* 2. 762. *H. & Arn.* 46. *Bab.* 36. *Lind.* 37.

ORDER IX. VIOLACEÆ.

Genus 1. VIOLA.

V. HIRTA. *Hairy Violet.* **Fig. 145.**
No stem. Leaves heart-shaped, rough with hairs. Bracts below the middle of the flower-stalk. Stipules membranous. Hedge-banks on chalk or limestone. 4 in. Perenn. April. Pale violet; scentless. ($\frac{2}{3}$) *E. B.* 1. 894. *E. B.* 2. 328. *H. & Arn.* 47. *Bab.* 37. *Lind.* 35.

V. ODORATA. *Sweet Violet.* **Fig. 146.**
No stem. Leaves heart-shaped, nearly smooth. Bracts above the middle of the stalk. Stipules membranous. Woods and hedge-banks; common. 5 in. Perenn. March and April. Deep violet or white; sweet-scented. ($\frac{2}{3}$) *E. B.* 1. 619. *E. B.* 2. 329. *H. & Arn.* 47. *Bab.* 37. *Lind.* 35.

V. PALUSTRIS. *Marsh Violet.* **Fig. 147.**
No stem. Leaves kidney-shaped or heart-shaped, smooth. Bracts near the middle of the stalk. Stipules membranous. Bogs. 4 in. Perenn. April. Pale lilac. ($\frac{2}{3}$) *E. B.* 1. 444. *E. B.* 2. 330. *H. & Arn.* 46. *Bab.* 36. *Lind.* 35.

V. CANINA. *Dog Violet.* **Fig. 148.**
Stem long, channelled. Leaves heart-shaped. Stipules membranous. Woods and banks; common. 6 in. Perenn. April–Aug. Blue. ($\frac{2}{3}$) *E. B.* 1. 620. *E. B.* 2. 331. *H. & Arn.* 47. *Bab.* 37. *Lind.* 35.

V. FLAVICORNIS. *Yellow-spurred Violet.* **Fig. 149.**
Stem rather woody, angular. Probably a variety of the preceding. Heaths. 3 in. Perenn. May and June. Violet; spur yellow. ($\frac{2}{3}$) *E. B. Supp.* 2736. *E. B.* 2. 331*. *Bab.* 38. *Lind.* 36.

V. LACTEA. *Cream-coloured Violet.* **Fig. 150.**
Leaves ovato-lanceolate. Stipules membranous. Variety of *canina*? Bogs. 6 in. Perenn. June. Yellowish white. ($\frac{2}{3}$) *E. B.* 1. 445. *E. B.* 2. 332. *H. & Arn.* 48. *Bab.* 38. *Lind.* 35.

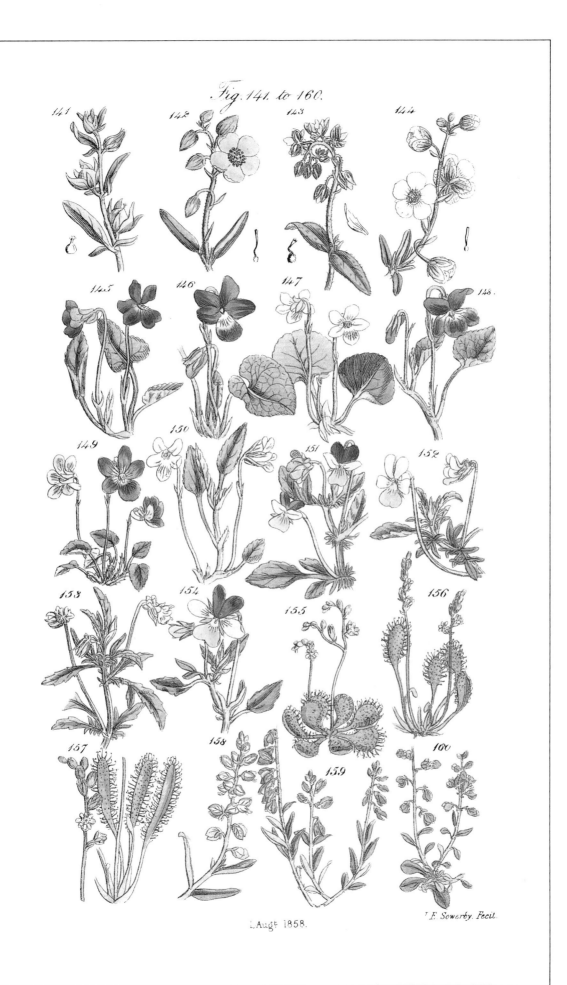

L.Augt 1858.

J.E.Sowerby. Fecit.

V. TRICOLOR. *Heart's-ease. Pansy.*   **Fig. 151.**
Stems angular, spreading. Leaves oblong, crenated. Stipules leafy, pinnatifid. Petals longer than the calyx. Fields; common. 6 in. Ann. May–Sept. Upper petals deep violet, lower yellow. ($\frac{2}{3}$) *E. B.* 1. 1287. *E. B.* 2. 333. *H. & Arn.* 49. *Bab.* 38. *Lind.* 36.

V. CURTISII. *Yellow Sea-side Pansy.*   **Fig. 152.**
Stems angular, decumbent. Leaves oblong, crenated. Stipules leafy, palmated. Sandy wastes near the sea. 6 in. Perenn. May–Aug. Lower petal deep yellow, upper ones straw-colour. ($\frac{2}{3}$) *E. B. Supp.* 2693. *E. B.* 2. 334*. *H. & Arn.* 49. *Bab.* 38. *Lind.* 320.

V. ARVENSIS. *Corn Pansy.*   **Fig. 153.**
Stems angular, spreading. Leaves oblong, crenated, smooth. Stipules leafy, pinnatifid. Petals shorter than the calyx. Fields; common. 6 in. Ann. May–Sept. Pale yellow. ($\frac{2}{3}$) *E. B. Supp.* 2712. *E. B.* 2. 333*. *H. & Arn.* 49. *Bab.* 39. *Lind.* 320.

V. LUTEA. *Mountain Pansy.*   **Fig. 154.**
Stems triangular. Leaves oblong, crenated, hairy. Stipules leafy, palmated. Petals large. Mountain pastures. 4 in. Perenn. May–Sept. Yellow or violet, very variable. ($\frac{2}{3}$) *E. B.* 1. 721. *E. B.* 2. 334. *H. & Arn.* 49. *Bab.* 38. *Lind.* 36.

ORDER X. DROSERACEÆ.

Genus 1. DROSERA.

D. ROTUNDIFOLIA. *Sun-dew.*   **Fig. 155.**
Leaves rounded, foot-stalks hairy. Bogs. 2–4 in. Perenn. July. White. ($\frac{2}{3}$) *E. B.* 1. 867. *E. B.* 2. 458. *H. & Arn.* 50. *Bab.* 39. *Lind.* 38.

D. LONGIFOLIA. *Long-leaved Sun-dew.*   **Fig. 156.**
Leaves obovate, foot-stalks smooth. Bogs. 2-6 in. Perenn. July. White. ($\frac{2}{3}$) *E. B.* 1. 868. *E. B.* 2. 459. *H. & Arn.* 50. *Lind.* 38.

D. ANGLICA. *Great Sun-dew.*   **Fig. 157.**
Leaves linear-oblong, foot-stalks smooth. Bogs. Perenn. July. Pinkish. ($\frac{2}{3}$) *E. B.* 1. 869. *E. B.* 2. 460. *H. & Arn.* 50. *Bab.* 39. *Lind.* 38.

ORDER XI. POLYGALACEÆ.

Genus 1. POLYGALA.

P. VULGARIS. *Milk-wort.*   **Fig. 158.**
Stems forming a spreading tuft. Leaves scattered, linear-lanceolate. Heaths. 2-6 in. Perenn. May–Sept. Blue, pink or white. ($\frac{2}{3}$) *E. B.* 1. 76. *E. B.* 2. 989. *H. & Arn.* 52. *Bab.* 40. *Lind.* 39.

P. OXYPTERA. *Milk-wort.*   **Fig. 159.**
Lower leaves small, obovate. A variety of *vulgaris.* Channel Islands. 6 in. Perenn. June–Sept. ($\frac{2}{3}$) *E. B. Supp.* 2827. *H. & Arn.* 52.

P. AMARA. *Broad-leaved Milk-wort.*   **Fig. 160.**
Lower leaves large, obovate, in a tuft; upper ones oblong. A variety of *vulgaris.* *E. B. Supp.* 2764. *E. B.* 2. 989*. *Bab.* 40. *Lind.* 320.

Order XII. FRANKENIACEÆ.
Genus 1. FRANKENIA.

F. LÆVIS. *Sea-heath.* **Fig. 161.**
Leaves linear, in whorls. Plant procumbent. Muddy salt marshes.
4 in. Perenn. July and Aug. Rose colour. ($\frac{2}{3}$) *E. B.* 1. 205.
E. B. 2. 463. *H. & Arn.* 53. *Bab.* 41. *Lind.* 39.

F. PULVERULENTA. *Powdery Sea-heath.* **Fig. 162.**
Leaves obtuse, rather indented at the apex, downy beneath. Coast
of Sussex; very rare. 4 in. Ann. July. Pale pink. ($\frac{2}{3}$) *E. B.*
1. 2222. *E. B.* 2. 464. *H. & Arn.* 53. *Bab.* 41. *Lind.* 39.

Order XIII. CARYOPHYLLACEÆ.
Genus 1. ELATINE.

E. TRIPETALA. *Water-wort.* **Fig. 163.**
Flowers stalked, seldom expanding. Petals 3. Stamens 6. Wet
sandy places or shallow water. 1 in. Ann. July and Aug. Pink.
($\frac{2}{3}$) *E. B.* 1. 955. *E. B.* 2. 578. *H. & Arn.* 54. *Bab.* 42. *Lind.* 48.

E. HYDROPIPER. *Octandrous Water-wort.* **Fig. 164.**
Flowers sessile. Petals 4. Stamens 8. Generally covered by the
water; rarely expanding; rare. 1 in. Ann. Aug. Pink. ($\frac{2}{3}$) *E. B.*
Supp. 2670. *E. B.* 2. 578*. *H. & Arn.* 54. *Bab.* 42. *Lind.* 321.

Genus 2. DIANTHUS.

D. ARMERIA. *Deptford Pink.* **Fig. 165.**
Flowers in clusters. Bracts lanceolate, downy, as long as the calyx.
Pastures. 1–1½ ft. Ann. July–Sept. Pink with white dots. ($\frac{1}{2}$)
E. B. 1. 317. *E. B.* 2. 614. *H. & Arn.* 56. *Bab.* 44. *Lind.* 44.

D. PROLIFER. *Proliferous Pink.* **Fig. 166.**
Flowers in clusters. Bracts ovate, membranous, longer than the
calyx. Gravelly pastures; rare. 9 in. Ann. July. Dark purple.
($\frac{1}{2}$) *E. B.* 1. 956. *E. B.* 2. 615. *H. & Arn.* 56. *Bab.* 44. *Lind.* 44.

D. CARYOPHYLLUS. *Clove Pink.* *Carnation.* **Fig. 167.**
Flowers solitary, large. Bracts very short. Petals unequally notched.
Stamens shorter than the calyx. Old walls. The origin of the garden
Pinks. 1–2 ft. Perenn. July. Pink. ($\frac{1}{2}$) *E. B.* 1. 214. *E. B.*
2. 616. *H. & Arn.* 56. *Bab.* 44. *Lind.* 44.

D. DELTOIDES. *Maiden Pink.* **Fig. 168.**
Stems procumbent. Flowers solitary. Bracts generally 2, ovato-
lanceolate. Heaths and sandy fields. 6–9 in. Perenn. July–Oct.
Pink or white, with a crimson ring. ($\frac{2}{3}$) *E. B.* 1. 61. *E. B.* 2. 617.
H. & Arn. 57. *Bab.* 45. *Lind.* 44.

D. CÆSIUS. *Mountain Pink.* *Cheddar Pink.* **Fig. 169.**
Stems single-flowered. Bracts roundish, short. Petals unequally
toothed. Stamens longer than the calyx. Cheddar Rocks, Somerset.
4–8 in. Perenn. July and Aug. Pale rose colour. ($\frac{2}{3}$) *E. B.* 1. 62.
E. B. 2. 618. *H. & Arn.* 57. *Bab.* 45. *Lind.* 44.

Genus 3. SAPONARIA.

S. OFFICINALIS. *Soapwort.* **Fig. 170.**
Leaves ovato-lanceolate. opposite. Calyx cylindrical. Flowers often
double. Hedge-banks and waste places. 2 ft. Perenn. Aug. Pink.
($\frac{1}{2}$) *E. B.* 1. 1060. *E. B.* 2. 613. *H. & Arn.* 57. *Bab.* 45. *Lind.* 45.

Genus 4. Cucubalus.

C. BACCIFER. *Berry-bearing Chickweed.* **Fig. 171.**
Stem straggling, branched. Fruit a succulent berry. South of Europe. Isle of Dogs near London, and Anglesey; scarcely wild. 1½ ft. Perenn. June and July. White; berries black. (⅔) *E. B.* 1. 1577. *E. B.* 2. 619. *Bab.* 45.

Genus 5. Silene.

S. ACAULIS. *Moss Campion. Cushion Pink.* **Fig. 172.**
Plant growing in mossy tufts. Leaves linear. Flowers solitary, on short stalks. High mountain summits. 1 in. Perenn. June and July. Deep pink or white. (⅔) *E. B.* 1. 1081. *E. B.* 2. 629. *H. & Arn.* 58. *Bab.* 47. *Lind.* 46.

S. INFLATA. *Bladder Campion.* **Fig. 173.**
Flowers numerous, in loose panicles. Calyx much inflated. Petals deeply cleft, with narrow segments Stem erect. Plant sometimes downy. Fields and way-sides; common. 1–2 ft. Perenn. June–Sept. White. (½) *E. B.* 1. 164. *E. B.* 2. 620. *H. & Arn.* 58. *Bab.* 46. *Lind.* 45.

S. MARITIMA. *Sea Campion.* **Fig. 174.**
Flowers solitary or few together. Calyx much inflated. Petals slightly cleft, with broad segments. Stems recumbent. Sea-coast. 4–9 in. Perenn. June–Sept. White. (½) *E. B.* 1. 957. *E. B.* 2. 621. *H. & Arn.* 58. *Bab.* 46. *Lind.* 45.

S. OTITES. *Spanish Catchfly.* **Fig. 175.**
Flowers generally diœcious, in whorls. Petals entire. Calyx slightly inflated. Stem erect, few-leaved. Dry fields in the Eastern counties. 6 in.–1 ft. Perenn. July and Aug. Pale yellow. (⅔) *E. B.* 1. 85. *E. B.* 2. 624. *H. & Arn.* 59. *Bab.* 46. *Lind.* 46.

S. ANGLICA. *English Catchfly.* **Fig. 176.**
Calyx slightly inflated. Petals small, slightly cleft. Flowers alternate, in the axils of the leaves. Lower capsules drooping. Plant hairy, viscid. Fields in dry soil. 6 in.–1 ft. Ann. June. White. (⅔) *E. B.* 1. 1178. *E. B.* 2. 622. *H. & Arn.* 59. *Bab.* 45. *Lind.* 45.

S. QUINQUEVULNERA. *Variegated Catchfly.* **Fig. 177.**
Petals entire, roundish. Flowers alternate. Plant hairy. Capsules erect. Sandy fields; not common. 1 ft. Ann. June–Aug. White, with deep red spot on each petal. (⅔) *E. B.* 1. 86. *E. B.* 2. 623. *H. & Arn.* 59. *Bab.* 46. *Lind.* 45.

S. NUTANS. *Nottingham Catchfly.* **Fig. 178.**
Flowers in drooping panicles. Petals deeply cleft, with linear segments. Calyx cylindrical. Leaves downy. Limestone rocks. 2 ft. Perenn. June and July. White. (½) *E. B.* 1. 465. *E. B.* 2. 625. *H. & Arn.* 59. *Bab.* 46. *Lind.* 46.

S. PATENS. *Dover Catchfly.* **Fig. 179.**
Flowers in erect panicles. Petals deeply cleft, with broad segments. Calyx long, club-shaped. Perhaps a variety of *nutans.* Dover cliffs. 1–2 ft. Perenn. July. White. (½) *E. B. Supp.* 2748. *E. B.* 2. 625*. *Bab.* 46.

S. CONICA. *Corn Catchfly.* **Fig. 180.**
Calyx inflated, conical, furrowed. Petals small, slightly cleft. Flowers in dichotomous panicles. Sandy places in Kent. 1 ft. Ann. July. Purple. (½) *E. B.* 1. 922. *E. B.* 2. 626. *H. & Arn.* 60. *Bab.* 46. *Lind.* 45.

Fig. 161 to 180.

S. NOCTIFLORA. *Night-flowering Catchfly.* **Fig. 181.**
Calyx with 10 hairy ribs, and very long linear teeth. Petals large, deeply cleft. Plant downy. Sandy fields. 1–2 ft. Ann. July. Pale pink or white, sweet-scented, opening at night. ($\frac{1}{2}$) *E. B.* 1. 291. *E. B.* 2. 627. *H. & Arn.* 60. *Bab.* 47. *Lind.* 46.

S. ARMERIA. *Lobel's Catchfly.* **Fig. 182.**
Flowers in rather close corymbs. Petals notched. Calyx club-shaped. Walls; doubtful native. 1$\frac{1}{2}$ ft. Ann. July and Aug. Purplish pink. ($\frac{1}{2}$) *E. B.* 1. 1398. *E. B.* 2. 628. *H. & Arn.* 60. *Bab.* 47. *Lind.* 46.

Genus 6. LYCHNIS.

L. FLOS-CUCULI. *Cuckoo Flower. Ragged Robin.* **Fig. 183.**
Petals with 4 long linear segments. Leaves lanceolate. Flower-stems viscid. Moist meadows; common. 1–2 ft. Perenn. June. Rose-colour; calyx and flower-stalks pink. ($\frac{2}{3}$) *E. B.* 1. 573. *E. B.* 2. 664. *H. & Arn.* 61. *Bab.* 48. *Lind.* 47.

L. VISCARIA. *German Catchfly.* **Fig. 184.**
Flowers large. Petals slightly cleft. Leaves linear-lanceolate. Flower-stems viscid. Dry alpine rocks; local. 1 ft. Perenn. June. Deep purplish pink or white. ($\frac{2}{3}$) *E. B.* 1. 788. *E. B.* 2. 667. *H. & Arn.* 61. *Bab.* 47. *Lind.* 47.

L. ALPINA. *Mountain Campion.* **Fig. 185.**
Plant tufted. Petals sharply cleft. Flowers in close corymbs. Clova Mountains, Angus. 6 in. Perenn. June and July. Pink. ($\frac{2}{3}$) *E. B.* 1. 2254. *E. B.* 2. 668. *H. & Arn.* 61. *Bab.* 47. *Lind.* 47.

L. DIURNA. *Campion.* **Fig. 186.**
Flowers usually diœcious. Petals deeply cleft. Plant hairy. Fig. *b.*, with broader petals and globular capsules, is a distinct species (*L. vespertina*). Fields and banks; common. 1–2 ft. Perenn. May–Aug. Rose-colour; *b.* white. ($\frac{2}{3}$) *E. B.* 1. 1579 & 1580. *E. B.* 2. 665 & 666. *H. & Arn.* 61. *Bab.* 48. *Lind.* 47.

Genus 7. AGROSTEMMA.

A. GITHAGO. *Corn Cockle.* **Fig. 187.**
Flowers large. Teeth of the calyx projecting beyond the corolla. Petals very slightly cleft. Plant covered with silky hairs. Corn-fields; common. 2–3 ft. Ann. July. Purple. ($\frac{1}{2}$) *E. B.* 1. 741. *E. B.* 2. 663. *H. & Arn.* 62. *Bab.* 48. *Lind.* 47.

Genus 8. BUFFONIA.

B. TENUIFOLIA. **Fig. 188.**
Leaves very narrow, dilated at the base. Stems straggling. Calyx with straight parallel furrows. Capsule scarcely as long as the calyx. A doubtful native. 6 in. Ann. June. White. ($\frac{2}{3}$) *E. B.* 1. 1313. *E. B.* 2. 234. *H. & Arn.* 64. *Bab.* 48. *Lind.* 47.

Genus 9. SAGINA.

S. PROCUMBENS. *Creeping Pearl-wort.* **Fig. 189.**
Stems creeping, smooth. Petals very short. Leaves linear, minutely pointed. Garden-walks and waste places; very common. 1–2 in. Perenn. May–Nov. White. *E. B.* 1. 880. *E. B.* 2. 249. *H. & Arn.* 63. *Bab.* 49. *Lind.* 49.

S. APETALA. *Annual Pearl-wort.* **Fig. 190.**
Stems nearly erect, hairy. Leaves bristle-pointed. Petals minute. Dry ground; very common. 1–3 in. Ann. May and June. Green. *E. B.* 1. 881. *E. B.* 2. 251. *H. & Arn.* 62. *Bab.* 49. *Lind.* 49.

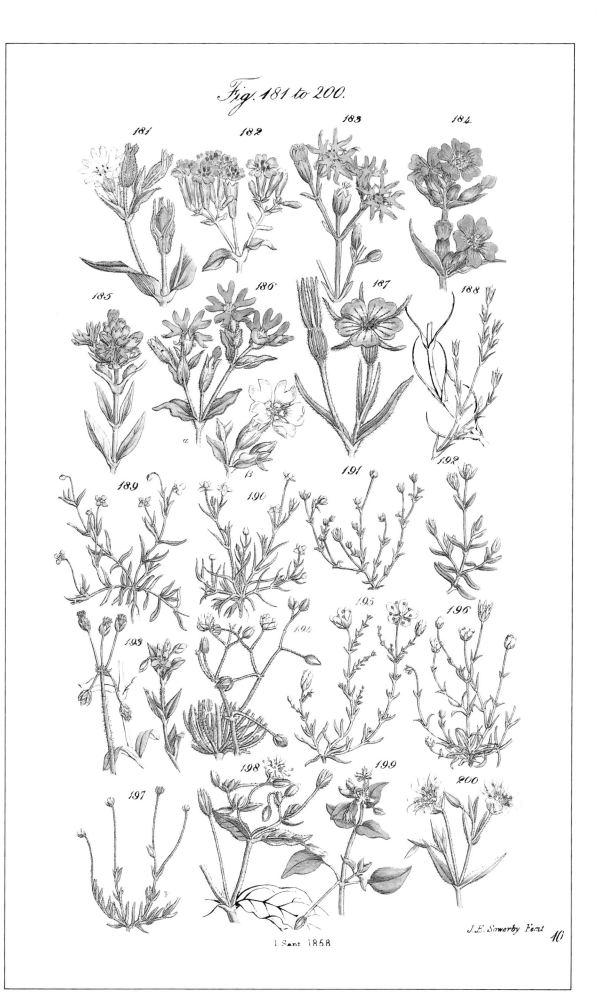

Fig. 181 to 200.

181   182   183   184

185   186   187   188

a   β   191   192

189   190

195   196

193   194

198   199   200

197

J.E. Sowerby Fecit

S. MARITIMA. *Sea Pearl-wort.* **Fig. 191.**
Stems nearly upright, smooth. Leaves short, obtuse. Petals wanting.
Sea-shore, and summit of Ben Nevis. 1–4 in. Ann. May–Aug. Green.
E. B. 1. 2195. *E. B.* 2. 250. *H. & Arn.* 63. *Bab.* 49. *Lind.* 49.

Genus 10. MŒNCHIA.

M. ERECTA. **Fig. 192.**
Leaves linear-lanceolate. Stem erect. Sandy places. 1–3 in. Ann.
May. White. *E. B.* 1. 609. *E. B.* 2. 252. *H. & Arn.* 70. *Bab.* 54.
Lind. 49.

Genus 11. HOLOSTEUM.

H. UMBELLATUM. *Jagged Chickweed.* **Fig. 193.**
Flowers in umbels. Leaves ovate. Upper part of the stem glaucous,
with glandular hairs. Walls near Norwich and Bury St. Edmunds.
3-4 in. Ann. April. Pink. ($\frac{2}{3}$) *E. B.* 1. 27. *E. B.* 2. 192.
H. & Arn. 70. *Bab.* 52. *Lind.* 50.

Genus 12. SPERGULA.

S. ARVENSIS. *Spurrey.* **Fig. 194.**
Leaves long, linear, in close whorls. Fruit-stalks reflexed. Plant
hairy. Corn-fields; very common. Cultivated in Holland for fodder.
6 in.–1 ft. Ann. June–Sept. White. ($\frac{2}{3}$) *E. B.* 1. 1535. *E. B.*
2. 677. *H. & Arn.* 155. *Bab.* 124. *Lind.* 48.

S. NODOSA. *Knotted Spurrey.* **Fig. 195.**
Leaves short, opposite; upper ones clustered. Petals large. Flowers
2 or 3 on each stem. Wet sandy places. 6 in. Perenn. July and
Aug. White. ($\frac{2}{3}$) *E. B.* 1. 694. *E. B.* 2. 678. *H. & Arn.* 64.
Bab. 50. *Lind.* 48.

S. SAGINOIDES. *Smooth Spurrey.* **Fig. 196.**
Leaves opposite. Flowers solitary, on long stalks. Capsules longer
than the calyx. Highland mountains. 1–3 in. Perenn. June and
July. White. ($\frac{2}{3}$) *E. B.* 1. 2105. *E. B.* 2. 679. *H. & Arn.* 64.
Bab. 50. *Lind.* 48.

S. SUBULATA. *Small Hairy Spurrey.* **Fig. 197.**
Leaves opposite. Flower-stalks solitary, very long. Plant rather
hairy. Capsules the same length as the calyx. Sandy places. 1–3 in.
Perenn. July and Aug. ($\frac{2}{3}$) *E. B.* 1. 1082. *E. B.* 2. 680. *H. &*
Arn. 64. *Bab.* 50. *Lind.* 48.

Genus 13. STELLARIA.

S. NEMORUM. *Wood Star-wort.* **Fig. 198.**
Lower leaves heart-shaped, with foot-stalks; upper ones ovate, sessile.
Plant hairy. Moist woods. 1-2 ft. Perenn. May and June. White.
($\frac{2}{3}$) *E. B.* 1. 92. *E. B.* 2. 630. *H. & Arn.* 69. *Bab.* 53. *Lind.* 52.

S. MEDIA. *Chickweed.* **Fig. 199.**
Leaves ovate; the lower ones with foot-stalks. Stems procumbent,
with a line of hairs on one side. A common weed. May be used as
an esculent. 6 in.–1 ft. Ann. All the year. White. ($\frac{2}{3}$) *E. B.*
1. 537. *E. B.* 2. 631. *H. & Arn.* 69. *Bab.* 53. *Lind.* 52.

S. HOLOSTEA. *Star-wort.* **Fig. 200.**
Leaves narrow-lanceolate, sessile. Petals inversely heart-shaped.
Stems erect. Hedge-banks. 1-2 ft. Perenn. May and June. White.
($\frac{2}{3}$) *E. B.* 1. 511. *E. B.* 2. 632. *H. & Arn.* 69. *Bab.* 53. *Lind.* 52.

S. GRAMINEA. *Lesser Star-wort.* **Fig. 201.**
Leaves lanceolate, sessile. Petals deeply cleft, with narrow lobes. Stems slender, erect. Hedge-banks and heaths. 1 ft. Perenn. June and July. White. ($\frac{2}{3}$) *E. B.* 1. 803. *E. B.* 2. 633. *H. & Arn.* 69. *Bab.* 53. *Lind.* 52.

S. GLAUCA. *Marsh Star-wort.* **Fig. 202.**
Leaves linear-lanceolate, glaucous. Petals deeply cleft. Stems erect. 1 ft. Perenn. Moist meadows; local. June and July. White. ($\frac{2}{3}$) *E. B.* 1. 825. *E. B.* 2. 634. *H. & Arn.* 69. *Bab.* 53. *Lind.* 52.

S. ULIGINOSA. *Bog Star-wort.* **Fig. 203.**
Leaves oblong-lanceolate. Petals shorter than the calyx. Ditches and wet places. 1 ft. Ann. June. White. ($\frac{2}{3}$) *E. B.* 1. 1074. *E. B.* 2. 635. *H. & Arn.* 70. *Bab.* 54. *Lind.* 51.

S. CERASTOIDES. *Alpine Star-wort.* **Fig. 204.**
Stems decumbent. Leaves elliptic-oblong, sessile. Petals deeply cleft, about the length of the calyx. Highland mountains. 6 in. Perenn. June. White. ($\frac{2}{3}$) *E. B.* 1. 911. *E. B.* 2. 637. *H. & Arn.* 73. *Bab.* 56. *Lind.* 53.

S. SCAPIGERA. *Many-stalked Star-wort.* **Fig. 205.**
Stem shorter than the flower-stalks. Leaves linear-lanceolate, crowded together. Flowers in a close irregular panicle. Moist places on mountains. 4 in. Perenn. June. ($\frac{2}{3}$) *E. B.* 1. 1269. *E. B.* 2. 636. *Bab.* 54. *Lind.* 52.

Genus 14. ARENARIA.

A. PEPLOIDES. *Sea Sand-wort. Sea Pimpernel.* **Fig. 206.**
Stem creeping, rather succulent. Leaves ovate, fleshy. Calyx without ribs. Flowers nearly sessile. Sandy sea-shores. 3 in. Perenn. July. White. ($\frac{2}{3}$) *E. B.* 1. 189. *E. B.* 2. 640. *H. & Arn.* 65. *Bab.* 50. *Lind.* 49.

A. TRINERVIS. *Plantain-leaved Sand-wort.* **Fig. 207.**
Plant downy. Leaves ovate, with foot-stalks. Calyx obscurely 3-ribbed. Moist woods. 1 ft. Ann. May and June. White. ($\frac{2}{3}$) *E. B.* 1. 1483. *E. B.* 2. 641. *H. & Arn.* 68. *Bab.* 51. *Lind.* 49.

A. SERPYLLIFOLIA. *Thyme-leaved Sand-wort.* **Fig. 208.**
Leaves ovate, sessile. Calyx hairy, 3 outer sepals 5-ribbed. Walls and dry places; common. 2–4 in. Ann. May–July. White. ($\frac{2}{3}$) *E. B.* 1. 923. *E. B.* 2. 642. *H. & Arn.* 67. *Bab.* 52. *Lind.* 49

A. CILIATA. *Fringed Sand-wort.* **Fig. 209.**
Stems procumbent, much branched, downy. Leaves spatulate, ciliated at the base. Flowers terminal, solitary. Petals large. Limestone cliffs; very rare. 3 in. Perenn. Aug. and Sept. ($\frac{2}{3}$) *E. B.* 1. 1745. *E. B.* 2. 646. *H. & Arn.* 67. *Bab.* 52. *Lind.* 50.

A. NORVEGICA. *Norway Sand-wort.* **Fig. 210.**
Leaves fleshy, spatulate, obovate. Sepals half as long as the corolla. Plant glabrous. Unst, Shetland. 3 in. Perenn. July and Aug. White. ($\frac{2}{3}$) *E. B. Supp.* 2852. *H. & Arn.* 67. *Bab.* 52.

A. VERNA. *Spring Sand-wort.*   **Fig. 211.**
Stems numerous, panicled above. Leaves awl-shaped. Petals the
length of the calyx. Mountain pastures. 4 in. Perenn. May-July.
White. ($\frac{2}{3}$) *E. B.* 1. 512. *E. B.* 2. 645. *H. & Arn.* 66. *Bab.* 51.
Lind. 50.

A. RUBELLA. *Little Red Sand-wort.*   **Fig. 212.**
Stems tufted, downy, usually one-flowered. Leaves linear, blunt.
Petals shorter than the calyx. Mountains; very rare. 2 in. Perenn.
May–Aug. White, anthers red. ($\frac{2}{3}$) *E. B. Supp.* 2638. *E. B.* 2. 646*.
H. & Arn. 66. *Bab.* 51.

A. TENUIFOLIA. *Fine-leaved Sand-wort.*   **Fig. 213.**
Stems slender, much branched. Leaves slender, awl-shaped. Petals
shorter than the calyx. Walls and sandy places. 5 in. Ann. June.
White. ($\frac{2}{3}$) *E. B.* 1. 219. *E. B.* 2. 643. *H. & Arn.* 66. *Bab.* 51.
Lind. 49.

A. FASTIGIATA. *Level-topped Sand-wort.*   **Fig. 214.**
Stem erect, densely corymbose when in fruit. Leaves very slender.
Flowers crowded. Petals small. Alpine rocks. 4 in. Ann. June.
White. ($\frac{2}{3}$) *E. B.* 1. 1744. *E. B.* 2. 644. *H. & Arn.* 67. *Bab.* 51.
Lind. 50.

A. RUBRA. *Red Sand-wort.*   **Fig. 215.**
Leaves with membranous stipules. Stems prostrate, hairy. Fields
and dry places; common. 2–3 in. Ann. July and Aug. Purple.
($\frac{2}{3}$) *E. B.* 1. 852. *E. B.* 2. 958. *H. & Arn.* 154. *Bab.* 124. *Lind.* 50.

A. MARINA. *Sea Sand-wort.*   **Fig. 216.**
Stems prostrate. Leaves with membranous stipules, fleshy, semi-
cylindrical. Sandy sea-shores; common. 2–4 in. Ann. June–Sept.
Purple. ($\frac{2}{3}$) *E. B.* 1. 958. *E. B.* 2. 639. *H. & Arn.* 154. *Bab.* 124.
Lind. 50.

Genus 15. CERASTIUM.

C. VULGATUM. *Broad-leaved Mouse-ear.*   **Fig. 217.**
Hairy, nearly erect, viscid above. Leaves roundish-ovate, pale green.
Petals equal to the calyx, deeply cleft. Fields and road-sides; common.
6 in. Ann. April–June. White. ($\frac{2}{3}$) *E. B.* 1. 789. *E. B.* 2. 669.
H. & Arn. 71. *Bab.* 54. *Lind.* 51.

C. VISCOSUM. *Narrow-leaved Mouse-ear.*   **Fig. 218.**
Hairy, spreading, viscid. Leaves oblong-lanceolate, dark green.
Petals rather shorter than the calyx, deeply cleft. Fields and way-
sides; common. 6 in. Perenn. May–Sept. ($\frac{2}{3}$) *E. B.* 1. 790.
E. B. 2. 670. *H. & Arn.* 71. *Bab.* 55. *Lind.* 51.

C. SEMIDECANDRUM. *Little Mouse-ear.*   **Fig. 219.**
Hairy, viscid, nearly erect. Leaves oblong-ovate. Petals shorter
than the calyx, slightly notched. Waste places and walls; very common. 1-3 in. Ann. March and April. White. ($\frac{2}{3}$) *E. B.* 1. 1630.
E. B. 2. 671. *H. & Arn.* 71. *Bab.* 55. *Lind.* 51.

C. TETRANDRUM. *Four-cleft Mouse-ear.*   **Fig. 220.**
Calyx 4-parted. Plant hairy, somewhat viscid. Probably a variety
of the preceding. Walls near the sea. 6 in. Ann. May. White ($\frac{2}{3}$)
E. B. 1. 166. *E. B.* 2. 672. *H. & Arn.* 72. *Bab.* 55. *Lind.* 51.

Fig. 201 to 220.

C. ARVENSE. *Field Chickweed.* **Fig. 221.**
Stems ascending. Leaves linear-lanceolate, generally downy. Petals large. Dry fields and banks. 5 in. Perenn. June and July. White. ($\frac{2}{3}$) *E. B.* 1. 93. *E. B.* 2. 673. *H. & Arn.* 72. *Bab.* 56. *Lind.* 51.

C. ALPINUM. *Mountain Chickweed.* **Fig. 222.**
Leaves elliptical-ovate, often covered with silky hairs. Petals large. Flowers in scanty panicles. Mountains. 3–5 in. Perenn. July and Aug. Pure white. ($\frac{2}{3}$) *E. B.* 1. 472. *E. B.* 2. 674. *H. & Arn.* 72. *Bab.* 56. *Lind.* 51.

C. LATIFOLIUM. *Broad-leaved Mountain Chickweed.* **Fig. 223.**
Leaves elliptical-ovate. Flowers terminal, usually solitary. Petals large. Plant covered with short rigid hairs. Mountains. 2–5 in. Perenn. June–Sept. White. ($\frac{2}{3}$) *E. B.* 1. 473. *E. B.* 2. 675. *H. & Arn.* 73. *Bab.* 56. *Lind.* 51.

C. AQUATICUM. *Water Chickweed.* **Fig. 224.**
Much like *Stellaria nemorum.* Straggling, hairy and viscid. Leaves heart-shaped, without foot-stalks. Petals about the length of the calyx. Styles 5. Watery places. 2 ft. Perenn. July. White. ($\frac{2}{3}$) *E. B.* 1. 538. *E. B.* 2. 676. *H. & Arn.* 68. *Bab.* 54. *Lind.* 51.

Genus 16. CHERLERIA.

C. SEDOIDES. *Moss Cyphel.* **Fig. 225.**
Plant in a close tuft. Leaves rather fleshy, light green. Petals minute. Mountain summits. 1 in. Perenn. June and July. Greenish. *E. B.* 1. 1212. *E. B.* 2. 647. *H. & Arn.* 65. *Bab.* 51. *Lind.* 48.

ORDER XIV. LINACEÆ.

Genus 1. LINUM.

L. USITATISSIMUM. *Common Flax.* **Fig. 226.**
Leaves lanceolate. Flowers large. Sepals ovate, with 3 ribs. Fields; not indigenous. Cultivated for its stems, which supply the flax of commerce, and its oily seeds (linseed). $1\frac{1}{2}$ ft. Ann. July. Purplish blue. ($\frac{1}{2}$) *E. B.* 1. 1357. *E. B.* 2. 453. *H. & Arn.* 74. *Bab.* 66. *Lind.* 53.

L. PERENNE. *Perennial Flax.* **Fig. 227.**
Leaves linear. Flowers large. Sepals with 5 obscure ribs, obovate, obtuse. Chalk and limestone hills. 2–3 ft. Perenn. June–Aug. Blue. ($\frac{1}{2}$) *E. B.* 1. 40. *E. B.* 2. 454. *H. & Arn.* 74. *Bab.* 66. *Lind.* 53.

L. ANGUSTIFOLIUM. *Narrow-leaved Flax.* **Fig. 228.**
Leaves linear-lanceolate. Calyx-leaves 3-ribbed, elliptical, pointed. Sandy and chalky pastures. 1 ft. Perenn. July. Pale blue. ($\frac{1}{2}$) *E. B.* 1. 381. *E. B.* 2. 455. *H. & Arn.* 74. *Bab.* 66. *Lind.* 53.

L. CATHARTICUM. *Little Flax.* **Fig. 229.**
Leaves opposite, obovate; upper ones lanceolate. Dry pastures; common. Cathartic. 4–6 in. Ann. June–Sept. White or yellowish. ($\frac{1}{2}$) *E. B.* 1. 382. *E. B.* 2. 456. *H. & Arn.* 74. *Bab.* 66. *Lind.* 54.

Genus 2. RADIOLA.

R. MILLEGRANA. *All-seed.* **Fig. 230.**
A small plant, easily known by its many-seeded, forked branches. Wet sandy places. 2 in. Ann. July and Aug. White. *E. B.* 1. 893. *E. B.* 2. 253. *H. & Arn.* 75. *Bab.* 66. *Lind.* 54.

Fig. 221 to 240

221   222   223   224
225   226   227   228
229   230   231   232
233   234   235   236
237   238   239   240

1 Sept. 1863.

J. E. Sowerby Fecit

12

Order XV. MALVACEÆ.
Genus 1. Lavatera.

L. arborea. *Tree Mallow.* **Fig. 231.**
Shrubby. Leaves downy, with 7 angles. Rocks on the sea-coast; rare. 3–8 ft. Bienn.? July–Oct. Rose-colour, purple in the centre. ($\frac{1}{2}$) *E. B.* 1. 1841. *E. B.* 2. 982. *H. & Arn.* 75. *Bab.* 58. *Lind.* 41.

Genus 2. Malva.

M. sylvestris. *Common Mallow.* **Fig. 232.**
Stems upright. Leaves with 7 acute lobes. Road-sides and waste ground; very common. 1–3 ft. Perenn. May–Aug. Rose-colour. ($\frac{1}{2}$) *E. B.* 1. 671. *E. B.* 2. 978. *H. & Arn.* 76. *Bab.* 57. *Lind.* 40.

M. rotundifolia. *Round-leaved Mallow.* **Fig. 233.**
Stems prostrate. Leaves roundish, bluntly 5-lobed. Waste ground; common. 6 in.–1 ft. Perenn.? June–Sept. Pale rose-colour. ($\frac{1}{2}$) *E. B.* 1. 1092. *E. B.* 2. 979. *H. & Arn.* 76. *Bab.* 57. *Lind.* 40.

M. moschata. *Musk Mallow.* **Fig. 234.**
Stem erect. Upper leaves in 5 deep, pinnatifid segments. Calyx hairy. Fields. 1–2 ft. Perenn. July and Aug. Rose-colour. ($\frac{1}{2}$) *E. B.* 1. 754. *E. B.* 2. 980. *H. & Arn.* 76. *Bab.* 57. *Lind.* 40.

Genus 3. Althæa.

A. officinalis. *Marsh Mallow.* **Fig. 235.**
Leaves soft and downy, slightly 3–5-lobed. Peduncles many-flowered, shorter than the leaves. Marshes near the sea. 4–6 ft. Perenn. July–Sept. Pale rose-colour. ($\frac{1}{2}$) *E. B.* 1. 147. *E. B.* 2. 981. *H. & Arn.* 77. *Bab.* 58. *Lind.* 41.

A. hirsuta. *Hairy Marsh Mallow.* **Fig. 236.**
Lower leaves roundish, obtusely lobed, serrated; upper ones acutely lobed, rough with hairs. Peduncles 1-flowered, longer than the leaves. Fields in Kent. 4–6 ft. June and July. Rose-colour. ($\frac{1}{2}$) *E. B. Supp.* 2674. *E. B.* 2. 981*. *H. & Arn.* 77. *Bab.* 58. *Lind.* 320.

Order XVI. TILIACEÆ.
Genus 1. Tilia.

T. europæa. *Lime. Linden-tree.* **Fig. 237.**
A tree. Leaves glabrous, obliquely heart-shaped, twice as long as the foot-stalks. Woods; scarcely wild. July. Yellowish. ($\frac{2}{3}$) *E. B.* 1. 610. *E. B.* 2. 763. *H. & Arn.* 78. *Bab.* 58. *Lind.* 54.

T. grandifolia. *Large-leaved Lime.* **Fig. 238.**
A tree. Leaves downy beneath, longer than their foot-stalks. Flowers 3 together. Woods; not native. July. Yellowish. ($\frac{2}{3}$) *E. B.* 1. 2720. *E. B.* 2. 763*. *H. & Arn.* 78. *Bab.* 59. *Lind.* 54.

T. parvifolia. *Small-leaved Lime.* **Fig. 239.**
A tree. Leaves smooth above, glaucous beneath, about the length of the foot-stalks. Umbels many-flowered. Woods. June and July. Yellowish. ($\frac{2}{3}$) *E. B.* 1. 1705. *E. B.* 2. 764. *H. & Arn.* 59. *Bab.* 78. *Lind.* 55.

Order XVII. HYPERICACEÆ.
Genus 1. Hypericum.

H. calycinum. *Large-flowered Tutsan.* **Fig. 240.**
Stem shrubby, square. Flowers very large, solitary. Bushy places; naturalized? 1 ft. Perenn. July–Sept. Bright yellow. ($\frac{1}{2}$) *E. B.* 1. 2017. *E. B.* 2. 1050. *H. & Arn.* 79. *Bab.* 59. *Lind.* 41.

H. Androsæmum. *Tutsan.* **Fig. 241.**
A shrub. Capsule berry-like, almost 1-celled. Bushy places. 2–3 ft. July and Aug. Yellow. ($\frac{2}{3}$) *E. B.* 1. 1225. *E. B.* 2. 1051. *H. & Arn.* 79. *Bab.* 59. *Lind.* 43.

H. Quadrangulum. *Square-stalked St. John's-wort.* **Fig. 242.**
Stem herbaceous, square, with sharp angles. Leaves with many pellucid dots. Sepals narrow. Bushy places; common. 1–2 ft. Perenn. July and Aug. Light yellow. ($\frac{2}{3}$) *E. B.* 1. 370. *E. B.* 2. 1052. *H. & Arn.* 80. *Bab.* 60. *Lind.* 42.

H. Perforatum. *Common St. John's-wort.* **Fig. 243.**
Stem 2-edged. Leaves with pellucid dots. Sepals narrow. Woods and hedge-banks; common. 9 in.–2 ft. Perenn. July and Aug. Bright yellow, dotted round the margin. ($\frac{2}{3}$) *E. B.* 1. 295. *E. B.* 2. 1053. *H. & Arn.* 80. *Bab.* 60. *Lind.* 42.

H. Dubium. **Fig. 244.**
Stem slightly square. Leaves without dots. Sepals broad. Hill woods; not common. 9 in.–2 ft. Perenn. July and Aug. Deep yellow. ($\frac{2}{3}$) *E. B.* 1. 296. *E. B.* 2. 1054. *H. & Arn.* 80. *Bab.* 60. *Lind.* 42.

H. Humifusum. *Trailing St. John's-wort.* **Fig. 245.**
Stem slender, trailing close to the ground. Leaves thin, pale green, dotted. Sandy and peaty places; common. 1–2 in. Perenn. June–Sept. Bright yellow; fruit red. *E. B.* 1. 1226. *E. B.* 2. 1055. *H. & Arn.* 80. *Bab.* 60. *Lind.* 42.

H. Montanum. *Hill St. John's-wort.* **Fig. 246.**
Stems erect, smooth. Leaves stem-clasping, dotted with black on the lower margin. Sepals with close black glandular serratures. Chalky or gravelly hills. 1–2 ft. Perenn. July. Pale yellow. ($\frac{2}{3}$) *E. B.* 1. 371. *E. B.* 2. 1056. *H. & Arn.* 81. *Bab.* 61. *Lind.* 42.

H. Barbatum. *Bearded St. John's-wort.* **Fig. 247.**
Stem slightly angular. Leaves with black dots beneath. Sepals fringed with long glandular hairs. A doubtful native. 1 ft. Perenn. Sept. Bright yellow. ($\frac{2}{3}$) *E. B.* 1. 1986. *E. B.* 2. 1057. *H. & Arn.* 81. *Bab.* 61. *Lind.* 42.

H. Linarifolium. *Narrow-leaved St. John's-wort.* **Fig. 248.**
Stem erect. Leaves linear. Sepals with many black dots and glandular serratures. Dry hills in Jersey and Devon. 6 in. Perenn. July and Aug. Yellow. ($\frac{2}{3}$) *E. B. Supp.* 2851. *H. & Arn.* 81. *Bab.* 61.

H. Hirsutum. *Hairy St. John's-wort.* **Fig. 249.**
Stem erect, round. Plant downy. Calyx with black glandular serratures. Dry woods on chalk. 1½–2 ft. Perenn. June and July. Golden yellow. ($\frac{2}{3}$) *E. B.* 1. 1156. *E. B.* 2. 1058. *H. & Arn.* 81. *Bab.* 61. *Lind.* 42.

H. Pulchrum. *Small St. John's-wort.* **Fig. 250.**
Stem erect, round. Leaves stem-clasping, smooth. Plant rather glaucous with a reddish tinge. Dry woods and heaths; common. 6 in.–1 ft. Perenn. July. Deep yellow, tipped with red outside · anthers red. ($\frac{2}{3}$) *E. B.* 1 1227. *E. B.* 2. 1059. *H. & Arn.* 81. *Bab.* 61. *Lind.* 42.

H. ELODES. *Water St. John's-wort.* Fig. 251.
Stems erect, round, creeping below. Leaves roundish-ovate, stem-clasping. Plant shaggy with hairs. Bogs and peaty pools. 6–9 in. Perenn. July and Aug. Pale yellow. ($\frac{2}{3}$) *E. B.* 1. 109. *E. B.* 2. 1060. *H. & Arn.* 82. *Bab.* 61. *Lind.* 42.

Genus 2. PARNASSIA.

P. PALUSTRIS. *Grass of Parnassus.* Fig. 252.
Root-leaves heart-shaped, with foot-stalks. Flowers solitary. Bogs. 3–10 in. Perenn. Aug.–Oct. White. ($\frac{1}{2}$) *E. B.* 1. 82. *E. B.* 2. 449. *H. & Arn.* 51. *Bab.* 40. *Lind.* 67.

ORDER XVIII. ACERACEÆ.
Genus 1. ACER.

A. PSEUDO-PLATANUS. *Sycamore.* Fig. 253.
A tree. Leaves 5-lobed, unequally serrated. Flowers in drooping racemes. Wings of fruit slightly diverging. Woods and hedges; naturalized. Wood white and soft. May. Greenish yellow. ($\frac{1}{2}$) *E. B.* 1. 303. *E. B.* 2. 562. *H. & Arn.* 82. *Bab.* 62. *Lind.* 55.

A. CAMPESTRE. *Maple.* Fig. 254.
A small tree. Leaves usually with 5 obtuse notched lobes. Flowers in erect, rather corymbose clusters. Wings of fruit diverging horizontally. Woods and hedges. Wood very hard. May and June. Greenish. ($\frac{2}{3}$) *E. B.* 1. 304. *E. B.* 2. 563. *H. & Arn.* 82. *Bab.* 62. *Lind.* 55.

ORDER XIX. GERANIACEÆ.
Genus 1. GERANIUM.

G. SANGUINEUM. *Crimson Crane's-bill.* Fig. 255.
Leaves opposite, roundish, very deeply 5- or 7-lobed; lobes trifid. Stalks single-flowered. Flowers large. Limestone pastures. 9 in. Perenn. June and July. Crimson-purple, blue when fading. ($\frac{1}{2}$) *E. B.* 1. 272. *E. B.* 2. 977. *H. & Arn.* 83. *Bab.* 63. *Lind.* 58.

G. PHÆUM. *Dusky Crane's-bill.* Fig. 256.
Stalks 2-flowered. Leaves alternate, with acute serrated lobes. Woods; rare. 1½ ft. Perenn. June. Blackish purple, rarely white. ($\frac{1}{2}$) *E. B.* 1. 322. *E. B.* 2. 965. *H. & Arn.* 83. *Bab.* 63. *Lind.* 56.

G. NODOSUM. *Knotty Crane's-bill.* Fig. 257.
Stems much swollen at the joints. Leaves opposite, 3–5-lobed, pointed. Fruit downy. Hertfordshire and Cumberland; scarcely wild. 1 ft. Perenn. May–Aug. Purple. ($\frac{1}{2}$) *E. B.* 1. 1091. *E. B.* 2. 966. *H. & Arn.* 83. *Bab.* 63. *Lind.* 56.

G. SYLVATICUM. *Wood Crane's-bill.* Fig. 258.
Stalks 2-flowered. Fruit hairy, keeled. Leaves 5–7-lobed, cut and serrated. Woods and meadows. 1–2 ft. Perenn. June and July. Bluish purple with crimson veins. ($\frac{1}{2}$) *E. B.* 1. 121. *E. B.* 2. 967. *H. & Arn.* 83. *Bab.* 64. *Lind.* 56.

G. PRATENSE. *Meadow Crane's-bill.* Fig. 259.
Leaves with 5–7 pinnatifid lobes. Flowers large; stamens dilated at the base. Moist pastures. 1–2 ft. Perenn. June and July. Purple-blue. ($\frac{1}{2}$) *E. B.* 1. 404. *E. B.* 2. 968. *H. & Arn.* 84. *Bab.* 63. *Lind.* 56.

G. PYRENAICUM. *Pyrenean Crane's-bill.* Fig. 260.
Leaves 3–7-lobed, kidney-shaped. Petals twice as long as the calyx. Meadows; local. 2–3 ft. Perenn. June and July. Lilac. ($\frac{1}{2}$) *E. B.* 1. 405. *E. B.* 2. 969. *H. & Arn.* 84. *Bab.* 63. *Lind.* 57.

Fig. 241 to 260.

13

G. LUCIDUM. *Shining Crane's-bill.*   **Fig. 261.**
Stems glossy, crimson. Leaves glossy, bright green, tipped with red, roundish, 5-lobed. Rocks and walls. 6 in. Ann. June–Sept. Rose-colour. ($\frac{2}{3}$) *E. B.* 1. 75. *E. B.* 2. 970. *H. & Arn.* 84. *Bab.* 64. *Lind.* 57.

G. ROBERTIANUM. *Herb Robert.*   **Fig. 262.**
Leaves ternate, with pinnatifid leaflets, shining green. Stems straggling, usually tinged with crimson, hairy. Hedge-banks; common. 1–1½ ft. Ann. May–Oct. Red with white streaks. ($\frac{2}{3}$) *E. B.* 1. 1486. *E. B.* 2. 971. *H. & Arn.* 85. *Bab.* 65. *Lind.* 57.

G. MOLLE. *Soft Crane's-bill. Dove's-foot.*   **Fig. 263.**
Leaves alternate, rounded, lobed, very downy. Petals notched. Dry pastures and waste ground; very common. 3–6 in. Ann. April–Aug. Pale purple. ($\frac{2}{3}$) *E. B.* 1. 778. *E. B.* 2. 972. *H. & Arn.* 85. *Bab.* 64. *Lind.* 57.

G. ROTUNDIFOLIUM. *Round-leaved Crane's-bill.*   **Fig. 264.**
Leaves opposite, rounded, lobed, downy. Petals entire, the length of the calyx. Pastures and waste ground. 3–6 in. Ann. June and July. Pink. ($\frac{2}{3}$) *E. B.* 1. 157. *E. B.* 2. 973. *H. & Arn.* 85. *Bab.* 64. *Lind.* 57.

G. PUSILLUM. *Small-flowered Crane's-bill.*   **Fig. 265.**
Leaves kidney-shaped, palmated, with trifid lobes. Petals notched. Waste ground; very common. 3 in. Ann. May–Sept. Purple. ($\frac{2}{3}$) *E. B.* 1. 385. *E. B.* 2. 974. *H. & Arn.* 85. *Bab.* 64. *Lind.* 57.

G. DISSECTUM. *Jagged Crane's-bill.*   **Fig. 266.**
Leaves palmate, with linear trifid lobes. Flower-stalks shorter than the leaves. Waste ground; common. 6 in. Ann. May and June. Deep pink. ($\frac{2}{3}$) *E. B.* 1. 753. *E. B.* 2. 975. *H. & Arn.* 85. *Bab.* 64. *Lind.* 57.

G. COLUMBINUM. *Long-stalked Crane's-bill.*   **Fig. 267.**
Leaves in 5 deeply lobed segments. Flower-stalks longer than the leaves. Fields and waysides; not common. 9 in. Ann. June and July. Purplish pink. ($\frac{2}{3}$) *E. B.* 1. 259. *E. B.* 2. 976. *H. & Arn.* 85. *Bab.* 64. *Lind.* 58.

Genus 2. ERODIUM.

E. CICUTARIUM. *Heron's-bill.*   **Fig. 268.**
Stems prostrate, hairy. Leaves pinnate, with pinnatifid lobes. Stalks many-flowered. Waste ground. 2–9 in. Ann. June–Sept. Pink, rarely white. ($\frac{2}{3}$) *E. B.* 1. 1768. *E. B.* 2. 962. *H. & Arn.* 86. *Bab.* 65. *Lind.* 58.

E. MOSCHATUM. *Musky Heron's-bill.*   **Fig. 269.**
Stems depressed, hairy. Leaves pinnate, with serrated lobes. Stalks many-flowered. Plant has a musk-like scent. Hilly pastures. 2–6 in. Ann. June and July. Pink. ($\frac{2}{3}$) *E. B.* 1. 902. *E. B.* 2. 963. *H. & Arn.* 86. *Bab.* 65. *Lind.* 58.

E. MARITIMUM. *Sea Heron's-bill.*   **Fig. 270.**
Stems depressed, hairy. Leaves simple, oval, slightly lobed. Stalks few-flowered. Flowers very small. Sandy shores; not common. 3–6 in. Perenn. May–Oct. Pale red. ($\frac{2}{3}$) *E. B.* 1. 646. *E. B.* 2. 964. *H. & Arn.* 86. *Bab.* 65. *Lind.* 58.

Fig. 261 to 280

261 262 263 264
265 266 267 268
269 270 271 272
273 274 275 276
277 278 279 280

1 Oct.r 1858.

J.E. Sowerby, fecit.

14

ORDER XX. BALSAMINACEÆ.
Genus 1. IMPATIENS.

I. NOLI-ME-TANGERE. *Yellow Balsam.* **Fig. 271.**
Spur loosely recurved. Watery shady places; local. Violently diuretic. 1–2 ft. Ann. July and Aug. Bright yellow with orange spots.
($\frac{1}{2}$) *E. B.* 1. 937. *E. B.* 2. 327. *H. & Arn.* 87. *Bab.* 67. *Lind.* 60.

I. FULVA. *Tawny Balsam.* **Fig. 272.**
Spur closely recurved. Banks of the Wey, Surrey. 2–3 ft. Ann. July. Orange, spotted with red. ($\frac{2}{3}$) *E. B. Supp.* 2794. *E. B.* 2. 327*. *H. & Arn.* 87. *Bab.* 67.

ORDER XXI. OXALIDACEÆ.
Genus 1. OXALIS.

O. ACETOSELLA. *Wood Sorrel. Shamrock.* **Fig. 273.**
Leaves springing from the root, ternate. Woods; very common. Leaves very acid. 4 in. Perenn. April and May. White. ($\frac{1}{2}$) *E. B.* 1. 762. *E. B.* 2. 661. *H. & Arn.* 88. *Bab.* 67. *Lind.* 59.

O. CORNICULATA. *Yellow Wood Sorrel.* **Fig. 274.**
Stems procumbent. Stalks 2-flowered. Moist places; rare. 2–4 in. Ann. June–Oct. Yellow. ($\frac{2}{3}$) *E. B.* 1. 1726. *E. B.* 2. 662. *H. & Arn.* 88. *Bab.* 68. *Lind.* 59.

ORDER XXII. STAPHYLEACEÆ.
Genus 1. STAPHYLEA.

S. PINNATA. *Bladder-nut.* **Fig. 275.**
A shrub with pinnate leaves and bladder-like fruit. A doubtful native. 5–6 ft. May and June. Greenish yellow. ($\frac{2}{3}$) *E. B.* 1. 1560. *E. B.* 2. 446. *H. & Arn.* 88. *Bab.* 68. *Lind.* 75.

ORDER XXIII. CELASTRACEÆ.
Genus 1. EUONYMUS.

E. EUROPÆUS. *Spindle-tree.* **Fig. 276.**
A bush. Leaves opposite. Flowers 4-parted. Hedges; common. May. Greenish; capsules crimson, with orange seeds. ($\frac{2}{3}$) *E. B.* 1. 362. *E. B.* 2. 337. *H. & Arn.* 91. *Bab.* 69. *Lind.* 74.

ORDER XXIV. RHAMNACEÆ.
Genus 1. RHAMNUS.

R. CATHARTICUS. *Buckthorn.* **Fig. 277.**
A bush with spiny branches. Flowers 4-cleft, in dense clusters. Thickets. Berries purgative. May. Green; berries black. ($\frac{1}{2}$) *E. B.* 1. 1629. *E. B.* 2. 335. *H. & Arn.* 92. *Bab.* 69. *Lind.* 73.

R. FRANGULA. *Alder Buckthorn.* **Fig. 278.**
A bush. Branches not spiny. Flowers in small clusters. Thickets. Berries purgative. May. Greenish white; berries dark purple. ($\frac{1}{2}$) *E. B.* 1. 250. *E. B.* 2. 336. *H. & Arn.* 92. *Bab.* 69. *Lind.* 62.

ORDER XXV. LEGUMINOSÆ.
Genus 1. ULEX.

U. EUROPÆUS. *Furze. Gorse. Whin.* **Fig. 279.**
An erect spiny shrub. Sepals ovate, with 2 ovate bracts. Commons and thickets; abundant. 3–6 ft. Dec.–May. Golden yellow. ($\frac{1}{2}$) *E. B.* 1. 742. *E. B.* 2. 990. *H. & Arn.* 94. *Bab.* 72. *Lind.* 77.

U. NANUS. *Dwarf Furze.* **Fig. 280.**
A spiny shrub, usually trailing. Sepals lanceolate, bracts minute. Heaths; abundant. 6 in.–2 ft. Aug.–Oct Yellow. ($\frac{1}{2}$) *E. B.* 1. 743. *E. B.* 2. 991. *H. & Arn.* 95. *Bab.* 72. *Lind.* 77.

Genus 2. Genista.

G. tinctoria. *Green-weed.* **Fig. 281.**
A little shrub. Leaves lanceolate, smooth. Flowers in erect racemes. Pastures and thickets. Bitter; yields a yellow dye. 1–2 ft. July and Aug. Bright yellow. ($\frac{2}{3}$) *E. B.* 1. 44. *E. B.* 2. 992. *H. & Arn.* 95. *Bab.* 72. *Lind.* 77.

G. pilosa. *Hairy Green-weed.* **Fig. 282.**
Stem prostrate. Leaves lanceolate, silky beneath. Flowers axillary. Dry heaths. 6–9 in. May and Sept. Yellow. ($\frac{2}{3}$) *E. B.* 1. 208. *E. B.* 2. 993. *H. & Arn.* 96. *Bab.* 72. *Lind.* 77.

G. anglica. *Needle Green-weed. Petty Whin.* **Fig. 283.**
A low shrub. Branches spiny. Leaves ovato-lanceolate. Boggy heaths. 1–2 ft. May–July. Bright yellow. ($\frac{2}{3}$) *E. B.* 1. 132. *E. B.* 2. 994. *H. & Arn.* 96. *Bab.* 73. *Lind.* 77.

Genus 3. Cytisus.

C. Scoparius. *Broom.* **Fig. 284.**
A shrub with angular branches and small ternate leaves. Woods and heaths; very common. Purgative and diuretic. 3–10 ft. May and June. Bright yellow. ($\frac{1}{2}$) *E. B.* 1. 1339. *E. B.* 2. 996. *H. & Arn.* 96. *Bab.* 73. *Lind.* 77.

Genus 4. Ononis.

O. spinosa. *Rest-Harrow.* **Fig. 285.**
Stem woody, spiny, nearly erect, slightly hairy. Sepals shorter than the pod. Heaths and dry commons; abundant. 1 ft. Perenn. June–Sept. Rose-colour or white. ($\frac{2}{3}$) *E. B.* 1. 682. *E. B.* 2. 995. *H. & Arn.* 96. *Bab.* 73. *Lind.* 78.

O. procurrens. *Trailing Rest-Harrow.* **Fig. 286.**
Stem rather woody, trailing, not spiny. Plant hairy all over. Sepals longer than the pod. Perhaps a variety of the last. Fields and waysides, especially on chalk. 6 in. Perenn. June–Sept. Rose-colour or white. ($\frac{2}{3}$) *E. B. Supp.* 2659. *H. & Arn.* 97. *Bab.* 73. *Lind.* 78.

O. reclinata. *Small Rest-Harrow.* **Fig. 287.**
Stem ascending, herbaceous. Plant hairy, viscid. Sepals shorter than the pods. Coast of Galloway and Channel Islands. 4–6 in. Ann. July. Pink. ($\frac{2}{3}$) *E. B. Supp.* 2838. *H. & Arn.* 97. *Bab.* 73.

Genus 5. Anthyllis.

A. vulneraria. *Kidney-vetch. Wound-wort.* **Fig. 288.**
Very hairy. Leaves pinnate. Flower-heads in pairs. Dry pastures. 6 in.–1 ft. Perenn. June–Aug. Yellow, rarely red or white. ($\frac{2}{3}$) *E. B.* 1. 104. *E. B.* 2. 997. *H. & Arn.* 97. *Bab.* 80. *Lind.* 78.

Genus 6. Medicago.

M. falcata. *Sickle Medick.* **Fig. 289.**
Stems procumbent. Leaflets narrow-obovate. Flowers in erect racemes. Pods sickle-shaped. Fields. 1 ft. Perenn. June and July. Pale yellow. ($\frac{2}{3}$) *E. B.* 1. 1016. *E. B.* 2. 1047. *H. & Arn.* 98. *Bab.* 74. *Lind.* 82.

M. sativa. *Lucerne. Purple Medick.* **Fig. 290.**
Stems erect. Leaflets oblong, toothed. Pods loosely spiral. Fields; not native. Cultivated for fodder. 1–2 ft. Perenn. June and July. Purple, streaked with white and green. ($\frac{2}{3}$) *E. B.* 1. 1749. *E. B.* 2. 1046. *H. & Arn.* 98. *Bab.* 74. *Lind.* 82.

M. LUPULINA. *Black Medick. Nonsuch.* **Fig. 291.**
Stems procumbent. Leaflets obovate. Pods kidney-shaped, rugged, one-seeded. Flowers in close ovate spikes. Fields; common. Cultivated for fodder. 6 in.–1 ft. Ann. May–Sept. Yellow. ($\frac{2}{3}$) *E. B.* 1. 971. *E. B.* 2. 1048. *H. & Arn.* 98. *Bab.* 74. *Lind.* 83.

M. MACULATA. *Spotted Medick.* **Fig. 292.**
Stems spreading. Leaflets obcordate. Pods coiled like a snail-shell, with long curved spines. Stalks few-flowered. Fields; common. 4–8 in. Ann. May and June. Yellow. ($\frac{2}{3}$) *E. B.* 1. 1616. *E. B.* 2. 1049. *H. & Arn.* 98. *Bab.* 74. *Lind.* 83.

M. DENTICULATA. *Reticulated Medick.* **Fig. 293.**
Stipules toothed. Pods spiral, flat, with spines. A variety of *maculata.* Sandy places. 4–8 in. Ann. April–July. Yellow. ($\frac{2}{3}$) *E. B. Supp.* 2634. *E. B.* 2. 1049**. *H. & Arn.* 99. *Bab.* 75. *Lind.* 324.

M. MINIMA. *Little Medick.* **Fig. 294.**
Hairy. Stipules nearly entire. Pods closely spiral, subglobose, spiny. A variety of *maculata.* Waste places; rare. 2–6 in. Ann. June and July. Yellow. ($\frac{2}{3}$) *E. B. Supp.* 2635. *E. B.* 2. 1049*. *H. & Arn.* 98. *Bab.* 74. *Lind.* 83.

Genus 7. MELILOTUS.

M. OFFICINALIS. *Yellow Melilot.* **Fig. 295.**
Stems erect. Petals nearly equal. Fields and waysides. Cultivated for fodder. 2–3 ft. Ann. June and July. Yellow. ($\frac{2}{3}$) *E. B.* 1. 1340. *E. B.* 2. 1026. *H. & Arn.* 99. *Bab.* 75. *Lind.* 79.

M. LEUCANTHA. *White Melilot.* **Fig. 296.**
Stems erect. Vexillum longer than the keel and wings. A variety of *officinalis?* Sandy fields. 2 ft. Ann. July. White. ($\frac{2}{3}$) *E. B.* 1. 2689. *E. B.* 2. 1026. *H. & Arn.* 99. *Bab.* 75. *Lind.* 324.

Genus 8. TRIFOLIUM.

T. ORNITHOPODIOIDES. *Bird's-foot Clover.* **Fig. 297.**
Stems spreading. Stalks 2- or 3-flowered. Pod 3-seeded, twice as long as the calyx. Heaths. 2–4 in. Ann. July. Pink. ($\frac{2}{3}$) *E. B.* 1. 1047. *E. B.* 2. 1027. *H. & Arn.* 100. *Bab.* 78. *Lind.* 82.

T. REPENS. *White Clover. Dutch Clover. Trefoil.* **Fig. 298.**
Stems creeping. Leaflets obcordate or obovate, usually with a dark spot at the base, bordered by a light line. Flowers in close round heads on long stalks. Legumes covered by the calyx, 4-seeded. Pastures; abundant. Grown for fodder. 2–9 in. Perenn. May–Sept. White. ($\frac{2}{3}$) *E. B.* 1. 1769. *E. B.* 2. 1028. *H. & Arn.* 100. *Bab.* 78. *Lind.* 79.

T. SUBTERRANEUM. *Subterraneous Trefoil.* **Fig. 299.**
Heads 3- or 4-flowered, with short palmated fibres growing from the apex of the stalk and covering the pods, which, when ripe, are often buried in the ground. Fields. 3 in. Ann. May. White. ($\frac{2}{3}$) *E. B.* 1. 1048. *E. B.* 2. 1029. *H. & Arn.* 103. *Bab.* 77. *Lind.* 80.

T. OCHROLEUCUM. *Sulphur-coloured Clover.* **Fig. 300.**
Stems ascending, downy. Leaflets obcordate. Pastures. 1–1½ ft. Perenn. July and Aug. Cream-colour. ($\frac{2}{3}$) *E. B.* 1. 1224. *E. B.* 2. 1030. *H. & Arn.* 101. *Bab.* 76. *Lind.* 80.

Fig. 281 to 300.

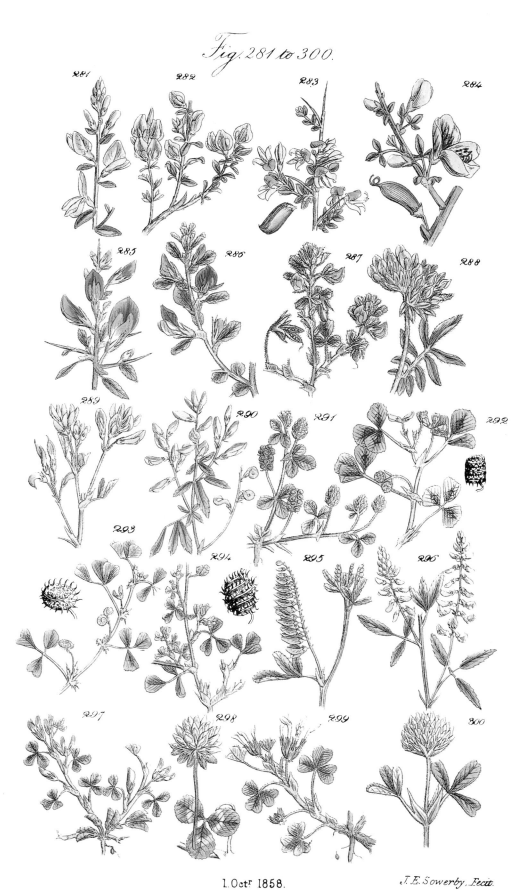

281 282 283 284
285 286 287 288
289 290 291 292
293 294 295 296
297 298 299 300

1. Octr 1858.

J.E. Sowerby, Fecit.

75

T. PRATENSE. *Red Clover. Red Trefoil.* **Fig. 301.**
Stems ascending, hairy. Leaflets elliptic, pointed. Lower tooth of the calyx the longest. Pastures. Cultivated for fodder. 1 ft. Perenn. May–Sept. Reddish purple. ($\frac{2}{3}$) *E. B.* 1. 1770. *E. B.* 2. 1031. *H. & Arn.* 101. *Bab.* 75. *Lind.* 80.

T. MEDIUM. *Purple Clover.* **Fig. 302.**
Stems branched, zigzag, hairy. Leaflets elliptic, pointed. Two lower teeth of the calyx equal in length. Pastures. Cultivated for fodder. 1–1½ ft. Perenn. July. Deep purple. ($\frac{2}{3}$) *E. B.* 1. 190. *E. B.* 2. 1032. *H. & Arn.* 101. *Bab.* 76. *Lind.* 80.

T. MARITIMUM. *Teasle-headed Trefoil.* **Fig. 303.**
Stems ascending. Leaflets oblong. Calyx-teeth enlarging after flowering. Salt marshes. 6–8 in. Ann. June and July. Pale purple. ($\frac{2}{3}$) *E. B.* 1. 220. *E. B.* 2. 1033. *H. & Arn.* 101. *Bab.* 77. *Lind.* 80.

T. STELLATUM. *Starry-headed Trefoil.* **Fig. 304.**
Stems spreading. Leaflets obcordate. Calyx-teeth very long. Shoreham; Sussex. 6–8 in. Ann. July and Aug. Rose-colour; calyx with a red circle at the base. ($\frac{2}{3}$) *E. B.* 1. 1545. *E. B.* 2. 1034. *H. & Arn.* 102. *Bab.* 76. *Lind.* 80.

T. ARVENSE. *Hare's-foot Trefoil.* **Fig. 305.**
Stems erect, branched. Head cylindrical, hairy. Calyx-teeth long, bristly. Corolla very small. Dry fields. 6 in.–1 ft. Ann. July and Aug. Pale purple. ($\frac{2}{3}$) *E. B.* 1. 944. *E. B.* 2. 1035. *H. & Arn.* 102. *Bab.* 76. *Lind.* 76.

T. SCABRUM. *Rough Trefoil.* **Fig. 306.**
Stems procumbent, hairy. Leaflets obcordate. Heads sessile, ovate. Calyx-tube cylindrical when in fruit. Dry fields. 4–6 in. Ann. June. Pale pink. ($\frac{2}{3}$) *E. B.* 1. 903. *E. B.* 2. 1036. *H. & Arn.* 102. *Bab.* 77. *Lind.* 80.

T. GLOMERATUM. *Round-headed Trefoil.* **Fig. 307.**
Stems prostrate, smooth. Heads of flower globose, sessile. Dry pastures. 4–6 in. Ann. July. Pale purple. ($\frac{2}{3}$) *E. B.* 1. 1063. *E. B.* 2. 1037. *H. & Arn.* 103. *Bab.* 78. *Lind.* 81.

T. STRIATUM. *Knotted Trefoil.* **Fig. 308.**
Downy. Stems ascending. Heads ovate, sessile. Calyx rather swollen when in fruit, striated. Sandy fields. 3–5 in. Ann. June. Pink. ($\frac{2}{3}$) *E. B.* 1. 1843. *E. B.* 2. 1038. *H. & Arn.* 102. *Bab.* 76. *Lind.* 82.

T. SUFFOCATUM. *Sand Trefoil.* **Fig. 309.**
Stems spreading. Heads roundish, sessile. Petals shorter than the calyx. Sea-shore, in loose sand. 1 in. Ann. July. White or pinkish. ($\frac{2}{3}$) *E. B.* 1. 1049. *E. B.* 2. 1039. *H. & Arn.* 103. *Bab.* 78. *Lind.* 79.

T. FRAGIFERUM. *Strawberry Trefoil.* **Fig. 310.**
Stems creeping. Heads globose, on long stalks. Calyx much inflated when in fruit, with the 2 upper teeth longest. Moist pastures. 3–6 in. Perenn. July. Pink; calyces reddish. ($\frac{2}{3}$) *E. B.* 1. 1050. *E. B.* 2. 1040. *H. & Arn.* 104. *Bab.* 78. *Lind.* 81.

Fig. 301 to 320.

301   302   303   304

305   306   307   308

309   310   311   312

313   314   315   316

317   318   319   320

1 Oct. 1858.

J. E. Sowerby. Fecit.

16

T. RESUPINATUM. *Reversed Trefoil.* **Fig. 311.**
Stem prostrate. Corolla with the vexillum curved downwards. Heads globose, on foot-stalks. Sea-coast; not native. 4 in. Ann. July. Pink. ($\frac{2}{3}$) *E. B. Supp.* 2789. *E. B.* 1. 1040. *H. & Arn.* 104. *Bab.* 79. *Lind.* 324.

T. PROCUMBENS. *Hop Trefoil.* **Fig. 312.**
Stem procumbent or erect. Heads ovate, many-flowered. Vexillum persistent. Dry fields; common. 4–8 in. Ann. June and July. Yellow, changing to brown. ($\frac{2}{3}$) *E. B.* 1. 945. *E. B.* 2. 1041. *H. & Arn.* 104. *Bab.* 79. *Lind.* 81.

T. MINUS. *Lesser Yellow Trefoil.* **Fig. 313.**
Stems procumbent. Heads few-flowered. Dry pastures. 4–9 in. Ann. June and July. Yellow. ($\frac{2}{3}$) *E. B.* 1. 1256. *E. B.* 2. 1042. *H. & Arn.* 105. *Bab.* 79. *Lind.* 81.

T. FILIFORME. *Slender Trefoil.* **Fig. 314.**
Stems procumbent. Flowers few together in lax racemes. Foot-stalks very slender. A variety of *minus.* Dry pastures. 2–6 in. Ann. July. Yellow. ($\frac{2}{3}$) *E. B.* 1. 1257. *E. B.* 2. 1042*. *H. & Arn.* 105. *Bab.* 79. *Lind.* 81.

Genus 9. LOTUS.

L. CORNICULATUS. *Bird's-foot Trefoil.* **Fig. 315.**
Stems recumbent, pithy. Heads depressed, few-flowered. Claw of the vexillum dilated. Dry pastures and heaths; common. 2–8 in. Perenn. June–Sept. Bright yellow; buds red. ($\frac{2}{3}$) *E. B.* 1. 2090. *E. B.* 2. 1043. *H. & Arn.* 105. *Bab.* 79. *Lind.* 81.

L. TENUIS. *Slender Bird's-foot Trefoil.* **Fig. 316.**
Stems prostrate, slender, nearly solid. Leaflets lanceolate. A variety of *corniculatus?* Pastures. 4–8 in. Perenn. July. Yellow. ($\frac{2}{3}$) *E. B. Supp.* 2615. *E. B.* 1. 1043*. *H. & Arn.* 105. *Bab.* 80. *Lind.* 82.

L. MAJOR. *Great Bird's-foot Trefoil.* **Fig. 317.**
Stems erect, tubular. Hairy. Heads many-flowered. Claw of the vexillum narrow. Bushy places. 1–2 ft. Perenn. June–Aug. Yellow. ($\frac{2}{3}$) *E. B.* 1. 2091. *E. B.* 2. 1044. *H. & Arn.* 106. *Bab.* 80. *Lind.* 82.

L. ANGUSTISSIMUS. *Little Bird's-foot Trefoil.* **Fig. 318.**
Hairy. Stems prostrate, slender. Flowers in pairs or solitary. Pods very long and slender. Southern coast; rare. 8 in. Ann. June. Yellow. ($\frac{2}{3}$) *E. B.* 1. 925. *E. B.* 2. 1045. *H. & Arn.* 106. *Bab.* 80. *Lind.* 82.

L. HISPIDUS. *Hairy Bird's-foot Trefoil.* **Fig. 319.**
Very hairy. Stems prostrate. Flowers 3 or 4 together. Probably a variety of *angustissimus.* Southern coast. 4–8 in. Ann. June and July. Yellow. ($\frac{2}{3}$) *E. B. Supp.* 2823. *H. & Arn.* 106. *Bab.* 80.

Genus 10. OXYTROPIS.

O. URALENSIS. **Fig. 320.**
Leaves tufted, silky. Heads few-flowered. Dry mountain pastures in Scotland. 2–6 in. Perenn. June and July. Purple. ($\frac{2}{3}$) *E. B.* 1. 466. *E. B.* 2. 1024. *H. & Arn.* 107. *Bab.* 80. *Lind.* 79.

O. CAMPESTRIS. Fig. 321.
Leaves tufted, rather silky. Heads many-flowered. Clova Mountains,
Angus. 2–4 in. Perenn. July. Pale yellow, wings purplish. ($\frac{2}{3}$)
E. B. 1. 2522. E. B. 2. 1025. H. & Arn. 107. Bab. 81. Lind. 79.

Genus 11. ASTRAGALUS.

A. GLYCYPHYLLOS. *Milk-Vetch.* Fig. 322.
Stem prostrate. Pods curved. Flowers in spikes. Woods and dry
fields. Leaves have a sweetish taste. 6 in.–2 ft. Perenn. July
Dingy yellow. ($\frac{2}{3}$) E. B. 1. 203. E. B. 2. 1022. H. & Arn. 107.
Bab. 81. Lind. 78.

A. HYPOGLOTTIS. *Purple Milk-Vetch.* Fig. 323.
Stem prostrate. Pods ovate. Flowers in round heads. Dry alpine
pastures. 2–6 in. Perenn. July. Purple. ($\frac{2}{3}$) E. B. 1. 274.
E. B. 2. 1023. H. & Arn. 108. Bab. 81. Lind. 78.

A. ALPINUS. *Mountain Milk-Vetch.* Fig. 324
Stem ascending. Pods elliptical, clothed with black hairs. Flowers
in scanty racemes. Clova Mountains, Angus. 6 in.–1 ft. Perenn.
July. White, tinged with purple. ($\frac{2}{3}$) E. B. Supp. 2717. E. B.
2. 1023*. H. & Arn. 108. Bab. 81. Lind. 323.

Genus 12. ORNITHOPUS.

O. PERPUSILLUS. *Bird's-foot.* Fig. 325.
Stems spreading. Pods jointed, compressed, curved. Foot-stalks
with a bract at the apex. Dry pastures; common. 2–6 in. Ann.
June. White streaked with red, keel green. ($\frac{2}{3}$) E. B. 1. 369.
E. B. 2. 1019. H. & Arn. 108. Bab. 86. Lind. 87.

O. EBRACTEATUS. *Joint-Vetch.* Fig. 326.
Stems prostrate. Pods jointed, cylindrical, curved. Foot-stalks
without bracts. Channel Islands and Scilly. Ann. July and Aug.
2–4 in. Yellow. ($\frac{2}{3}$) E. B. Supp. 2844. H. & Arn. 108. Bab. 86.
Lind. 324.

Genus 13. HIPPOCREPIS.

H. COMOSA. *Horse-shoe Vetch.* Fig. 327.
Flowers in umbels. Pods jointed; the joints curved like a horse-
shoe. Chalky hills. 4–6 in. Perenn. May–Aug. Yellow. ($\frac{2}{3}$)
E. B. 1. 31. E. B. 2. 1020. H. & Arn. 109. Bab. 86. Lind. 88.

Genus 14. ONOBRYCHIS.

O. SATIVA. *Saintfoin.* Fig. 328.
Stems elongated. Pods one-seeded. Plant hairy. Chalk hills.
Cultivated for fodder. 1–2 ft. Perenn. June and July. Crimson
and white. ($\frac{2}{3}$) E. B. 1. 96. E. B. 2. 1021. H. & Arn. 109.
Bab. 87. Lind. 88.

Genus 15. VICIA.

V. SYLVATICA. *Wood Vetch.* Fig. 329.
Stems climbing. Leaflets oval. Stipules deeply toothed at the base.
Flowers in racemes. Woods and hedges. 5–6 ft. Perenn. July.
White with blue streaks. ($\frac{2}{3}$) E. B. 1. 79. E. B. 2. 1008. H. &
Arn. 112. Bab. 82. Lind. 84.

V. CRACCA. *Tufted Vetch.* Fig. 330.
Stem slender, climbing. Leaflets lanceolate. Stipules entire. Flowers
in close racemes. Hedges; very common. 3–5 ft. Perenn. July
and Aug. Purplish blue. ($\frac{2}{3}$) E. B. 1. 1168. E. B. 2. 1009. H. &
Arn. 112. Bab. 83. Lind. 84.

V. SATIVA. *Vetch. Tare.* **Fig. 331.**
Leaves elliptic-oblong. Flowers sessile, axillary, usually in pairs. Fields; a doubtful native. Cultivated for fodder. 1–2 ft. Ann. June. Purple. ($\frac{2}{3}$) *E. B.* 1. 334. *E. B.* 2. 1010. *H. & Arn.* 110. *Bab.* 84. *Lind.* 84.

V. ANGUSTIFOLIA. **Fig. 332.**
Upper leaves lanceolate, lower linear. Flowers usually solitary. A variety of *sativa.* Fields. Ann. June. Deep purple. ($\frac{2}{3}$) *E. B. Supp.* 2614. *E. B.* 2. 1010*. *H. & Arn.* 110. *Bab.* 84. *Lind.* 324.

V. BOBARTII. **Fig. 333.**
Upper leaflets linear, lower obcordate. Flowers usually solitary. A variety of *sativa.* Fields. Ann. June and July. Purple. ($\frac{2}{3}$) *E. B. Supp.* 2708. *E. B.* 2. 1010**. *H. & Arn.* 110. *Bab.* 84. *Lind.* 84.

V. LATHYROIDES. *Spring Vetch.* **Fig. 334.**
Stems procumbent. Leaflets obcordate. Tendrils very short. Flowers solitary. Fields and waysides. 4–5 in. Ann. April and May. Purple or white. ($\frac{2}{3}$) *E. B.* 1. 30. *E. B.* 2. 1011. *H. & Arn.* 110. *Bab.* 84. *Lind.* 84.

V. LUTEA. *Yellow Vetch.* **Fig. 335.**
Stems spreading. Leaflets elliptic-lanceolate. Flowers solitary, vexillum smooth. Sea-coast. 4 in.–2 ft. Perenn. June and July. Pale yellow, tinged with purple. ($\frac{2}{3}$) *E. B.* 1. 481. *E. B.* 2. 1012. *H. & Arn.* 111. *Bab.* 84. *Lind.* 85.

V. HYBRIDA. *Hairy-flowered Vetch.* **Fig. 336.**
Stems ascending. Leaflets obcordate or obovate. Vexillum hairy. Glastonbury Tor, Somersetshire, and near Lincoln. 1–2 ft. Perenn. June and July. Yellow with purple veins. ($\frac{2}{3}$) *E. B.* 1. 482. *E. B.* 2. 1013. *H. & Arn.* 111. *Bab.* 83. *Lind.* 85.

V. LÆVIGATA. *Smooth-podded Vetch.* **Fig. 337.**
Stems ascending. Plant smooth. Flowers solitary. Pods smooth. Beach at Weymouth. 6 in.–1 ft. Perenn. July–Sept. Pale purple or whitish. ($\frac{2}{3}$) *E. B.* 1. 483. *E. B.* 2. 1014. *H. & Arn.* 110. *Bab.* 83. *Lind.* 85.

V. SEPIUM. *Bush Vetch.* **Fig. 338.**
Stems climbing. Leaflets ovate. Flowers in short clusters. Pods smooth. Thickets; common. 1–2 ft. Perenn. May–July. Purple. ($\frac{2}{3}$) *E. B.* 1. 1515. *E. B.* 2. 1015. *H. & Arn.* 110. *Bab.* 83. *Lind.* 85.

V. BITHYNICA. **Fig. 339.**
Stems climbing. Upper leaflets very long, linear-lanceolate, lower elliptic-lanceolate. Flowers solitary, on long stalks. Bushy places; rare. 1–2 ft. Perenn. July and Aug. Purple, keel and wings whitish. ($\frac{2}{3}$) *E. B.* 1. 1842. *E. B.* 2. 1046. *H. & Arn.* 111. *Bab.* 83. *Lind.* 85.

Genus 16. ERVUM.

E. TETRASPERMUM. *Tine-Tare.* **Fig. 340.**
Stems very slender, climbing. Flowers mostly in pairs. Pods smooth, 4-seeded. Corn-fields and thickets. 1–2 ft. Ann. June and July. Pale purple. ($\frac{2}{3}$) *E. B.* 1. 1223. *E. B.* 2. 1017. *H. & Arn.* 112. *Bab.* 82. *Lind.* 83.

Fig. 321 to 340.

321 322 323 324
325 326 327 328
329 330 331 332
333 334 335 336
337 338 339 340

1. Nov.r 1858.

J. E. Sowerby, Exit.

17

E. HIRSUTUM.   *Hairy Tine-Tare.*   **Fig. 341.**
Stems very slender, climbing. Flowers several together. Pods hairy, 2-seeded. Corn-fields and thickets. 2–3 ft. Ann. June and July. Bluish white. ($\frac{2}{3}$) *E. B.* 1. 970. *E. B.* 2. 1018. *H. & Arn.* 113. *Bab.* 81. *Lind.* 83.

Genus 17. LATHYRUS.

L. APHACA.   *Yellow Vetchling.*   **Fig. 342.**
Leaves usually absent. *Stipules* very large and leaf-like, sagittate, glaucous. Fields ; rare. Seeds poisonous. 1–2 ft. Ann. June–Aug. Yellow. ($\frac{2}{3}$) *E.B.* 1. 1167. *E. B.* 2. 1000. *H. & Arn.* 113. *Bab.* 84. *Lind.* 86.

L. NISSOLIA.   *Crimson Vetchling.*   **Fig. 343.**
Stem erect. Leaves simple, linear-lanceolate, without tendrils. Stipules minute. Pods very long. Woods and banks. 2 ft. Ann. May and June. Crimson. ($\frac{2}{3}$) *E. B.* 1. 112. *E. B.* 2. 1001. *H. & Arn.* 113. *Bab.* 85. *Lind.* 86.

L. HIRSUTUS.   *Rough-podded Vetchling.*   **Fig. 344.**
Stems spreading, winged, hairy. Tendrils with 2 leaflets. Pods oblong, hairy. Fields ; rare. 1–2 ft. Ann. July. Pale purple, vexillum crimson. ($\frac{2}{3}$) *E. B.* 1. 1255. *E. B.* 2. 1002. *H. & Arn.* 113. *Bab.* 85. *Lind.* 86.

L. PRATENSIS.   *Meadow Vetchling.*   **Fig. 345.**
Stems angular, climbing. Tendrils with 2 leaflets. Stipules large, arrow-shaped. Meadows and bushy places. 6 in.–3 ft. Perenn. July and Aug. Yellow. ($\frac{2}{3}$) *E.B.* 1. 670. *E. B.* 2. 1003. *H. & Arn.* 114. *Bab.* 85. *Lind.* 86.

L. SYLVESTRIS.   *Narrow-leaved Everlasting Pea.*   **Fig. 346.**
Stem winged, climbing. Leaflets 3-ribbed, linear-lanceolate. Thickets. 3–6 ft. Perenn. July and Aug. Greenish and purple. ($\frac{2}{3}$) *E. B.* 1. 805. *E. B.* 2. 1004. *H. & Arn.* 114. *Bab.* 85. *Lind.* 85.

L. LATIFOLIUS.   *Everlasting Pea.*   **Fig. 347.**
Stem winged, climbing. Leaflets elliptical, broad. Woods and thickets; naturalized ? 4–8 ft. Perenn. July and Aug. Rose-colour. ($\frac{1}{2}$) *E. B.* 1. 1108. *E. B.* 2. 1005. *H. & Arn.* 114. *Bab.* 85. *Lind.* 85.

L. PALUSTRIS.   *Marsh Vetchling.*   **Fig. 348.**
Stem winged, climbing. Tendrils with 2–4 pairs of leaflets. Meadows and boggy woods. 2–4 ft. Perenn. June–Sept. Purplish blue. ($\frac{1}{2}$) *E. B.* 1. 169. *E. B.* 2. 1006. *H. & Arn.* 114. *Bab.* 85. *Lind.* 86.

Genus 18. PISUM.

P. MARITIMUM.   *Sea-side Pea.*   **Fig. 349.**
Stem angular, procumbent. Leaflets numerous, alternate. Glaucous. Sea-coast. 1–2 ft. Perenn. July and Aug. Purple with crimson veins. ($\frac{1}{2}$) *E. B.* 1. 1046. *E. B.* 2. 1007. *H. & Arn.* 114. *Bab.* 85. *Lind.* 84.

Genus 19. OROBUS.

O. TUBEROSUS.   *Bitter Vetch.*   **Fig. 350.**
Stem simple, erect. Stipules half-arrow-shaped, toothed at the base. Woods and thickets ; common. Tuberous roots edible. 6 in.– 1 ft. Perenn. May–July. Purple ; blue when fading. ($\frac{2}{3}$) *E. B.* 1. 1153. *E. B.* 2. 998. *H. & Arn.* 115. *Bab.* 86. *Lind.* 87

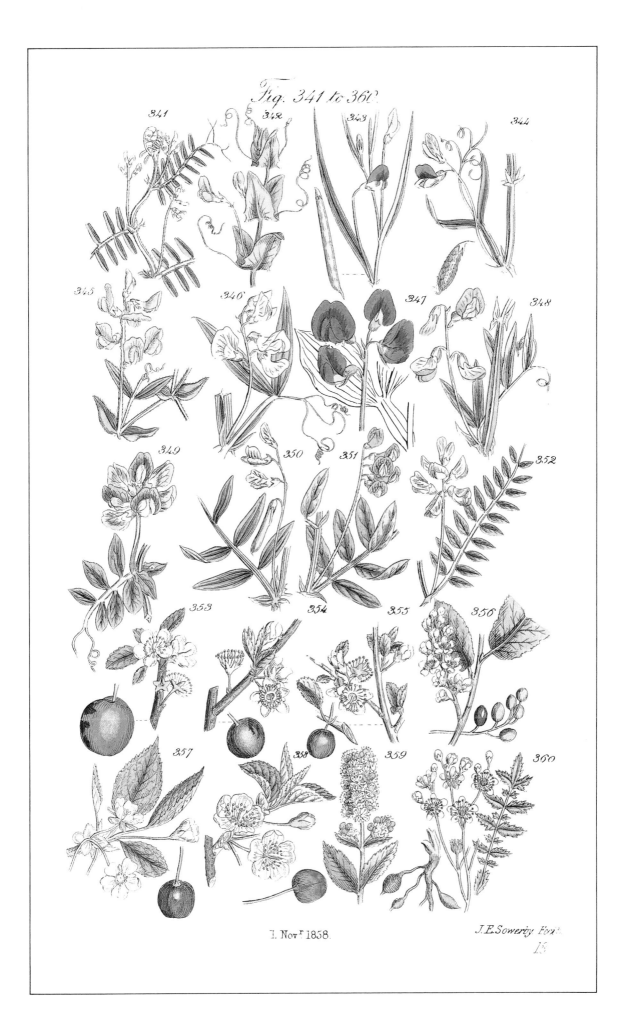

Fig. 341 to 360.

341 342 343 344

345 346 347 348

349 350 351 352

353 354 355 356

357 358 359 360

1. Nov.ʳ 1858.

J.E.Sowerby Penˣ

O. NIGER. *Black Bitter Vetch.* **Fig. 351.**
Stem branched, erect. Stipules linear-lanceolate. Rocks in the Highlands. 1–1½ ft. Perenn. June and July. Crimson and purple. ($\frac{2}{3}$) *E. B. Supp.* 2788. *E. B.* 2. 998*. *H. & Arn.* 115. *Bab.* 86. *Lind.* 87.

O. SYLVATICUS. *Wood Bitter Vetch.* **Fig. 352.**
Stem branched, hairy, decumbent. Stipules half-arrow-shaped. Leaves hairy, with many leaflets. Mountain woods. 1–2 ft. Perenn. May and June. Whitish with purple streaks. ($\frac{2}{3}$) *E. B.* 1. 518. *E. B.* 2. 999. *H. & Arn.* 112. *Bab.* 82. *Lind.* 87.

ORDER XXVI. ROSACEÆ.

Genus 1. PRUNUS.

P. DOMESTICA. *Wild Plum.* **Fig. 353.**
A small tree. Branches without thorns. Peduncles solitary or in pairs. Woods and hedges; scarcely wild. The origin of the garden Plums. May. White; fruit purple or black, with bloom. ($\frac{1}{2}$) *E. B.* 1. 1783. *E. B.* 2. 690. *H. & Arn.* 117. *Bab.* 89. *Lind.* 90.

P. INSITITIA. *Wild Bullace.* **Fig. 354.**
A small tree. Branches terminating in a spine. Peduncles mostly in pairs. Leaves downy beneath. Thickets and hedges. Fruit austere. The origin of the Bullace Plum. April. White; fruit black, with bloom. ($\frac{1}{2}$) *E. B.* 1. 841. *E. B.* 2. 691. *H. & Arn.* 117. *Bab.* 89. *Lind.* 90.

P. SPINOSA. *Sloe. Blackthorn.* **Fig. 355.**
A bush. Branches ending in a spine. Peduncles solitary. Thickets and hedges; very common. Leaves poisonous; fruit very austere. March and April. White; fruit black, with bloom. ($\frac{2}{3}$) *E. B.* 1. 842. *E. B.* 2. 692. *H. & Arn.* 117. *Bab.* 89. *Lind.* 90.

P. PADUS. *Bird Cherry.* **Fig. 356.**
A small tree. Flowers in long racemes. Woods and hedges. Fruit bitter. May. White; fruit black, without bloom. ($\frac{2}{3}$) *E. B.* 1. 1383. *E. B.* 2. 688. *H. & Arn.* 118. *Bab.* 90. *Lind.* 90.

P. AVIUM. *Wild Cherry.* **Fig. 357.**
A tree. Flowers in lax umbels. Sepals rather pointed. Leaves drooping, downy beneath. Woods and hedges. The origin of the garden Cherry. May. White; fruit black or red, without bloom. ($\frac{1}{2}$) *E. B.* 1. 706. *E. B.* 2. 689. *H. & Arn.* 118. *Bab.* 90. *Lind.* 90.

P. CERASUS. *Morello Cherry.* **Fig. 358.**
A bush. Flowers in spreading umbels. Sepals blunt and rounded. Leaves glabrous, not drooping. Woods. Fruit acid. May. White; fruit red. ($\frac{1}{2}$) *E. B. Supp.* 2863. *H. & Arn.* 118. *Bab.* 90. *Lind.* 325.

Genus 2. SPIRÆA.

S. SALICIFOLIA. *Willow-leaved Dropwort.* **Fig. 359.**
A shrub. Leaves elliptic-lanceolate. Flowers in terminal racemes. Mountain woods. 3–4 ft. July and Aug. Rose-colour. ($\frac{2}{3}$) *E. B.* 1. 284. *E. B.* 2. 702. *H. & Arn.* 119. *Bab.* 90. *Lind.* 89.

S. FILIPENDULA. *Common Dropwort.* **Fig. 360.**
Herbaceous. Leaves interruptedly pinnated. Flowers in a cymose panicle. Pastures on chalk or limestone. 1 ft. Perenn. July. White or pinkish. ($\frac{2}{3}$) *E. B.* 1. 284. *E. B.* 2. 703. *H. & Arn.* 119. *Bab.* 90. *Lind.* 89.

S. ULMARIA. *Meadow-sweet.* **Fig. 361.**
Herbaceous. Leaves interruptedly pinnate, the terminal leaflet large
and lobed. Flowers in proliferous cymes. Meadows; common. 2–
4 ft. Perenn. June and July. Yellowish white. ($\frac{2}{3}$) *E. B.* 1. 960.
E. B. 2. 704. *H. & Arn.* 119. *Bab.* 90. *Lind.* 89.

Genus 3. DRYAS.

D. OCTOPETALA. *Mountain Avens.* **Fig. 362.**
Stem woody, creeping. Leaves oblong, crenated, downy beneath.
Petals 8. Mountain pastures. 6 in. Perenn. June and July.
White, stamens yellow. ($\frac{1}{2}$) *E. B.* 1. 451. *E. B.* 2. 745. *H. &*
Arn. 119. *Bab.* 109. *Lind.* 99.

Genus 4. GEUM.

G. URBANUM. *Common Avens.* **Fig. 363.**
Root-leaves lyrato-pinnate. Flowers erect. Styles naked. Woods
and hedge-banks. 1–2 ft. Perenn. June–Aug. Yellow. ($\frac{2}{3}$)
E. B. 1. 1400. *E. B.* 2. 742. *H. & Arn.* 120. *Bab.* 109. *Lind.* 98.
G. RIVALE. *Water Avens.* **Fig. 364.**
Root-leaves lyrate or pinnate. Flowers drooping. Styles hairy.
Marshes and river-banks. 1 ft. Perenn. June and July. Dull
purplish red. ($\frac{2}{3}$) *E. B.* 1. 106. *E. B.* 2. 743. *H. & Arn.* 120.
Bab. 109. *Lind.* 98.

Genus 5. RUBUS.

R. IDÆUS. *Raspberry.* **Fig. 365.**
Stems biennial, woody, erect, round, downy, with straight prickles.
Leaves pinnate, of 3 or 5 leaflets, white and cottony beneath. Mountain
woods. Fruit edible. 4 ft. June. Greenish white; fruit red. ($\frac{2}{3}$)
E. B. 1. 2442. *E. B.* 2. 719. *H. & Arn.* 123. *Bab.* 95. *Lind.* 92.
R. SUBERECTUS. *Red-fruited Bramble.* **Fig. 366.**
Stems biennial, woody, round, nearly erect, with few prickles. Leaves
digitate or pinnate, not white beneath. Moist thickets and commons.
Fruit edible. 3–4 ft June–Aug. White; fruit red. ($\frac{2}{3}$) *E. B.*
1. 2572. *E. B.* 2. 720. *H. & Arn.* 124. *Bab.* 96. *Lind.* 92.
R. PLICATUS. **Fig. 367.**
Stems biennial, woody, nearly erect, not rooting, somewhat angular,
with curved prickles. Leaves digitate, with 5 stalked cordato-ovate
leaflets. A variety of *fruticosus*? 3 ft. July and Aug. White or
pinkish; fruit black. ($\frac{2}{3}$) *E. B. Supp.* 2714. *E. B.* 2. 720*. *H. &*
Arn. 124. *Bab.* 96. *Lind.* 92.
R. CARPINIFOLIUS. **Fig. 368.**
Stems decumbent, somewhat angular, with curved prickles. Leaves
digitate, with 5 stalked ovate pointed leaflets. Panicle compact, hairy.
A variety of *fruticosus*. July and Aug. Deep pink. ($\frac{2}{3}$) *E. B.*
Supp. 2664. *E. B.* 2. 721* ter. *H. & Arn.* 125. *Bab.* 99. *Lind.* 93.
R. RHAMNIFOLIUS. **Fig. 369.**
Stems arched, somewhat angular, with straight prickles. Leaves
digitate, with 5 stalked somewhat cordate leaflets. Panicle spreading.
A variety of *fruticosus*. July and Aug. Pinkish. ($\frac{2}{3}$) *E. B. Supp.*
2604. *E. B.* 2. 721*. *H. & Arn.* 124. *Bab.* 98. *Lind.* 94.
R. FRUTICOSUS. *Bramble. Blackberry.* **Fig. 370.**
Stems biennial, woody, arched or procumbent, often rooting, angular,
with prickles only at the angles. Leaves digitate, usually with 5 leaflets. Calyx reflexed from the fruit. Its *varieties* are endless. Fruit
edible. Thickets and commons; abundant. 2–6 ft. July and Aug.
Pink or white; fruit black when ripe. ($\frac{2}{3}$) *E. B.* 1. 715. *E. B.*
2. 721. *H. & Arn.* 121. *Bab.* 96–107. *Lind.* 92–95.

R. LEUCOSTACHYS.   **Fig. 371.**

Stems arched, angular and furrowed, hairy. Prickles straight. Leaves
with 3 or 5 stalked, somewhat cordate, coriaceous leaflets, white beneath.
Panicle elongated and slender, hairy. A variety of *fruticosus.* July
and Aug. Deep pink. ($\frac{2}{3}$) *E. B. Supp.* 2631. *E. B.* 2. 721* *bis.*
H. & Arn. 126. *Bab.* 99. *Lind.* 95.

R. MACROPHYLLUS.   **Fig. 372.**

Prickles very few and small, equal. Leaves large, with 3–5 stalked
elliptical leaflets. A variety of *fruticosus.* July and Aug. Greenish
white. ($\frac{2}{3}$) *E. B. Supp.* 2625. *E. B.* 2. 721* *quar.* *H. & Arn.* 124.
Bab. 101. *Lind.* 93.

R. KÖHLERI.   **Fig. 373.**

Stems decurved. Prickles numerous, unequal. Leaves with 5 stalked
ovate or elliptical leaflets. Panicles much divided, long, rigid, naked
at the end. A variety of *fruticosus.* July and Aug. Pale pink. ($\frac{2}{3}$)
E. B. Supp. 2605. *E. B.* 2. 723*. *H. & Arn.* 128. *Bab.* 103. *Lind.* 93.

R. CORYLIFOLIUS.   **Fig. 374.**

Stem decurved, roundish. Prickles unequal, scattered. Leaves with
5 ovate leaflets, the outer ones sessile. Calyx spreading or reflexed.
A variety of *fruticosus* or *cæsius?* July and Aug. White; fruit black,
large-grained. ($\frac{2}{3}$) *E. B.* 1. 827. *E. B.* 2. 723. *H. & Arn.* 122.
Bab. 106. *Lind.* 93.

R. CÆSIUS. *Dewberry.*   **Fig. 375.**

Stems biennial, woody, trailing, angular, glaucous. Prickles straight,
unequal, passing into setæ. Leaves mostly with 3 leaflets, the lateral
ones sessile. Calyx embracing the fruit. Fruit large-grained. *Varieties*
numerous. Heaths and banks. 1–3 ft. June and July. White or
pale pink; fruit black, with a glaucous bloom. ($\frac{2}{3}$) *E. B.* 1. 826.
E. B. 2. 722. *H. & Arn.* 122. *Bab.* 107. *Lind.* 94.

R. SAXATILIS. *Stone Bramble.*   **Fig. 376.**

Stems nearly herbaceous, creeping; flowering branches erect. Leaves
ternate. Panicle cymose. Rocky woods. Fruit edible. 6–10 in.
June. Greenish white; fruit red. ($\frac{2}{3}$) *E. B.* 1. 2233. *E. B.* 2. 724.
H. & Arn. 122. *Bab.* 107. *Lind.* 95.

R. ARCTICUS. *Arctic Bramble.*   **Fig. 377.**

Stems erect, rather woody, very slender, without prickles, generally
one-flowered. Leaves ternate. Mountain moors; very rare. Fruit
edible. 4–6 in. June. Deep rose-colour; fruit red. ($\frac{2}{3}$) *E. B.*
1. 1585. *E. B.* 2. 725. *H. & Arn.* 123. *Bab.* 108. *Lind.* 95.

R. CHAMÆMORUS. *Cloud-berry.*   **Fig. 378.**

Stems simple, herbaceous, single-flowered. Leaves simple, lobed.
Flowers unisexual. Mountain moors. Fruit edible. 6–8 in. June.
White; fruit orange. ($\frac{2}{3}$) *E. B.* 1. 716. *E. B.* 2. 726. *H. & Arn.* 123.
Bab. 108. *Lind.* 95.

Genus 6. FRAGARIA.

F. VESCA. *Wild Strawberry.*   **Fig. 379.**

Hairs of the pedicels closely pressed. Woods; abundant. Fruit edible.
4–9 in. Perenn. May–Aug. White; fruit red or white. ($\frac{2}{3}$) *E. B.*
1. 1524. *E. B.* 2. 727. *H. & Arn.* 130. *Bab.* 95. *Lind.* 95.

F. ATROVIRENS.   **Fig. 380.**

A variety of *vesca*, with larger fruit and more rounded leaves.
Northumberland. 4–6 in. Perenn. May–July. White; fruit white
or red. ($\frac{2}{3}$) *E. B. Supp.* 2742. *E. B.* 2. 727*. *Lind.* 96.

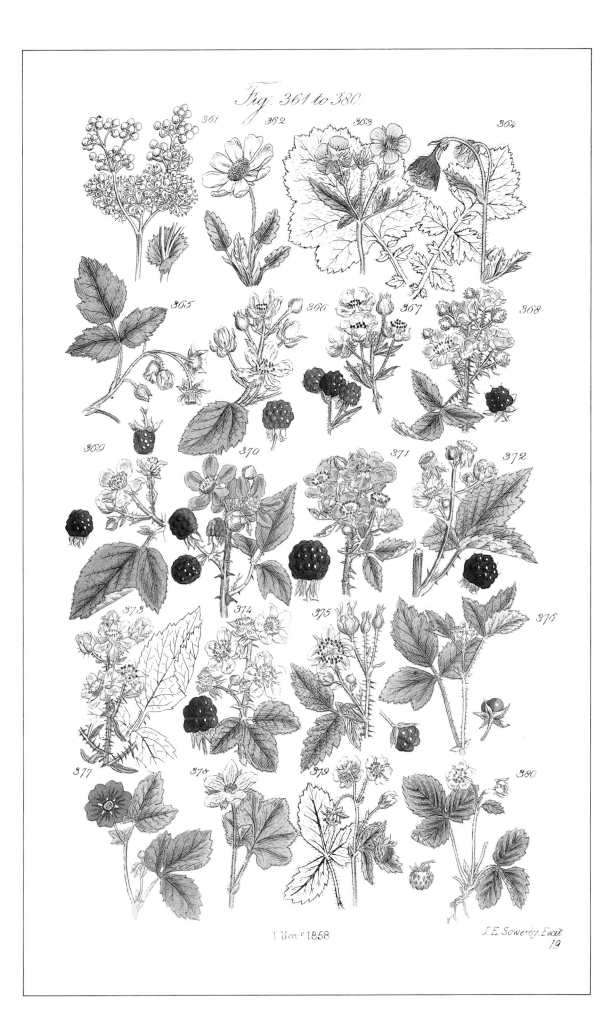

Fig. 361 to 380.

361   362   363   364

365   366   367   368

369   370   371   372

373   374   375   376

377   378   379   380

1 Nov.r 1858   J. E. Sowerby, Fecit.
19

F. ELATIOR. *Hautboy Strawberry.* **Fig. 381.**
Hairs of the peduncles and pedicels all spreading, somewhat deflexed.
Woods; local. Fruit edible. 6 in.–1 ft. Perenn. June–Sept.
White; fruit red, sweet-scented. ($\frac{2}{3}$) *E. B.* 1. 2197. *E. B.* 2. 728.
H. & Arn. 130. *Bab.* 95. *Lind.* 96.

Genus 7. COMARUM.

C. PALUSTRE. *Marsh Cinque-foil.* **Fig. 382.**
Lower leaves pinnate, with deeply serrated leaflets, glaucous beneath.
Bogs and marshes. Root astringent; yields a yellow die. 1 ft. Perenn.
July and Aug. Dingy purple. ($\frac{2}{3}$) *E. B.* 1. 172. *E. B.* 2. 744.
H. & Arn. 130. *Bab.* 94. *Lind.* 97.

Genus 8. POTENTILLA.

P. FRUTICOSA. *Shrubby Cinque-foil.* **Fig. 383.**
Stem shrubby. Leaves pinnate; leaflets entire, hairy. Mountain
thickets. 3–4 ft. June and July. Bright yellow. ($\frac{2}{3}$) *E. B.* 1. 861.
E. B. 2. 730. *H. & Arn.* 131. *Bab.* 94. *Lind.* 96.

P. ANSERINA. *Goose-weed. Silver-weed.* **Fig. 384.**
Stem creeping. Leaves interruptedly pinnate, silky. Stalks single-
flowered. Meadows and road-sides; very common. 2–4 in. Perenn.
June and July. Bright yellow. ($\frac{2}{3}$) *E. B.* 1. 861. *E. B.* 2. 730.
H. & Arn. 131. *Bab.* 93. *Lind.* 96.

P. RUPESTRIS. *Strawberry-flowered Cinque-foil.* **Fig. 385.**
Stems erect, dichotomous. Leaves lyrato-pinnate; leaflets ovate,
serrated. Rocks in Wales; very rare. 1 ft. Perenn. June. White.
($\frac{2}{3}$) *E. B.* 1. 2058. *E. B.* 2. 731. *H. & Arn.* 131. *Bab.* 93. *Lind.* 96.

P. ARGENTEA. *Hoary Cinque-foil.* **Fig. 386.**
Stems decumbent. Leaves quinate; leaflets wedge-shaped, jagged,
white and downy beneath. Commons and pastures; local. 6–8 in.
Perenn. June–Sept. Yellow. ($\frac{2}{3}$) *E. B.* 1. 89. *E. B.* 2. 732.
H. & Arn. 131. *Bab.* 93. *Lind.* 96.

P. VERNA. *Spring Cinque-foil.* **Fig. 387.**
Stems decumbent. Root-leaves quinate; leaflets obovate, serrated,
hairy. Flowers 2 or 3 together. Hill-pastures. 4 in. Perenn.
April and May. Yellow. ($\frac{2}{3}$) *E. B.* 1. 37. *E. B.* 2. 733. *H. &*
Arn. 131. *Bab.* 93. *Lind.* 97.

P. ALPESTRIS. *Alpine Cinque-foil.* **Fig. 388.**
Stems ascending. Root-leaves quinate; leaflets wedge-shaped, deeply
serrated, hairy. Mountains. 4–6 in. Perenn. June and July.
Orange-yellow. ($\frac{2}{3}$) *E. B.* 1. 561. *E. B.* 2. 734. *H. & Arn.* 132.
Bab. 93. *Lind.* 96.

P. OPACA. *Saw-leaved Cinque-foil.* **Fig. 389.**
Stems decumbent. Root-leaves with 7 wedge-shaped deeply serrated
leaflets; stem ones ternate. Mountains; rare. 6 in. Perenn. June
and July. Deep yellow. ($\frac{2}{3}$) *E. B.* 1. 2449. *E. B.* 2. 735. *H. &*
Arn. 132. *Bab.* 93. *Lind.* 97.

P. ALBA. *White rock Cinque-foil.* **Fig. 390.**
Stems very slender, procumbent. Root-leaves quinate; leaflets oblong,
silky beneath. Mountains. 4–6 in. Perenn. June–Sept. White. ($\frac{2}{3}$)
E. B. 1. 1384. *E. B.* 2. 736. *H. & Arn.* 133. *Bab.* 94. *Lind.* 97.

Fig. 381 to 400.

381 382 383 384 385 386 387 388 389 390 391 392 393 394 395 396 397 398 400

Nov.¹ 1 1858.

J.E.Sowerby, fecit

20

P. REPTANS. *Creeping Cinque-foil.* **Fig. 391.**
Stems filiform, creeping, rooting at the joints. Leaves quinate, on long petioles. Peduncles axillary, single-flowered. Meadows and road-sides; very common. 4 in. Perenn. June–Sept. Yellow. ($\frac{2}{3}$) *E. B.* 1. 862. *E. B.* 2. 737. *H. & Arn.* 132. *Bab.* 93. *Lind.* 97.

P. TRIDENTATA. *Trifid Cinque-foil.* **Fig. 392.**
Stem erect, panicled. Leaves ternate, smooth above, hairy beneath, 3-toothed at the apex. Mountains; very rare. 6 in. Perenn. May and June. White. ($\frac{2}{3}$) *E. B.* 1. 2389. *E. B.* 2. 738. *H. & Arn.* 133. *Bab.* 94. *Lind.* 97.

P. FRAGARIASTRUM. *Barren Strawberry.* **Fig. 393.**
Stems creeping. Leaves ternate, very hairy on both sides. Hedge-banks and woods; common. 2–4 in. Perenn. April and May. White. ($\frac{2}{3}$) *E. B.* 1. 1785. *E. B.* 2. 739. *H. & Arn.* 133. *Bab.* 94. *Lind.* 97.

Genus 9. TORMENTILLA.

T. OFFICINALIS. *Common Tormentil.* **Fig. 394.**
Stems filiform, prostrate. Leaves ternate, sessile; leaflets deeply serrated; stipules cut. Heaths; common. Astringent. 2–6 in. Perenn. June and July. Yellow. ($\frac{2}{3}$) *E. B.* 1. 863. *E. B.* 2. 740. *H. & Arn.* 132. *Bab.* 94. *Lind.* 97.

T. REPTANS. *Trailing Tormentil.* **Fig. 395.**
Stems prostrate. Leaves ternate or quinate, with foot-stalks. Hedge-banks and fields. 4 in. June and July. Yellow. ($\frac{2}{3}$) *E. B.* 1. 864. *E. B.* 2. 741. *H. & Arn.* 133. *Bab.* 94. *Lind.* 98.

Genus 10. SIBBALDIA.

S. PROCUMBENS. **Fig. 396.**
Leaves ternate; leaflets wedge-shaped, with 3 teeth. Glaucous. Mountains. 4 in. Perenn. July. Yellow. ($\frac{2}{3}$) *E. B.* 1. 897. *E. B.* 2. 457. *H. & Arn.* 134. *Bab.* 92. *Lind.* 98.

Genus 11. AGRIMONIA.

A. EUPATORIA. *Agrimony.* **Fig. 397.**
Stem-leaves interruptedly pinnate. Flowers in terminal spikes. Fields and way-sides. Astringent and tonic. 2 ft. Perenn. June and July. Yellow. ($\frac{2}{3}$) *E. B.* 1. 1335. *E. B.* 2. 684. *H. & Arn.* 136. *Bab.* 91. *Lind.* 99.

Genus 12. ALCHEMILLA.

A. VULGARIS. *Lady's Mantle.* **Fig. 398.**
Leaves lobed, plaited, serrated. Dry hill-pastures 6–10 in. Perenn. May–Aug. Green. ($\frac{2}{3}$) *E. B.* 1. 597. *E. B.* 2. 230. *H. & Arn.* 134. *Bab.* 92. *Lind.* 103.

A. ALPINA. *Alpine Lady's Mantle.* **Fig. 399.**
Leaves digitate, serrated, silky beneath. Mountains. 6 in. Perenn. July. Green. ($\frac{2}{3}$) *E. B.* 1. 244. *E. B.* 2. 231. *H. & Arn.* 134. *Bab.* 92. *Lind.* 103.

A. ARVENSIS. *Field Lady's Mantle.* **Fig. 400.**
Leaves 3-lobed, lobes deeply cut. Flowers axillary. Fields; common. 3–4 in. Ann. May–Aug. Green. ($\frac{2}{3}$) *E. B.* 1. 1011. *E. B.* 2. 232. *H. & Arn.* 135. *Bab.* 92. *Lind.* 103.

Genus 13. Sanguisorba.

S. officinalis. *Burnet.* **Fig. 401.**

Flowers in ovate spikes. Leaves pinnate. Pastures. 1–2 ft. Perenn. June–Aug. Dark purple. ($\frac{2}{3}$) *E. B.* 1. 1312. *E. B.* 2. 233. *H. & Arn.* 135. *Bab.* 91. *Lind.* 103.

Genus 14. Poterium.

P. Sanguisorba. *Salad Burnet.* **Fig. 402.**

Flowers in globular heads, monœcious; stamens very long. Leaves pinnate. Chalky and sandy pastures; abundant. 4 in.–2 ft. Perenn. July. Green, stamens purple. ($\frac{2}{3}$) *E. B.* 1. 860. *E. B.* 2. 1320. *H. & Arn.* 135. *Bab.* 91. *Lind.* 103.

Genus 15. Rosa.

R. cinnamomea. *Cinnamon Rose.* **Fig. 403.**

Stems with a few scattered prickles. Leaflets oblong-lanceolate, simply serrated, downy beneath. Fruit small, nearly globular. A doubtful native. 6 ft. May. Purplish pink; fruit red. ($\frac{1}{2}$) *E. B.* 1. 2388. *E. B.* 2. 705. *H. & Arn.* 137. *Bab.* 110.

R. Dicksonii. *Dickson's Rose.* **Fig. 404.**

Stems blood-red, with a few slender prickles. Leaflets ovato-lanceolate, downy, with double serratures, folded together. Fruit large, ovate. Ireland. May and June. Deep purple-pink. ($\frac{1}{2}$) *E. B. Supp.* 2707. *E. B.* 2. 705*. *H. & Arn.* 137. *Bab.* 110. *Lind.* 99.

R. rubella. *Red-fruited Dwarf Rose.* **Fig. 405.**

Branches covered with small prickles and glandular setæ. Fruit oblong, pendulous. Sandy sea-coasts. 6 in.–2 ft. June and July. Pale pink or cream-colour; fruit crimson. ($\frac{1}{2}$) *E. B.* 1. 2521. *E. B.* 2. 706. *H. & Arn.* 138. *Bab.* 110. *Lind.* 98.

R. spinosissima. *Burnet Rose.* **Fig. 406.**

Prickles crowded, very unequal. Leaflets almost round. Fruit globose, erect. Sandy shores and heaths. 4 in.–2 ft. May and June. Pink or cream-colour; fruit dark purple when ripe. ($\frac{1}{2}$) *E. B.* 1. 187. *E. B.* 2. 707. *H. & Arn.* 137. *Bab.* 110. *Lind.* 99.

R. hibernica. *Irish Rose.* **Fig. 407.**

Prickles scattered, unequal. Leaflets elliptical, simply serrate, hairy beneath. Sepals pinnate. Fruit nearly globular. Ireland. 6 ft. June–Nov. Pale pink; fruit red. ($\frac{1}{2}$) *E. B.* 1. 2196. *E. B.* 2. 708. *H. & Arn.* 138. *Bab.* 110. *Lind.* 100.

R. Wilsonii. *Wilson's Rose.* **Fig. 408.**

Prickles crowded, unequal, mixed with setæ. Sepals simple. Fruit ovate, with setæ. Caernarvonshire. 3 ft. July. Deep pink; fruit orange-red. ($\frac{1}{2}$) *E. B. Supp.* 2723. *E. B.* 2. 708*. *H. & Arn.* 138. *Bab.* 111. *Lind.* 325.

R. involuta. *Unexpanded Rose.* **Fig. 409.**

Prickles crowded, very unequal, mixed with setæ. Leaves doubly serrate, hairy. Sepals simple. Petals rarely opening. Fruit globular, rough with setæ. Hebrides. 2 ft. June. Pale pink; fruit dark red. ($\frac{1}{2}$) *E. B.* 1. 2068. *E. B.* 2. 709. *H. & Arn.* 138. *Bab.* 111. *Lind.* 100.

R. Sabini. *Sabine's Rose.* **Fig. 410.**

Prickles nearly straight, scattered, unequal. Leaves doubly serrate, hairy. Sepals pinnate. Fruit rough with setæ, variable in form. Flowers very large. Its varieties are numerous. Thickets. 8–10 ft. June. Pink of various shades; fruit dark red. ($\frac{1}{2}$) *E. B. Supp.* 2594. *E. B.* 2. 709*. *H. & Arn.* 138. *Bab.* 111. *Lind.* 100.

R. Doniana.   Fig. 411.
A variety of *Sabini*. Leaves densely pubescent. Sepals nearly simple.
($\frac{1}{2}$) *E. B. Supp.* 2601. *E. B.* 2. 709* *bis.* *H. & Arn.* 138. *Bab.* 111.
Lind. 100.

R. villosa. *Apple Rose.*   Fig. 412.
A variety of *Sabini*. Sepals nearly simple. Larger prickles curved.
Fruit very large, with stiff prickles. 8 ft. June. Pink; fruit dark
crimson. ($\frac{1}{2}$) *E. B.* 1. 583. *E. B.* 2. 709* *ter.* *H. & Arn.* 138.
Bab. 111. *Lind.* 100.

R. mollis. *Soft-leaved Rose.*   Fig. 413.
Root-shoots erect. Prickles equal, straight. Leaflets ovate, downy
on both sides. Sepals nearly simple, converging. Fruit globose.
Mountain thickets; common. 6 ft. June and July. Red or deep
pink, rarely white. ($\frac{1}{2}$) *E. B.* 1. 2459. *E. B.* 2. 710. *H. & Arn.* 139.
Bab. 111. *Lind.* 100.

R. tomentosa. *Downy Dog-Rose.*   Fig. 414.
Root-shoots arched. Sepals much divided, diverging. A variety of
mollis. Hedges and thickets. 6 ft. June and July. Pink; fruit
red. ($\frac{1}{2}$) *E. B.* 1. 990. *E. B.* 2. 711. *H. & Arn.* 139. *Bab.* 111.
Lind. 100.

R. scabriuscula.   Fig. 415.
A variety of *tomentosa*. Leaflets nearly smooth above. Sepals mostly
simple. ($\frac{1}{2}$) *E. B.* 1. 1896. *E. B.* 2. 711*. *H. & Arn.* 139.
Bab. 111. *Lind.* 100.

R. inodora. *Scentless Briar.*   Fig. 416.
Prickles nearly equal, very much hooked. Leaflets hairy. Fruit
elliptical or nearly globular. Sepals much divided, deciduous before
the fruit is ripe. Thickets. 6 ft. June and July. Pale pink; fruit
red. ($\frac{1}{2}$) *E. B.* 1. 2570. *E. B.* 2. 712. *H. & Arn.* 139. *Bab.* 111.
Lind. 101.

R. micrantha. *Small-flowered Briar.*   Fig. 417.
Prickles equal, curved. Leaflets hairy. Sepals pinnate, elongated,
deciduous. Fruit oblong-ovate. 6 ft. June and July. Pale pink;
fruit red. ($\frac{1}{2}$) *E. B.* 1. 2490. *E. B.* 2. 713. *H. & Arn.* 139. *Bab.* 112.
Lind. 101.

R. rubiginosa. *Sweet Briar. Eglantine.*   Fig. 418.
Prickles very numerous, unequal; the larger ones curved. Leaflets
with many brown glands beneath. Sepals elongated, persistent. Fruit
pear-shaped. Thickets. Leaves sweet-scented. 4–6 ft. June and
July. Deep pink; fruit orange-red. ($\frac{1}{2}$) *E. B.* 1. 991. *E. B.* 2.
714. *H. & Arn.* 139. *Bab.* 112. *Lind.* 101.

R. sepium. *Small-leaved Sweet Briar.*   Fig. 419.
Prickles numerous, unequal. Leaves small, acute at both ends. Sepals
elongated, persistent. Fruit ovate. A variety of *rubiginosa*. 3–4 ft.
June. Pale pink. ($\frac{1}{2}$) *E. B. Supp.* 2653. *E. B.* 2. 714*. *H. &
Arn.* 140. *Lind.* 101.

R. canina. *Dog Rose.*   Fig. 420.
Prickles equal, hooked. Leaflets ovate, acute, simply serrated, smooth
on both sides. Fruit ovate, smooth. Sepals pinnate, deciduous. Thickets
and hedges; abundant. Its *varieties* are very numerous. 4–8 ft.
June. Pink; fruit deep red. ($\frac{1}{2}$) *E. B.* 1. 992. *E. B.* 2. 715.
H. & Arn. 140. *Bab.* 112. *Lind.* 101.

Fig. 401 to 420.

401　40.　403　404

405　406　407　408

409　410　411　412

413　414　415　416

417　418　419　420

1 Dec: 1858
J.E. Sowerby. Fec.

R. SARMENTACEA.   **Fig. 421.**

A variety of *canina*. Leaflets doubly serrated, glandular at the edges. Hedges and thickets. ($\frac{1}{2}$) *E. B. Supp.* 2595. *E. B.* 2. 715*. *H. & Arn.* 140. *Bab.* 112. *Lind.* 102.

R. DUMETORUM.   **Fig. 422.**

A variety of *canina*. Leaflets slightly hairy on both sides, simply serrated. ($\frac{1}{2}$) *E. B. Supp.* 2610. *E. B.* 2. 715* *bis*. *H. & Arn.* 140. *Bab.* 112. *Lind.* 102.

R. FORSTERI.   **Fig. 423.**

A variety of *canina*. Leaflets more or less downy beneath, simply serrated. ($\frac{1}{2}$) *E. B. Supp.* 2611. *E. B.* 2. 715* *ter*. *H. & Arn.* 140. *Bab.* 112. *Lind.* 102.

R. CÆSIA.   *Glaucous Dog-Rose.*   **Fig. 424.**

Prickles numerous, hooked. Leaflets doubly serrated, downy and glaucous on both sides. Sepals pinnate. Fruit oblong, smooth. Scotland and North of England. 5 ft. June and July. Pale pink; fruit red. ($\frac{1}{2}$) *E. B.* 1. 2367. *E. B.* 2. 716. *H. & Arn.* 140. *Bab.* 113. *Lind.* 102.

R. SYSTYLA.   **Fig. 425.**

Root-shoots nearly erect, arched. Prickles hooked. Styles forming a column above the fruit. Thickets. 8–12 ft. July. Pink. ($\frac{1}{2}$) *E. B.* 1. 1895. *E. B.* 2. 717. *H. & Arn.* 140. *Bab.* 113. *Lind.* 102.

R. ARVENSIS.   *Trailing Dog-Rose.*   **Fig. 426.**

Root-shoots long, trailing. Prickles hooked. Leaflets smooth above, glaucous beneath. Styles forming a column above the fruit. Hedgebanks and heaths; common. 1–4 ft. June and July. White, on purplish stalks. ($\frac{1}{2}$) *E. B.* 1. 188. *E. B.* 2. 718. *H. & Arn.* 140. *Bab.* 112. *Lind.* 102.

Genus 16. MESPILUS.

M. GERMANICA.   *Medlar.*   **Fig. 427.**

A tree. Branches thorny. Leaves lanceolate, downy. Flowers solitary, nearly sessile. Hedges; rare. Fruit edible. May and June. White. ($\frac{1}{2}$) *E. B.* 1. 1523. *E. B.* 2. 694. *H. & Arn.* 141. *Bab.* 113. *Lind.* 104.

Genus 17. CRATÆGUS.

C. OXYACANTHA.   *Hawthorn. May.*   **Fig. 428.**

A thorny bush. Leaves deeply cleft. Flowers corymbose. Thickets and hedges; abundant. 4–20 ft. May. White or pink; fruit red. ($\frac{1}{2}$) *E. B.* 1. 2504. *E. B.* 2. 693. *H. & Arn.* 141. *Bab.* 113. *Lind.* 104.

Genus 18. COTONEASTER.

C. VULGARIS.   **Fig. 429.**

A shrub. Leaves oval, entire, downy beneath. Cliffs on the Caernarvonshire coast. 2–4 ft. May. White; fruit red. ($\frac{1}{2}$) *E. B. Supp.* 2713. *E. B.* 2. 694*. *H. & Arn.* 142. *Bab.* 113. *Lind.* 104.

Genus 19. PYRUS.

P. COMMUNIS.   *Wild Pear.*   **Fig. 430.**

A tree. Leaves simple, ovate, serrated. Flowers corymbose. Fruit large, turbinate. Woods and hedges. The origin of the garden Pear. April and May. White. ($\frac{1}{2}$) *E. B.* 1. 1784. *E. B.* 2. 695 *H. & Arn.* 142. *Bab.* 114. *Lind.* 105.

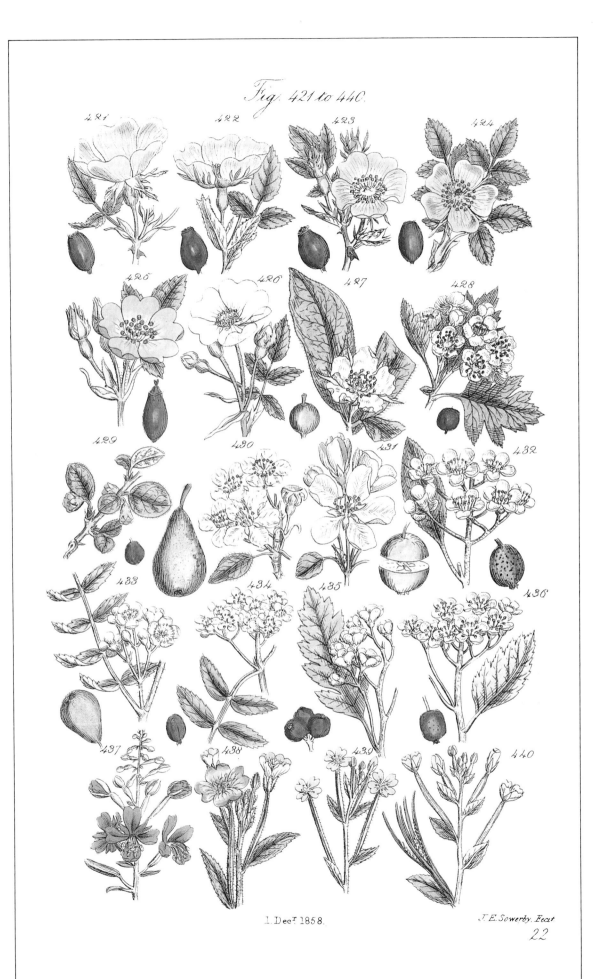

Fig. 421 to 440.

421 422 423 424
425 426 427 428
429 430 431 432
433 434 435 436
437 438 439 440

1. Decʳ 1858.

J.E.Sowerby, Fecit

22

P. MALUS. *Wild Apple. Crab.* **Fig. 431.**
A tree. Leaves simple, ovate, serrated. Flowers in a sessile umbel. Fruit large, globose. Woods and thickets. Fruit very acid. The origin of the garden Apple. May. Rose-colour and white. ($\frac{1}{2}$) *E. B.* 1. 179. *E. B.* 2. 696. *H. & Arn.* 142. *Bab.* 114. *Lind.* 105.

P. TORMINALIS. *Wild Service-tree.* **Fig. 432.**
A tree. Leaves ovate or cordate, 7-lobed, serrated. Flowers in a corymbose cyme. Fruit small, round or ovate. Hedges and woods. Fruit edible. May. White; fruit greenish brown. ($\frac{1}{2}$) *E. B.* 1. 298. *E. B.* 2. 697. *H. & Arn.* 142. *Bab.* 114. *Lind.* 105.

P. DOMESTICA. *Service-tree.* **Fig. 433.**
A tree. Leaves pinnate, downy beneath. Flowers in panicles. Fruit pear-shaped. Woods; rare. Fruit edible. May. White; fruit green or pink. ($\frac{1}{2}$) *E. B.* 1. 350. *E. B.* 2. 698. *H. & Arn.* 142. *Bab.* 114. *Lind.* 105.

P. AUCUPARIA. *Mountain Ash. Rowan-tree.* **Fig. 434.**
A tree. Leaves pinnate. Flowers in corymbs. Fruit globose. Mountain woods. May. White; fruit bright red. ($\frac{1}{2}$) *E. B.* 1. 337. *E. B.* 2. 699. *H. & Arn.* 143. *Bab.* 114. *Lind.* 106.

P. PINNATIFIDA. **Fig. 435.**
A tree. Leaves deeply pinnatifid, downy beneath. Flowers in corymbs. Fruit globose. Western Islands. May. White; fruit scarlet. ($\frac{1}{2}$) *E. B.* 1. 2331. *E. B.* 2. 700. *H. & Arn.* 143. *Lind.* 105.

P. ARIA. *White Beam-tree.* **Fig. 436.**
A tree. Leaves ovate, cut, serrated, very hoary beneath. Flowers in flat corymbs. Rocky woods. May. White; fruit red. ($\frac{1}{2}$) *E. B.* 1. 1858. *E. B.* 2. 701. *H. & Arn.* 143. *Lind.* 105.

ORDER XXVII. ONAGRACEÆ.

Genus 1. EPILOBIUM.

E. ANGUSTIFOLIUM. *French Willow-herb. Rose-Bay.* **Fig. 437.**
Leaves scattered, linear-lanceolate, smooth. Petals unequal. Stamens bent down. Moist shady places. 3–6 ft. Perenn. July and Aug. Deep pink. ($\frac{1}{2}$) *E. B.* 1. 1947. *E. B.* 2. 542. *H. & Arn.* 144. *Bab.* 116. *Lind.* 108.

E. HIRSUTUM. *Great Hairy Willow-herb.* **Fig. 438.**
Leaves ovato-lanceolate, stem-clasping. Plant hairy. Petals equal. Stigma 4-cleft. Flowers large. Wet places; common. 4–5 ft. July. Pink. ($\frac{1}{2}$) *E. B.* 1. 838. *E. B.* 2. 543. *H. & Arn.* 144. *Bab.* 117. *Lind.* 108.

E. PARVIFLORUM. *Small-flowered Willow-herb.* **Fig. 439.**
Leaves sessile, lanceolate, downy on both sides. Stigma 4-cleft. Flowers small. Wet places; common. 1–1½ ft. Perenn. July. Pale pink. ($\frac{2}{3}$) *E. B.* 1. 795. *E. B.* 2. 544. *H. & Arn.* 144. *Bab.* 117. *Lind.* 108.

E. MONTANUM. *Broad-leaved Willow-herb.* **Fig. 440.**
Leaves ovate, with short petioles. Plant usually tinged with crimson. Stigma 4-cleft. Dry places and walls; common. 3 in.–1 ft. Perenn. July. Rose-colour. ($\frac{2}{3}$) *E. B.* 1. 1177. *E. B.* 2. 545. *H. & Arn.* 114. *Bab.* 117. *Lind.* 108.

E. ROSEUM. *Smooth-leaved Willow-herb.* **Fig. 441.**
Leaves ovato-lanceolate, with petioles. Stem slightly angular. Stigma entire. A common weed. 1–1½ ft. Perenn. July. Pale rose-colour. ($\frac{2}{3}$) *E. B.* 1. 693. *E. B.* 2. 546. *H. & Arn.* 145. *Bab.* 118. *Lind.* 108.

E. TETRAGONUM. *Square-stalked Willow-herb.* **Fig. 442.**
Leaves sessile, lanceolate. Stem 4-angled. Stigma entire. Wet places; common. 1–2 ft. Perenn. July. Pale pink. ($\frac{2}{3}$) *E. B.* 1. 1948. *E. B.* 2. 547. *H. & Arn.* 145. *Bab.* 118. *Lind.* 108.

E. PALUSTRE. *Marsh Willow-herb.* **Fig. 443.**
Leaves sessile, linear-lanceolate. Stem round. Stigma entire. Marshes and bogs. 1 ft. Perenn. July. Pale pink. ($\frac{2}{3}$) *E. B.* 1. 346. *E. B.* 2. 548. *H. & Arn.* 145. *Bab.* 118. *Lind.* 108.

E. ALSINIFOLIUM. *Chickweed Willow-herb.* **Fig. 444.**
Leaves nearly sessile, ovate. Stem decumbent. Stigma entire. By mountain streams. 6 in.–1 ft. Perenn. July. Pink. ($\frac{2}{3}$) *E. B.* 1. 2000. *E. B.* 2. 549. *H. & Arn.* 145. *Bab.* 119. *Lind.* 108.

E. ALPINUM. *Alpine Willow-herb.* **Fig. 445.**
Leaves nearly sessile, elliptic-lanceolate, obtuse. Stem decumbent. Stigma entire. By mountain streams. 2–4 in. Perenn. July. Pink. ($\frac{2}{3}$) *E. B.* 1. 2001. *E. B.* 2. 550. *H. & Arn.* 146. *Bab.* 118. *Lind.* 108.

Genus 2. ŒNOTHERA.

Œ. BIENNIS. *Evening Primrose.* **Fig. 446.**
Stem rough. Flowers sessile, in a terminal spike. Waste ground and sandy coasts. 3–4 ft. Bienn. July–Oct. Yellow. ($\frac{1}{2}$) *E. B.* 1. 1534. *E. B.* 2. 541. *H. & Arn.* 146. *Bab.* 119. *Lind.* 109.

Genus 3. ISNARDIA.

I. PALUSTRIS. **Fig. 447.**
Stem procumbent, rooting. Flowers axillary, apetalous. Bogs. 2–4 in. Ann. May–Aug. Green. ($\frac{2}{3}$) *E. B. Supp.* 2593. *E. B.* 2. 233*. *H. & Arn.* 146. *Bab.* 119. *Lind.* 109.

Genus 4. CIRCÆA.

C. LUTETIANA. *Enchanter's Nightshade.* **Fig. 448.**
Stem erect. Leaves ovate, downy. Shady woods, common. 1–½ ft. Perenn. June and July. Pale pink. ($\frac{2}{3}$) *E. B.* 1. 1056. *E. B.* 2. 7. *H. & Arn.* 147. *Bab.* 119. *Lind.* 110.

C. ALPINA. *Alpine Enchanter's Nightshade.* **Fig. 449.**
Stem ascending. Leaves heart-shaped. Shady places on mountains. 4–8 in. Perenn. July and Aug. Pale pink. ($\frac{2}{3}$) *E. B.* 1. 1057. *E. B.* 2. 7*. *H. & Arn.* 147. *Bab.* 119. *Lind.* 110.

ORDER XXVIII. HALORAGACEÆ.

Genus 1. HIPPURIS.

H. VULGARIS. *Mare's-tail.* **Fig. 450.**
Leaves linear, in whorls. Flowers axillary, sessile. Pools and ditches 4 in.–1 ft. Perenn. May and June. Anther reddish. ($\frac{2}{3}$) *E. B* 1. 763. *E. B.* 2. 3. *H. & Arn.* 148. *Bab.* 120. *Lind.* 110.

Genus 2. MYRIOPHYLLUM.

M. SPICATUM. *Water-Milfoil.*   **Fig. 451.**
Spikes leafless. Leaves submersed, 4 in a whorl; with long linear lobes. Ditches and pools. Perenn. July and Aug. Reddish. ($\frac{2}{3}$)
E. B. 1. 83. *E. B.* 2. 1316. *H. & Arn.* 120. *Bab.* 148. *Lind.* 110.

M. VERTICILLATUM.   **Fig. 452.**
Spike leafy. Flowers in axillary whorls. Leaves submersed, 5 in a whorl. Ponds and ditches; local. Perenn. July. Greenish. ($\frac{2}{3}$)
E. B. 1. 218. *E. B.* 2. 1317. *H. & Arn.* 148. *Bab.* 120. *Lind.* 110.

M. ALTERNIFLORUM.   **Fig. 453.**
Fertile flowers in the axils of the upper leaves; sterile ones alternate, in spikes. Ponds; local. Perenn. July. Reddish. ($\frac{2}{3}$) *E. B. Supp.* 2854. *H. & Arn.* 149. *Bab.* 120. *Lind.* 110.

ORDER XXIX. LYTHRACEÆ.

Genus 1. LYTHRUM.

L. SALICARIA. *Purple Loosestrife.*   **Fig. 454.**
Leaves opposite, lanceolate. Flowers in leafy spikes. Stamens 12. Wet places; common. 3–4 ft. Perenn. July and Aug. Purple. ($\frac{2}{3}$)
E. B. 1. 1061. *E. B.* 2. 682. *H. & Arn.* 149. *Bab.* 115. *Lind.* 72.

L. HYSSOPIFOLIUM. *Hyssop-leaved Loosestrife.*   **Fig. 455.**
Leaves alternate, linear-lanceolate. Flowers axillary. Stamens 6. Ditches and wet places; rare. 6 in. Ann. Aug. Purple. ($\frac{2}{3}$)
E. B. 1. 292. *E. B.* 2. 683. *H. & Arn.* 149. *Bab.* 115. *Lind.* 72.

Genus 2. PEPLIS.

P. PORTULA. *Water Purslane.*   **Fig. 456.**
Leaves opposite, obovate. Flowers axillary, solitary. Watery places. 2 in. Ann. July and Aug. Reddish. ($\frac{2}{3}$) *E. B.* 1. 1211. *E. B.* 2. 465. *H. & Arn.* 149. *Bab.* 115. *Lind.* 72.

ORDER XXX. TAMARICACEÆ.

Genus 1. TAMARIX.

T. GALLICA. *Tamarisk.*   **Fig. 457.**
A slender shrub. Flowers in lateral spikes. Cliffs on the southern coast. 4–8 ft. July. Pale pink. ($\frac{2}{3}$) *E. B.* 1. 1318. *E. B.* 2. 447. *H. & Arn.* 150. *Bab.* 116. *Lind.* 62.

ORDER XXXI. CUCURBITACEÆ.

Genus 1. BRYONIA.

B. DIOICA. *Bryony.*   **Fig. 458.**
Stems climbing. Leaves palmate, rough. Diœcious. Hedges; common. Acrid. Perenn. May. Green; berries red. ($\frac{2}{3}$) *E. B.* 1. 439. *E. B.* 2. 1312. *H. & Arn.* 151. *Bab.* 121. *Lind.* 329.

ORDER XXXII. PORTULACEÆ.

Genus 1. MONTIA.

M. FONTANA. *Water Blinks.*   **Fig. 459.**
Stem creeping, rooting. Leaves opposite. Watery places; common. 1 in. Ann. April and May. Reddish. ($\frac{2}{3}$) *E. B.* 1. 1206. *E. B.* 2. 191. *H. & Arn.* 151. *Bab.* 121. *Lind.* 63.

ORDER XXXIII. ILLECEBRACEÆ.

Genus 1. CORRIGIOLA.

C. LITTORALIS. *Strapwort.*   **Fig. 460.**
Stems prostrate. Leaves linear-oblong. Flowers in corymbs. Sandy wastes; rare. 1–2 in. Ann. July and Aug. White. ($\frac{2}{3}$) *E. B.* 1. 668. *E. B.* 2. 448. *H. & Arn.* 152. *Bab.* 123. *Lind.* 60.

Fig. 441 to 460.

441   442   443   444

445   446   447   448

449   450   451   452

453   454   455   456

457   458   459   460

1 Dec.r 1858.

J.E.Sowerby

23

Genus 2. HERNIARIA.

H. GLABRA. *Rupture-wort.* **Fig. 461.**
Stems prostrate. Flowers in leafy spikes. Leaves glabrous. Sandy places. 2–4 in. Perenn. July and Aug. Green. ($\frac{2}{3}$) *E. B.* 1. 206. *E. B.* 2. 348. *H. & Arn.* 153. *Bab.* 123. *Lind.* 61.

H. HIRSUTA. **Fig. 462.**
Flowers in axillary clusters. Leaves hairy. A variety of *glabra?* Sandy places; rare. 2–4 in. Perenn. July and Aug. Green. ($\frac{2}{3}$) *E. B.* 1. 1379. *E. B.* 2. 348*. *H. & Arn.* 153. *Bab.* 123. *Lind.* 61.

H. CILIATA. **Fig. 463.**
Flowers in axillary clusters on the lateral branches. Leaves ciliated. A variety of *glabra.* Cornwall and Guernsey. 2–4 in. Perenn. July. Green. ($\frac{2}{3}$) *E. B. Supp.* 2857. *H. & Arn.* 153. *Bab.* 123. *Lind.* 322.

Genus 3. ILLECEBRUM.

I. VERTICILLATUM. *Whorled Knot-grass.* **Fig. 464.**
Stems procumbent. Leaves opposite, with membranous stipules. Flowers in whorls. Bogs in Cornwall and Devon. 4 in. Perenn. July. Pinkish. ($\frac{2}{3}$) *E. B.* 1. 895. *E. B.* 2. 345. *H. & Arn.* 154. *Bab.* 123. *Lind.* 61.

Genus 4. POLYCARPON.

P. TETRAPHYLLUM. *Four-leaved All-seed.* **Fig. 465.**
Leaves usually in fours. Flowers in panicles, with 3 stamens. Southern coasts. 4 in. Ann. May–Sept. Greenish. ($\frac{2}{3}$) *E. B.* 1. 1031. *E. B.* 2. 193. *H. & Arn.* 154. *Bab.* 124. *Lind.* 61.

ORDER XXXIV. CRASSULACEÆ.
Genus 1. TILLÆA.

T. MUSCOSA. **Fig. 466.**
Leaves succulent. Flowers axillary, usually 3-cleft. Sandy wastes. 2 in. Ann. May and June. Reddish. ($\frac{2}{3}$) *E. B.* 1. 116. *E. B.* 2. 254. *H. & Arn.* 156. *Bab.* 125. *Lind.* 63.

Genus 2. COTYLEDON.

C. UMBILICUS. *Penny-wort.* **Fig. 467.**
Root tuberous. Leaves peltate, depressed in the centre. Flowers pendulous. Moist rocks and walls. 4 in.–1 ft. June–Aug. Greenish. ($\frac{2}{3}$) *E. B.* 1. 325. *E. B.* 2. 648. *H. & Arn.* 156. *Bab.* 128. *Lind.* 64.

C. LUTEA. *Great Penny-wort.* **Fig. 468.**
Root creeping. Lower leaves only peltate. Flowers erect. Not native. 1–1½ ft. Perenn. July. Bright yellow. ($\frac{2}{3}$) *E. B.* 1. 1522. *E. B.* 2. 649. *H. & Arn.* 156. *Bab.* 128. *Lind.* 64.

Genus 3. SEMPERVIVUM.

S. TECTORUM. *Houseleek.* **Fig. 469.**
Leaves broad, succulent, in close tufts. Offsets spreading. Walls and roofs; scarcely wild. 6–8 in. Perenn. July. Pink. ($\frac{2}{3}$) *E. B.* 1. 1320. *E. B.* 2. 687. *H. & Arn.* 156. *Bab.* 127. *Lind.* 65.

Genus 4. RHODIOLA.

R. ROSEA. *Rose-root.* **Fig. 470.**
Flowers 4-cleft. Diœcious. Leaves ovate, glaucous, serrated. Mountain rocks. 6–8 in. Perenn. Yellow. ($\frac{2}{3}$) *E. B.* 1. 508. *E. B.* 2. 1395 *H. & Arn.* 157. *Bab.* 126. *Lind.* 64.

Fig. 461 to 480

461   462   463   464
465   466   467   468
469   470   471   472
473   474   475   476
477   478   479   480

1 Dec.r 1858.

J.E. Sowerby. fecit.

24

Genus 5. SEDUM.

S. TELEPHIUM. *Orpine.* **Fig. 471.**
Stems erect. Leaves ovate, flat, serrated. Hedge-banks and waste places. 1–2 ft. Perenn. July. Purple. ($\frac{2}{3}$) *E. B.* 1. 1319. *E. B.* 2. 650. *H. & Arn.* 157. *Bab.* 126. *Lind.* 64.

S. DASYPHYLLUM. *Thick-leaved Stonecrop.* **Fig. 472.**
Stems flaccid. Leaves ovate, very fleshy, glaucous. Flowers in scanty panicles. Rocks. 1–3 in. Perenn. July. Pink or white. ($\frac{2}{3}$) *E. B.* 1. 656. *E. B.* 2. 651. *H. & Arn.* 157. *Bab.* 126. *Lind.* 64.

S. ANGLICUM. *Mountain Stonecrop.* **Fig. 473.**
Leaves close, alternate, ovate, fleshy, spurred at the base. Flowers in 2-branched cymes. Mountain and sea-side rocks; common. 1–2 in. Perenn. July. White or pinkish. ($\frac{2}{3}$) *E. B.* 1. 171. *E. B.* 2. 652. *H. & Arn.* 157. *Bab.* 127. *Lind.* 64.

S. ALBUM. *White Stonecrop.* **Fig. 474.**
Leaves scattered, cylindrical, fleshy. Flowers in many-branched panicles. Rocks and walls. 2–4 in. Perenn. July. White; anthers red. ($\frac{2}{3}$) *E. B.* 1. 1578. *E. B.* 2. 656. *H. & Arn.* 158. *Bab.* 126. *Lind.* 65.

S. VILLOSUM. *Hairy Stonecrop.* **Fig. 475.**
Stem erect. Leaves alternate, slightly hairy and viscid. Flowers corymbose. Moist rocks. Perenn. June and July. White. ($\frac{2}{3}$) *E. B.* 1. 394. *E. B.* 2. 655. *H. & Arn.* 158. *Bab.* 126. *Lind.* 65.

S. ACRE. *Stonecrop. Wall-Pepper.* **Fig. 476.**
Leaves close, alternate, fleshy, somewhat ovate, spurred at the base, bright green. Flowers in trifid cymes. Walls and rocks; common. Acrid. 1–2 in. Perenn. June. Bright yellow. ($\frac{2}{3}$) *E. B.* 1. 839. *E. B.* 2. 653. *H. & Arn.* 158. *Bab.* 127. *Lind.* 64.

S. SEXANGULARE. *Tasteless Stonecrop.* **Fig. 477.**
Leaves in 6 rows, nearly cylindrical, fleshy. Cyme 3-branched. Old walls and sandy places; not common. 1–3 in. Perenn. July. Yellow. ($\frac{2}{3}$) *E. B.* 1. 1946. *E. B.* 2. 654. *H. & Arn.* 158. *Bab.* 127. *Lind.* 64.

S. REFLEXUM. *Crooked Stonecrop.* **Fig. 478.**
Stems straggling. Leaves awl-shaped, spurred at the base, scattered; the lower ones recurved. Sepals ovate. Walls and roofs. 6 in.–1 ft. Perenn. July. Yellow. ($\frac{2}{3}$) *E. B.* 1. 695. *E. B.* 2. 657. *H. & Arn.* 158. *Bab.* 127. *Lind.* 65.

S. GLAUCUM. *Glaucous Stonecrop.* **Fig. 479.**
Leaves awl-shaped, scattered, glaucous. Sepals lanceolate. Walls and dry places. 6 in.–1 ft. Perenn. July and Aug. Yellow. ($\frac{2}{3}$) *E. B.* 1. 2477. *E. B.* 2. 658. *H. & Arn.* 158. *Bab.* 127. *Lind.* 65.

S. RUPESTRE. *Rock Stonecrop.* **Fig. 480.**
Leaves awl-shaped, erect, spurred at the base; those of the branches in 5 close rows. Sepals elliptical. Rocks; rare. 6 in.–1 ft. Perenn. Yellow. ($\frac{2}{3}$) *E. B.* 1. 170. *E. B.* 2. 659. *H. & Arn.* 158. *Bab.* 127. *Lind.* 65.

S. Forsterianum. *Welsh Stonecrop.* **Fig. 481.**
Leaves semicylindrical, spurred at the base, in many rows, clustered. Sepals short and rounded. Rocks. 6 in.–1 ft. Perenn. July. Yellow. ($\frac{1}{2}$) *E. B.* 1. 1802. *E. B.* 2. 660. *H. & Arn.* 159. *Bab.* 127. *Lind.* 65.

Order XXXV. GROSSULARIACEÆ.

Genus 1. Ribes.

R. rubrum. *Red Currant.* **Fig. 482.**
A shrub. Branches without thorns. Clusters of flowers pendulous, smooth. Woods in the North. Fruit edible. 2–4 ft. May. Green; fruit red. ($\frac{2}{3}$) *E. B.* 1. 1289. *E. B.* 2. 338. *H. & Arn.* 159. *Bab.* 128. *Lind.* 106.

R. petræum. *Rock Currant.* **Fig. 483.**
A shrub. Not thorny. Clusters slightly hairy; erect in flower, pendulous in fruit. Bracts shorter than the flower-stalk. Northern woods. 4 ft. May. Yellowish; fruit red. ($\frac{2}{3}$) *E. B.* 1. 705. *E. B.* 2. 339. *H. & Arn.* 159. *Bab.* 128. *Lind.* 106.

R. spicatum. *Acid Mountain Currant.* **Fig. 484.**
A shrub. Not thorny. Clusters erect. Bracts shorter than the flowers. Yorkshire mountains. 4 ft. May. Green; fruit red. ($\frac{2}{3}$) *E. B.* 1. 1290. *E. B.* 2. 340. *H. & Arn.* 159. *Bab.* 129. *Lind.* 106.

R. alpinum. *Tasteless Mountain Currant.* **Fig. 485.**
A shrub. Not thorny. Diœcious. Clusters upright. Bracts longer than the flowers. Leaves deeply lobed. Mountain woods. 4 ft. May. Green; fruit red. ($\frac{2}{3}$) *E. B.* 1. 704. *E. B.* 2. 341. *H. & Arn.* 160. *Bab.* 128. *Lind.* 107.

R. nigrum. *Black Currant.* **Fig. 486.**
A shrub. Not thorny. Clusters hairy, pendulous; few-flowered, with a solitary flower at the base. Leaves glandulous at the back. River-sides and swampy thickets. 4–6 ft. May. Greenish; fruit black. ($\frac{2}{3}$) *E. B.* 1. 1291. *E. B.* 2. 342. *H. & Arn.* 160. *Bab.* 128. *Lind.* 107.

R. Grossularia. *Gooseberry.* **Fig. 487.**
A shrub. Branches with thorns beneath each leaf. Stalks short, few-flowered. Fruit hairy. Hedges and thickets. Fruit edible. 4 ft. April and May. Greenish; fruit green. ($\frac{2}{3}$) *E. B.* 1. 1292. *E. B.* 2. 343. *H. & Arn.* 160. *Bab.* 128. *Lind.* 107.

R. Uva-crispa. *Smooth Gooseberry.* **Fig. 488.**
Fruit smooth, and yellowish when ripe. A mere variety of *Grossularia*. *E. B.* 1. 2057. *E. B.* 2. 343*. *H. & Arn.* 160. *Bab.* 128. *Lind.* 107.

Order XXXVI. SAXIFRAGACEÆ.

Genus 1. Saxifraga.

S. Geum. *Kidney-leaved Saxifrage.* **Fig. 489.**
Leaves roundish, kidney-shaped, acutely crenate, rather hairy, with long petioles. Varieties numerous. South of Ireland. 6–9 in. Perenn. June. Cream-colour. ($\frac{2}{3}$) *E. B.* 1. 1561. *E. B.* 2. 594. *H. & Arn.* 161. *Bab.* 130. *Lind.* 70.

S. hirsuta. *Hairy Saxifrage.* **Fig. 490.**
Leaves ovate, acutely serrated, hairy on both sides; with long petioles. South of Ireland. 6 in.–1 ft. Perenn. June. White spotted with red. ($\frac{2}{3}$) *E. B.* 1. 2322. *E. B.* 2. 595. *H. & Arn.* 161. *Bab.* 129. *Lind.* 71

S. UMBROSA. *London Pride. None-so-pretty.* **Fig. 491.**
Leaves obovate, smooth, crenated; petioles short and dilated. Mountains. 6–10 in. Perenn. June. White spotted with red and yellow. ($\frac{2}{3}$) *E. B.* 1. 663. *E. B.* 2. 596. *H. & Arn.* 161. *Bab.* 129. *Lind.* 71.

S. STELLARIS. *Starry Saxifrage.* **Fig. 492.**
Leaves oblong, wedge-shaped, serrated, sessile, in a star-like tuft. Panicle few-flowered. Mountains. 2–6 in. Perenn. June–Aug. White, yellow at the base. ($\frac{2}{3}$) *E. B.* 1. 167. *E. B.* 2. 597. *H. & Arn.* 162. *Bab.* 130. *Lind.* 71.

S. NIVALIS. *Alpine Saxifrage.* **Fig. 493.**
Leaves roundish-obovate, crenated, with short dilated petioles. Calyx spreading, half-inferior. Mountain summits. 2–6 in. Perenn. July and Aug. White. ($\frac{2}{3}$) *E. B.* 1. 440. *E. B.* 2. 598. *H. & Arn.* 162. *Bab.* 132. *Lind.* 68.

S. HIRCULUS. *Yellow Marsh Saxifrage.* **Fig. 494.**
Stems erect, leafy. Stem-leaves lanceolate, entire, alternate. Calyx inferior. Bogs. 6–9 in. Perenn. Aug. Bright yellow, with red dots. ($\frac{2}{3}$) *E. B.* 1. 1009. *E. B.* 2. 599. *H. & Arn.* 162. *Bab.* 130. *Lind.* 67.

S. AIZOIDES. *Yellow Mountain Saxifrage.* **Fig. 495.**
Stem branched, decumbent. Leaves linear-lanceolate, toothed. Calyx half-inferior. Boggy places on mountains. 5–8 in. Perenn. June–Nov. Yellow with red dots. ($\frac{2}{3}$) *E. B.* 1. 39. *E. B.* 2. 600. *H. & Arn.* 163. *Bab.* 130. *Lind.* 67.

S. OPPOSITIFOLIA. *Purple Saxifrage.* **Fig. 496.**
Leaves opposite, ovate, hairy at the edges. Flowers solitary at the ends of the branches. Mountain summits. 1–4 in. Perenn. March and April. Purple. ($\frac{2}{3}$) *E. B.* 1. 9. *E. B.* 2. 601. *H. & Arn.* 162. *Bab.* 133. *Lind.* 69.

S. GRANULATA. *Meadow Saxifrage.* **Fig. 497.**
Leaves kidney-shaped, lobed; lower ones on long petioles. Root tuberous. Meadows; common. 6 in.–1 ft. Perenn. May and June. White. ($\frac{2}{3}$) *E. B.* 1. 500. *E. B.* 2. 602. *H. & Arn.* 163. *Bab.* 132. *Lind.* 68.

S. CERNUA. *Drooping Saxifrage.* **Fig. 498.**
Leaves kidney-shaped, palmately lobed, with petioles; upper ones with bulbs in the axils. Mountain rocks. 3–5 in. Perenn. June–Aug. White. ($\frac{2}{3}$) *E. B.* 1. 664. *E. B.* 2. 603. *H. & Arn.* 163. *Bab.* 132. *Lind.* 68.

S. RIVULARIS. *Alpine Brook Saxifrage.* **Fig. 499.**
Lower leaves lobed, with long petioles; upper ones lanceolate, entire. Moist rocks. 2–4 in. Perenn. July–Sept. White. ($\frac{2}{3}$) *E. B.* 1. 2275. *E. B.* 2. 604. *H. & Arn.* 163. *Bab.* 132. *Lind.* 68.

S. TRIDACTYLITES. *Rue-leaved Saxifrage.* **Fig. 500.**
Leaves wedge-shaped, 3–5-cleft, alternate. Walls and dry places; common. 1–6 in. Ann. May and June. White. ($\frac{2}{3}$) *E. B.* 1. 501. *E. B.* 2. 501. *H. & Arn.* 163. *Bab.* 132.

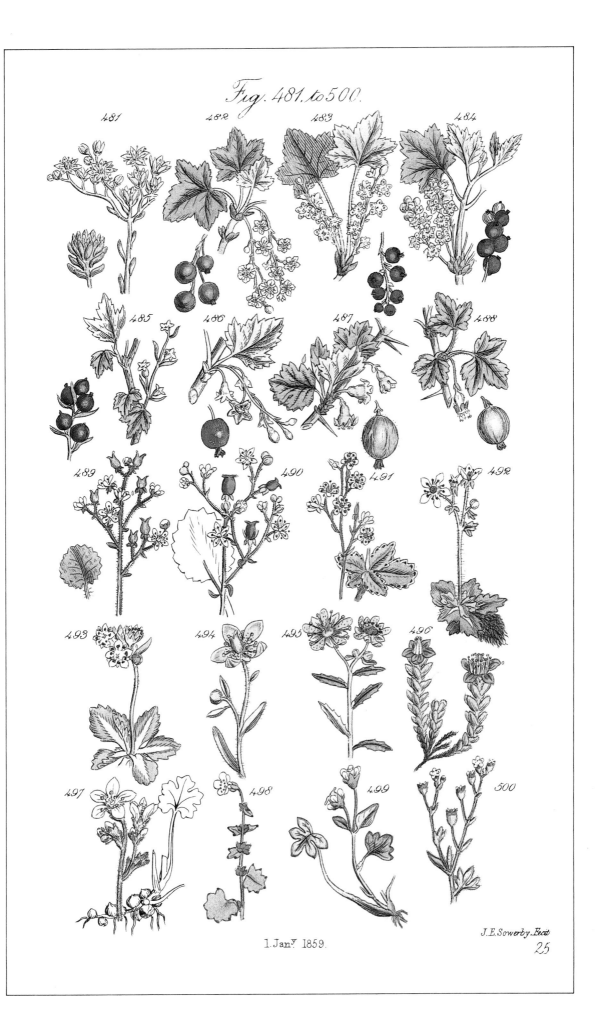

Fig. 481. to 500.

481 482 483 484
485 486 487 488
489 490 491 492
493 494 495 496
497 498 499 500

J.E.Sowerby.Fecit

S. MUSCOIDES. *Moss Saxifrage.* Fig. **501.**
Root-leaves tufted, linear or trifid, glutinous. Corymbs few-flowered. Calyx superior. Highland mountains. 2–3 in. Perenn. May and June. Yellowish. ($\frac{2}{3}$) *E. B.* 1. 2314. *E. B.* 2. 606. *H. & Arn.* 164. *Lind.* 68.

S. CÆSPITOSA. *Palmate Saxifrage.* Fig. **502.**
Root-leaves tufted, palmate, 3–5-cleft, hairy. Calyx half-inferior, hairy. Mountains. 2–4 in. Perenn. May and June. Yellowish-white. ($\frac{2}{3}$) *E. B.* 1. 455. *E. B.* 2. 607. *H. & Arn.* 164. *Bab.* 130. *Lind.* 69.

S. HIRTA. *Hairy Saxifrage.* Fig. **503.**
Root-leaves tufted, 3–5-cleft, very hairy. Shoots ascending. Sepals acute. Petals obovate. Mountains. 6–8 in. Perenn. June and July. White. ($\frac{2}{3}$) *E. B.* 1. 2291. *E. B.* 2. 608. *H. & Arn.* 164. *Bab.* 131. *Lind.* 69.

S. PLATYPETALA. *Broad-flowered Saxifrage.* Fig. **504.**
Leaves 3- or 5-cleft; segments linear, hairy. Shoots procumbent. Sepals ovate. Petals broad and rounded. 4–8 in. Perenn. May–July. White. ($\frac{2}{3}$) *E. B.* 1. 2276. *E. B.* 2. 609. *H. & Arn.* 164. *Bab.* 131. *Lind.* 69.

S. HYPNOIDES. *Ladies' Cushion.* Fig. **505.**
Root-leaves 3–5-cleft; those of the shoots linear. Shoots long, procumbent. Varieties numerous. Mountains; common. 3–5 in. Perenn. May–July. White. ($\frac{2}{3}$) *E. B.* 1. 454. *E. B.* 2. 610. *H. & Arn.* 164. *Bab.* 131. *Lind.* 69.

S. ELONGELLA. *Long-stalked Saxifrage.* Fig. **506.**
Leaves 3- or 5-cleft. Shoots short and erect. Flower-stalks very long, leafless. A variety of *hypnoides?* Moist rocks; rare. 4–6 in. Perenn. May. White. ($\frac{2}{3}$) *E. B.* 1. 2277. *E. B.* 2. 611. *H. & Arn.* 164. *Bab.* 131. *Lind.* 70.

S. PEDATIFIDA. *Geranium-leaved Saxifrage.* Fig. **507.**
Leaves with very long petioles, 3-cleft, the lateral segments 2- or 3-lobed. Flowers in a cymose panicle. 6–10 in. Perenn. May. White. ($\frac{2}{3}$) *E. B.* 1. 2278. *E. B.* 2. 612. *H. & Arn.* 165. *Bab.* 131. *Lind.* 70.

Genus 2. CHRYSOSPLENIUM.

C. ALTERNIFOLIUM. *Golden Saxifrage.* Fig. **508.**
A somewhat succulent creeping plant. Leaves alternate. Moist places; not common. 1–4 in. Perenn. March and April. Yellow. ($\frac{2}{3}$) *E. B.* 1. 54. *E. B.* 2. 593. *H. & Arn.* 165. *Bab.* 133. *Lind.* 66.

C. OPPOSITIFOLIUM. *Opposite-leaved Golden Saxifrage.* Fig. **509.**
Stem creeping, succulent. Leaves opposite, light-yellowish green. Moist places. 1–6 in. Perenn. May–July. Yellow. ($\frac{2}{3}$) *E. B.* 1. 490. *E. B.* 2. 592. *H. & Arn.* 165. *Bab.* 133. *Lind.* 67.

ORDER XXXVII. UMBELLIFERÆ.

Genus 1. HYDROCOTYLE.

H. VULGARIS. *Marsh Penny-wort.* Fig. **510.**
Leaves peltate, orbicular. Umbels with about 5 nearly sessile flowers. Moist places; common. 2–4 in. Perenn. May and June. Pinkish. ($\frac{1}{2}$) *E. B.* 1. 751. *E. B.* 2. 379. *H. & Arn.* 169. *Bab.* 139. *Lind.* 128.

Fig. 501 to 520

501   502   503   504
505   506   507   508
509   510   511   512
513   514   515   516
517   518   519   520

J.E.Sowerby, Fecit.

Genus 2. SANICULA.

S. EUROPÆA. *Wood Sanicle.*   **Fig. 511.**
Root-leaves simple, deeply lobed, dark green. Flowers sessile. Woods ;
common. 1 ft. Perenn. May and June. White. ($\frac{1}{2}$) *E. B* 1. 98.
E. B. 2. 380. *H. & Arn.* 169. *Bab.* 139. *Lind.* 127.

Genus 3. ERYNGIUM.

E. MARITIMUM. *Sea Holly. Eryngo.*   **Fig. 512.**
Root-leaves roundish, spiny. Plant very glaucous. Sandy coasts.
6 in.–2 ft. Perenn. July. Blue. ($\frac{1}{2}$) *E. B.* 1. 718. *E. B.* 2. 381.
H. & Arn. 169. *Bab.* 139. *Lind.* 127.

E. CAMPESTRE. *Field Eryngo.*   **Fig. 513.**
Root-leaves 2- or 3-pinnatifid, spiny. Waste ground ; rare. 2 ft.
Perenn. July and Aug. Purplish. ($\frac{1}{2}$) *E. B.* 1. 57. *E. B.* 2. 382.
H. & Arn. 140. *Lind.* 127.

Genus 4. CICUTA.

C. VIROSA. *Water Hemlock.*   **Fig. 514.**
Leaves biternate, with linear-lanceolate leaflets. Umbels opposite the
leaves. Ditches. Very poisonous. 3–4 ft Perenn. Aug. White. ($\frac{1}{2}$)
E. B. 1. 479. *E. B.* 2. 383. *H. & Arn.* 170. *Bab.* 140. *Lind.* 123.

Genus 5. APIUM.

A. GRAVEOLENS. *Smallage. Wild Celery.*   **Fig. 515.**
Leaves pinnate or ternate ; the lower ones on long petioles with
roundish leaflets ; upper leaflets wedge-shaped. Stem furrowed.
Marshes. Rather acrid. 3–4 ft. Bienn. June–Aug. White. ($\frac{1}{2}$)
E. B. 1. 1210. *E. B.* 2. 384. *H. & Arn.* 170. *Bab.* 140. *Lind.* 123.

Genus 6. PETROSELINUM.

P. SATIVUM. *Parsley.*   **Fig. 516.**
Stem striated. Leaves tripinnate, shining ; the lower ones with
roundish leaflets. Old walls ; scarcely wild. 1–3 ft. Bienn. June
and July. Pale yellow. ($\frac{1}{2}$) *E. B. Supp.* 2793. *E. B.* 2. 384*.
H. & Arn. 171. *Bab.* 140.

P. SEGETUM. *Corn Parsley.*   **Fig. 517.**
Leaves pinnate, with roundish serrated leaflets. Umbels scanty,
drooping. Chalky fields. 1$\frac{1}{2}$ ft. Bienn. Aug. Pink. ($\frac{1}{2}$) *E. B.*
1. 228. *E. B.* 2. 385. *H. & Arn.* 171. *Bab.* 140. *Lind.* 123.

Genus 7. TRINIA.

T. GLABERRIMA. *Honewort.*   **Fig. 518.**
Leaves tripinnate, with linear leaflets, pale glaucous green. Flowers
diœcious. Limestone rocks. 1–2 ft. Perenn. May and June.
White. ($\frac{1}{2}$) *E. B.* 1. 1209. *E. B.* 2. 386. *H. & Arn.* 171. *Bab.* 140.
Lind. 124.

Genus 8. HELOSCIADIUM.

H. NODIFLORUM. *Marsh-wort.*   **Fig. 519.**
Stem procumbent. Leaflets ovate, serrated. Umbels sessile, opposite the
leaves. Ditches ; common. 6–8 in. Perenn. July and Aug. White. ($\frac{1}{2}$)
E. B. 1. 639. *E. B.* 2. 387. *H. & Arn.* 172. *Bab.* 141. *Lind.* 122.

H. REPENS. *Creeping Marsh-wort.*   **Fig. 520.**
Stem creeping. Leaflets roundish, deeply toothed. Umbels stalked.
Watery places. 4–6 in. Perenn. July and Aug. White. ($\frac{1}{2}$)
E. B. 1. 1431. *E. B.* 2. 388. *H. & Arn.* 172. *Bab.* 141. *Lind.* 122.

H. INUNDATUM. *Water Marsh-Wort.*   **Fig. 521.**
Stem creeping. Lower leaves in hair-like segments. Umbels of 2
rays. In shallow water. 2–4 in. Perenn. July. White. ($\frac{1}{2}$)
E. B. 1. 227. *E. B.* 2. 389. *H. & Arn.* 172. *Bab.* 141. *Lind.* 122.

Genus 9. SISON.

S. AMOMUM. *Hedge Stone-wort.*   **Fig. 522.**
Leaves pinnate; upper ones ternate. Umbels generally of 4 or 5
rays. Hedge-banks. Has a strong pungent odour. 2–3 ft. Bienn. Aug.
White. ($\frac{1}{2}$) *E. B.* 1. 954. *E. B.* 2. 390. *H. & Arn.* 172. *Bab.* 141.
Lind. 122.

Genus 10. ÆGOPODIUM.

Æ. PODAGRARIA. *Gout Weed. Herb Gerarde.*   **Fig. 523.**
Root-leaves 2-ternate; upper ones ternate; leaflets ovate, pointed.
Waste places and gardens. 2 ft. Perenn. May and June. White.
( ) *E. B.* 1. 940. *E. B.* 2. 391. *H. & Arn.* 172. *Bab.* 141. *Lind.* 123.

Genus 11. CARUM.

C. CARUI. *Caraway.*   **Fig. 524.**
Stem branched. Leaves doubly pinnate; segments linear. Pastures;
naturalized. Seeds aromatic. 1–2 ft. Bienn. June. White. ($\frac{1}{2}$)
E. B. 1. 1503. *E. B.* 2. 392. *H. & Arn.* 173. *Bab.* 141. *Lind.* 122.

C. VERTICILLATUM. *Whorled Caraway.*   **Fig. 525.**
Leaflets with linear segments in whorls. Salt marshes; rare. 1–
1$\frac{1}{2}$ ft. Perenn. July. Pinkish. ($\frac{1}{2}$) *E. B.* 1. 395. *E. B.* 2. 393.
H. & Arn. 173. *Bab.* 173. *Lind.* 122.

Genus 12. BUNIUM.

B. BULBOCASTANUM. *Large Earth-nut.*   **Fig. 526.**
Lower leaves bipinnate on long foot-stalks. Fruit oblong, with reflexed styles. Involucrum of many leaves. Chalky pastures. Tuberous
root edible. 1–2 ft. Perenn. June. White. ($\frac{1}{2}$) *E. B. Supp.* 2862.
Bab. 142.

B. FLEXUOSUM. *Earth-nut.*   **Fig. 527.**
Lower leaves triternate, on long foot-stalks. Fruit oval with erect
styles. Involucrum of few leaves or absent. Fields; common. Tubers
edible. 1–1$\frac{1}{2}$ ft. Perenn. June. White. ($\frac{1}{2}$) *E. B.* 1. 988.
E. B. 2. 394. *H. & Arn.* 174. *Bab.* 142. *Lind.* 121.

Genus 13. PIMPINELLA.

P. SAXIFRAGA. *Burnet-Saxifrage.*   **Fig. 528.**
Leaves pinnate; lower ones with roundish leaflets; upper with linear
segments. Dry fields; common. 1 ft. Perenn. July and Aug. White.
($\frac{1}{2}$) *E. B.* 1. 407. *E. B.* 2. 395. *H. & Arn.* 174. *Bab.* 142. *Lind.* 121.

P. MAGNA. *Great Burnet-Saxifrage.*   **Fig. 529.**
Leaves pinnate; leaflets all ovate, serrated, sometimes 3-lobed. Woods.
2–3 ft. Perenn. Aug. and Sept. White. ($\frac{1}{2}$) *E. B.* 1. 408.
E. B. 2. 396. *H. & Arn.* 174. *Bab.* 142. *Lind.* 121.

Genus 14. SIUM.

S. LATIFOLIUM. *Water Parsnip.*   **Fig. 530.**
Leaves pinnate; leaflets equally serrated. Umbels terminal. Ditches
and river-sides. Poisonous. 4–5 ft. Perenn. July and Aug. White. ($\frac{1}{2}$)
E. B. 1. 204. *E. B.* 2. 397. *H. & Arn.* 174. *Bab.* 142. *Lind.* 127

S. ANGUSTIFOLIUM. *Narrow-leaved Water-Parsnip.* **Fig. 531.**
Leaves pinnate; leaflets unequally lobed and serrated. Umbels opposite the leaves. Ditches. Poisonous. 8 in.–1 ft. Perenn. July
and Aug. White. ($\frac{1}{2}$) *E. B.* 1. 139. *E. B.* 2. 398. *H. & Arn.* 175.
Bab. 142. *Lind.* 121.

Genus 15. BUPLEURUM.

B. ODONTITIS. *Narrow-leaved Hare's-ear.* **Fig. 532.**
Leaves lanceolate. Involucrum of 3 or 4 leaves. Rocks in Devon
and Channel Islands. 2–9 in. Ann. July. Yellow. ($\frac{1}{2}$) *E. B.*
1. 2468. *E. B.* 2. 399. *H. & Arn.* 175. *Bab.* 143. *Lind.* 120.

B. ROTUNDIFOLIUM. *Hare's-ear.* **Fig. 533.**
Leaves oval, perfoliate, glaucous. Involucrum wanting; involucels
of 4 or 5 broad pointed leaves. Corn fields. 18 in. Ann. June and
July. Yellow. ($\frac{1}{2}$) *E. B.* 1. 99. *E. B.* 2. 400. *H. & Arn.* 175.
Bab. 143. *Lind.* 120.

B. TENUISSIMUM. *Slender Hare's-ear.* **Fig. 534.**
Leaves linear. Umbels simple, alternate. Muddy sea-shores. 2–
4 in. Ann. Aug. and Sept. Yellow. ($\frac{1}{2}$) *E. B.* 1. 478. *E. B.*
2. 401. *H. & Arn.* 175. *Bab.* 143. *Lind.* 120.

B. FALCATUM. *Long-leaved Hare's-ear.* **Fig. 535.**
Lower leaves obovate, with very long stalks; upper linear-lanceolate.
Near Ongar, Essex. 1–4 ft. Perenn. July and Aug. Yellow. ($\frac{1}{2}$)
E. B. Supp. 2763. *E. B.* 2. 401*. *H. & Arn.* 175. *Bab.* 143. *Lind.* 326.

Genus 16. ŒNANTHE.

Œ. FISTULOSA. *Water-Dropwort.* **Fig. 536.**
Stem-leaves pinnate, tubular. Root throwing out runners. Styles
very long when in fruit. Ditches. Poisonous. 2–3 ft. Perenn.
July and Aug. Pinkish. ($\frac{1}{2}$) *E. B.* 1. 363. *E. B.* 2. 402. *H. &*
Arn. 176. *Bab.* 143. *Lind.* 119.

Œ. PIMPINELLOIDES. *Parsley Water-Dropwort.* **Fig. 537.**
Root-leaflets wedge-shaped, cleft; stem ones linear, very long. In-
volucrum of several leaves. Salt marshes. *Roots* edible. 2–3 ft.
Perenn. July. White. ($\frac{1}{2}$) *E. B.* 1. 347. *E. B.* 2. 403. *H. &*
Arn. 176. *Bab.* 143. *Lind.* 119.

Œ. PEUCEDANIFOLIA. *Sulphur-weed Dropwort.* **Fig. 538.**
Leaflets all linear. Primary involucrum wanting. Marshes. Roots
unwholesome. 1½–2 ft. Perenn. June. Pink. ($\frac{1}{2}$) *E. B.* 1. 348.
E. B. 2. 404. *H. & Arn.* 177. *Bab.* 144. *Lind.* 120.

Œ. CROCATA. *Hemlock Dropwort.* **Fig. 539.**
Leaflets all wedge-shaped, many-cleft. Fruit linear-oblong with
slender ridges. River-sides. Much like *Celery* before flowering.
Very poisonous. 3–5 ft. Perenn. July. White. ($\frac{1}{2}$) *E. B.* 1. 2313.
E. B. 2. 405. *H. & Arn.* 177. *Bab.* 144. *Lind.* 120.

Œ. PHELLANDRIUM. *Fine-leaved Water Dropwort.* **Fig. 540.**
Leaflets with many narrow wedge-shaped segments. Subaqueous
leaves hair-like. Fruit ovate, with broad ridges. Ditches. 2–3 ft.
Perenn. June and July. Pinkish. ($\frac{1}{2}$) *E. B.* 1. 684. *E. B.* 2. 406.
H. & Arn. 177. *Bab.* 144. *Lind.* 120.

Fig. 521 to 540

521 522 523 524
525 526 527 528
529 530 531 532
533 534 535 536
537 538 539 540

1 Jan.ʸ 1859.

J. E. Sowerby Fecit
27

Genus 17. Æthusa.

Æ. Cynapium. *Fool's Parsley.* **Fig. 541.**
Leaflets all wedge-shaped, with lanceolate segments, dark glossy green. Leaves of involucels long, pointing downwards. A common weed. Poisonous. 6 in.–2 ft. Ann. July and Aug. White. ($\frac{1}{2}$) *E. B.* 1. 1192. *E. B.* 2. 407. *H. & Arn.* 178. *Bab.* 145. *Lind.* 119.

Genus 18. Fœniculum.

F. vulgare. *Fennel.* **Fig. 542.**
Leaves biternate with nearly filiform leaflets. Chalky fields and way-sides. A culinary herb. 3–6 ft. Perenn. July and Aug. Yellow. ($\frac{1}{2}$) *E. B.* 1. 1208. *E. B.* 2. 408. *H. & Arn.* 178. *Bab.* 145. *Lind.* 119.

Genus 19. Seseli.

S. Libanotis. *Mountain Stone-Parsley.* **Fig. 543.**
Stem furrowed. Leaves 2-pinnate, cut. Involucrum many-leaved. Chalky hills. $1\frac{1}{2}$–2 ft. Perenn. Aug. White. ($\frac{1}{2}$) *E. B.* 1. 138. *E. B.* 2. 409. *H. & Arn.* 179. *Bab.* 145. *Lind.* 119.

Genus 20. Ligusticum.

L. scoticum. *Scottish Lovage.* **Fig. 544.**
Leaves biternate; leaflets broad, serrated. Involucrum of about 6 nar-row leaves. Northern sea-cliffs. Eaten in Scotland. 2 ft. July. White. ($\frac{1}{2}$) *E. B.* 1. 1207. *E. B.* 2. 410. *H. & Arn.* 179. *Bab.* 145. *Lind.* 118.

Genus 21. Silaus.

S. pratensis. *Pepper Saxifrage.* **Fig. 545.**
Leaflets deeply pinnatifid; segments linear-lanceolate, dark green. Involucrum 1 or 2-leaved. Moist meadows. 1-2 ft. Perenn. June–Aug. Yellow. ($\frac{1}{2}$) *E. B.* 1. 2142. *E. B.* 2. 418. *H. & Arn.* 179. *Bab.* 146. *Lind.* 118.

Genus 22. Meum.

M. Athamanticum. *Spignel.* **Fig. 546.**
Leaflets all in numerous bristle-like segments. Umbels with involu-crum. Mountain pastures. $1\frac{1}{2}$ ft. Perenn. June and July. Pale yellow. ($\frac{1}{2}$) *E. B.* 1. 2249. *E. B.* 2. 412. *H. & Arn.* 180. *Bab.* 146. *Lind.* 118.

Genus 23. Crithmum.

C. maritimum. *Samphire.* **Fig. 547.**
Plant succulent. Leaves lanceolate, fleshy. Rocky sea-shores. An aromatic esculent. 6 in.–$1\frac{1}{2}$ ft. Perenn. Aug. White. ($\frac{1}{2}$) *E. B.* 1. 819. *E. B.* 2. 413. *H. & Arn.* 180. *Bab.* 146. *Lind.* 146.

Genus 24. Angelica.

A. Archangelica. *Garden Angelica.* **Fig. 548.**
Terminal leaflet 3-lobed. Umbels globular, without involucrum. Plant bright green. Not indigenous. Aromatic. 4–6 ft. Bienn. June–Sept. Bright green. ($\frac{1}{2}$) *E. B.* 1. 2561. *E. B.* 2. 414. *H. & Arn.* 180. *Bab.* 146. *Lind.* 117.

A. sylvestris. *Wild Angelica.* **Fig. 549.**
Leaflets equal, sometimes lobed at the base. Stems usually reddish. Watery places; common. 2–4 ft. Perenn. July. Pinkish. ($\frac{1}{2}$) *E. B.* 1. 1128. *E. B.* 2. 415. *H. & Arn.* 180. *Bab.* 146. *Lind.* 117.

Genus 25. Peucedanum.

P. officinale. *Sed Hog's Fennel.* **Fig. 550.**
Leaflets linear, filiform. Leaves of the involucrum few, deciduous. Salt marshes; rare. Plant fœtid. 3 ft. Perenn. July–Sept. Yellow. ($\frac{1}{2}$) *E. B.* 1. 1767. *E. B.* 2. 416. *H. & Arn.* 181. *Bab.* 147. *Lind.* 117.

Fig. 541 to 560.

541 542 543 544
545 546 547 548
549 550 551 552
553 554 555 556
557 558 559 560

1 Jan.ʸ 1859

J. E. Sowerby.

P. **palustre.** *Milk Parsley. Hog's Fennel.* **Fig. 551.**
Leaves tripinnate; leaflets pinnatifid, with lanceolate segments. Marshes. Has a fœtid milky juice. 4–5 ft. Perenn. July. White. ($\frac{1}{2}$) *E. B.* 1. 229. *E. B.* 2. 417. *H. & Arn.* 181. *Bab.* 147. *Lind.* 116.

P. **Ostruthium.** *Master-wort.* **Fig. 552.**
Leaves biternate; leaflets broad, ovate. Involucrum wanting. Moist pastures; a doubtful native. 2 ft. Perenn. May–July. White. ($\frac{1}{2}$) *E. B.* 1. 1380. *E. B.* 2. 418. *H. & Arn.* 181. *Bab.* 147. *Lind.* 116.

Genus 26. Pastinaca.

P. **sativa.** *Wild Parsnip.* **Fig. 553.**
Leaves simply pinnate, serrated, downy beneath. Fields and road-sides. Variety cultivated for its edible root. 3–4 ft. Bienn. July. Yellow. ($\frac{1}{2}$) *E. B.* 1. 556. *E. B.* 2. 419. *H. & Arn.* 182. *Bab.* 147. *Lind.* 116.

Genus 27. Heracleum.

H. **Sphondylium.** *Cow-Parsnip.* **Fig. 554.**
Leaves pinnate, leaflets pinnatifid, cut and serrated. Petals unequal. Fields; common. 4–5 ft. Bienn. July. White. ($\frac{1}{2}$) *E. B.* 1. 939. *E. B.* 2. 420. *H. & Arn.* 182. *Bab.* 147. *Lind.* 116.

Genus 28. Tordylium.

T. **officinale.** *Small Hart-wort.* **Fig. 555.**
Leaflets ovate, cut, crenated. Involucels about as long as the flowers. Radiant petals in pairs, unequal. A doubtful native. 1 ft. Ann. June and July. White. ($\frac{1}{2}$) *E. B.* 1. 2440. *E. B.* 2. 421. *H. & Arn.* 182. *Bab.* 147. *Lind.* 115.

T. **maximum.** *Great Hart-wort.* **Fig. 556.**
Leaflets lanceolate, serrated and notched. Involucels shorter than the umbels. A doubtful native. 2 ft. Ann. June and July. Pink. ($\frac{1}{2}$) *E. B.* 1. 1173. *E. B.* 2. 422. *H. & Arn.* 182. *Bab.* 147. *Lind.* 115.

Genus 29. Daucus.

D. **Carota.** *Wild Carrot. Bird's-nest.* **Fig. 557.**
Leaflets pinnatifid, with linear-lanceolate acute segments. Umbels concave when in fruit. Bristles of the fruit slender. Fields; common on the chalk. Variety cultivated for its edible root. 1–3 ft. Bienn. July. White. ($\frac{1}{2}$) *E. B.* 1. 1174. *E. B.* 2. 423. *H. & Arn.* 187. *Bab.* 148. *Lind.* 113.

D. **maritima.** *Sea-side Carrot.* **Fig. 558.**
Leaves pinnatifid, fleshy, with rounded segments. Umbels convex in fruit. Bristles of fruit flattened. Southern coast. 1–2 ft. Bienn. July and Aug. White. ($\frac{1}{2}$) *E. B.* 1. 2560. *E. B.* 2. 424. *H. & Arn.* 187. *Bab.* 148. *Lind.* 113.

Genus 30. Caucalis.

C. **daucoides.** *Small Bur-Parsley.* **Fig. 559.**
Primary umbels of about 3 rays, without involucrum. Leaves 2- or 3-pinnate, segments pinnatifid. Corn-fields; local. 1½ ft. Ann. June. Pink. ($\frac{1}{2}$) *E. B.* 1. 197. *E. B.* 2. 425. *H. & Arn.* 188. *Bab.* 148. *Lind.* 114.

C. **latifolia.** *Great Bur-Parsley.* **Fig. 560.**
Primary umbels of about 3 rays, with a membranous involucrum. Leaves pinnate, with deeply serrated leaflets. Corn-fields. 3 ft. Ann. July. Pink. ($\frac{1}{2}$) *E. B.* 1. 198. *E. B.* 2. 426. *H. & Arn.* 188. *Bab.* 148. *Lind.* 114.

Genus 31. Torilis.

T. Anthriscus. *Upright Hedge-Parsley.* **Fig. 561.**
Leaves bipinnate; leaflets cut and serrated. Involucrum many-leaved.
A common weed. 2–3 ft. Ann. July. Pink. ($\frac{2}{3}$) *E. B.* 1. 987.
E. B. 2. 427. *H. & Arn.* 188. *Bab.* 148. *Lind.* 114.

T. infesta. *Spreading Hedge-Parsley.* **Fig. 562.**
Leaves pinnate; leaflets pinnatifid, cut and serrated. Primary invo-
lucrum wanting, or of only one leaf. A common weed. 1 ft. Ann.
July. White or pink. ($\frac{2}{3}$) *E. B.* 1. 1314. *E. B.* 2. 428. *H. &*
Arn. 188. *Bab.* 149. *Lind.* 114.

T. nodosa. *Knotted Hedge-Parsley.* **Fig. 563.**
Stem prostrate. Umbels lateral, simple, nearly sessile. Fields and
banks; common. 6 in.–1 ft. Ann. May–July. Pink. ($\frac{2}{3}$) *E. B.*
1. 199. *E. B.* 2. 429. *H. & Arn.* 189. *Bab.* 149. *Lind.* 114.

Genus 32. Scandix.

S. Pecten-Veneris. *Venus's Comb. Shepherd's Needle.* **Fig. 564.**
Fruit nearly smooth, with a very long beak. Leaflets in linear seg-
ments. A common weed. 6 in.–1 ft. Ann. June–Aug. White.
($\frac{2}{3}$) *E. B.* 1. 1397. *E. B.* 2. 430. *H. & Arn.* 185. *Bab.* 149. *Lind.* 125.

Genus 33. Anthriscus.

A. sylvestris. *Chervil. Cow-Parsley.* **Fig. 565.**
Umbels terminal, stalked. Stem hairy below. Leaves tripinnate;
leaflets pinnatifid. Hedge-banks; very common. 3–4 ft. Perenn.
April and May. White. ($\frac{2}{3}$) *E. B.* 1. 752. *E. B.* 2. 431. *H. &*
Arn. 185. *Bab.* 149. *Lind.* 124.

A. Cerefolium. *Garden Chervil.* **Fig. 566.**
Umbels sessile, lateral. Leaves bipinnate; leaflets pinnatifid, pale
green. Waste ground. 1½–2 ft. Ann. June. White. ($\frac{2}{3}$) *E. B.*
1. 1268. *E. B.* 2. 432. *H. & Arn.* 185. *Bab.* 149. *Lind.* 124.

A. vulgaris. *Common Chervil.* **Fig. 567.**
Umbels stalked, lateral. Leaves tripinnate; segments pinnatifid.
Stem nearly smooth. Banks and road-sides. 6 in.–3 ft. Ann. May.
White. ($\frac{2}{3}$) *E. B.* 1. 818. *E. B.* 2. 433. *H. & Arn.* 185. *Bab.* 149.
Lind. 124.

Genus 34. Chærophyllum.

C. temulentum. *Rough Chervil.* **Fig. 568.**
Stem spotted with purple, rough with hairs. Umbels drooping.
Hedge-banks; common. Poisonous? 1½–3 ft. Bienn. July. White.
($\frac{2}{3}$) *E. B.* 1. 1521. *E. B.* 2. 434. *H. & Arn.* 186. *Bab.* 150.
Lind. 125.

C. aureum. *Yellow-seeded Chervil.* **Fig. 569.**
Stem angular, hairy. Leaves tripinnate; leaflets sharply pinnatifid,
pointed. Fields; not common. 3 ft. Perenn. June. White; seeds
yellow. ($\frac{2}{3}$) *E. B.* 1. 2103. *E. B.* 2. 435. *H. & Arn.* 186. *Bab.* 150.
Lind. 125.

C. aromaticum. *Broad-leaved Chervil.* **Fig. 570.**
Leaflets undivided, ovate, serrated. Near Guthrie Forfar. 2–3 ft.
Perenn. June. White. ($\frac{2}{3}$) *E. B. Supp.* 2636. *E. B.* 2. 435*.
H. & Arn. 186. *Bab.* 150. *Lind.* 125.

Genus 35. Myrrhis.

M. odorata. *Sweet Cicely.* **Fig. 571.**
Leaves tripinnate; leaflets cut and pinnatifid. Fruit with sharp elevated ribs. North of England. Aromatic. 2 ft. Perenn. May and June. White. ($\frac{2}{3}$) *E. B.* 1. 697. *E. B.* 2. 436. *H. & Arn.* 187. *Bab.* 150. *Lind.* 125.

Genus 36. Echinophora.

E. spinosa. *Prickly Samphire.* **Fig. 572.**
Leaves bipinnatifid, with spinous segments. Involucrum spinous. Sandy coasts; rare. 1 ft. Perenn. July. White. ($\frac{2}{3}$) *E. B.* 1. 2413. *E. B.* 2. 437. *H. & Arn.* 189. *Bab.* 150. *Lind.* 126.

Genus 37. Conium.

C. maculatum. *Hemlock.* **Fig. 573.**
Stem polished, spotted with purple. Leaves dark glossy green, tripinnate. Fruit with waved ridges. Hedge-banks. Very poisonous. 2–4 ft. Bienn. June and July. White. ($\frac{2}{3}$) *E. B.* 1. 1191. *E. B.* 2. 438. *H. & Arn.* 183. *Bab.* 150. *Lind.* 126.

Genus 38. Physospermum.

P. cornubiense. *Cornish Bladder-seed.* **Fig. 574.**
Root-leaves 2- or 3-ternate, cut; stem ones ternate, entire. Fields in Cornwall. $1\frac{1}{2}$–2 ft. Perenn. July. White. ($\frac{2}{3}$) *E. B.* 1. 683. *E. B.* 2. 439. *H. & Arn.* 184. *Bab.* 151. *Lind.* 126.

Genus 39. Smyrnium.

S. Olusatrum. *Alexanders.* **Fig. 575.**
Stem-leaves ternate, serrated; bright yellow-green. Sea-side and waste ground. 3–4 ft. Bienn. May and June. Yellow. ($\frac{2}{3}$) *E. B.* 1. 230. *E. B.* 2. 440. *H. & Arn.* 184. *Bab.* 151. *Lind.* 126.

Genus 40. Coriandrum.

C. sativum. *Coriander.* **Fig. 576.**
Seed globular. Lower leaflets wedge-shaped. Fields and waste places. Seeds aromatic. 2 ft. Ann. June. White. ($\frac{2}{3}$) *E. B.* 1. 67. *E. B.* 2. 441. *H. & Arn.* 183. *Bab.* 151. *Lind.* 115.

Order XXXVIII. ARALIACEÆ.

Genus 1. Adoxa.

A. moschatellina. *Moschatel.* **Fig. 577.**
Root-leaves ternate, deeply lobed, few in number. Flowers in a small terminal head. Woods and hedge-banks. Has a musky scent. 8 in. Perenn. April. Pale yellow. ($\frac{2}{3}$) *E. B.* 1. 453. *E. B.* 2. 577. *H. & Arn.* 190. *Bab.* 152. *Lind.* 67.

Genus 2. Hedera.

H. Helix. *Ivy.* **Fig. 578.**
Leaves ovate or cordate with angular lobes. Stems climbing by rooting fibres. Perenn. Oct. Pale green; berries black when ripe. ($\frac{2}{3}$) *E. B.* 1. 1267. *E. B.* 2. 344. *H. & Arn.* 190. *Bab.* 152. *Lind.* 133.

Order XXXIX. CORNACEÆ.

Genus 1. Cornus.

C. sanguinea. *Cornel-tree. Dogwood.* **Fig. 579.**
A shrub. Leaves opposite, ovate. Flowers in cymes. Hedges; common. 4–6 ft. June. White; berries black. ($\frac{2}{3}$) *E. B.* 1. 249. *E. B.* 2. 227. *H. & Arn.* 191. *Bab.* 152. *Lind.* 133.

C. suecica. *Dwarf Cornel.* **Fig. 580.**
Herbaceous, creeping. Flowers in terminal umbels. Alpine pastures. 6 in. Perenn. June and July. Purple. ($\frac{2}{3}$) *E. B.* 1. 310. *E. B.* 2. 228. *H. & Arn.* 191. *Bab.* 152. *Lind.* 133.

Fig. 561 to 580.

1 Feb. 1859.

J. E. Sowerby, Fecit.

23

ORDER XL. LORANTHACEÆ.
Genus 1. VISCUM.

V. ALBUM. *Mistletoe.* **Fig. 581.**
A parasitic shrub. Stems forked. Leaves opposite. Diœcious.
On apple and other trees. March–May. Yellowish; berries white.
($\frac{2}{3}$) *E. B.* 1. 1470. *E. B.* 2. 1386. *H. & Arn.* 191. *Bab.* 153. *Lind.* 133.

ORDER XLI. CAPRIFOLIACEÆ.
Genus 1. SAMBUCUS.

S. EBULUS. *Dwarf Elder. Dane-wort.* **Fig. 582.**
Leaflets lanceolate. Stem herbaceous. Cymes with 3 branches.
Waste ground. Violently purgative. 2–3 ft. Perenn. July. Pink;
berries black. ($\frac{2}{3}$) *E. B.* 1. 475. *E. B.* 2. 444. *H. & Arn.* 192.
Bab. 154. *Lind.* 132.

S. NIGRA. *Common Elder.* **Fig. 583.**
A large shrub. Leaflets ovate. Cymes with 5 principal branches.
Hedges; common. Bark and leaves cathartic. 8–15 ft. June.
White; berries black. ($\frac{2}{3}$) *E. B.* 1. 476. *E. B.* 2. 445. *H. & Arn.* 192.
Bab. 154. *Lind.* 132.

Genus 2. VIBURNUM.

V. LANTANA. *Meal-tree.* **Fig. 584.**
A shrub. Leaves heart-shaped, serrated, downy beneath. Hedges
and thickets. 6–12 ft. June. White; berries purple when ripe.
($\frac{2}{3}$) *E. B.* 1. 331. *E. B.* 2. 442. *H. & Arn.* 193. *Bab.* 154. *Lind.* 132.

V. OPULUS. *Guelder Rose.* **Fig. 585.**
A large shrub. Leaves 3-lobed, serrated. Outer flowers barren, with
one large 5-lobed petal. Woods. 10–15 ft. June. White; berries
red. ($\frac{2}{3}$) *E. B.* 1. 332. *E. B.* 2. 443. *H. & Arn.* 193. *Bab.* 154.
Lind. 132.

Genus 3. LONICERA.

L. CAPRIFOLIUM. *Perfoliate Honeysuckle.* **Fig. 586.**
A climbing shrub. Upper leaves united round the stem. Woods;
rare. May and June. White or purple. ($\frac{2}{3}$) *E. B.* 1. 799. *E. B.* 2. 324.
H. & Arn. 193. *Bab.* 154. *Lind.* 131.

L. PERICLYMENUM. *Honeysuckle. Woodbine.* **Fig. 587.**
A climbing shrub. Leaves separate. Flowers in terminal heads.
Woods; common. June and July. Pale yellow, red outside. ($\frac{2}{3}$)
E. B. 1. 800. *E. B.* 2. 325. *H. & Arn.* 193. *Bab.* 154. *Lind.* 131.

L. XYLOSTEUM. *Upright Honeysuckle.* **Fig. 588.**
A shrub. Flower-stalks 2-flowered. Thickets in Sussex. June.
Pale yellow. ($\frac{2}{3}$) *E. B.* 1. 916. *E. B.* 2. 326. *H. & Arn.* 193.
Bab. 155. *Lind.* 132.

Genus 4. LINNÆA.

L. BOREALIS. **Fig. 589.**
A small creeping shrub. Leaves opposite. Flowers in pairs, drooping.
Northern Pine-woods. 6–8 in. Perenn. May and June. White or
pale rose-colour. ($\frac{2}{3}$) *E. B.* 1. 433. *E. B.* 2. 884. *H. & Arn.* 194.
Bab. 155. *Lind.* 132.

ORDER XLII. RUBIACEÆ.
Genus 1. RUBIA.

R. PEREGRINA. *Wild Madder.* **Fig. 590.**
Leaves 4 in a whorl, oval, with prickles on the margin, evergreen.
Shady thickets. 8 in. Perenn. July. White. ($\frac{2}{3}$) *E. B.* 1. 851.
E. B. 2. 218. *H. & Arn.* 195. *Bab.* 159. *Lind.* 131.

Fig. 581 to 600.

I. Feb. 1859.

J. E. Sowerby, fecit.

30.

Genus 2. Galium.

G. cruciatum. *Cross-wort.* **Fig. 591.**
Leaves 4 in a whorl, ovate, hairy. Bunches of flowers lateral, with
2 leaves. Hedges and thickets. 1 ft. Perenn. June. Yellow. ($\frac{2}{3}$)
E. B. 1. 143. *E. B.* 2. 203. *H. & Arn.* 195. *Bab.* 156. *Lind.* 128.

G. verum. *Yellow Bed-straw.* **Fig. 592.**
Leaves 8 in a whorl, linear, channelled, rough. Flowers in close
panicles. Dry fields; common. 6 in.–2 ft. Perenn. July and Aug.
Yellow. ($\frac{2}{3}$) *E.B.* 1. 660. *E. B.* 2. 204. *H. & Arn.* 195. *Bab.* 158.
Lind. 130.

G. palustre. *White Water Bed-straw.* **Fig. 593.**
Leaves chiefly 4 in a whorl, obovate. Stems weak and spreading.
Ditches. 1–4 ft. Perenn. July and Aug. White. ($\frac{2}{3}$) *E.B.* 1. 1857.
E. B. 2. 205. *H. & Arn.* 196. *Bab.* 159. *Lind.* 128.

G. Witheringii. *Rough Heath Bed-straw.* **Fig. 594.**
Leaves 5 in a whorl, lanceolate, fringed with bristles. Stem upright,
hairy. Boggy heaths. 1 ft. Perenn. July. Pale yellow. ($\frac{2}{3}$)
E. B. 1. 2206. *E. B.* 2. 206. *H. & Arn.* 196. *Bab.* 159. *Lind.* 128.

G. saxatile. *Smooth Heath Bed-straw.* **Fig. 595.**
Leaves 6 in a whorl, obovate. Stem prostrate, much branched.
Heaths; common. 2–6 in. Perenn. June–Sept. White. ($\frac{2}{3}$) *E. B.*
1. 815. *E. B.* 2. 207. *H. & Arn.* 195. *Bab.* 158. *Lind.* 128.

G. uliginosum. *Rough Marsh Bed-straw.* **Fig. 596.**
Leaves 6 in a whorl, lanceolate, rigid, their edges rough with reflexed
prickles. Wet places. 1 ft. Perenn. July and Aug. White. ($\frac{2}{3}$)
E. B. 1. 1972. *E. B.* 2. 208. *H. & Arn.* 196. *Bab.* 159. *Lind.* 129.

G. erectum. *Upright Bed-straw.* **Fig. 597.**
Leaves 8 in a whorl, lanceolate, veiny, bristle-pointed with marginal
prickles pointing forward. Hedges. 1 ft. Perenn. June. White.
($\frac{2}{3}$) *E. B.* 1. 2067. *E. B.* 2. 209. *H. & Arn.* 196. *Bab.* 157. *Lind.* 129.

G. cinereum. *Grey Bed-straw.* **Fig. 598.**
Leaves 6 or 8 in a whorl, linear, with marginal prickles. A variety
of *erectum.* Scotland; rare. 1 ft. Perenn. July. White. ($\frac{2}{3}$)
E. B. Supp. 2783. *E. B.* 2. 209*. *H. & Arn.* 196. *Bab.* 157. *Lind.* 129.

G. aristatum. *Bearded Bed-straw.* **Fig. 599.**
Leaves 6 in a whorl, stalked, lanceolate, with minute marginal prickles.
A variety of *erectum.* Angus-shire. 1 ft. Perenn. July. White.
($\frac{2}{3}$) *E. B. Supp.* 2784. *E. B.* 2. 209**. *H. & Arn.* 196. *Bab.* 157.
Lind. 129.

G. saccharatum. *Rough-fruited Bed-straw.* **Fig. 600.**
Leaves 6 in a whorl, lanceolate, with prickles pointing forward.
Flower-stalks axillary, 3-flowered. Corn-fields; rare. 1 ft. Ann.
June–Aug. White. ($\frac{2}{3}$) *E. B.* 1. 2173. *E. B.* 2. 210. *H. &*
Arn. 197. *Bab.* 156. *Lind.* 129.

G. TRICORNE. *Corn Bed-straw.* **Fig. 601.**
Leaves about 8 in a whorl. Stem and leaves rough with reflexed prickles. Flower-stalks axillary, 3-flowered. Fruit rough, drooping. Dry fields. 1 ft. Ann. July. White. ($\frac{2}{3}$) *E. B.* 1. 1641. *E. B.* 2. 211. *H. & Arn.* 198. *Bab.* 156. *Lind.* 129.

G. SPURIUM. *Smooth-fruited Corn Bed-straw.* **Fig. 602.**
Leaves about 8 in a whorl. Flower-stalks axillary, many-flowered. Fruit smooth, erect. Forfar. 1–2 ft. Ann. June and July. White. ($\frac{2}{3}$) *E. B.* 1. 1871. *E. B.* 2. 212. *H. & Arn.* 198. *Bab.* 157. *Lind.* 129.

G. PUSILLUM. *Little Mountain Bed-straw.* **Fig. 603.**
Leaves 8 in a whorl, linear-lanceolate. Panicles terminal, forked. Fruit very smooth. Limestone hills. 3–10 in. Perenn. July and Aug. White. ($\frac{2}{3}$) *E. B.* 1. 74. *E. B.* 2. 213. *H. & Arn.* 196. *Bab.* 158. *Lind.* 129.

G. MOLLUGO. *Great Hedge Bed-straw.* **Fig. 604.**
Leaves 8 in a whorl, oval, bristle-pointed. Flowers in loose spreading panicles. Seeds smooth, globular. Hedges. 1–4 ft. Perenn. July and Aug. White. ($\frac{2}{3}$) *E. B.* 1. 1673. *E. B.* 2. 214. *H. & Arn.* 197. *Bab.* 158. *Lind.* 130.

G. ANGLICUM. *Wall Bed-straw.* **Fig. 605.**
Leaves about 6 in a whorl, lanceolate, pointed, fringed with prickles. Stems straggling. Flower-stalks forked, terminal. 6–8 in. Ann. June and July. White. ($\frac{2}{3}$) *E. B.* 1. 384. *E. B.* 2. 215. *H. & Arn.* 197. *Bab.* 157. *Lind.* 130.

G. BOREALE. *Cross-leaved Bed-straw.* **Fig. 606.**
Leaves 4 in a whorl, ovate-lanceolate, not hairy. Stem erect. Rocky places. 1 ft. Perenn. July. White. ($\frac{2}{3}$) *E. B.* 1. 105. *E. B.* 2. 216. *H. & Arn.* 197. *Bab.* 156. *Lind.* 130.

G. APARINE. *Goose-grass. Cleavers.* **Fig. 607.**
Leaves 8 in a whorl, lanceolate, keeled, rough. Stem weak, prickly. Fruit covered with hooked bristles. Hedge-banks; abundant. Ann. May–Aug. White. ($\frac{2}{3}$) *E. B.* 1. 816. *E. B.* 2. 217. *H. & Arn.* 198. *Bab.* 157. *Lind.* 130.

Genus 3. SHERARDIA.

S. ARVENSIS. *Field Madder.* **Fig. 608.**
All the leaves whorled. Flowers terminal. Fields; common. 4–6 in. Ann. June–Aug. Purplish blue. ($\frac{2}{3}$) *E. B.* 1. 891. *E. B.* 2. 200. *H. & Arn.* 199. *Bab.* 156. *Lind.* 130.

Genus 4. ASPERULA.

A. ODORATA. *Woodruff.* **Fig. 609.**
Leaves 8 in a whorl, lanceolate. Tufts of flowers on long stalks. Dry woods; common. 6–8 in. Perenn. May. White. ($\frac{2}{3}$) *E. B.* 1. 755. *E. B.* 2. 201. *H. & Arn.* 199. *Bab.* 156. *Lind.* 130.

A. ARVENSIS. *Field Woodruff.* **Fig. 610.**
Leaves 6–10 in a whorl, linear-lanceolate. Near Davenport. 6–10 in. Ann. May–July. Blue. ($\frac{2}{3}$) *E. B. Supp.* 2792. *E. B.* 2. 201*. *H. & Arn.* 199. *Bab.* 156.

A. CYNANCHICA. *Squinancy-wort.* **Fig. 611.**
Lower leaves 4 in a whorl, upper ones in pairs. Dry banks. 6 in.
Perenn. July. Pink. ($\frac{2}{3}$) *E. B.* 1. 33. *E. B.* 2. 202. *H. &*
Arn. 199. *Bab.* 155. *Lind.* 130.

ORDER XLIII. VALERIANACEÆ.

Genus 1. CENTRANTHUS.

C. RUBRA. *Red Valerian.* **Fig. 612.**
Leaves lanceolate, entire. Stamen 1. Spur of flower long. Chalky
banks and old walls. 1½ ft. Perenn. June–Aug. Red. ($\frac{2}{3}$) *E. B.*
1. 1531. *E. B.* 2. 37. *H. & Arn.* 200. *Bab.* 160. *Lind.* 139.

Genus 2. VALERIANA.

V. DIOICA. *Marsh Valerian.* **Fig. 613.**
Flowers diœcious. Root-leaves ovate, those of the stem pinnate.
Moist meadows. 1 ft. Perenn. June. Pink. ($\frac{2}{3}$) *E. B.* 1. 628.
E. B. 2. 38. *H. & Arn.* 200. *Bab.* 160. *Lind.* 138.

V. OFFICINALIS. *Great Wild Valerian.* **Fig. 614.**
Leaves all pinnate ; leaflets lanceolate. Moist places ; common. Root
aromatic and antispasmodic. 3–4 ft. Perenn. June. Pink. ($\frac{2}{3}$)
E. B. 1. 698. *E. B.* 2. 39. *H. & Arn.* 200. *Bab.* 160. *Lind.* 138.

V. PYRENAICA. *Heart-leaved Valerian.* **Fig. 615.**
Stem-leaves heart-shaped ; the upper ones pinnated. A doubtful
native. 3 ft. Perenn. July. Pink. ($\frac{2}{3}$) *E. B.* 1. 1591. *E. B.*
2. 40. *H. & Arn.* 201. *Bab.* 160. *Lind.* 138.

Genus 3. FEDIA.

F. OLITORIA. *Corn Salad.* **Fig. 616.**
Flowers in round heads. Leaves tongue-shaped. Fruit subglobose.
A common weed. 6 in. Ann. April–June. Blue. ($\frac{2}{3}$) *E. B.* 1. 811.
E. B. 2. 41. *H. & Arn.* 201. *Bab.* 161. *Lind.* 23.

F. DENTATA. *Lamb's Lettuce.* **Fig. 617.**
Flowers in the forks of the stem. Fruit ovate. Leaves linear, tongue-
shaped. Corn-fields. 1 ft. Ann. June and July. Purple. ($\frac{2}{3}$)
E. B. 1. 1370. *E. B.* 2. 42. *H. & Arn.* 202. *Bab.* 161. *Lind.* 138.

F. AURICULA. **Fig. 618.**
Upper leaves somewhat pinnatifid at the base. Fruit subglobose. A
variety of *dentata*? Corn-fields. 1 ft. Ann. June and July. Purple.
($\frac{2}{3}$) *E. B. Supp.* 2809. *H. & Arn.* 202. *Bab.* 161. *Lind.* 327.

F. CARINATA. **Fig. 619.**
Fruit oblong. Leaves entire, oblong or spatulate. A variety of
dentata. Corn-fields and gardens. 8 in. Ann. June and July.
Purple. ($\frac{2}{3}$) *E. B. Supp.* 2810. *H. & Arn.* 201. *Bab.* 161. *Lind.* 327.

ORDER XLIV. DIPSACEÆ.

Genus 1. DIPSACUS.

D. FULLONUM. *Fuller's Teasle.* **Fig. 620.**
Leaves connected at the base. Scales of the receptacle broad, hooked.
Involucrum spreading. Heads used for dressing cloth. Waste places ;
not native. 4 ft. Bienn. July. Purple. ($\frac{2}{3}$) *E. B.* 1. 2080. *E. B.*
2. 194. *H. & Arn.* 203. *Bab.* 162. *Lind.* 139.

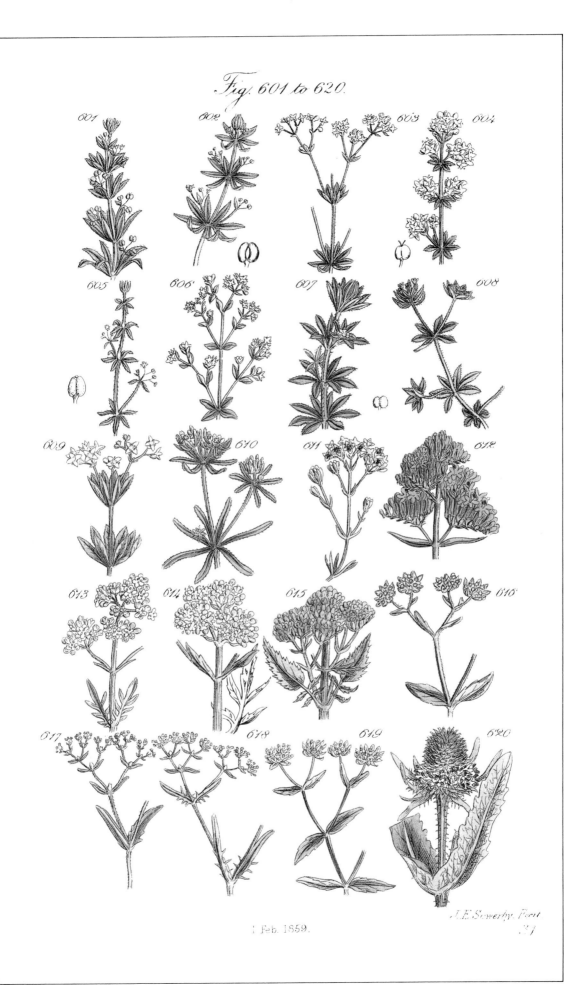

Fig. 601 to 620.

J.E. Sowerby, Pinxt

D. sylvestris. *Wild Teasle.* **Fig. 621.**
Leaves often connected at the base. Scales of receptacle narrow, straight. Ditch-banks and way-sides; common. 4 ft. Bienn. July. Purple. ($\frac{2}{3}$) *E. B.* 1. 1032. *E. B.* 2. 195. *H. & Arn.* 203. *Bab.* 16. *Lind.* 139.

D. pilosus. *Small Teasle.* **Fig. 622.**
Leaves with foot-stalks, ternate, with small leaflets. Shady places on a chalky soil. 4 ft. Bienn. Aug. and Sept. White. ($\frac{2}{3}$) *E. B.* 1. 877. *E. B.* 2. 196. *H. & Arn.* 203. *Bab.* 163. *Lind.* 139.

Genus 2. Scabiosa.

S. succisa. *Devil's-bit.* **Fig. 623.**
Corolla 4-cleft, regular. Heads of flowers nearly globular. Commons; very common. 1 ft. Perenn. Aug.–Oct. Blue. ($\frac{2}{3}$) *E. B.* 1. 878. *E. B.* 2. 197. *H. & Arn.* 204. *Bab.* 163. *Lind.* 139.

S. arvensis. *Field Scabious.* **Fig. 624.**
Corolla 4-cleft. Marginal flowers radiant. Leaves pinnatifid. Corn-fields and pastures; common. 2–3 ft. Perenn. July. Purple. ($\frac{2}{3}$) *E. B.* 1. 659. *E. B.* 2. 198. *H. & Arn.* 204. *Bab.* 163. *Lind.* 140.

S. columbaria. *Small Scabious.* **Fig. 625.**
Corolla 5-cleft, irregular. Upper leaves pinnatifid, with linear segments. Pastures. 1–1½ ft. Perenn. June–Aug. Purple. ($\frac{2}{3}$) *E. B.* 1. 134. *E. B.* 2. 199. *H. & Arn.* 204. *Bab.* 163. *Lind.* 140.

Order XLV. COMPOSITÆ.

Genus 1. Tragopogon.

T. pratensis. *Yellow Goat's-beard.* **Fig. 626.**
Leaves channelled, pointed, dilated at the base. Peduncle thickened upwards. Involucrum about equal to the florets. Meadows. 1–2 ft. Bienn. June and July. Yellow. ($\frac{2}{3}$) *E. B.* 1. 434. *E. B.* 2. 1061. *H. & Arn.* 209. *Bab.* 193. *Lind.* 161.

T. porrifolius. *Purple Goat's-beard. Salsify.* **Fig. 627.**
Leaves straight from the base. Involucrum longer than the florets. Moist meadows; not native. Roots esculent. 3–4 ft. Bienn. May and June. Purple. ($\frac{2}{3}$) *E. B.* 1. 638. *E. B.* 2. 1062. *H. & Arn.* 209. *Bab.* 193. *Lind.* 161.

Genus 2. Helminthia.

H. echioides. *Ox-tongue.* **Fig. 628.**
Involucrum double; outer one spiny at the margin. Lower leaves lanceolate, spiny. Hedge-banks. 2–3 ft. Ann. June and July. Yellow. ($\frac{2}{3}$) *E. B.* 1. 972. *E. B.* 2. 1063. *H. & Arn.* 209. *Bab.* 194. *Lind.* 158.

Genus 3. Picris.

P. hieracioides. *Yellow Succory.* **Fig. 629.**
Stem rough with hooked bristles. Leaves rough, lanceolate, wavy. Foot-stalks with many bracts. Road-sides; common. 2–3 ft. Bienn. July and Aug. Yellow. ($\frac{2}{3}$) *E. B.* 1. 196. *E. B.* 2. 1064. *H. & Arn.* 210. *Bab.* 193. *Lind.* 158.

Genus 4. Sonchus.

S. alpinus. *Blue Sow-Thistle.* **Fig. 630.**
Leaves lyrate; terminal lobe triangular. Stems covered with glandular hairs. Scottish mountains. 3–4 ft. Perenn. July and Aug. Blue. ($\frac{2}{3}$) *E. B.* 1. 2425. *E. B.* 2. 1065. *H. & Arn.* 213. *Bab.* 196. *Lind.* 156.

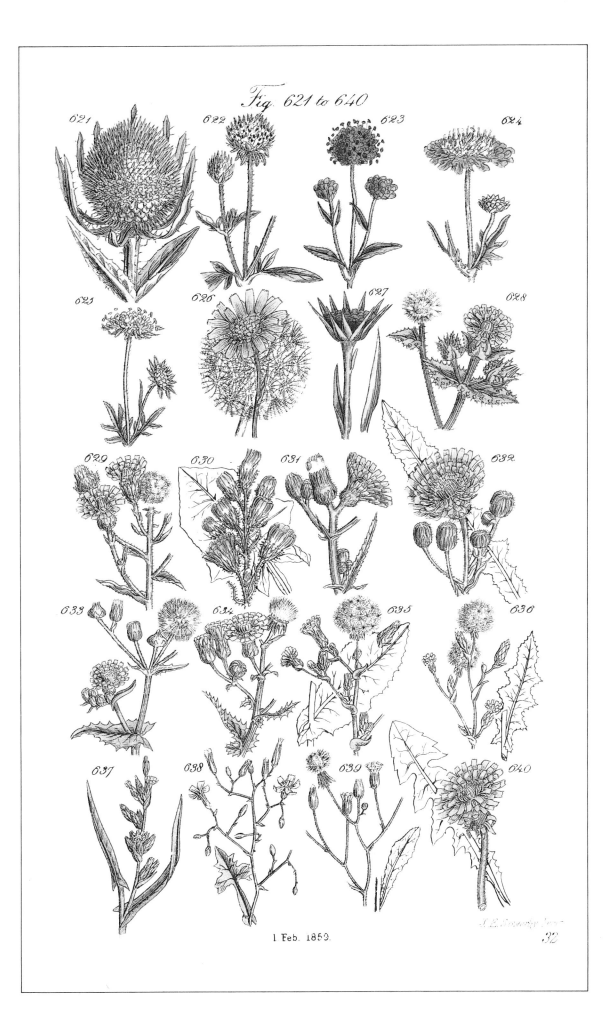

Fig. 621 to 640

S. PALUSTRIS. *Marsh Sow-Thistle.*   **Fig. 631.**
Leaves runcinate; upper ones arrow-shaped, with very long lobes.
Involucrum hairy. River-sides; rare. 7–8 ft. Perenn. July. Yellow.
($\frac{2}{3}$) *E. B.* 1. 935. *E. B.* 2. 1066. *H. & Arn.* 213. *Bab.* 195. *Lind.* 156.

S. ARVENSIS. *Corn Sow-Thistle.*   **Fig. 632.**
Creeping at the root. Lower leaves runcinate; upper ones entire.
Involucrum hairy. Corn-fields; common. 3–4 ft. Perenn. Aug.
Golden yellow. ($\frac{2}{3}$)   *E. B.* 1. 674. *E. B.* 2. 1067. *H. & Arn.* 213.
Bab. 195. *Lind.* 156.

S. OLERACEUS. *Sow-Thistle.*   **Fig. 633.**
Leaves more or less pinnatifid; lower ones with foot-stalks. Invo-
lucrum smooth. A common weed. 1–3 ft. Ann. June–Oct. Yellow.
($\frac{2}{3}$) *E. B.* 1. 843. *E. B.* 2. 1068. *H. & Arn.* 213. *Bab.* 195. *Lind.* 156.

S. ASPER. *Rough Sow-Thistle.*   **Fig. 634.**
Leaves with rounded bases; lower ones sessile, spiny at the margin.
A mere variety of *oleraceus.* ($\frac{2}{3}$) *E. B. Supp.* 2765. *E. B.* 2. 1068*.
H. & Arn. 214. *Bab.* 195. *Lind.* 328.

Genus 5. LACTUCA.

L. VIROSA. *Wild Lettuce.*   **Fig. 635.**
Leaves horizontal, oblong, finely toothed. Stem prickly. Flowers
in panicles. Hedge-banks; common. Very narcotic. 3–4 ft. Bienn.
Aug. Yellow. ($\frac{2}{3}$) *E. B.* 1. 1957. *E. B.* 2. 1069. *H. & Arn.* 212.
Bab. 194. *Lind.* 156.

L. SCARIOLA. *Prickly Lettuce.*   **Fig. 636.**
Leaves nearly erect, lobed, prickly. Flowers in a terminal panicle.
Waste places. 2–3 ft. Bienn. Aug. Yellow. ($\frac{2}{3}$) *E. B.* 1. 268.
E. B. 2. 1070. *H. & Arn.* 212. *Bab.* 194. *Lind.* 156.

L. SALIGNA. *Small Lettuce.*   **Fig. 637.**
Root-leaves lanceolate, entire; upper ones linear-lanceolate, sagittate.
Flowers nearly sessile. Near the sea. 6 in.–1 ft. Bienn. Aug.
Pale yellow. ($\frac{2}{3}$)   *E. B.* 1. 707. *E. B.* 2. 1071. *H. & Arn.* 212.
Bab. 194. *Lind.* 157.

Genus 6. PRENANTHES.

P. MURALIS. *Ivy-leaved Wall-Lettuce.*   **Fig. 638.**
Leaves lyrate; terminal lobe large and angular. Florets 5. Walls
and cliffs. 1 ft. Perenn. July and Aug. Pale yellow. ($\frac{2}{3}$) *E. B.*
1. 457. *E. B.* 2. 1072. *H. & Arn.* 212. *Bab.* 194. *Lind.* 157.

P. HIERACIIFOLIA. *Hawk-weed Wall-Lettuce.*   **Fig. 639.**
Leaves oblong-obovate, downy, toothed. Panicle corymbose, spread-
ing. Near Forfar. 1 ft. Ann. June–Sept. Yellow, anthers brown. ($\frac{2}{3}$)
E. B. 1. 2325. *E. B.* 2. 1073. *H. & Arn.* 214. *Bab.* 197. *Lind.* 158.

Genus 7. LEONTODON.

L. TARAXACUM. *Dandelion.*   **Fig. 640.**
Leaves runcinate, smooth, all springing from the root. Outer scales
of involucrum reflexed. A common weed. Diuretic. 6 in. Perenn.
April–Oct. Bright yellow. ($\frac{1}{2}$)   *E. B.* 1. 510. *E. B.* 2. 1074. *H. &*
Arn. 216. *Bab.* 195. *Lind.* 157.

L. PALUSTRE. *Marsh Dandelion.* **Fig. 641.**
Leaves sinuated and toothed. Outer scales of involucrum erect. A variety of *Taraxacum.* Marshes. 6 in. Perenn. May–Sept. Yellow. ($\frac{1}{2}$) *E. B.* 1. 553. *E. B.* 2. 1075. *H. & Arn.* 216. *Bab.* 195. *Lind.* 157.

Genus 8. APARGIA.

A. HISPIDA. *Rough Hawk-bit.* **Fig. 642.**
Leaves with hooked teeth, hairy. Stem single-flowered. Involucrum hairy. Dry pastures and heaths; common. 6 in. Perenn. June and July. Bright yellow. ($\frac{1}{2}$) *E. B.* 1. 554. *E. B.* 2. 1076. *H. & Arn.* 210. *Bab.* 192. *Lind.* 162.

A. TARAXACI. *Dandelion Hawk-bit.* **Fig. 643.**
Leaves smooth, runcinate. Involucrum hairy. Stem single-flowered. Mountains. 1 ft. Perenn. Aug. Deep yellow. ($\frac{1}{2}$) *E. B.* 1. 1109. *E. B.* 2. 1077. *H. & Arn.* 210. *Bab.* 193. *Lind.* 162.

A. AUTUMNALIS. *Autumnal Hawk-bit.* **Fig. 644.**
Leaves nearly smooth, pinnatifid. Stem branched, with many scaly bracts. Meadows; abundant. 1 ft. Perenn. Aug. and Sept. Yellow. ($\frac{1}{2}$) *E. B.* 1. 830. *E. B.* 2. 1078. *H. & Arn.* 210. *Bab.* 193. *Lind.* 162.

Genus 9. THRINCIA.

T. HIRTA. *Hairy Hawk-bit.* **Fig. 645.**
Leaves lanceolate, slightly toothed, hairy. Stems single-flowered. Gravelly commons; frequent. 6–8 in. Perenn. July and Aug. Bright yellow, orange outside. ($\frac{1}{2}$) *E. B.* 1. 555. *E. B.* 2. 1079. *H. & Arn.* 211. *Bab.* 192. *Lind.* 162.

Genus 10. HIERACIUM.

H. ALPINUM. *Alpine Hawkweed* **Fig. 646.**
Very hairy. Stem with 1 or 2 bracts, single-flowered. Leaves oblong-lanceolate, nearly entire. Involucrum shaggy. Mountains. 6 in. Perenn. Aug. Deep yellow. ($\frac{1}{2}$) *E. B.* 1. 1110. *E. B.* 2. 1080. *H. & Arn.* 219. *Bab.* 199. *Lind.* 159.

H. HALLERI. **Fig. 647.**
Hairy. Stem 1-flowered, with 1 or 2 leaves near the base. Leaves lanceolate, nearly entire. A variety of *alpinum.* Mountains. Perenn. Aug. Yellow. ($\frac{1}{2}$) *E. B.* 1. 2379. *E. B.* 2. 1081. *H. & Arn.* 218. *Bab.* 202? *Lind.* 160.

H. PILOSELLA. *Mouse-ear Hawkweed.* **Fig. 648.**
Scions creeping. Stem hairy, leafless, 1-flowered. Leaves elliptic-lanceolate, entire, very hairy, downy beneath. Dry places; very common. 6 in. Perenn. May–Aug. Lemon-yellow. ($\frac{1}{2}$) *E. B.* 1. 1093. *E. B.* 2. 1082. *H. & Arn.* 217. *Bab.* 198. *Lind.* 159.

H. DUBIUM. **Fig. 649.**
Scions creeping. Stem nearly smooth, loosely corymbose. Leaves elliptic-lanceolate, nearly entire, with long hairs. Mountains; rare. 1 ft. Perenn. July. Yellow. ($\frac{1}{2}$) *E. B.* 1. 2332. *E. B.* 2. 1083. *Lind.* 159.

H. AURICULA. **Fig. 650.**
Scions short. Stem leafless, scape-like, hairy, densely corymbiferous. Leaves lanceolate, nearly entire, hairy. Near Grassmere. 8 in. Perenn. July. Yellow. ($\frac{1}{2}$) *E. B.* 1. 2368. *E. B.* 2. 1084. *Lind.* 159.

H. AURANTIACUM. *Orange Hawkweed.* **Fig. 651.**
Scions creeping. Stem nearly leafless, hairy, densely corymbose.
Leaves elliptical, entire, hairy. Flowers numerous. Northern woods.
8 in.–1 ft. Perenn. June–Aug. Deep orange. ($\frac{1}{2}$) *E. B.* 1. 1469.
E. B. 2. 1085. *H. & Arn.* 217. *Bab.* 198. *Lind.* 159.

H. LAWSONI. *Glaucous Hawkweed.* **Fig. 652.**
Hairy. Stem simply branched, few-leaved. Leaves elliptic-lanceolate,
glaucous. Peduncles with black glandular hairs. Mountains. 1 ft.
Perenn. Aug. Yellow. ($\frac{1}{2}$) *E. B.* 1. 2083. *E. B.* 2. 1086. *Bab.* 201.
Lind. 160.

H. PULMONARIUM. **Fig. 653.**
Hairy. Stem somewhat corymbose, 2–6-flowered. Leaves lanceolate,
deeply toothed; teeth pointing forward. Rocky places. 1 ft. Perenn.
Aug. Yellow. ($\frac{1}{2}$) *E. B.* 1. 2307. *E. B.* 2. 1087. *H. & Arn.* 220.
Lind. 159.

H. MURORUM. *Wall Hawkweed.* **Fig. 654.**
Hairy. Stem corymbose, bearing a single leaf. Leaves ovate or
heart-shaped. Dry woods and walls; common. 2 in.–2 ft. Perenn.
Aug. Deep yellow. ($\frac{1}{2}$) *E. B.* 1. 2082. *E. B.* 2. 1088. *H. &*
Arn. 221. *Bab.* 203. *Lind.* 159.

H. SYLVATICUM. *Wood Hawkweed.* **Fig. 655.**
Stem branched upwards, many-leaved. Leaves ovate-lanceolate, with
teeth at the base pointing upwards. Dry woods; common. 1–2 ft.
Perenn. July and Aug. Yellow. ($\frac{1}{2}$) *E. B.* 1. 2031. *E. B.* 2. 1089.
H. & Arn. 223. *Bab.* 204. *Lind.* 159.

H. MACULATUM. *Spotted Hawkweed.* **Fig. 656.**
Leaves more deeply toothed, spotted with purple. A variety of
sylvaticum. Dry woods. 1–2 ft. Perenn. July and Aug. Yellow.
($\frac{1}{2}$) *E. B.* 1. 2121. *E. B.* 2. 1090. *H. & Arn.* 223. *Bab.* 204.
Lind. 159.

H. PALUDOSUM. *Succory-leaved Hawkweed.* **Fig. 657.**
Stem angular, hollow, panicled. Leaves smooth, oblong-ovate,
toothed, stem-clasping. Involucrum covered with black bristles.
Shady places; common. 2–3 ft. Perenn. July and Aug. Bright
yellow. ($\frac{1}{2}$) *E. B.* 1. 1094. *E. B.* 2. 1091. *H. & Arn.* 215. *Bab.* 197.
Lind. 160.

H. MOLLE. *Soft Hawkweed.* **Fig. 658.**
Stem hollow, panicled. Leaves hairy, lanceolate, stem-clasping;
lower ones elliptical, stalked. Northern woods. 1–2 ft. Perenn.
July and Aug. Yellow. ($\frac{1}{2}$) *E. B.* 1. 2210. *E. B.* 2. 1092. *H. &*
Arn. 215. *Bab.* 197. *Lind.* 160.

H. CERINTHOIDES. **Fig. 659.**
Stem solid, corymbose. Leaves hairy, slightly toothed, oblong;
lower ones with petioles. Involucrum hairy. Highland rocks. 2 ft.
Perenn. Aug. Bright yellow. ($\frac{1}{2}$) *E. B.* 1. 2378. *E. B.* 2. 1093.
H. & Arn. 218. *Bab.* 201? *Lind.* 160.

H. AMPLEXICAULE. **Fig. 660.**
Stem corymbose, with glandular hairs. Leaves toothed; lower ones
oblong-ovate, with petioles; stem ones cordate, stem-clasping. Clova
Mountains. 6 in.–1 ft. Perenn. Aug. Yellow. ($\frac{1}{2}$) *E. B. Supp.* 2690.
E. B. 2. 1093*. *H. & Arn.* 219. *Lind.* 160.

Fig. 641 to 660.

641 642 643 644

645 646 647 648

649 650 651 652

653 654 655 656

657 658 659 660

1 March. 1859.

J.E.Sowerby. Fecit

33

H. SABAUDUM. *Shrubby Hawkweed.* **Fig. 661.**
Stem erect, much branched, very leafy, many-flowered. Leaves ovate-lanceolate, toothed, hairy beneath. Woods; common. 2–3 ft. Perenn. July–Sept. Yellow. ($\frac{1}{2}$) *E. B.* 1. 349. *E. B.* 2. 1094. *H. & Arn.* 227. *Bab.* 207. *Lind.* 160.

H. DENTICULATUM. **Fig. 662.**
Stem erect, solid, many-flowered. Leaves sessile, elliptic-lanceolate, glaucous beneath. Peduncles cottony. Northern woods. 3 ft. Perenn. Aug. Yellow. ($\frac{1}{2}$) *E. B.* 1. 2122. *E. B.* 2. 1095. *H. & Arn.* 224. *Bab.* 205. *Lind.* 160.

H. PRENANTHOIDES. **Fig. 663.**
Stem erect, many-flowered. Leaves elliptic-oblong; upper ones cordate, stem-clasping. Scotland. 3–4 ft. Perenn. Aug. Yellow. ($\frac{1}{2}$) *E. B.* 1. 2235. *E. B.* 2. 1096. *H. & Arn.* 224. *Bab.* 205. *Lind.* 161.

H. UMBELLATUM. *Narrow-leaved Hawkweed.* **Fig. 664.**
Stem erect, simple, very leafy. Leaves linear-lanceolate, nearly smooth. Flowers in terminal umbel-like corymbs. Dry woods; common. 2–3 ft. Perenn. Aug. and Sept. Yellow. ($\frac{1}{2}$) *E. B.* 1. 1771. *E. B.* 2. 1097. *H. & Arn.* 226. *Bab.* 206. *Lind.* 161.

Genus 11. CREPIS.

C. TECTORUM. *Smooth Hawk's-beard.* **Fig. 665.**
Stem smooth, purple at the joints. Upper leaves linear-lanceolate; lower runcinate. Walls and dry places; common. 6 in.–2 ft. Ann. June–Sept. Yellow. ($\frac{1}{2}$) *E. B.* 1. 1111. *E. B.* 2. 1098. *H. & Arn.* 214. *Bab.* 197. *Lind.* 158.

C. BIENNIS. *Rough Hawk's-beard.* **Fig. 666.**
Stem and leaves hairy. Root-leaves somewhat lyrate; upper pinnatifid, with toothed lobes. Dry pastures. 2–4 ft. Bienn. June and July. Yellow. ($\frac{1}{2}$) *E. B.* 1. 149. *E. B.* 2. 1099. *H. & Arn.* 214. *Bab.* 197. *Lind.* 158.

Genus 12. BORKHAUSIA.

B. FŒTIDA. *Stinking Hawk's-beard.* **Fig. 667.**
Stem hairy, spreading. Leaves pinnatifid, hairy, sessile. Involucrum with deciduous scales at the base. Chalky fields. 6 in.–1 ft. Bienn. June and July. Yellow. ($\frac{1}{2}$) *E. B.* 1. 406. *E. B.* 2. 1100. *H. & Arn.* 215. *Bab.* 196. *Lind.* 158.

Genus 13. HYPOCHŒRIS.

H. MACULATA. *Spotted Cat's-ear.* **Fig. 668.**
Stems simple, hairy; generally 1-flowered. Leaves ovate-oblong, all growing from the root, spotted with brown beneath. Dry pastures. 6–8 in. Perenn. July and Aug. Yellow. ($\frac{1}{2}$) *E. B.* 1. 225. *E. B.* 2. 1101. *H. & Arn.* 212. *Bab.* 192. *Lind.* 161.

H. GLABRA. *Smooth Cat's-ear.* **Fig. 669.**
Nearly smooth. Stems branched, leafy. Leaves waved or toothed. Dry pastures. 4 in.–1 ft. Ann. July and Aug. Yellow. ($\frac{1}{2}$) *E. B.* 1. 575. *E. B.* 2. 1102. *H. & Arn.* 211. *Bab.* 191. *Lind.* 161.

H. RADICATA. *Long-rooted Cat's-ear.* **Fig. 670.**
Stems branched, not leafy, smooth. Leaves runcinate, rough with hairs. Meadows; very common. 1 ft. Perenn. June–Sept. Yellow. ($\frac{1}{2}$) *E. B.* 1. 831. *E. B.* 2. 1103. *H. & Arn.* 211. *Bab.* 192. *Lind.* 161.

Fig. 661 to 680

1. March. 1859

Genus 14. LAPSANA.

L. COMMUNIS. *Nipple-wort.* **Fig. 671.**
Stem branched, panicled. Leaves ovate, toothed with foot-stalks.
Peduncles slender. A common weed. 2–3 ft. Ann. July and Aug.
Pale yellow. ($\frac{1}{2}$) *E. B.* 1. 844. *E. B.* 2. 1104. *H. & Arn.* 227.
Bab. 191. *Lind.* 157.

L. PUSILLA. *Dwarf Nipple-wort.* **Fig. 672.**
Leaves all from the root. Stem branched, peduncles thickened up-
wards. Sandy fields. 6–8 in. Ann. June and July. Bright yellow.
($\frac{1}{2}$) *E. B.* 1. 95. *E. B.* 2. 1105. *H. & Arn.* 227. *Bab.* 191. *Lind.* 157.

Genus 15. CICHORIUM.

C. INTYBUS. *Chicory. Succory.* **Fig. 673.**
Leaves runcinate. Flowers sessile, in pairs. Chalky or dry fields
and way-sides. Roots used as a substitute for coffee. 1–3 ft. Perenn.
July–Sept. Bright blue. ($\frac{1}{2}$) *E. B.* 1. 537. *E. B.* 2. 1106. *H. &*
Arn. 228. *Bab.* 191. *Lind.* 162.

Genus 16. ARCTIUM.

A. LAPPA. *Burdock.* **Fig. 674.**
Leaves heart-shaped, with petioles, very large. Scales of involucrum
hooked. Waste places and road-sides; abundant. 3–4 ft. Bienn.
July and Aug. Purple or white. ($\frac{1}{2}$) *E. B.* 1. 1228. *E. B.* 2. 1107.
H. & Arn. 229. *Bab.* 184. *Lind.* 154.

A. TOMENTOSUM. *Downy-headed Burdock.* **Fig. 675.**
Involucrum cottony. A variety of *Lappa.* Way-sides. 1–4 ft.
Bienn. July and Aug. Purple. ($\frac{1}{2}$) *E. B.* 1. 2478. *E. B.* 2. 1108.
H. & Arn. 229. *Bab.* 185. *Lind.* 154.

Genus 17. SERRATULA.

S. TINCTORIA. *Saw-wort.* **Fig. 676.**
Leaves pinnatifid, or nearly entire, with sharp serratures. Woods;
common. Yields a yellow dye. 2–3 ft. Perenn. Aug. and Sept.
Purple. ($\frac{1}{2}$) *E. B.* 1. 38. *E. B.* 2. 1109. *H. & Arn.* 229. *Bab.* 185.
Lind. 154.

Genus 18. SAUSSUREA.

S. ALPINA. **Fig. 677.**
Leaves undivided, cottony beneath. Flowers in an umbel-like cluster.
Moist alpine rocks. 6–10 in. Perenn. Aug. Purple. ($\frac{1}{2}$) *E. B.*
1. 599. *E. B.* 2. 1110. *H. & Arn.* 230. *Bab.* 183. *Lind.* 154.

Genus 19. CARDUUS.

C. NUTANS. *Musk Thistle.* **Fig. 678.**
Leaves decurrent, deeply waved, spinous. Flowers drooping. Waste
ground. 2–3 ft. Ann. July and Aug. Deep purple. ($\frac{1}{2}$) *E. B.*
1. 1112. *E. B.* 2. 1111. *H. & Arn.* 230. *Bab.* 188. *Lind.* 155.

C. ACANTHOIDES. *Welted Thistle.* **Fig. 679.**
Leaves decurrent, very spinous. Flowers in heads, nearly sessile.
Road-sides; common. 3–5 ft. Ann. July. Purple or white. ($\frac{1}{2}$)
E. B. 1. 973. *E. B.* 2. 1112. *H. & Arn.* 230. *Bab.* 188. *Lind.* 155.

C. TENUIFLORUS. *Slender-flowered Thistle.* **Fig. 680.**
Leaves decurrent, pinnatifid, spinous, rather cottony beneath. Waste
places. 2–4 ft. Ann. June and July. Pale rose-colour. ($\frac{1}{2}$) *E. B.*
1. 412. *E. B.* 2. 1113. *H. & Arn.* 230. *Bab.* 188. *Lind.* 156.

Genus 20. SILYBUM.

S. MARIANUM. *Milk Thistle.* **Fig 681.**
Leaves waved, spinous, glossy green with white veins. Spines of involucrum very large, recurved. Waste places. 4–5 ft. Bienn. July. Purple. ($\frac{1}{2}$) *E. B.* 1. 976. *E. B.* 2. 1114. *H. & Arn.* 231. *Bab.* 190. *Lind.* 154.

Genus 21. CNICUS.

C. LANCEOLATUS. *Spear Thistle.* **Fig. 682.**
Stem hairy, furrowed. Leaves spinous, cottony beneath. Involucrum ovate, with lanceolate spreading scales. Flowers solitary. Waste places; common. 3–4 ft. Bienn. July and Aug. Purple. ($\frac{1}{2}$) *E. B.* 1. 107. *E. B.* 2. 1115. *H. & Arn.* 231. *Bab.* 188. *Lind.* 152.

C. PALUSTRIS. *Marsh Thistle.* **Fig. 683.**
Leaves decurrent, pinnatifid, toothed, spinous. Involucrum ovate, scales nearly smooth. Flowers in close clusters. Marshes. 3–6 ft. Bienn. July and Aug. Purple or white. ($\frac{1}{2}$) *E. B.* 1. 974. *E. B.* 2. 1116. *H. & Arn.* 231. *Bab.* 189. *Lind.* 152.

C. ARVENSIS. *Common Thistle.* **Fig. 684.**
Root creeping. Stem panicled, solid. Leaves sessile, pinnatifid, spinous, deep shining green, nearly smooth. A common weed. 1–3 ft. Perenn. July. Pale purple or whitish. ($\frac{1}{2}$) *E. B.* 1. 975. *E. B.* 2. 1117. *H. & Arn.* 231. *Bab.* 189. *Lind.* 153.

C. ERIOPHORUS. *Woolly-headed Thistle.* **Fig. 685.**
Stem very thick, furrowed. Leaves deeply pinnatifid, downy beneath. Involucrum spherical, woolly. Limestone pastures and waste places. 3–4 ft. July and Aug. Purple or white. ($\frac{1}{2}$) *E. B.* 1. 386. *E. B.* 2. 1118. *H. & Arn.* 232. *Bab.* 189. *Lind.* 153.

C. TUBEROSUS. *Tuberous Plume Thistle.* **Fig. 686.**
Root creeping, tuberous. Stem 1- or 2-flowered, not prickly. Leaves pinnatifid, with small prickles. Woods. 2 ft. Perenn. Aug. Bright purple. ($\frac{1}{2}$) *E. B.* 1. 2562. *E. B.* 2. 1119. *H. & Arn.* 232. *Bab.* 190. *Lind.* 153.

C. HETEROPHYLLUS. *Dark Plume Thistle.* **Fig. 687.**
Stems downy, mostly 1-flowered. Leaves lanceolate, not prickly. Northern pastures. 2–3 ft. Perenn. July and Aug. Dark purple. ($\frac{1}{2}$) *E. B.* 1. 675. *E. B.* 2. 1120. *H. & Arn.* 232. *Bab.* 190. *Lind.* 153.

C. PRATENSIS. *Meadow Plume Thistle.* **Fig. 688.**
Stems downy, 1-flowered. Leaves lanceolate, green above, cottony beneath, with small spines. Involucrum cottony. Wet meadows and heaths. 1 ft. Perenn. July. Dull purple. ($\frac{1}{2}$) *E. B.* 1. 177. *E. B.* 2. 1121. *H. & Arn.* 232. *Bab.* 189. *Lind.* 153.

C. ACAULIS. *Dwarf Plume Thistle.* **Fig. 689.**
Stemless. Involucrum smooth, sessile. Chalk pastures; abundant. 2 in. Perenn. July. Purple. ($\frac{1}{2}$) *E. B.* 1. 161. *E. B.* 2. 1122. *H. & Arn.* 233. *Bab.* 190. *Lind.* 153.

Genus 22. ONOPORDUM.

O. ACANTHIUM. *Cotton Thistle.* **Fig. 690.**
Stem winged. Leaves sinuated, spinous, white and cottony. Scales of involucrum spreading. Waste places. 4–6 ft. Bienn. Aug. Purple. ($\frac{1}{2}$) *E. B.* 1. 977. *E. B.* 2. 1123. *H. & Arn.* 233. *Bab.* 187. *Lind.* 152.

Genus 23. CARLINA.

C. VULGARIS. *Carline Thistle.* **Fig. 691.**
Stem downy, corymbose, many-flowered. Leaves waved, with unequal spines. Inner scales of involucrum pale yellow, membranaceous. Dry pastures. 3 in.–1 ft. Bienn. June and July. Florets red, anthers yellow. ($\frac{1}{2}$) *E. B.* 1. 1144. *E. B.* 2. 1124. *H. & Arn.* 234. *Bab.* 184. *Lind.* 154.

Genus 24. BIDENS.

B. CERNUA. *Nodding Bur Marigold.* **Fig. 692.**
Leaves lanceolate, deeply serrated. Flowers drooping. Ditches. 1–2 ft. Ann. June–Sept. Yellow. ($\frac{1}{2}$) *E. B.* 1. 1114. *E. B.* 2. 1125. *H. & Arn.* 238. *Bab.* 174. *Lind.* 151.

B. TRIPARTITA. *Bur Marigold.* **Fig. 693.**
Leaves tripartite. Flowers rather drooping. Ditches; very common. 1–3 ft. Ann. July–Sept. Yellow. ($\frac{1}{2}$) *E. B.* 1. 1113. *E. B.* 2. 1126. *H. & Arn.* 238. *Bab.* 173. *Lind.* 151.

Genus 25. EUPATORIUM.

E. CANNABINUM. *Hemp Agrimony.* **Fig. 694.**
Leaves opposite, pinnate, deeply serrated. Flowers in dense terminal corymbs. Ditches; common. 2–3 ft. Perenn. July and Aug. Pink. ($\frac{1}{2}$) *E. B.* 1. 428. *E. B.* 2. 1127. *H. & Arn.* 240. *Bab.* 170. *Lind.* 142.

Genus 26. CHRYSOCOMA.

C. LINOSYRIS. *Goldilocks.* **Fig. 695.**
Leaves linear, smooth, glaucous. Cliffs on the south coast. 1$\frac{1}{2}$–2 ft. Perenn. Aug. and Sept. Yellow. ($\frac{1}{2}$) *E. B.* 1. 2505. *E. B.* 2. 1128. *H. & Arn.* 240. *Bab.* 172. *Lind.* 142.

Genus 27. DIOTIS.

D. MARITIMA. *Cotton-weed.* **Fig. 696.**
Plant covered with a dense cottony down. Flowers in terminal corymbs. Sandy shores. 1 ft. Perenn. Aug. and Sept. Yellow. ($\frac{1}{2}$) *E. B.* 1. 141. *E. B.* 2. 1129. *H. & Arn.* 238. *Bab.* 176. *Lind.* 149.

Genus 28. TANACETUM.

T. VULGARE. *Tansy.* **Fig. 697.**
Leaves bipinnatifid, serrated. Flowers in a flat corymb. Fields. 1–3 ft. Perenn. July and Aug. Yellow. ($\frac{1}{2}$) *E. B.* 1. 1229. *E. B.* 2. 1130. *H. & Arn.* 238. *Bab.* 178. *Lind.* 149.

Genus 29. ARTEMISIA.

A. CAMPESTRIS. *Field Southernwood.* **Fig. 698.**
Stems twiggy, procumbent before flowering. Leaves bipinnatifid, with linear segments. Dry heaths. 1 ft. Perenn. Aug. Yellow. ($\frac{1}{2}$) *E. B.* 1. 338. *E. B.* 2. 1131. *H. & Arn.* 239. *Bab.* 177. *Lind.* 149.

A. MARITIMA. *Sea Wormwood.* **Fig. 699.**
Erect. Leaves downy, bipinnatifid, with linear segments. Flowers in drooping racemes. Sea-shore. 1–1$\frac{1}{2}$ ft. Perenn. Sept. Yellowish. ($\frac{1}{2}$) *E. B.* 1. 1706. *E. B.* 2. 1132. *H. & Arn.* 239. *Bab.* 177. *Lind.* 149.

A. GALLICA. **Fig. 700.**
Racemes closer, erect. A variety of *maritima*. Sea-shore and salt marshes. 1$\frac{1}{2}$ ft. Perenn. Sept. Yellow or brownish. ($\frac{1}{2}$) *E. B.* 1. 1001. *E. B.* 2. 1132*. *H. & Arn.* 239. *Bab.* 178. *Lind.* 149.

Fig. 681 to 700.

681 682 683 684

685 686 687 688

689 690 691 692

693 694 695 696

697 698 699 700

A. ABSINTHIUM. *Wormwood.* **Fig. 701.**
Leaves bipinnatifid, with lanceolate segments, downy. Waste places.
1 ft. Perenn. Aug. Dingy yellow. ($\frac{1}{2}$) *E. B.* 1. 1230. *E. B.* 2. 1133.
H. & Arn. 239. *Bab.* 177. *Lind.* 149.

A. VULGARIS. *Mugwort.* **Fig. 702.**
Leaves pinnatifid, with unequally cut segments, downy beneath. Hedge-
banks. 3–4 ft. Perenn. Aug. Reddish or yellow. ($\frac{1}{2}$) *E. B.* 1. 978.
E. B. 2. 1134. *H. & Arn.* 239. *Bab.* 178. *Lind.* 149.

A. CÆRULESCENS. *Lavender Mugwort.* **Fig. 703.**
Leaves lanceolate, hoary; lowermost pinnatifid. Flowers erect. Sea-
coast; a doubtful native. 2–3 ft. Perenn. Aug. Yellow or brownish.
($\frac{1}{2}$) *E. B.* 1. 2426. *E. B.* 2. 1135. *H. & Arn.* 240. *Bab.* 178.
Lind. 149.

Genus 30. ANTENNARIA.

A. MARGARITACEA. *Pearly Everlasting.* **Fig. 704.**
Stems branched above. Leaves linear-lanceolate, cottony. Flowers
in flat corymbs. Moist meadows; not native. 1–3 ft. Perenn. Aug.
Involucrum pearly white, florets yellow. ($\frac{1}{2}$) *E. B.* 1. 2018. *E. B.*
2. 1136. *H. & Arn.* 241. *Bab.* 180. *Lind.* 144.

A. DIOICA. *Cat's-foot.* **Fig. 705.**
Shoots procumbent. Stems unbranched, white and cottony. Leaves
green above, cottony beneath. Dry heaths. 2–6 in. Perenn. June
and July. White or rose-colour. ($\frac{1}{2}$) *E. B.* 1. 267. *E. B.* 2. 1137.
H. & Arn. 241. *Bab.* 180. *Lind.* 144.

Genus 31. GNAPHALIUM.

G. LUTEO-ALBUM. *Jersey Cudweed.* **Fig. 706.**
Leaves half stem-clasping, linear-oblong, woolly on both sides. Dry
fields. 1 ft. Ann. July and Aug. Pale yellow. ($\frac{1}{2}$) *E. B.* 1. 1002.
E. B. 2. 1138. *H. & Arn.* 241. *Bab.* 179. *Lind.* 145.

G. SYLVATICUM. *Highland Cudweed.* **Fig. 707.**
Stem simple, nearly erect, downy. Leaves lanceolate, tapering at the
base. Flowers axillary, sessile. Mountains. 1–1$\frac{1}{2}$ ft. Perenn. Aug.
Yellow. ($\frac{1}{2}$) *E. B.* 1. 913. *E. B.* 2. 1139. *H. & Arn.* 242. *Bab.* 180.
Lind. 145.

G. SUPINUM. *Dwarf Cudweed.* **Fig. 708.**
Stem decumbent, simple or branched at the base. Leaves linear,
downy on both sides. Flowers solitary or in a spike-like raceme.
Highland mountains. 2–4 in. Perenn. July and Aug. Yellow.
($\frac{1}{2}$) *E. B.* 1. 1193. *E. B.* 2. 1140. *H. & Arn.* 242. *Bab.* 180.
Lind. 145.

G. ULIGINOSUM. *Marsh Cudweed.* **Fig. 709.**
Stem much branched, spreading. Leaves linear-lanceolate, downy
on both sides. Flowers in crowded leafy tufts. Watery places. 9 in.
Ann. Aug. and Sept. Yellowish brown. ($\frac{1}{2}$) *E. B.* 1. 1194. *E. B.* 2.
1141. *H. & Arn.* 242. *Bab.* 180. *Lind.* 145.

G. GALLICUM. *Narrow-leaved Cudweed.* **Fig. 710.**
Stem erect, branched. Leaves linear, acute, downy. Flowers in
axillary clusters. Dry fields; rare. 9 in. Ann. July and Aug.
Brownish yellow. ($\frac{1}{2}$) *E. B.* 1. 2369. *E. B.* 2. 1142. *H. & Arn.* 243.
Bab. 180. *Lind.* 145.

Fig 701 to 720.

701 702 703 704
705 706 707 708
709 710 711 712
713 714 715 716
717 718 719 720

J.E. Sowerby. Fecit.

1. March. 1859.

36

G. MINIMUM. *Least Cudweed.* **Fig. 711.**
Stem branched, forked, the branches spreading. Leaves lanceolate, flat, cottony. Flowers in terminal and lateral clusters. Dry ground; common. 2–6 in. Ann. July and Aug. Yellow. ($\frac{1}{2}$) *E. B.* 1. 1157. *E. B.* 2. 1143. *H. & Arn.* 243. *Bab.* 179. *Lind.* 145.

G. GERMANICUM. *Common Cudweed.* **Fig. 712.**
Stem proliferous at the summit. Leaves lanceolate, downy. Heads globose, many-flowered. 6–9 in. Ann. June and July. Pale yellow. ($\frac{1}{2}$) *E. B.* 1. 946. *E. B.* 2. 1144. *H. & Arn.* 243. *Bab.* 178. *Lind.* 145.

Genus 32. CONYZA.

C. SQUARROSA. *Spikenard.* **Fig. 713.**
Leaves ovate-lanceolate, downy. Scales of involucrum leafy, recurved. Chalky fields. 2–3 ft. Bienn. Sept. and Oct. Yellow. ($\frac{1}{2}$) *E. B.* 1. 1195. *E. B.* 2. 1145. *H. & Arn.* 250. *Bab.* 172. *Lind.* 142.

Genus 33. ERIGERON.

E. CANADENSE. *Canada Flea-bane.* **Fig. 714.**
Stem hairy. Leaves lanceolate. Flowers in panicles. Waste ground; naturalized? 6 in.–2 ft. Ann. Aug. and Sept. Yellowish. ($\frac{1}{2}$) *E. B.* 1. 2019. *E. B.* 2. 1146. *H. & Arn.* 244. *Bab.* 171. *Lind.* 144.

E. ACRE. *Blue Flea-bane.* **Fig. 715.**
Leaves lanceolate. Flowers in racemes. Dry pastures. 1–1½ ft. Bienn. Aug. Outer florets purplish, inner yellow. ($\frac{1}{2}$) *E. B.* 1. 1158. *E. B.* 2. 1147. *H. & Arn.* 245. *Bab.* 171. *Lind.* 145.

E. ALPINUM. *Alpine Flea-bane.* **Fig. 716.**
Stem mostly 1-flowered. Leaves lanceolate. Outer florets radiate. Highland mountains. 2–5 in. Perenn. July. Pale purple. ($\frac{1}{2}$) *E. B.* 1. 464. *E. B.* 2. 1148. *H. & Arn.* 246. *Bab.* 171. *Lind.* 144.

E. UNIFLORUM. **Fig. 717.**
Involucrum woolly. Outer florets erect. A variety of *alpinum.* Highland mountains. 2–6 in. Perenn. July. Purple. ($\frac{1}{2}$) *E. B.* 1. 2416. *E. B.* 2. 1148*. *H. & Arn.* 246. *Bab.* 171. *Lind.* 144.

Genus 34. TUSSILAGO.

T. FARFARA. *Colt's-foot.* **Fig. 718.**
Root creeping. Leaves cordate, angular, downy beneath; appearing after the flowers. Clayey banks; abundant. 4 in.–1 ft. Perenn. March and April. Golden yellow. ($\frac{1}{2}$) *E. B.* 1. 429. *E. B.* 2. 1149. *H. & Arn.* 245. *Bab.* 170. *Lind.* 147.

Genus 35. PETASITES.

P. VULGARIS. *Butter-bur.* **Fig. 719.**
Leaves very large, heart-shaped, downy beneath. Flowers in a close panicle, appearing before the leaves. Banks of rivers and wet meadows. 3–6 in. Perenn. April and May. Pale lilac. ($\frac{1}{2}$) *E. B.* 1. 431. *E. B.* 2. 1150. *H. & Arn.* 244. *Bab.* 170. *Lind.* 147.

Genus 36. SENECIO.

S. VULGARIS. *Groundsel.* **Fig. 720.**
Leaves pinnatifid, with obtuse segments. Flowers panicled, without rays. A common weed. 4 in.–1 ft. Ann. All the year. Yellow. ($\frac{1}{2}$) *E. B.* 1. 747. *E. B.* 2. 1151. *H. & Arn.* 247. *Bab.* 181. *Lind.* 146.

S. viscosus. *Stinking Groundsel.* **Fig. 721.**
Stem with many spreading branches. Leaves pinnatifid, viscid. Ray-florets revolute. Waste ground. Has a fœtid smell. 1–2 ft. Ann. July and Aug. Yellow. (⅔) *E. B.* 1. 32. *E. B.* 2. 1152. *H. & Arn.* 248. *Bab.* 181. *Lind.* 146.

S. sylvaticus. *Mountain Groundsel.* **Fig. 722.**
Stem erect, straight. Leaves sessile, pinnatifid, lobed. Ray-florets often wanting. Dry pastures. 1–2 ft. Ann. July. Yellow. (⅔) *E. B.* 1. 748. *E. B.* 2. 1153. *H. & Arn.* 248. *Bab.* 181. *Lind.* 146.

S. lividus. **Fig. 723.**
Leaves dilated at the base, pinnatifid and toothed. A variety of *sylvaticus.* Barren heaths. 1–2 ft. Ann. Sept. Yellow. (⅔) *E. B.* 1. 2515. *E. B.* 2. 1154. *H. & Arn.* 247. *Bab.* 182. *Lind.* 146.

S. squalidus. **Fig. 724.**
Leaves pinnatifid, with distant segments. Rays spreading. Walls and waste places. 1–2 ft. Ann. June–Oct. Yellow. (⅔) *E. B.* 1. 600. *E. B.* 2. 1155. *H. & Arn.* 248. *Bab.* 182. *Lind.* 146.

S. tenuifolius. *Hoary Ragwort.* **Fig. 725.**
Stem erect, cottony. Leaves closely pinnatifid, downy beneath. Banks and way-sides. 1–3 ft. Perenn. July and Aug. Yellow. (⅔) *E. B.* 1. 574. *E. B.* 2. 1156. *H. & Arn.* 248. *Bab.* 182. *Lind.* 146.

S. Jacobæa. *Common Ragwort.* **Fig. 726.**
Stem erect, branched, furrowed. Leaves bipinnatifid, with spreading toothed segments; lower ones somewhat lyrate. Rays spreading, toothed. Dry places; common. 2–3 ft. Perenn. July and Aug. Deep yellow. (⅔) *E. B.* 1. 1130. *E. B.* 2. 1157. *H. & Arn.* 248. *Bab.* 182. *Lind.* 146.

S. aquaticus. *Marsh Ragwort.* **Fig. 727.**
Leaves lyrate, smooth, serrated. Rays spreading, elliptical. Wet places; common. 1–3 ft. Perenn. July–Oct. Yellow. (⅔) *E. B.* 1. 1131. *E. B.* 2. 1158. *H. & Arn.* 248. *Bab.* 182. *Lind.* 146.

S. paludosus. *Great Ragwort, Bird's-tongue.* **Fig. 728.**
Stem quite straight, hollow, rather woolly. Leaves lanceolate, serrated. Fens and ditches; rare. 5–6 ft. Perenn. June and July. Yellow. (⅔) *E. B.* 1. 650. *E. B.* 2. 1159. *H. & Arn.* 248. *Bab.* 183. *Lind.* 146.

S. Saracenicus. *Broad-leaved Ragwort.* **Fig. 729.**
Stem erect, little branched. Leaves lanceolate, serrated. Corymbs terminal. Moist meadows; rare. 3–5 ft. Perenn. July and Aug. Yellow. (⅔) *E. B.* 1. 2211. *E. B.* 2. 1160. *H. & Arn.* 248. *Bab.* 183. *Lind.* 147.

Genus 37. Aster.

A. Tripolium. *Sea Starwort. Sea Aster.* **Fig. 730.**
Stem smooth. Leaves linear-lanceolate, fleshy. Flowers in corymbs. Muddy sea-shores and salt marshes; common. 6 in.–3 ft. Perenn. Aug. and Sept. Disk yellow, rays blue or purple. (⅔) *E. B.* 1 87. *E. B.* 2. 1161. *H. & Arn.* 246. *Bab.* 171. *Lind.* 143.

Genus 38. SOLIDAGO.

S. VIRGAUREA. *Golden-rod.* **Fig. 731.**
Stem-leaves lanceolate; lower ones elliptical. Flowers in rather close panicles. Woods and heaths; common. 1–3 ft. Perenn. July–Sept. Yellow. ($\frac{2}{3}$) *E. B.* 1. 301. *E. B.* 2. 1162. *H. & Arn.* 246. *Bab.* 172. *Lind.* 144.

Genus 39. INULA.

I. HELENIUM. *Elecampane.* **Fig. 732.**
Leaves ovate or lanceolate, downy beneath, very large. Flowers large, terminal. 3–6 ft. Perenn. July and Aug. Yellow. ($\frac{1}{2}$) *E. B.* 1. 1546. *E. B.* 2. 1163. *H. & Arn.* 250. *Bab.* 172. *Lind.* 143.

Genus 40. PULICARIA.

P. DYSENTERICA. *Flea-bane.* **Fig. 733.**
Stem and leaves woolly. Leaves oblong, stem-clasping. Ditches; common. 1 ft. Perenn. Aug. and Sept. Deep yellow. ($\frac{2}{3}$) *E. B.* 1. 1115. *E. B.* 2. 1164. *H. & Arn.* 251. *Bab.* 173. *Lind.* 143.

P. VULGARIS. *Small Flea-bane.* **Fig. 734.**
Stem hairy, much branched. Leaves lanceolate. Rays very short. 6 in.–1 ft. Ann. Aug. and Sept. Yellow. ($\frac{2}{3}$) *E. B.* 1. 1196. *E. B.* 2. 1165. *H. & Arn.* 251. *Bab.* 173. *Lind.* 143.

Genus 41. LIMBARDA.

L. CRITHMOIDES. *Golden Samphire.* **Fig. 735.**
Leaves linear, fleshy, 3-pointed. Salt marshes; common. 1 ft. Perenn. Aug. Deep yellow. ($\frac{2}{3}$) *E. B.* 1. 68. *E. B.* 2. 1166. *H. & Arn.* 250. *Bab.* 173. *Lind.* 143.

Genus 42. CINERARIA.

C. PALUSTRIS. *Marsh Flea-wort.* **Fig. 736.**
Stem shaggy, much branched, hollow. Leaves broadly lanceolate. Fens; local. 2–3 ft. Perenn. June and July. Yellow. ($\frac{2}{3}$) *E. B.* 1. 151. *E. B.* 2. 1167. *H. & Arn.* 249. *Bab.* 183. *Lind.* 147.

C. CAMPESTRIS. *Field Flea-wort.* **Fig. 737.**
Herb woolly. Root-leaves oval. Flowers in an umbel. 6 in.–1 ft. Perenn. May and June. Yellow. ($\frac{2}{3}$) *E. B.* 1. 152. *E. B.* 2. 1168. *H. & Arn.* 249. *Bab.* 183. *Lind.* 147.

Genus 43. DORONICUM.

D. PLANTAGINEUM. *Greater Leopard's-bane.* **Fig. 738.**
Lower leaves stalked, heart-shaped; upper sessile. A doubtful native. 2 ft. Perenn. May and June. Bright yellow. ($\frac{1}{2}$) *E. B.* 1. 630. *E. B.* 2. 1169. *H. & Arn.* 250. *Bab.* 181. *Lind.* 327.

D. PARDALIANCHES. *Common Leopard's-bane.* **Fig. 739.**
Leaves heart-shaped; lower on long petioles, upper on winged petioles dilated at the base. Moist woods; scarcely native. 2–3 ft. Perenn. June–Sept. Yellow. ($\frac{1}{2}$) *E. B. Supp.* 2654. *E. B.* 2. 1169*. *H. & Arn.* 249. *Bab.* 181. *Lind.* 147.

Genus 44. BELLIS.

B. PERENNIS. *Daisy.* **Fig. 740.**
Root creeping. Leaves spatulate, crenated. Pastures; abundant. 1–8 in. Perenn. April–Oct. White tipped with crimson. ($\frac{2}{3}$) *E. B.* 1. 424. *E. B.* 2. 1170. *H. & Arn.* 251. *Bab.* 172. *Lind.* 148.

Fig. 721 to 740.

721 722 723 724
725 726 727 728
729 730 731 732
733 734 735 736
737 738 739 740

1, April, 1859.

J E Sowerby, Fecit

37

Genus 45. CHRYSANTHEMUM.

C. LEUCANTHEMUM. *Ox-eye Daisy.* **Fig. 741.**
Stem branched. Root-leaves obovate, with petioles. Dry pastures;
common. 2 ft. Perenn. June and July. White. ($\frac{1}{2}$) *E. B.* 1. 601.
E. B. 2. 1171. *H. & Arn.* 252. *Bab.* 176. *Lind.* 148.

C. SEGETUM. *Corn Marigold.* **Fig. 742.**
Leaves glaucous, deeply notched. Peduncles thickened upwards.
Corn-fields; common. 1–2 ft. Ann. June–Aug. Yellow. ($\frac{2}{3}$) *E. B.* 1.
540. *E. B.* 2. 1172. *H. & Arn.* 252. *Bab.* 176. *Lind.* 140.

Genus 46. PYRETHRUM.

P. PARTHENIUM. *Feverfew.* **Fig. 743.**
Stem erect. Leaves bipinnatifid, with petioles. Rays shorter than
the disk. Waste places; frequent. 1–2 ft. Perenn. July. White. ($\frac{2}{3}$)
E. B. 1. 1231. *E. B.* 2. 1173. *H. & Arn.* 252. *Bab.* 177. *Lind.* 148.

P. INODORUM. *Corn Feverfew.* **Fig. 744.**
Stem spreading. Leaves bipinnatifid, with hair-like segments.
Fields; common. 1 ft. Ann. Aug. and Sept. White. ($\frac{2}{3}$) *E. B.* 1.
676. *E. B.* 2. 1174. *H. & Arn.* 252. *Bab.* 177. *Lind.* 148.

P. MARITIMUM. *Sea-side Feverfew.* **Fig. 745.**
Stem spreading, branched. Leaves bipinnatifid, with linear segments.
Sandy sea-shores. 1 ft. Perenn. July. White. ($\frac{2}{3}$) *E. B.* 1. 979.
E. B. 2. 1175. *H. & Arn.* 252. *Bab.* 177. *Lind.* 148.

Genus 47. MATRICARIA.

M. CHAMOMILLA. *Wild Chamomile.* **Fig. 746.**
Leaves smooth, bipinnatifid, with hair-like segments. Receptacle
conical. Corn-fields; common. 1 ft. Ann. July and Aug. White.
($\frac{2}{3}$) *E. B.* 1. 1232. *E. B.* 2. 1176. *H. & Arn.* 253. *Bab.* 177.
Lind. 149.

Genus 48. ANTHEMIS.

A. MARITIMA. *Sea Chamomile.* **Fig. 747.**
Stems prostrate. Leaves bipinnatifid, with fleshy segments; somewhat hairy. Scales of receptacle prominent, pointed. Rocky coasts.
4–8 in. Ann. July. White. ($\frac{2}{3}$) *E. B.* 1. 2370. *E. B.* 2. 1177.
H. & Arn. 253. *Bab.* 178. *Lind.* 149.

A. NOBILIS. *Common Chamomile.* **Fig. 748.**
Stems procumbent. Leaves bipinnatifid, with linear segments,
downy. Dry pastures. Tonic. 6 in. Perenn. Aug. and Sept.
White. ($\frac{2}{3}$) *E. B.* 1. 980. *E. B.* 2. 1178. *H. & Arn.* 253. *Bab.* 175.
Lind. 150.

A. ARVENSIS. *Corn Chamomile.* **Fig. 749.**
Stem erect. Leaves bipinnatifid, with linear-lanceolate segments.
Receptacle conical. Corn-fields. 1 ft. Bienn. July. White. ($\frac{2}{3}$) *E. B.*
1. 602. *E. B.* 2. 1179. *H. & Arn.* 254. *Bab.* 174. *Lind.* 150.

A. COTULA. *Stinking Chamomile.* **Fig. 750.**
Stem erect, branched. Leaves bipinnatifid, smooth. Receptacle
conical. A common weed. 6 in.–1 ft. Ann. July and Aug. White.
($\frac{2}{3}$) *E. B.* 1. 1772. *E. B.* 2. 1180. *H. & Arn.* 254. *Bab.* 174.
Lind. 150.

Fig. 741 to 760.

741 742 743 744
745 746 747 748
749 750 751 752
753 754 755 756
757 758 759 760

1, April, 1859.

J. E. Sowerby, Fecit.

38

A. TINCTORIA. *Ox-eye Chamomile.* **Fig. 751.**
Stem erect, corymbose, cottony. Leaves bipinnatifid, with serrated segments, downy beneath. Dry fields; rare. 1–1½ ft. Bienn.? July and Aug. Yellow. (⅔) *E. B.* 1. 1472. *E. B.* 2. 1181. *H. & Arn.* 254. *Bab.* 174. *Lind.* 150.

Genus 49. ACHILLEA.

A. PTARMICA. *Sneeze-wort. Goose-wort.* **Fig. 752.**
Leaves linear-lanceolate, minutely serrated. Corymbs flat. Moist pastures. 1–2 ft. Perenn. July and Aug. White. (⅔) *E. B.* 1. 757. *E. B.* 2. 1182. *H. & Arn.* 254. *Bab.* 175. *Lind.* 151.

A. SERRATA. **Fig. 753.**
Leaves linear-lanceolate, downy, deeply serrated. Corymbs nearly simple. Near Matlock, Derby. 1 ft. Perenn. Aug. Pale yellow. (⅔) *E. B.* 1. 2531. *E. B.* 2. 1183. *H. & Arn.* 255. *Bab.* 175. *Lind.* 151.

A. MILLEFOLIUM. *Yarrow. Milfoil.* **Fig. 754.**
Stems furrowed. Leaves bipinnatifid, hairy; segments linear. Pastures and way-sides; very common. 1–2 ft. Perenn. June–Aug. White. (⅔) *E. B.* 1. 758. *E. B.* 2. 1184. *H. & Arn.* 255. *Bab.* 176. *Lind.* 151.

A. TOMENTOSA. *Golden Milfoil.* **Fig. 755.**
Leaves woolly, pinnatifid; segments linear. Dry hill-pastures; not common. 6–8 in. Perenn. May–Oct. Golden yellow. (⅔) *E. B.* 1. 2532. *E. B.* 2. 1185. *H. & Arn.* 255. *Bab.* 175. *Lind.* 151.

Genus 50. CENTAUREA.

C. JACEA. *Brown Knapweed.* **Fig. 756.**
Leaves linear-lanceolate; those of the root broader. Scales of involucrum pinnatifid, dark brown. 2–3 ft. Perenn. Aug. and Sept. Bright purple. (⅔) *E. B.* 1. 1678. *E. B.* 2. 1186. *H. & Arn.* 234 *Bab.* 185. *Lind.* 155.

C. NIGRA. *Black Knapweed.* **Fig. 757.**
Lower leaves somewhat lyrate; upper ovate-lanceolate. Scales of involucrum pectinated, black. Pastures and way-sides; very common. 2–3 ft. Perenn. June–Sept. Purple. (⅔) *E. B.* 1. 278. *E. B.* 2. 1187. *H. & Arn.* 235. *Bab.* 186. *Lind.* 155.

C. CYANUS. *Corn-flower. Blue-bottle.* **Fig. 758.**
Leaves linear-lanceolate. Scales of involucrum serrated. Flowers radiant. Corn-fields; very common. 2–3 ft. Ann. July and Aug. Inner florets purple, outer brilliant blue. (⅔) *E. B.* 1. 277. *E. B.* 2. 1188. *H. & Arn.* 236. *Bab.* 186. *Lind.* 155.

C. SCABIOSA. *Great Knapweed.* **Fig. 759.**
Leaves pinnatifid, with lanceolate segments. Flowers radiant. Scales of involucrum ovate, rather downy. Corn-fields and pastures. 2–3 ft. Perenn. July and Aug. Purple. (⅔) *E. B.* 1. 56. *E. B.* 2. 1189. *H. & Arn.* 235. *Bab.* 186. *Lind.* 155.

C. ISNARDI. *Jersey Star-Thistle.* **Fig. 760.**
Leaves somewhat pinnatifid, the lobes spiny. Scales of involucrum with palmated spines. Channel Islands. 1 ft. Perenn. July and Aug. Pale purple. (⅔) *E. B.* 1. 2256. *E. B.* 2. 1190. *H. & Arn.* 237. *Bab.* 187. *Lind.* 155.

C. Calcitrapa. *Common Star-Thistle.* **Fig. 761.**
Heads lateral, sessile. Scales of involucrum lengthened into long spines. Waste places; local. 1–2 ft. Ann. July–Sept. Pale purple. ($\frac{2}{3}$) *E. B.* 1. 125. *E. B.* 2. 1191. *H. & Arn.* 236. *Bab.* 187. *Lind.* 155.

C. solstitialis. *Yellow Star-Thistle.* **Fig. 762.**
Leaves lanceolate, not spiny. Flowers terminal. Scales of involucrum spiny. Waste places. 2 ft. Ann. June–Oct. Yellow. ($\frac{2}{3}$) *E. B.* 1. 243. *E. B.* 2. 1192. *H. & Arn.* 236. *Bab.* 187. *Lind.* 155.

Genus 51. Xanthium.

X. strumarium. *Bur-weed.* **Fig. 763.**
Monœcious. Leaves 3-lobed at the base, angular, and toothed. Fruit covered with hooked spines. Waste ground; scarcely wild. 1–2 ft. Ann. Aug. and Sept. Greenish. ($\frac{2}{3}$) *E. B.* 1. 2544. *E. B.* 2. 1310. *H. & Arn.* 256. *Bab.* 208. *Lind.* 151.

Order XLVI. CAMPANULACEÆ.

Genus 1. Campanula.

C. rotundifolia. *Blue-bell. Hair-bell.* **Fig. 764.**
Stem slender. Root-leaves roundish heart-shaped; stem-leaves linear. Heaths; abundant. 8 in.–2 ft. Perenn. July–Sept. Blue. ($\frac{2}{3}$) *E. B.* 1. 866. *E. B.* 2. 296. *H. & Arn.* 258. *Bab.* 210. *Lind.* 136.

C. patula. *Spreading Bell-flower.* **Fig. 765.**
Root-leaves oval; others lanceolate. Corolla spreading. Segments of the calyx toothed. Woods. 1 ft. Bienn. July. Purplish blue. ($\frac{2}{3}$) *E. B.* 1. 42. *E. B.* 2. 297. *H. & Arn.* 257. *Bab.* 211. *Lind.* 136.

C. Rapunculus. *Rampion Bell-flower.* **Fig. 766.**
Leaves elliptic-lanceolate. Panicle erect. Segments of calyx entire. Banks and fields. 3 ft. Bienn. July and Aug. Pale blue. ($\frac{2}{3}$) *E. B.* 1. 283. *E. B.* 2. 298. *H. & Arn.* 257. *Bab.* 211. *Lind.* 136.

C. persicifolia. *Peach-leaved Bell-flower.* **Fig. 767.**
Root-leaves oblong, stalked; upper linear-lanceolate, sessile. Corolla spreading. Calyx-segments entire. Woods; very rare. 2 ft. Perenn. July. Blue. ($\frac{2}{3}$) *E. B. Supp.* 2773. *E. B.* 2. 298*. *H. & Arn.* 257. *Bab.* 210. *Lind.* 136.

C. latifolia. *Giant Bell-flower.* **Fig. 768.**
Leaves ovate-lanceolate. Racemes erect. Shady places. 3–4 ft. Perenn. Aug. Blue, pink, or white. ($\frac{2}{3}$) *E. B.* 1. 302. *E. B.* 2. 299. *H. & Arn.* 258. *Bab.* 210. *Lind.* 136.

C. rapunculoides. *Creeping Bell-flower.* **Fig. 769.**
Root-leaves heart-shaped, on foot-stalks; upper lanceolate. Flowers drooping to one side. Calyx reflexed. Northern corn-fields. 1 ft. Perenn. July and Aug. Pale blue. ($\frac{2}{3}$) *E. B.* 1. 1369. *E. B.* 2. 300. *H. & Arn.* 258. *Bab.* 210. *Lind.* 136.

C. Trachelium. *Nettle-leaved Bell-flower.* **Fig. 770.**
Leaves cordate, on foot-stalks, serrated. Flower-stalks axillary, with 1–3 flowers. Woods and hedges; common. 2–3 ft. Perenn. July and Aug. Deep blue. ($\frac{2}{3}$) *E. B.* 1. 12 *E. B.* 2. 301. *H. & Arn.* 258. *Bab.* 210. *Lind.* 136.

C. GLOMERATA. *Clustered Bell-flower.* **Fig. 771.**
Leaves ovate, crenated. Flowers sessile, in a terminal cluster.
Chalky pastures. 6 in.–1 ft. Perenn. July and Aug. Purple-blue.
($\frac{2}{3}$) *E. B.* 1. 90. *E. B.* 2. 302. *H. & Arn.* 258. *Bab.* 209. *Lind.* 136.

C. HEDERACEA. *Ivy-leaved Bell-flower.* **Fig. 772.**
Trailing; stem very slender. Leaves heart-shaped, angular. Bogs.
4 in. Perenn. June–Aug. Blue. ($\frac{2}{3}$) *E. B.* 1. 73. *E. B.* 2. 303.
H. & Arn. 259. *Bab.* 211. *Lind.* 136.

C. HYBRIDA. *Corn Bell-flower.* **Fig. 773.**
Leaves oblong, crenated. Corolla shorter than the calyx. Corn-
fields. 6–9 in. Ann. Aug. Purplish. ($\frac{2}{3}$) *E. B.* 1. 375. *E. B.* 2.
304. *H. & Arn.* 259. *Bab.* 211. *Lind.* 135.

Genus 2. PHYTEUMA.

P. ORBICULARE. *Rampion.* **Fig. 774.**
Flowers in a round head. Lower leaves heart-shaped, on long
petioles. Chalk-hills; local. 1 ft. Perenn. Aug. Purple. ($\frac{2}{3}$)
E. B. 1. 142. *E. B.* 2. 305. *H. & Arn.* 259. *Bab.* 209. *Lind.* 135.

P. SPICATUM. *Spiked Rampion.* **Fig. 775.**
Flowers in a cylindrical spike. Lower leaves ovate-heart-shaped.
Hedges; rare. 3 ft. Perenn. Aug. Cream-colour. ($\frac{2}{3}$) *E. B.*
Supp. 2598. *E. B.* 2. 305*. *H. & Arn.* 259. *Bab.* 209. *Lind.* 135.

Genus 3. JASIONE.

J. MONTANA. *Sheep's Scabious.* **Fig. 776.**
Flowers in round heads, with a circle of ovate bracts beneath. Dry
pastures; common. 6 in.–1 ft. Ann. June and July. Blue. ($\frac{2}{3}$)
E. B. 1. 882. *E. B.* 2. 306. *H. & Arn.* 260. *Bab.* 209.

ORDER XLVII. LOBELIACEÆ.

Genus 1. LOBELIA.

L. DORTMANNA. *Water Lobelia.* **Fig. 777.**
Leaves nearly cylindrical, composed of 2 tubes. Flowers rise above
the water. Alpine lakes. Perenn. July. Light blue. ($\frac{2}{3}$) *E. B.* 1.
140. *E. B.* 2. 307. *H. & Arn.* 261. *Bab.* 209. *Lind.* 137.

L. URENS. *Acrid Lobelia.* **Fig. 778.**
Lower leaves obovate, on foot-stalks. Flowers in a terminal raceme.
Heaths in Devonshire. 1 ft. Perenn. Sept. Light blue. ($\frac{2}{3}$) *E. B.* 1.
953. *E. B.* 2. 308. *H. & Arn.* 261. *Bab.* 209. *Lind.* 137.

ORDER XLVIII. VACCINIACEÆ.

Genus 1. VACCINIUM.

V. MYRTILLUS. *Bilberry. Whortle-berry.* **Fig. 779.**
Shrubby. Peduncles solitary, 1-flowered. Leaves ovate, serrated.
Heaths; common. Fruit edible. 1–2 ft. May. Pink; berries black.
($\frac{2}{3}$) *E. B.* 1. 456. *E. B.* 2. 551. *H. & Arn.* 261. *Bab.* 216. *Lind.* 134.

V. ULIGINOSUM. *Bog Whortle-berry.* **Fig. 780.**
Shrubby. Peduncles in clusters, 1-flowered. Leaves obovate, entire. Northern bogs. 1 ft. May. Pink; berries black. ($\frac{2}{3}$) *E. B.* 1.
581. *E. B.* 2. 552. *H. & Arn.* 262. *Bab.* 216. *Lind.* 134.

Fig. 761 to 780.

1. April 1859.

J.E. Sowerby, Fecit.

39

V. Vitis Idæa. *Cow-berry.*   **Fig. 781.**
Shrubby. Leaves obovate, evergreen, glossy, dotted beneath. Flowers in terminal racemes. Dry heaths. 4–9 in. May. Pink; fruit red. ($\frac{2}{3}$) *E. B.* 1. 598. *E. B.* 2. 553. *H. & Arn.* 262. *Bab.* 216. *Lind.* 134.

Genus 2. Oxycoccus.

O. palustris. *Cranberry.*   **Fig. 782.**
A slender trailing shrub. Peduncles 1-flowered, terminal. Leaves ovate, evergreen. Bogs. Fruit edible. 2–4 in. June. Pink; berries red. ($\frac{2}{3}$) *E. B.* 1. 319. *E. B.* 2. 554. *H. & Arn.* 262. *Bab.* 84. *Lind.* 134.

Order XLIX. ERICACEÆ.

Genus 1. Erica.

E. Tetralix. *Cross-leaved Heath.*   **Fig. 783.**
A shrub. Leaves 4 in a whorl, ciliated. Corolla ovate, as long as the style. Flowers in round tufts. Heaths; common. 6 in.–1 ft. July–Sept. Pink. ($\frac{2}{3}$) *E. B.* 1. 1014. *E. B.* 2. 557. *H. & Arn.* 265. *Bab.* 214. *Lind.* 174.

E. cinerea. *Common Heath.*   **Fig. 784.**
A shrub. Leaves 3 in a whorl. Corolla ovate, shorter than the style. Flowers in racemes. Heaths; abundant. 6 in.–2 ft. July– Oct. Purple-red. ($\frac{2}{3}$) *E. B.* 1. 1015. *E. B.* 2. 558. *H. & Arn.* 266. *Bab.* 214. *Lind.* 174.

E. mediterranea. *Mediterranean Heath.*   **Fig. 785.**
A shrub. Branches upright. Leaves 4 in a whorl. Flowers axillary. West of Ireland. 1–4 ft. April. Pink; anthers brown. ($\frac{2}{3}$) *E. B. Supp.* 2774. *E. B.* 2. 558*. *H. & Arn.* 266. *Bab.* 215. *Lind.* 330.

E. vagans. *Cornish Heath.*   **Fig. 786.**
A shrub. Corolla bell-shaped. Flowers in the middle of the shoots. Cornwall. 1–2 ft. July and Aug. Pink. ($\frac{2}{3}$) *E. B.* 1. 3. *E. B.* 2. 559. *H. & Arn.* 266. *Bab.* 215. *Lind.* 174.

E. ciliaris. *Fringe-leaved Heath.*   **Fig. 787.**
A shrub. Flowers in terminal one-sided racemes. Leaves fringed with hairs. Cornwall. 1 ft. July and Aug. Deep pink. ($\frac{2}{3}$) *E. B. Supp.* 2618. *E. B.* 2. 559*. *H. & Arn.* 265. *Bab.* 215. *Lind.* 174.

Genus 2. Calluna.

C. vulgaris. *Ling. Heather.*   **Fig. 788.**
A shrub. Leaves imbricated in 4 rows. Heaths; abundant. 6 in.– 4 ft. June–Oct. Pink. ($\frac{2}{3}$) *E. B.* 1. 1013. *E. B.* 2. 560. *H. & Arn.* 267. *Bab.* 214. *Lind.* 173.

Genus 3. Menziesia.

M. cærulea.   **Fig. 789.**
A shrub. Leaves scattered, linear. Flowers 5-cleft. Highland moors. 6 in.–1 ft. June and July. Bluish purple. ($\frac{2}{3}$) *E. B.* 1. 2469. *E. B.* 2. 555. *H. & Arn.* 267. *Bab.* 215. *Lind.* 173.

M. polifolia. *St. Dabeoc's Heath.*   **Fig. 790.**
A shrub. Leaves ovate, white beneath. Flowers 4-cleft. West of Ireland. 1 ft. July–Sept. Deep pink. ($\frac{2}{3}$) *E. B.* 1. 35. *E. B.* 2. 556. *H. & Arn.* 267. *Bab.* 215. *Lind.* 173.

Fig. 781 to 800.

1 April 1859.

J.E. Sowerby, Fec.

Genus 4. AZALEA.

A. PROCUMBENS.   **Fig. 791.**
A small, procumbent, Heath-like shrub. Flowers in terminal clusters. Mountains. 2–4 in. July. Pink. ($\frac{2}{3}$) *E. B.* 1. 865. *E. B.* 2. 289. *H. & Arn.* 267. *Bab.* 216. *Lind.* 172.

Genus 5. ANDROMEDA.

A. POLIFOLIA. *Marsh Cistus.*   **Fig. 792.**
A shrub. Leaves alternate, lanceolate, revolute, glaucous beneath. Flowers in terminal clusters. Bogs. 1 ft. June. Pink. ($\frac{2}{3}$) *E. B.* 1. 713. *E. B.* 2. 586. *H. & Arn.* 268. *Bab.* 213. *Lind.* 173.

Genus 6. ARBUTUS.

A. UNEDO. *Strawberry-tree.*   **Fig. 793.**
A tree or large bush. Leaves smooth, serrated. Panicles terminal. South of Ireland. Sept. and Oct. Pinkish; berries red. ($\frac{2}{3}$) *E. B.* 1. 2377. *E. B.* 2. 587. *H. & Arn.* 268. *Bab.* 213. *Lind.* 174.

Genus 7. ARCTOSTAPHYLOS.

A. ALPINA. *Black Bear-berry.*   **Fig. 794.**
Stems procumbent. Leaves wrinkled, serrated, deciduous. **Dry mountain heaths.** 4–6 in. Perenn. May. Pinkish; berries black. ($\frac{2}{3}$) *E. B.* 1. 2030. *E. B.* 2. 588. *H. & Arn.* 269. *Bab.* 213. *Lind.* 174.

A. UVA-URSI. *Red Bear-berry.*   **Fig. 795.**
Evergreen. Stems procumbent. Leaves obovate, entire, revolute at the margin. Stony heaths. Astringent. 4–6 in. Perenn. May. Pink; berries red. ($\frac{2}{3}$) *E. B.* 1. 714. *E. B.* 2. 589. *H. & Arn.* 269. *Bab.* 213. *Lind.* 174.

Order L. PYROLACEÆ.

Genus 1. PYROLA.

P. ROTUNDIFOLIA. *Round-leaved Winter-green.*   **Fig. 796.**
Stamens ascending; style twice as long, declining. Leaves roundish. Moist woods; rare. 10 in. Perenn. July and Aug. White. ($\frac{2}{3}$) *E. B.* 1. 213. *E. B.* 2. 581. *H. & Arn.* 270. *Bab.* 217. *Lind.* 175.

P. MEDIA. *Winter-green.*   **Fig. 797.**
Stamens inflexed, shorter than the style. Calyx shorter than the stamens. Moist woods. 6–8 in. Perenn. July. White. ($\frac{2}{3}$) *E. B.* 1. 1945. *E. B.* 2. 582. *H. & Arn.* 270. *Bab.* 217. *Lind.* 175.

P. MINOR. *Lesser Winter-green.*   **Fig. 798.**
Stamens equal to the style. Stigma with 5 divergent rays. Moist alpine woods. 6–10 in. Perenn. July. Pink. ($\frac{2}{3}$) *E. B.* 1. 2543. *E. B.* 2. 583. *H. & Arn.* 271. *Bab.* 217. *Lind.* 175.

P. SECUNDA. *Serrated Winter-green.*   **Fig. 799.**
Leaves ovate-lanceolate, serrated. Racemes one-sided. Fir woods in Scotland. 6–8 in. July. Greenish white. ($\frac{2}{3}$) *E. B.* 1. 517. *E. B.* 2. 584. *H. & Arn.* 270. *Bab.* 217. *Lind.* 175.

P. UNIFLORA. *Single-flowered Winter-green.*   **Fig. 800.**
Stem bearing a solitary flower. Leaves orbicular. Moist alpine woods. 4–6 in. Perenn. July. White. ($\frac{2}{3}$) *E. B.* 1. 146. *E. B.* 2. 585. *H. & Arn.* 270. *Bab.* 217. *Lind.* 175.

Order LI. MONOTROPACEÆ.
Genus 1. MONOTROPA.

M. HYPOPITYS. *Yellow Bird's-nest.* **Fig. 801.**

A brownish parasitic plant, without leaves. Flowers in an erect raceme, drooping at the top. Roots of beech and fir trees. 6–9 in. Perenn. June and July. Dull yellow. ($\frac{2}{3}$) *E. B.* 1. 69. *E. B.* 2. 580. *H. & Arn.* 271. *Bab.* 218. *Lind.* 176.

Order LII. AQUIFOLIACEÆ.
Genus 1. ILEX.

I. AQUIFOLIUM. *Holly.* **Fig. 802.**

A small bushy evergreen tree. Lower leaves waved, with spiny teeth; upper entire, ovate. Woods and thickets. 6–20 ft. May. White; berries scarlet. ($\frac{2}{3}$) *E. B.* 1. 496. *E. B.* 2. 235. *H. & Arn.* 272. *Bab.* 218. *Lind.* 176.

Order LIII. OLEACEÆ.
Genus 1. LIGUSTRUM.

L. VULGARE. *Privet.* **Fig. 803.**

A shrub. Leaves elliptic-lanceolate, nearly evergreen. Hedges and thickets. 4–8 ft. June. White. ($\frac{2}{3}$) *E. B.* 1. 764. *E. B.* 2. 5. *H. & Arn.* 273. *Bab.* 219. *Lind.* 171.

Genus 2. FRAXINUS.

F. EXCELSIOR. *Ash.* **Fig. 804.**

A tree. Leaves pinnate, serrated. Flowers without calyx or corolla. Woods and hedgerows; common. April. ($\frac{2}{3}$) *E. B.* 1. 1692. *E. B.* 2. 6. *H. & Arn.* 273. *Bab.* 219. *Lind.* 171.

F. HETEROPHYLLA. *Simple-leaved Ash.* **Fig. 805.**

Most of the leaves simple, ovate-lanceolate. A variety of *excelsior*. ($\frac{2}{3}$) *E. B.* 1. 2476. *E. B.* 2. 6*. *H. & Arn.* 276. *Bab.* 219. *Lind.* 171.

Order LIV. APOCYNACEÆ.
Genus 1. VINCA.

V. MINOR. *Lesser Periwinkle.* **Fig. 806.**

Stems procumbent. Leaves elliptic-lanceolate; evergreen. Thickets; not common. 4–6 in. Perenn. April–July. Blue. ($\frac{2}{3}$) *E. B.* 1. 917. *E. B.* 2. 293. *H. & Arn.* 274. *Bab.* 219. *Lind.* 176.

V. MAJOR. *Greater Periwinkle.* **Fig. 807.**

Stems erect at first, trailing when long. Leaves ovate, large; evergreen usually. Hedges. May and June. Purplish blue. ($\frac{2}{3}$) *E. B.* 1. 514. *E. B.* 2. 295. *H. & Arn.* 274. *Bab.* 219. *Lind.* 176.

Order LV. GENTIANACEÆ.
Genus 1. EXACUM.

E. FILIFORME. *Gentianella.* **Fig. 808.**

Stem filiform, branched. Leaves sessile. Flowers on long foot-stalks. Bogs; local. 4–6 in. Ann. July. Yellow. ($\frac{2}{3}$) *E. B.* 1. 235. *E. B.* 2. 219. *H. & Arn.* 275. *Bab.* 222. *Lind.* 176.

Genus 2. ERYTHRÆA.

E. CENTAURIUM. *Centaury.* **Fig. 809.**

Stem elongated, little branched. Leaves ovate-lanceolate, 3-ribbed. Calyx half as long as the tube of the corolla. Dry pastures; common. 6 in.–1 ft. Ann. June–Sept. Pink. ($\frac{2}{3}$) *E. B.* 1. 417. *E. B.* 2. 320. *H. & Arn.* 221. *Bab.* 276. *Lind.* 177.

E. LITTORALIS. *Tufted Centaury.* **Fig. 810.**

Stem simple. Leaves linear-obovate, 3-ribbed, tufted. Flowers nearly sessile. Sea-coast. 2–4 in. Ann. July. Pink. ($\frac{2}{3}$) *E. B.* 1. 2305. *E. B.* 2. 321. *H. & Arn.* 221. *Bab.* 221. *Lind.* 178.

E. LATIFOLIA. *Broad-leaved Centaury.* **Fig. 811.**
Stem branched, very short. Flowers in a dense tuft. Leaves broad, elliptical, with 5 or 7 ribs. A variety of *Centaurium?* Sea-coast; local. 1–3 in. Ann. July. Pink. ($\frac{2}{3}$) *E. B. Supp.* 2719. *E. B.* 2. 321*. *H. & Arn.* 276. *Bab.* 221. *Lind.* 178.

E. PULCHELLA. *Dwarf Centaury.* **Fig. 812.**
Stem branched, short. Leaves ovate, with 3 or 5 ribs. A variety of *Centaurium.* Dry places. 2–4 in. Ann. Sept. Pink. ($\frac{2}{3}$) *E. B.* 1. 458. *E. B.* 2. 322. *H. & Arn.* 276. *Bab.* 221. *Lind.* 178.

Genus 3. GENTIANA.

G. PNEUMONANTHE. *Marsh Gentian. Calathian Violet.* **Fig. 813.**
Leaves nearly linear. Flowers 2 or more together, on short stalks. Wet heaths; local. 4–8 in. Perenn. Aug. Deep blue with greenish streaks. ($\frac{2}{3}$) *E. B.* 1. 20. *E. B.* 2. 373. *H. & Arn.* 277. *Bab.* 223. *Lind.* 178.

G. ACAULIS. *Dwarf Gentian.* **Fig. 814.**
Leaves oblong-lanceolate. Flowers large, solitary, bell-shaped, as long as the stem. Near Haverfordwest; not native. 4–6 in. Perenn. May–July. Deep blue. ($\frac{1}{2}$) *E. B.* 1. 1594. *E. B.* 2. 374. *Lind.* 178.

G. VERNA. *Spring Gentian.* **Fig. 815.**
Leaves ovate, clustered. Flowers solitary; corolla salver-shaped, with rounded lobes. Mountains; rare. 2–3 in. Perenn. April. Bright blue. ($\frac{1}{2}$) *E. B.* 1. 493. *E. B.* 2. 375. *H. & Arn.* 277. *Bab.* 222. *Lind.* 178.

G. NIVALIS. *Small Alpine Gentian.* **Fig. 816.**
Leaves elliptical. Flowers several; corolla funnel-shaped; the segments with small bifid lobes at the base. Mountain tops; rare. 1–3 in. Ann. July and Aug. Blue. ($\frac{2}{3}$) *E. B.* 1. 896. *E. B.* 2. 376. *H. & Arn.* 277. *Bab.* 222. *Lind.* 178.

G. AMARELLA. *Autumn Gentian.* **Fig. 817.**
Stem much branched. Corolla 5-cleft. Segments of the calyx equal. Limestone pastures. 4–6 in. Ann. or bienn. Aug. and Sept. Purplish blue. ($\frac{2}{3}$) *E. B.* 1. 236. *E. B.* 2. 377. *H. & Arn.* 277. *Bab.* 222. *Lind.* 179.

G. CAMPESTRIS. *Field Gentian.* **Fig. 818.**
Stem branched. Corolla 4-cleft. Outer segments of the calyx very large. Hill-pastures; common on the chalk. 2–6 in. Ann. Aug. and Sept. Purple. ($\frac{2}{3}$) *E. B.* 1. 237. *E. B.* 2. 378. *H. & Arn.* 278. *Bab.* 278. *Lind.* 178.

Genus 4. CHLORA.

C. PERFOLIATA. *Yellow-wort.* **Fig. 819.**
Leaves ovate, glaucous, perfoliate. Chalky hills; common. 3 in.–1 ft. Ann. July–Sept. Bright yellow. ($\frac{2}{3}$) *E. B.* 1. 60. *E. B.* 2. 561. *H. & Arn.* 278. *Bab.* 221. *Lind.* 179.

Genus 5. MENYANTHES.

M. TRIFOLIATA. *Bog-bean. Marsh Trefoil.* **Fig. 820.**
Leaves ternate, the stalks sheathing the stem. Petals fringed with filaments within. Bogs. Bitter and sudorific. 8 in. Perenn. June. White tipped with pink. ($\frac{2}{3}$) *E. B.* 1. 494. *E. B.* 2. 280. *H. & Arn.* 278. *Bab.* 223. *Lind.* 179.

Fig. 801. to 820.

1. April 1859

J.E.Sowerby. Fec.

4

Genus 6. VILLARSIA.

V. NYMPHÆOIDES. *Fringed Water-lily.*   **Fig. 821.**
Leaves floating, heart-shaped. Petals fringed. Pools and slow rivers.
Perenn. Aug. Yellow. ($\frac{2}{3}$) *E. B.* 1. 217. *E. B.* 2. 281. *H. & Arn.*
279. *Bab.* 223. *Lind.* 180.

Genus 7. SWERTIA.

S. PERENNIS. *Marsh Felwort.*   **Fig. 822.**
Flowers erect, corymbose. Root-leaves ovate. Mountain bogs; a
doubtful native. 8 in.–1 ft. Perenn. Aug. Blue. ($\frac{2}{3}$) *E.B.* 1. 1441.
E. B. 2. 372. *Lind.* 179.

ORDER LVI. POLEMONIACEÆ.
Genus 1. POLEMONIUM.

P. CÆRULEUM. *Jacob's Ladder.*   **Fig. 823.**
Leaves pinnate. Calyx longer than the tube of the corolla. Bushy
places; rare. 1 ft. Perenn. May and June. Pale blue or white.
($\frac{2}{3}$) *E. B.* 1. 14. *E. B.* 2. 295. *H. & Arn.* 279. *Bab.* 224. *Lind.* 168.

ORDER LVII. CONVOLVULACEÆ.
Genus 1. CONVOLVULUS.

C. ARVENSIS. *Small Bind-weed.*   **Fig. 824.**
Stem climbing or trailing. Leaves arrow-shaped. Bracts minute.
Hedge-banks; abundant. Perenn. June and July. Pink. ($\frac{1}{2}$)
E. B. 1. 312. *E. B.* 2. 290. *H. & Arn.* 280. *Bab.* 224. *Lind.* 167.

C. SEPIUM. *Great Bind-weed.*   **Fig. 825.**
Stem climbing. Leaves arrow-shaped. Bracts very large, heart-
shaped, close. Hedges and ditch-banks; abundant. Perenn. July
and Aug. White. ($\frac{1}{2}$) *E. B.* 1. 313. *E. B.* 2. 291. *H. & Arn.* 281.
Bab. 224. *Lind.* 167.

C. SOLDANELLA. *Sea Bind-weed.*   **Fig. 826.**
Stem trailing. Leaves angular, kidney-shaped. Bracts large, ovate,
close. Sandy shores; local. Perenn. July. Rose-colour. ($\frac{1}{2}$) *E. B.* 1.
314. *E. B.* 2. 292. *H. & Arn.* 281. *Bab.* 225. *Lind.* 167.

Genus 2. CUSCUTA.

C. EUROPÆA. *Greater Dodder.*   **Fig. 827.**
A twining thread-like plant, without leaves. Segments of corolla
reflexed. Stamens without scales. Parasitic on thistles and other
plants. 2 ft. Ann. August. Reddish. ($\frac{2}{3}$) *E. B.* 1. 378. *E. B.* 2.
370. *H. & Arn.* 281. *Bab.* 225. *Lind.* 168.

C. EPITHYMUM. *Common Dodder.*   **Fig. 828.**
Twining, without leaves. Stamens with a fringed scale at the base.
Parasitic on Heath and Thyme; common. 4 in.–1 ft. Perenn. Aug.
Reddish. ($\frac{2}{3}$) *E. B.* 1. 55. *E. B.* 2. 371. *H. & Arn.* 282. *Bab.* 225.
Lind. 168.

C. EPILINUM. *Flax Dodder.*   **Fig. 829.**
Flower-heads on short peduncles, with a broad ovate bract. Corolla-
segments erect. A variety of *europæa?* 2 ft. Ann. Aug. Reddish.
($\frac{2}{3}$) *E. B. Supp.* 2850. *H. & Arn.* 282. *Bab.* 225. *Lind.* 329.

ORDER LVIII. BORAGINACEÆ.
Genus 1. ECHIUM.

E. VULGARE. *Viper-grass.*   **Fig. 830.**
Leaves lanceolate. Plant covered with stiff prickly hairs. Flowers
in short lateral spikes. Dry fields. 1–1½ ft. Bienn. June–Aug. Blue.
($\frac{2}{3}$) *E. B.* 1. 181. *E. B.* 2. 274. *H. & Arn.* 283. *Bab.* 229. *Lind.* 163.

Fig. 821 to 840

1 May 1889

J.E. Sowerby. Fecit.

42

E. VIOLACEUM. *Purple Viper-grass.* **Fig. 831.**
Leaves ovate-oblong; upper ones oblong-cordate. Flowers in elongated lateral spikes. Sandy fields, Jersey. 1–1½ ft. Bienn. July. Purple-blue. (⅔) *E. B. Supp.* 2798. *H. & Arn.* 284. *Bab.* 229. *Lind.* 163.

Genus 2. PULMONARIA.

P. OFFICINALIS. *Lungwort.* **Fig. 832.**
Root-leaves ovate, generally spotted with white. Woods; rare. 6 in.–1 ft. Perenn. May. Purple. (⅔) *E. B.* 1. 118. *E. B.* 2. 267. *H. & Arn.* 284. *Bab.* 229. *Lind.* 163.

P. ANGUSTIFOLIA. *Narrow-leaved Lungwort.* **Fig. 833.**
Leaves lanceolate, sometimes spotted. Woods; rare. 1 ft. Perenn. May. Purple. (⅔) *E. B.* 1. 1628. *E. B.* 2. 268. *H. & Arn.* 284. *Bab.* 229. *Lind.* 164.

Genus 3. LITHOSPERMUM.

L. OFFICINALE. *Gromwell.* **Fig. 834.**
Leaves lanceolate, broad. Seeds polished, even. Fields and waste ground. 1–1½ ft. Perenn. June. Pale yellow. (⅔) *E. B.* 1. 134. *E. B.* 2. 259. *H. & Arn.* 285. *Bab.* 230. *Lind.* 16₁.

L. ARVENSE. *Corn Gromwell.* **Fig. 835.**
Leaves lanceolate, obtuse. Seeds rugged. Fields; common. 1 ft. Ann. May–July. White. (⅔) *E. B.* 1. 123. *E. B.* 2. 260. *H. & Arn.* 285. *Bab.* 230. *Lind.* 164.

L. PURPURO-CÆRULEUM. *Creeping Gromwell.* **Fig. 836.**
Barren stems prostrate. Corolla much longer than the calyx. Seeds nearly even. Fields; not common. 1½ ft. Perenn. June–Aug. Purple-blue. (⅔) *E. B.* 1. 117. *E. B.* 2. 261. *H. & Arn.* 285. *Bab.* 230. *Lind.* 164.

L. MARITIMUM. *Sea Gromwell.* **Fig. 837.**
Leaves ovate, fleshy, glaucous. Stems procumbent. Seeds keeled. Sandy coasts. 8 in.–1 ft. Perenn. May and June. Purple. (⅔) *E. B.* 1. 368. *E. B.* 2. 262. *H. & Arn.* 285. *Bab.* 230. *Lind.* 164.

Genus 4. MYOSOTIS.

M. PALUSTRIS. *Forget-me-not.* **Fig. 838.**
Leaves bright green, hairy. Limb of corolla longer than the tube. Style equal to the calyx. Calyx open when in fruit. Ditches; common. 1 ft. Perenn. June–Aug. Bright blue with yellow eye. (⅔) *E. B.* 1. 1973. *E. B.* 2. 255. *H. & Arn.* 286. *Bab.* 230. *Lind.* 165.

M. REPENS. *Creeping Forget-me-not.* **Fig. 839.**
Limb of corolla longer than the tube. Style shorter than the calyx. Calyx closed when in fruit. Moist peaty places. 8 in. Perenn. June and July. Blue. (⅔) *E. B. Supp.* 2703. *E. B.* 2. 255*. *H. & Arn.* 286. *Bab.* 231.

M. CÆSPITOSA. *Tufted Forget-me-not.* **Fig. 840.**
Limb of corolla equal to the tube. Style very short. Hairs on the stem adpressed. Watery places; common. 8 in. Ann.? July. Blue. (⅔) *E. B. Supp.* 2661. *E. B.* 2. 255**. *H. & Arn.* 286. *Bab.* 231. *Lind.* 165.

M. ALPESTRIS. *Alpine Forget-me-not.* **Fig. 841.**
Limb of corolla longer than the tube. Style $\frac{1}{2}$ as long as the calyx. Calyx open, very hairy. Root-leaves on long stalks. Mountains. 4 in.– 1 ft. Perenn. July and Aug. Bright blue with yellow eye. ($\frac{2}{3}$) *E. B.* 1. 2559. *E. B.* 2. 256. *H. & Arn.* 287. *Bab.* 231. *Lind.* 166.

M. SYLVATICA. *Wood Forget-me-not.* **Fig. 842.**
Limb of corolla longer than the tube. Style nearly as long as the calyx. Calyx closed when in fruit. Root-leaves on short stalks. Shady places. 1 ft. Perenn. July. Bright blue. ($\frac{2}{3}$) *E. B. Supp.* 2630. *E. B.* 2. 256*. *H. & Arn.* 287. *Bab.* 231. *Lind.* 166.

M. ARVENSIS. *Field Forget-me-not.* **Fig. 843.**
Limb of corolla as long as the tube, concave. Calyx closed. Style very short. Dry places; common. 4–8 in. Ann. May–Aug. Light blue. ($\frac{2}{3}$) *E. B. Supp.* 2629. *E. B.* 2. 256**. *H. & Arn.* 287. *Bab.* 231. *Lind.* 166.

M. COLLINA. *Early Forget-me-not.* **Fig. 844.**
Flowers very small. Calyx open, as long as the pedicels. Corolla-limb shorter than the tube. Dry fields and walls; common. 4–6 in. Ann. April–Aug. Blue. ($\frac{2}{3}$) *E. B.* 1. 2558. *E. B.* 2. 257. *H. & Arn.* 288. *Bab.* 232.

M. VERSICOLOR. *Changeable Forget-me-not.* **Fig. 845.**
Flowers very small. Calyx closed, longer than the pedicels. Limb of corolla shorter than the tube. Dry places. 2–6 in. Ann. May–July. Yellow; afterwards blue. ($\frac{2}{3}$) *E. B.* 1. 480. *E. B.* 2. 258. *H. & Arn.* 288. *Bab.* 232. *Lind.* 166.

Genus 5. ANCHUSA.

A. OFFICINALIS. *Alkanet.* **Fig. 846.**
Leaves oblong-lanceolate. Flowers in one-sided spikes. Waste ground; rare. 1–2 ft. Perenn. June and July. Purple. ($\frac{2}{3}$) *E. B.* 1. 662. *E. B.* 2. 263. *H. & Arn.* 288. *Bab.* 228. *Lind.* 165.

A. SEMPERVIRENS. *Evergreen Alkanet.* **Fig. 847.**
Leaves ovate. Flower-stalks axillary. Waste ground; local. 1 ft. Perenn. May and June. Deep blue. ($\frac{2}{3}$) *E. B.* 1. 45. *E. B.* 2. 264. *H. & Arn.* 289. *Bab.* 228. *Lind.* 165.

Genus 6. LYCOPSIS.

L. ARVENSIS. *Bugloss.* **Fig. 848.**
Leaves lanceolate, hairy. Calyx erect when in flower. Fields; common. 1 ft. Ann. June. Bright blue. ($\frac{2}{3}$) *E. B.* 1. 938. *E. B.* 2. 273. *H. & Arn.* 289. *Bab.* 229. *Lind.* 165.

Genus 7. SYMPHYTUM.

S. OFFICINALE. *Comfrey.* **Fig. 849.**
Leaves ovate-lanceolate. Stem winged. Watery places; common. 2–3 ft. Perenn. May–Sept. Yellowish; sometimes purple. ($\frac{2}{3}$) *E. B.* 1. 817. *E. B.* 2. 269. *H. & Arn.* 289. *Bab.* 229. *Lind.* 165.

S. TUBEROSUM. *Tuberous Comfrey.* **Fig. 850.**
Leaves ovate. Stem slightly winged. Root tuberous. Wet places; rare. 2 ft. Perenn. July and Aug. Yellowish. ($\frac{2}{3}$) *E. B.* 1. 1502. *E. B.* 2. 270. *H. & Arn.* 290. *Bab.* 229. *Lind.* 165.

Genus 8. Borago.

B. officinalis. *Common Borage.* **Fig. 851.**
Lower leaves obovate. Plant covered with prickly hairs. Waste ground.
6 in.–1 ft. Bienn. June–Aug. Bright light blue. ($\frac{2}{3}$) *E. B.* 1. 36.
E. B. 2. 271. *H. & Arn.* 290. *Bab.* 228. *Lind.* 164.

Genus 9. Asperugo.

A. procumbens. *Madwort.* **Fig. 852.**
Procumbent. Leaves lanceolate, bristly. Waste places; rare. 6 in.–
1 ft. Ann. June and July. Purple. ($\frac{2}{3}$) *E. B.* 1. 661. *E. B.* 2.
272. *H. & Arn.* 290. *Bab.* 227. *Lind.* 165.

Genus 10. Cynoglossum.

C. officinale. *Hound's-tongue.* **Fig. 853.**
Leaves lanceolate, broad, downy, sessile. Waste ground; common.
Narcotic. 2 ft. Bienn. July. Purplish red. ($\frac{2}{3}$) *E. B.* 1. 921.
E. B. 2. 265. *H. & Arn.* 291. *Bab.* 228. *Lind.* 166.

C. sylvaticum. *Green-leaved Hound's-tongue.* **Fig. 854.**
Leaves shining green, slightly hairy; lower ones on very long stalks.
Shady places. 2 ft. Bienn. June and July. Purple. ($\frac{2}{3}$) *E. B.*
1. 1642. *E. B.* 2. 266. *H. & Arn.* 291. *Bab.* 228. *Lind.* 166.

Order LIX. SOLANACEÆ.

Genus 1. Datura.

D. Stramonium. *Thorn-apple.* **Fig. 855.**
Leaves ovate, angular, and sinuated. Fruit spiny. Waste ground;
not native. Narcotic. 6 in.–2 ft. Ann. July–Sept. White. ($\frac{2}{3}$) *E. B.*
1. 1288. *E. B.* 2. 315. *H. & Arn.* 292. *Bab.* 234. *Lind.* 180.

Genus 2. Hyoscyamus.

H. niger. *Henbane.* **Fig. 856.**
Leaves downy, sinuated, stem-clasping. Flowers sessile. Waste
ground. Poisonous. 6 in.–1 ft. Ann. July. Dingy yellow with
purple veins. ($\frac{2}{3}$) *E. B.* 1. 591. *E. B.* 2. 316. *H. & Arn.* 292.
Bab. 233. *Lind.* 181.

Genus 3. Atropa.

A. Belladonna. *Dwale. Deadly Nightshade.* **Fig. 857.**
Stem herbaceous. Leaves ovate. Flowers solitary. Waste ground.
Very poisonous. 2–3 ft. Perenn. June. Dull purple; berries black.
($\frac{2}{3}$) *E. B.* 1. 592. *E. B.* 2. 317. *H. & Arn.* 293. *Bab.* 233. *Lind.* 182.

Genus 4. Solanum.

S. Dulcamara. *Woody Nightshade. Bittersweet.* **Fig. 858.**
A climbing shrub. Leaves heart-shaped. Flowers in drooping
clusters. Hedges; abundant. Poisonous. 2–6 ft. June–Aug. Bright
purple, stamens yellow; berries red. ($\frac{2}{3}$) *E. B.* 1. 565. *E. B.* 2. 318.
H. & Arn. 293. *Bab.* 233. *Lind.* 182.

S. nigrum. *Garden Nightshade.* **Fig. 859.**
Stem herbaceous. Leaves ovate, waved. Flower in drooping umbels.
A common weed. Narcotic. 4 in.–1 ft. Ann. June–Sept. White;
berries black. ($\frac{2}{3}$) *E. B.* 1. 566. *E. B.* 2. 319. *H. & Arn.* 293.
Bab. 233. *Lind.* 182.

Order LX. OROBANCHACEÆ.

Genus 1. Orobanche.

O. major. *Broom-rape.* **Fig. 860.**
Stem simple. Tube of corolla inflated; upper lip entire; lower in
3 equal segments. Stamens smooth. Roots of Broom and Furze. 1 ft.
May–July. Purplish brown. ($\frac{2}{3}$) *E. B.* 1. 421. *E. B.* 2. 885. *H.*
& Arn. 294. *Bab.* 234. *Lind.* 193.

Fig. 841 to 860.

841   842   843   844
845   846   847   848
849   850   851   852
853   854   855   856
857   858   859   860

1 July, 1859.

J. E. Sowerby, Fecit.

43

O. **CARYOPHYLLACEA.** *Clove-scented Broom-rape.* **Fig. 861.**
Stem simple. Corolla-tube inflated; upper lip emarginate. Stamens hairy. On the roots of *Galium.* 1 ft. July and Aug. Purple-brown. ($\frac{2}{3}$) *E. B. Supp.* 2. 639. *E. B.* 2. 885*. *H. & Arn.* 294. *Bab.* 235. *Lind.* 331.

O. **RUBRA.** *Red Broom-rape.* **Fig. 862.**
Stem simple. Upper lip of corolla cleft. Stamen fringed on one side. On Thyme. 6 in.–1 ft. July. Purplish red. ($\frac{2}{3}$) *E. B.* 1. 1786. *E. B.* 2. 888. *H. & Arn.* 295. *Bab.* 234. *Lind.* 194.

O. **ELATIOR.** *Tall Broom-rape.* **Fig. 863.**
Stem simple. Corolla funnel-shaped. Stamens downy. On *Centaurea* and other plants. 1–1½ ft. July and Aug. Yellowish brown. ($\frac{2}{3}$) *E. B.* 1. 568. *E. B.* 2. 886. *H. & Arn.* 295. *Bab.* 235. *Lind.* 194.

O. **MINOR.** *Lesser Broom-rape.* **Fig. 864.**
Stem simple. Corolla cylindrical; upper lip entire; lower with 3 curled segments. Stamens ciliated. On Clover. 5–8 in. July. Pale violet. ($\frac{2}{3}$) *E. B.* 1. 422. *E. B.* 2. 887. *H. & Arn.* 296. *Bab.* 236. *Lind.* 194.

O. **HEDERÆ.** *Ivy Broom-rape.* **Fig. 865.**
Stem simple. Tube of corolla curved; upper lip 2-lobed. On Ivy-roots. 6–8 in. June–Aug. Yellowish brown. ($\frac{2}{3}$) *E. B. Supp.* 2859. *H. & Arn.* 296. *Bab.* 235.

O. **CÆRULEA.** *Purple Broom-rape.* **Fig. 866.**
Stem simple. Flowers with 3 bracts. On *Artemisia.* 6–8 in. July. Purple. ($\frac{2}{3}$) *E. B.* 1. 423. *E. B.* 2. 889. *H. & Arn.* 297. *Bab.* 236. *Lind.* 194.

O. **RAMOSA.** *Branched Broom-rape.* **Fig. 867.**
Stem branched. Flowers with 3 bracts. On Hemp. 8–10 in. Aug. and Sept. Pale blue or yellowish. ($\frac{2}{3}$) *E. B.* 1. 184. *E. B.* 2. 890. *H. & Arn.* 297. *Bab.* 237. *Lind.* 194.

Genus 2. LATHRÆA.

L. **SQUAMARIA.** *Tooth-wort.* **Fig. 868.**
Stem simple. Flowers in one-sided pendulous racemes. Parasitic on tree-roots. 6–10 in. Perenn. April and May. Purple. ($\frac{2}{3}$) *E. B.* 1. 50. *E. B.* 2. 864. *H. & Arn.* 298. *Bab.* 237. *Lind.* 194.

ORDER LXI. SCROPHULARIACEÆ.

Genus 1. VERONICA.

V. **SPICATA.** *Spiked Speedwell.* **Fig. 869.**
Stem ascending. Flowers in terminal spikes. Leaves opposite, crenated, obtuse. Dry pastures. 8 in. Perenn. July and Aug. Blue. ($\frac{2}{3}$) *E. B.* 1. 2. *E. B.* 2. 8. *H. & Arn.* 299. *Bab.* 247. *Lind.* 188.

V. **HYBRIDA.** *Welsh Speedwell.* **Fig. 870.**
Leaves very broad, obtuse. A variety of *spicata.* Mountain-pastures. 6–8 in. Perenn. July and Aug. Blue. ($\frac{2}{3}$) *E. B.* 1. 673. *E. B.* 2. 9. *H. & Arn.* 299. *Bab.* 247. *Lind.* 188.

Fig. 861 to 880.

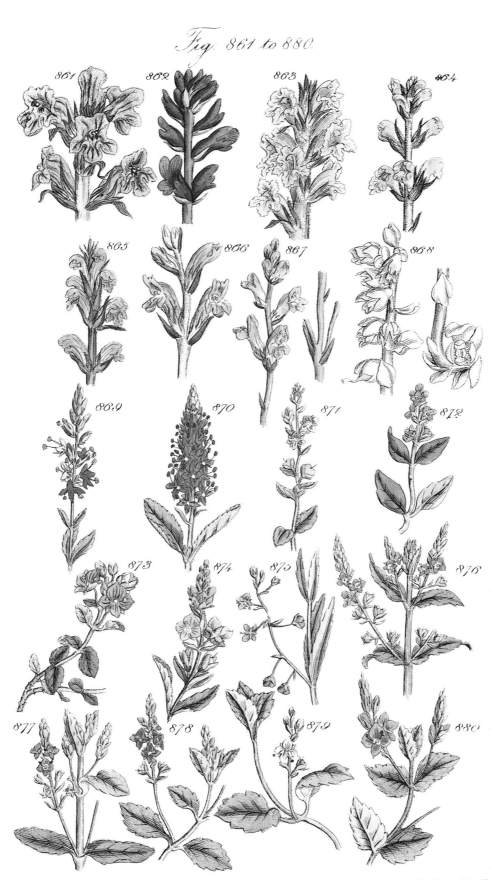

861 862 863 864
865 866 867 868
869 870 871 872
873 874 875 876
877 878 879 880

1 July. 1859.

J.E.Sowerby. Fecit

44

V. SERPYLLIFOLIA. *Thyme-leaved Speedwell.* **Fig. 871.**
Flowers in spiked racemes. Leaves ovate, 3-ribbed, smooth. Capsule shorter than the style. Pastures; abundant. 4–6 in. Perenn. June. Blue. ($\frac{2}{3}$) *E. B.* 1. 1075. *E. B.* 2. 13. *H. & Arn.* 299. *Bab.* 248. *Lind.* 188.

V. ALPINA. *Alpine Speedwell.* **Fig. 872.**
Racemes corymbose, few-flowered. Leaves elliptic-ovate. Calyx hairy. Mountains. 2–4 in. Perenn. July and Aug. Blue. ($\frac{2}{3}$) *E. B.* 1. 484. *E. B.* 2. 12. *H. & Arn.* 299. *Bab.* 248. *Lind.* 188.

V. SAXATILIS. *Blue Rock Speedwell.* **Fig. 873.**
Stems spreading. Corymb terminal, few-flowered. Leaves elliptical. Mountains. 2–4 in. Perenn. July. Light blue. ($\frac{2}{3}$) *E. B.* 1. 1027. *E. B.* 2. 11. *H. & Arn.* 247. *Bab.* 300. *Lind.* 188.

V. FRUTICULOSA. *Shrubby Speedwell.* **Fig. 874.**
Stems woody, branched at the base. Spike terminal, many-flowered. Highland mountains. 8–10 in. Perenn. July. Pink. ($\frac{2}{3}$) *E. B.* 1. 1028. *E. B.* 2. 10. *H. & Arn.* 300. *Bab.* 247. *Lind.* 188.

V. SCUTELLATA. *Marsh Speedwell.* **Fig. 875.**
Clusters lateral, alternate. Fruit-stalks reflexed. Leaves linear. Bogs. 8 in. Perenn. July and Aug. Pink. ($\frac{2}{3}$) *E. B.* 1. 782. *E. B.* 2. 15. *H. & Arn.* 300. *Bab.* 246. *Lind.* 188.

V. ANAGALLIS. *Water Speedwell.* **Fig. 876.**
Stems erect. Leaves lanceolate, serrated, glossy. Clusters lateral. Ditches. 6 in.–1 ft. Perenn. July. Blue. ($\frac{2}{3}$) *E. B.* 1. 781. *E. B.* 2. 14*. *H. & Arn.* 300. *Bab.* 246. *Lind.* 188.

V. BECCABUNGA. *Brooklime.* **Fig. 877.**
Stems creeping. Leaves oval, flat, glossy. Clusters lateral. Ditches; abundant. 6–8 in. Perenn. June and July. Blue. ($\frac{2}{3}$) *E. B.* 1. 655. *E. B.* 2. 14. *H. & Arn.* 300. *Bab.* 246. *Lind.* 188.

V. OFFICINALIS. *Common Speedwell.* **Fig. 878.**
Stem procumbent. Leaves elliptical, serrated, rough. Clusters lateral, spiked. Flower-stalks shorter than their bracts. Dry places; common. 4–6 in. Perenn. May–Aug. Blue. ($\frac{2}{3}$) *E. B.* 1. 765. *E. B.* 2. 16. *H. & Arn.* 301. *Bab.* 247. *Lind.* 189.

V. MONTANA. *Mountain Speedwell.* **Fig. 879.**
Stem procumbent, hairy. Clusters lateral, few-flowered. Leaves ovate, serrated. Shady woods; not common. 4–6 in. Perenn. May–July. Pale blue ($\frac{2}{3}$) *E. B.* 1. 766. *E. B.* 2. 18. *H. & Arn.* 301. *Bab.* 247. *Lind.* 189.

V. CHAMÆDRYS. *Germander Speedwell.* **Fig. 880.**
Stem trailing, with a line of hairs on each side. Leaves ovate, sessile, rough, serrated. Clusters lateral. Banks; abundant. 4 in. Perenn. May and June. Bright blue ($\frac{2}{3}$) *E. B.* 1. 623. *E. B.* 2. 17. *H. & Arn.* 306. *Bab.* 247. *Lind.* 189.

V. HIRSUTA. *Hairy Speedwell.*   **Fig. 881.**
Stem procumbent, hairy. Leaves ovate-lanceolate. Capsule ovate, entire. A variety of *officinalis?* Heaths in Ayrshire. 2–4 in. Perenn. June. Blue. ($\frac{2}{3}$) *E. B. Supp.* 2673. *H. & Arn.* 301. *Bab.* 247. *Lind.* 189.

V. HEDERIFOLIA. *Ivy-leaved Speedwell.*   **Fig. 882.**
Stem procumbent. Leaves 5-lobed. Flowers solitary. A common weed. 2–5 in. Ann. April–Aug. Pale blue. ($\frac{2}{3}$) *E. B.* 1. 784. *E. B.* 2. 21. *H. & Arn.* 301. *Bab.* 249. *Lind.* 189.

V. AGRESTIS. *Germander Chickweed.*   **Fig. 883.**
Stem procumbent. Leaves stalked, ovate, crenated. Sepals oblong, blunt. Plant pale green. A common weed. 2–6 in. Ann. April–Sept. Pale blue. ($\frac{2}{3}$) *E. B. Supp.* 2603. *E. B.* 2. 18*. *H. & Arn.* 302. *Bab.* 249. *Lind.* 189.

V. POLITA. *Grey Speedwell.*   **Fig. 884.**
Stem procumbent. Leaves cordate-ovate, deeply serrated. Sepals ovate, acute. Plant greyish green. A common weed. 2–6 in. Ann. May–Sept. Pale blue. ($\frac{2}{3}$) *E. B.* 1. 783. *E. B.* 2. 19. *H. & Arn.* 302. *Bab.* 249. *Lind.* 331.

V. BUXBAUMII.   **Fig. 885.**
Stem procumbent. Leaves cordate-ovate, deeply serrated. Sepals lanceolate, acute. Flowers large. Fields. 6–8 in. Ann. April–Sept. Blue. ($\frac{2}{3}$) *E. B. Supp.* 2769. *H. & Arn.* 302. *Bab.* 249. *Lind.* 331.

V. ARVENSIS. *Wall Speedwell.*   **Fig. 886.**
Stem erect. Leaves ovate, serrated; floral ones lanceolate. Flowers nearly sessile. A common weed. 2–5 in. Ann. May. Blue. ($\frac{2}{3}$) *E. B.* 1. 734. *E. B.* 2. 20. *H. & Arn.* 302. *Bab.* 248. *Lind.* 189.

V. VERNA. *Vernal Speedwell.*   **Fig. 887.**
Stem erect. Leaves pinnatifid. Flower-stalks shorter than the calyx. Dry fields; rare. 1–3 in. Ann. April and May. Blue. ($\frac{2}{3}$) *E. B.* 1. 25. *E. B.* 2. 23. *H. & Arn.* 303. *Bab.* 248. *Lind.* 189.

V. TRIPHYLLOS. *Trifid Speedwell.*   **Fig. 888.**
Stem erect. Upper leaves in deep finger-like segments. Flower-stalks longer than the calyx. Sandy fields; rare. 4–6 in. Ann. May. Deep blue. ($\frac{2}{3}$) *E. B.* 1. 25. *E. B.* 2. 23. *H. & Arn.* 303. *Bab.* 248. *Lind.* 189.

Genus 2. BARTSIA.

B. ALPINA. *Alpine Painted-cup.*   **Fig. 889.**
Stem square. Leaves opposite, ovate-cordate. Flowers in a terminal spike. Alpine pastures; rare. 6–8 in. Perenn. June and July. Purple. ($\frac{2}{3}$) *E. B.* 1. 361. *E. B.* 2. 855. *H. & Arn.* 303. *Bab.* 245. *Lind.* 190.

B. VISCOSA. *Marsh Painted-cup.*   **Fig. 890.**
Stem round. Leaves lanceolate, with rounded serratures. Flowers axillary. Moist pastures. 6 in.–1 ft. Ann. Aug. Yellow. ($\frac{2}{3}$) *E. B.* 1. 1045. *E. B.* 2. 856. *H. & Arn.* 304. *Bab.* 245. *Lind.* 190.

B. **Odontites.** *Red Eye-bright.* **Fig. 891.**
Stem square. Leaves lanceolate, serrated. Flowers in one-sided
racemes. A common weed. 6 in.–1 ft. Ann. July–Sept. Purple.
($\frac{2}{3}$) *E. B.* 1. 1415. *E. B.* 2. 857. *H. & Arn.* 304. *Bab.* 246. *Lind.* 191.

Genus 3. Euphrasia.

E. **officinalis.** *Eye-bright.* **Fig. 892.**
Stem erect. Leaves ovate, deeply toothed. Dry pastures; common.
1–8 in. Ann. July–Sept. White or pinkish. ($\frac{2}{3}$) *E. B.* 1. 1416.
E. B. 2. 858. *H. & Arn.* 304. *Bab.* 245. *Lind.* 191.

Genus 4. Rhinanthus.

R. **Crista-galli.** *Yellow-rattle.* **Fig. 893.**
Stem simple or slightly branched. Leaves lanceolate, serrated.
Flowers in loose spikes. Meadows. 1–2 ft. Ann. June. Yellow,
with two blue spots on the upper lip. ($\frac{2}{3}$) *E. B.* 1. 657. *E. B.* 2. 859.
H. & Arn. 305. *Bab.* 244. *Lind.* 190.

R. **major.** *Large Yellow-rattle.* **Fig. 894.**
Stem much branched. Leaves linear-lanceolate, serrated. Flowers
in crowded spikes. Corn-fields. 1$\frac{1}{2}$–2 ft. Ann. July and Aug.
Yellow, with a purple spot on the upper lip. ($\frac{2}{3}$) *E. B. Supp.* 2737.
E. B. 2. 859*. *H. & Arn.* 305. *Bab.* 244. *Lind.* 190.

Genus 5. Melampyrum.

M. **cristatum.** *Crested Cow-Wheat.* **Fig. 895.**
Leaves linear-lanceolate. Flowers in dense 4-sided spikes. Bracts
heart-shaped, pointed, toothed at the base. Woods and fields. 1 ft.
Ann. July. Yellow; bracts rose-coloured at the base. ($\frac{2}{3}$) *E. B.*
1. 41. *E. B.* 2. 860. *H. & Arn.* 306. *Bab.* 243. *Lind.* 195.

M. **arvense.** *Purple Cow-Wheat.* **Fig. 896.**
Flowers in loose spikes. Bracts pinnatifid. Fields; local. 1–1$\frac{1}{2}$ ft.
Ann. July. Yellow and purple; bracts purple at the base. ($\frac{2}{3}$)
E. B. 1. 53. *E. B.* 2. 861. *H. & Arn.* 306. *Bab.* 243. *Lind.* 195.

M. **pratense.** *Yellow Cow-Wheat.* **Fig. 897.**
Flowers axillary, unilateral. Upper bracts pinnatifid at the base.
Woods. 1–1$\frac{1}{2}$ ft. Ann. June–Aug. Pale yellow. ($\frac{2}{3}$) *E. B.* 1. 113.
E. B. 2. 862. *H. & Arn.* 306. *Bab.* 243. *Lind.* 195.

M. **sylvaticum.** *Wood Cow-Wheat.* **Fig. 898.**
Flowers axillary, unilateral. Bracts entire. Alpine woods; rare.
1 ft. Ann. July. Yellow. ($\frac{2}{3}$) *E. B.* 1. 804. *E. B.* 2. 863. *H. &
Arn.* 306. *Bab.* 244. *Lind.* 195.

Genus 6. Pedicularis.

P. **palustris.** *Marsh Red-rattle. Louse-wort.* **Fig. 899.**
Stem solitary, branched above. Calyx ovate, hairy. Marshes.
8 in.–1 ft. Perenn.? June and July. Pink or white. ($\frac{3}{4}$) *E. B.*
1. 399. *E. B.* 2. 865. *H. & Arn.* 307. *Bab.* 244. *Lind.* 190.

P. **sylvatica.** *Dwarf Red-rattle. Louse-wort.* **Fig. 900.**
Stem branched, spreading. Calyx oblong, smooth. Moist pastures
and bogs; common. 3–8 in. Perenn. June and July. Pink or
white. ($\frac{2}{3}$) *E. B.* 1. 400. *E. B.* 2. 866. *H. & Arn.* 307. *Bab.* 244.
Lind. 190.

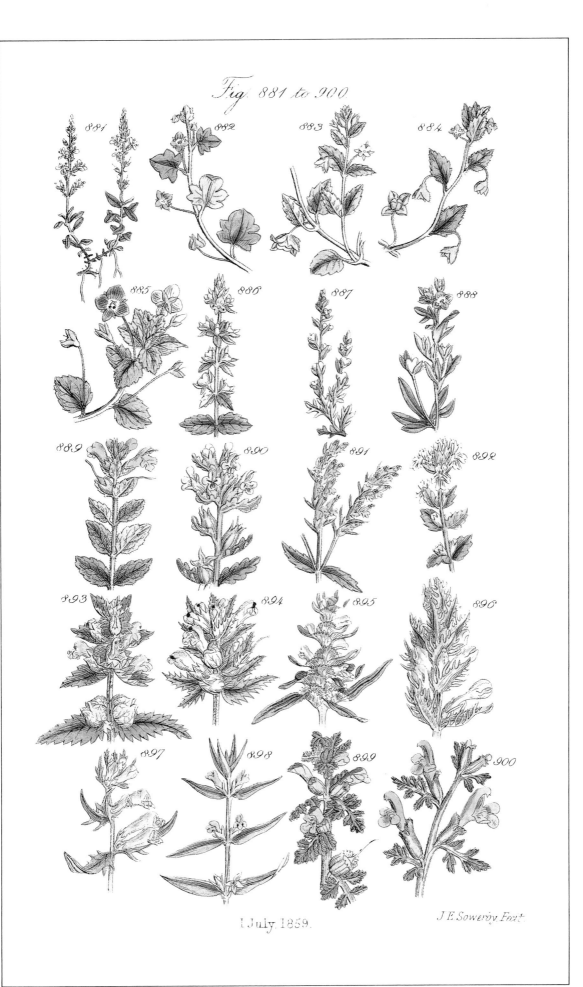

Fig. 881 to 900.

1 July 1859.

J.E.Sowerby, Fecit.

Genus 7. SCROPHULARIA.

S. NODOSA. *Knotty Fig-wort.* **Fig. 901.**
Root tuberous. Stem with obtuse angles. Leaves cordate, acute, smooth. Woods; common. 2–3 ft. Perenn. July. Greenish purple. ($\frac{2}{3}$) *E. B.* 1. 1544. *E. B.* 2. 876. *H. & Arn.* 307. *Bab.* 242. *Lind.* 193.

S. AQUATICA. *Water Fig-wort.* **Fig. 902.**
Stem winged at the angles. Leaves ovate, blunt, glabrous. Ditches; common. 3–4 ft. Perenn. July. Greenish; lips dark purple. ($\frac{2}{3}$) *E. B.* 1. 854. *E. B.* 2. 877. *H. & Arn.* 854. *Bab.* 242. *Lind.* 193.

S. SCORODONIA. *Balm-leaved Fig-wort.* **Fig. 903.**
Plant downy. Leaves heart-shaped, serrated. Panicle leafy. Ditches in Ireland and the southern counties. 2 ft. Perenn. July. Purplish. ($\frac{2}{3}$) *E. B.* 1. 2209. *E. B.* 2. 878. *H. & Arn.* 308. *Bab.* 242. *Lind.* 193.

S. VERNALIS. *Yellow Fig-wort.* **Fig. 904.**
Plant downy. Leaves broadly cordate, pale green. Flowers in leafy cymes. Shady places. 2 ft. Perenn.? April and May. Yellow. ($\frac{2}{3}$) *E. B.* 1. 567. *E. B.* 2. 879. *H. & Arn.* 308. *Bab.* 243. *Lind.* 193.

Genus 8. DIGITALIS.

D. PURPUREA. *Foxglove.* **Fig. 905.**
Leaves ovate-lanceolate, rugged, crenated, downy. Woods and hedge-banks; common in hilly districts. Very poisonous. 2–5 ft. Bienn. June and July. Crimson, speckled within; rarely white. ($\frac{1}{2}$) *E. B.* 1. 1297. *E. B.* 2. 880. *H. & Arn.* 309. *Bab.* 240. *Lind.* 192.

Genus 9. ANTIRRHINUM.

A. MAJUS. *Snapdragon.* **Fig. 906.**
Leaves lanceolate. Flowers in spiked racemes. Sepals ovate, shorter than the corolla. Old walls; common, but not indigenous. 1–2 ft. Perenn. June–Sept. Purple, pink, or white. ($\frac{1}{2}$) *E. B.* 1. 129. *E. B.* 2. 874. *H. & Arn.* 309. *Bab.* 240. *Lind.* 192.

A. ORONTIUM. *Calf's-snout.* **Fig. 907.**
Leaves linear-lanceolate. Flowers sessile, in lax spikes. Sepals linear, longer than the corolla. Corn-fields; not common. 6 in.–1 ft. Ann. July and Aug. Pink. ($\frac{2}{3}$) *E. B.* 1. 1155. *E. B.* 2. 875. *H. & Arn.* 309. *Bab.* 240. *Lind.* 192.

Genus 10. LINARIA.

L. CYMBALARIA. *Ivy-leaved Snapdragon.* **Fig. 908.**
Stems trailing, very long and slender. Leaves cordate, 5-lobed. Walls; common, but not indigenous. 2–4 in. Perenn. June–Nov. Purple. ($\frac{2}{3}$) *E. B.* 1. 502. *E. B.* 2. 867. *H. & Arn.* 310. *Bab.* 240. *Lind.* 191.

L. SPURIA. *Fluellen.* **Fig. 909.**
Stems procumbent. Leaves ovate, downy. Dry fields. 2–4 in. Ann. July–Sept. Violet and yellow. ($\frac{2}{3}$) *E. B.* 1. 691. *E. B.* 2. 868. *H. & Arn.* 310. *Bab.* 241. *Lind.* 191.

L. ELATINE. *Sharp-leaved Fluellen.* **Fig. 910.**
Stems procumbent. Leaves cordate-hastate, acute. Dry fields. 2–4 in. Ann. June–Sept. Violet and yellow. ($\frac{2}{3}$) *E. B.* 1. 692. *E. B.* 2. 869. *H. & Arn.* 310. *Bab.* 240. *Lind.* 191.

Fig. 901 to 920.

901   902   903   904

905   906   907   908

909   910   911   912

913   914   915   916

917   918   919   920

1 July 1859.

J. E. Sowerby, Fecit.

46

L. REPENS. *Creeping Toad-Flax.* **Fig. 911.**
Stem erect, with creeping runners. Leaves linear, glaucous. Calyx smooth, as long as the spur. Rocks near the sea. 1–2 ft. Perenn. July–Sept. Pale blue, with streaks; lower lip sometimes pink. ($\frac{2}{3}$) E. B. 1. 1253. E. B. 2. 870. H. & Arn. 310. Bab. 241. Lind. 191.

L. VULGARIS. *Toad-Flax. Butter-and-Eggs.* **Fig. 912.**
Stems erect. Leaves linear-lanceolate, glaucous. Calyx smooth, shorter than the spur. Hedges; common. 1–2 ft. Perenn. June and July. Bright yellow and orange. ($\frac{2}{3}$) E. B. 1. 658. E. B. 2. 871 & 872. H. & Arn. 311. Bab. 242. Lind. 191.

L. MINOR. *Small Toad-Flax.* **Fig. 913.**
Stem erect, much-branched. Leaves linear-lanceolate. Flowers axillary. Calyx longer than the spur. Chalky fields; local. 4–8 in. Ann. June and July. Purple and yellow. ($\frac{2}{3}$) E. B. 1. 2014. E. B. 2. 873. H. & Arn. 312. Bab. 241. Lind. 192.

L. PELISERIANA. *Purple Toad-Flax.* **Fig. 914.**
Stem erect, little-branched. Leaves linear. Flowers in racemes. Sepals linear, twice as long as the capsule. Jersey. 1 ft. Ann. June. Purple. ($\frac{2}{3}$) E. B. Supp. 2832. H. & Arn. 311. Bab. 241.

Genus 11. LIMOSELLA.

L. AQUATICA. *Mudwort.* **Fig. 915.**
Leaves spatulate, on long stalks. Petals shorter than the tube of the calyx. Muddy places. 1–2 in. Ann. July–Sept. Rose-colour. ($\frac{2}{3}$) E. B. 1. 357. E. B. 2. 882. H. & Arn. 312. Bab. 243. Lind. 192.

Genus 12. SIBTHORPIA.

S. EUROPÆA. *Cornish Money-wort.* **Fig. 916.**
Stems creeping and rooting. Leaves alternate, kidney-shaped, nearly orbicular. Flowers minute, axillary, on short peduncles. Moist places; local. $\frac{1}{2}$ in. Perenn. June–Oct. Pinkish. ($\frac{2}{3}$) E. B. 1. 649. E. B. 2. 881. H. & Arn. 312. Bab. 246. Lind. 192.

Genus 13. VERBASCUM.

V. THAPSUS. *Great Mullein.* **Fig. 917.**
Leaves decurrent, woolly on both sides. Stem simple. Flowers sessile, densely crowded. Hedge-banks. 4–6 ft. Bienn. July and Aug. Deep yellow. ($\frac{1}{2}$) E. B. 1. 549. E. B. 2. 309. H. & Arn. 313. Bab. 238. Lind. 181.

V. LYCHNITIS. *White Mullein.* **Fig. 918.**
Leaves nearly smooth on the upper side. Stem angular, panicled. Chalky places; local. 4–5 ft. Bienn. June. Pale yellow. ($\frac{1}{2}$) E. B. 1. 58. E. B. 2. 310. H. & Arn. 314. Bab. 239. Lind. 181.

V. PULVERULENTUM. *Hoary Mullein.* **Fig. 919.**
Leaves covered with mealy wool. Stem round, panicled. Waste ground and hedge-banks. 3–4 ft. Bienn. July. Bright yellow. ($\frac{1}{2}$) E. B. 1. 487. E. B. 2. 311. H. & Arn. 314. Bab. 239. Lind. 181.

V. NIGRUM. *Dark Mullein.* **Fig. 920.**
Leaves oblong heart-shaped, on foot-stalks, dark green, slightly downy. Flowers in a raceme. Hedge-banks. 3 ft. Perenn. June–Oct. Yellow. ($\frac{1}{2}$) E. B. 1. 59. E. B. 2. 312. H. & Arn. 314. Bab. 239. Lind. 181.

V. VIRGATUM. *Large-flowered Mullein.* **Fig. 921.**
Leaves oblong-lanceolate, toothed, sessile; root ones downy, somewhat lyrate. Stem branched. Flowers clustered, nearly sessile. Banks; rare. 5–6 ft. Bienn. Aug. Yellow. ($\frac{1}{2}$) *E. B.* 1. 550. *E. B.* 2. 313. *H. & Arn.* 314. *Bab.* 240. *Lind.* 181.

V. BLATTARIA. *Moth Mullein.* **Fig. 922.**
Leaves stem-clasping, oblong, serrated, smooth. Flowers distant. Banks; rare. 3–4 ft. Ann. July–Nov. Yellow. ($\frac{1}{2}$) *E. B.* 1. 393. *E. B.* 2. 314. *H. & Arn.* 313. *Bab.* 240. *Lind.* 181.

ORDER LXII. LABIATÆ.
Genus 1. LYCOPUS.

L. EUROPÆUS. *Gipsy-wort.* **Fig. 923.**
Leaves very deeply serrated. Flowers in dense whorls. Ditches and pool-sides. 1–2 ft. Perenn. June–Sept. White. ($\frac{2}{3}$) *E. B.* 1. 1105. *E. B.* 2. 30. *H. & Arn.* 316. *Bab.* 254. *Lind.* 198.

Genus 2. SALVIA.

S. PRATENSIS. *Meadow Clary.* **Fig. 924.**
Leaves oblong, heart-shaped at the base. Corolla thrice as long as the calyx. Hedge-banks; rare. 3 ft. Perenn. June. Purple. ($\frac{1}{2}$) *E. B.* 1. 153. *E. B.* 2. 31. *H. & Arn.* 317. *Bab.* 254. *Lind.* 197.

S. VERBENACA. *Wild Clary.* **Fig. 925.**
Leaves serrated and crenated. Corolla-tube equal to the calyx. Dry fields and hedge-banks. 1–2 ft. Perenn. June–Oct. Purple. ($\frac{1}{2}$) *E. B.* 1. 154. *E. B.* 2. 32. *H. & Arn.* 317. *Bab.* 254. *Lind.* 197.

Genus 3. MENTHA.

M. SYLVESTRIS. *Horse Mint.* **Fig. 926.**
Leaves ovate-oblong, very acute, deeply serrated, downy beneath. Spikes nearly cylindrical. Bracts awl-shaped. Calyx very hairy. Moist ground. 2–4 ft. Perenn. Aug. and Sept. Pale lilac. ($\frac{2}{3}$) *E. B.* 1. 686. *E. B.* 2. 802. *H. & Arn.* 318. *Bab.* 252. *Lind.* 199.

M. ROTUNDIFOLIA. *Round-leaved Mint.* **Fig. 927.**
Leaves elliptical, obtuse, wrinkled, sharply serrated, shaggy beneath. Spikes interrupted. Bracts lanceolate. Moist places. 1–2 ft. Perenn. Aug. and Sept. Reddish. ($\frac{2}{3}$) *E. B.* 1. 446. *E. B.* 2. 803. *H. & Arn.* 318. *Bab.* 252. *Lind.* 199.

M. VIRIDIS. *Spear Mint.* **Fig. 928.**
Leaves lanceolate, acute, serrated, glabrous. Spikes interrupted. Bracts awl-shaped. Moist places. A culinary herb. 1–1$\frac{1}{2}$ ft. Perenn. Aug. and Sept. Reddish purple. ($\frac{2}{3}$) *E. B.* 1. 2424. *E. B.* 2. 804. *H. & Arn.* 318. *Bab.* 252. *Lind.* 199.

M. PIPERITA. *Pepper-Mint.* **Fig. 929.**
Leaves ovate-lanceolate, acute, deeply serrated, rather hairy. Spikes interrupted below. Bracts lanceolate. Calyx smooth at the base, glandular. Watery places. 1 ft. Perenn. Aug. and Sept. Pale purple. ($\frac{2}{3}$) *E. B.* 1. 686. *E. B.* 2. 805. *H. & Arn.* 319. *Bab.* 253. *Lind.* 199.

M. CRISPA. *Curled Mint.* **Fig. 930.**
Leaves cordate, rugged, crisped at the margin, with long pointed teeth. A variety of *piperita.* Wet places. 1 ft. Aug. and Sept. Purplish red. ($\frac{2}{3}$) *E. B. Supp.* 2785. *E. B.* 2. 805. *H. & Arn.* 319. *Bab.* 253. *Lind.* 199.

M. CITRATA. *Bergamot Mint.* **Fig. 931.**
Leaves cordate-ovate, acute, sharply serrated, smooth, stalked. Whorls distant. Calyx glabrous. Wet places; rare. 1 ft. Perenn. Aug. and Sept. Purple. ($\frac{2}{3}$) *E. B.* 1. 1025. *E. B.* 2. 806. *H. & Arn.* 319. *Bab.* 253. *Lind.* 200.

M. HIRSUTA. *Water Mint. Hairy Mint.* **Fig. 932.**
Leaves ovate, serrated, hairy, stalked. Flowers in dense heads. Calyx hairy. Wet places; common. 1–2 ft. Perenn. Aug. and Sept. Pale purple. ($\frac{2}{3}$) *E. B.* 1. 447. *E. B.* 2. 807. *H. & Arn.* 319. *Bab.* 253. *Lind.* 200.

M. SATIVA. **Fig. 933.**
Leaves ovate or ovate-lanceolate. Flowers in dense, distant whorls. A variety of *hirsuta*. Wet places. 1–2 ft. Perenn. Aug. and Sept. Pale purple. ($\frac{2}{3}$) *E. B.* 1. 448. *E. B.* 2. 808. *H. & Arn.* 319. *Bab.* 253. *Lind.* 200.

M. ACUTIFOLIA. *Sharp-leaved Mint.* **Fig. 934.**
Leaves ovate-lanceolate, tapering at each end. Flowers whorled. Calyx hairy all over, hairs of the pedicels spreading. Wet places; rare. 1–2 ft. Perenn. July and Aug. Reddish purple. ($\frac{2}{3}$) *E. B.* 1. 2415. *E. B.* 2. 809. *H. & Arn.* 320. *Bab.* 253. *Lind.* 200.

M. RUBRA. *Red Mint.* **Fig. 935.**
Stem upright, zigzag. Leaves ovate, sharply serrated, glabrous. Flowers whorled. Pedicels and lower part of the calyx smooth. Watery places. 2–6 ft. Sept. Purplish red. ($\frac{2}{3}$) *E. B.* 1. 1413. *E. B.* 2. 810. *H. & Arn.* 320. *Bab.* 253. *Lind.* 200.

M. GENTILIS. *Bushy Red Mint.* **Fig. 936.**
Stem much-branched, spreading. Leaves ovate, hairy, stalked. Flowers whorled. Pedicels smooth. 1–2 ft. Perenn. Aug. and Sept. Reddish purple. ($\frac{2}{3}$) *E. B.* 1. 2118. *E. B.* 2. 811. *H. & Arn.* 320. *Bab.* 253. *Lind.* 201.

M. GRACILIS. *Narrow-leaved Red Mint.* **Fig. 937.**
Stem upright, much-branched. Leaves ovate-lanceolate, acute. A variety of *gentilis*. 1 ft. Perenn. Sept. Reddish. ($\frac{2}{3}$) *E. B.* 1. 449. *E. B.* 2. 812. *H. & Arn.* 320. *Bab.* 253. *Lind.* 199.

M. ARVENSIS. *Corn Mint.* **Fig. 938.**
Stem branched, spreading. Leaves ovate, hairy. Flowers whorled. Calyx bell-shaped, hairy. Corn-fields. 8–10 in. Perenn. July–Sept. Purple. ($\frac{2}{3}$) *E. B.* 1. 2119. *E. B.* 2. 813. *H. & Arn.* 320. *Bab.* 254. *Lind.* 200.

M. AGRESTIS. *Field Mint.* **Fig. 939.**
Stem erect. Leaves heart-shaped, serrated, rugged. A variety of *arvensis*. Corn-fields. 8–10 in. Perenn. Aug. and Sept. Purple. ($\frac{2}{3}$) *E. B.* 1. 2120. *E. B.* 2. 814. *H. & Arn.* 320. *Bab.* 254. *Lind.* 200.

M. PULEGIUM. *Penny-royal.* **Fig. 940.**
Stem prostrate. Leaves ovate, downy. Flowers whorled. Calyx downy all over. Wet places; naturalized. 4–8 in. Perenn. Aug. and Sept. Pale purple. ($\frac{2}{3}$) *E. B.* 1. 1026. *E. B.* 2. 815. *H. & Arn.* 320. *Bab.* 254. *Lind.* 201.

Fig 921 to 940.

921 922 923 924
925 926 927 928
929 930 931 932
933 934 935 936
937 938 939 940

J. E. Sowerby. Fecit.
47.

Genus 4. THYMUS.

T. SERPYLLUM. *Wild Thyme.* **Fig. 941.**
Stems branched, decumbent. Leaves ovate, hairy, sometimes very woolly. Flowers in heads. Heaths and hedge-banks; abundant. 1–2 in. Perenn. June–Sept. Reddish. ($\frac{2}{3}$) *E. B.* 1. 1514. *E. B.* 2. 816. *H. & Arn.* 321. *Bab.* 255. *Lind.* 201.

Genus 5. ORIGANUM.

O. VULGARE. *Marjoram.* **Fig. 942.**
Flowers in roundish heads, panicled. Leaves ovate, entire. Hedge-banks and bushy places; abundant on the chalk. $1\frac{1}{2}$–2 ft. Perenn. July and Aug. Rose-colour. ($\frac{2}{3}$) *E. B.* 1. 1143. *E. B.* 2. 817. *H. & Arn.* 322. *Bab.* 255. *Lind.* 201.

Genus 6. TEUCRIUM.

T. SCORODONIA. *Germander. Wood-Sage.* **Fig. 943.**
Stem erect. Leaves heart-shaped, crenated, downy, with foot-stalks. Flowers in one-sided racemes. Woods and commons; abundant. 1–2 ft. Perenn. July–Sept. Pale yellow. ($\frac{2}{3}$) *E. B.* 1. 1543. *E. B.* 2. 818. *H. & Arn.* 322. *Bab.* 262. *Lind.* 198.

T. SCORDIUM. *Water Germander.* **Fig. 944.**
Stem procumbent. Leaves oblong, sessile. Flowers axillary, in pairs. Wet meadows; local. 9 in.–1 ft. Perenn. July. Pink. ($\frac{2}{3}$) *E. B.* 1. 828. *E. B.* 2. 819. *H. & Arn.* 322. *Bab.* 262. *Lind.* 198.

T. CHAMÆDRYS. *Wall Germander.* **Fig. 945.**
Stems ascending, roundish. Leaves ovate, tapering to a stalk. Flowers axillary, three together. Old walls; naturalized. 9 in. Perenn. June–Nov. Purplish red. ($\frac{2}{3}$) *E. B.* 1. 680. *E. B.* 2. 820. *H. & Arn.* 323. *Bab.* 262. *Lind.* 198.

Genus 7. AJUGA.

A. REPTANS. *Bugle.* **Fig. 946.**
Plant nearly smooth. Stem solitary, with creeping runners. Lower lip of corolla 4-cleft. Woods; abundant. 6 in.–1 ft. Perenn. May and June. Blue, pink, or white. ($\frac{2}{3}$) *E. B.* 1. 489. *E. B.* 2. 821. *H. & Arn.* 323. *Bab.* 263. *Lind.* 197.

A. PYRAMIDALIS. *Pyramidal Bugle.* **Fig. 947.**
Hairy. Stem without runners. Root-leaves very large, obovate; whorls crowded in a pyramidal form. Highland pastures. 2–6 in. Perenn. June. Bluish, with darker streaks. ($\frac{2}{3}$) *E. B.* 1. 1270. *E. B.* 2. 822. *H. & Arn.* 323. *Bab.* 263. *Lind.* 198.

A. ALPINA. *Mountain Bugle.* **Fig. 948.**
Leaves nearly smooth. Stem without runners. Whorls distant. Mountains; rare. 2–6 in. Perenn. June and July. Pale blue or pink. ($\frac{2}{3}$) *E. B.* 1. 477. *E. B.* 2. 823. *H. & Arn.* 324. *Bab.* 263. *Lind.* 197.

A. CHAMÆPITYS. *Ground Pine. Yellow Bugle.* **Fig. 949.**
Hairy. Stem spreading, branched. Leaves in three linear segments. Flowers solitary. Chalky fields; local. 6–8 in. Ann. April and May. Yellow, with red dots. ($\frac{2}{3}$) *E. B.* 1. 77. *E. B.* 2. 824. *H. & Arn.* 324. *Bab.* 263. *Lind.* 198.

Genus 8. BALLOTA.

B. NIGRA. *Black Horehound.* **Fig. 950.**
Leaves ovate, deeply serrated. Hedges and waste ground. 2–3 ft. Perenn. July and Aug. Purple. ($\frac{2}{3}$) *E. B.* 1. 46. *E. B.* 2. 825. *H. & Arn.* 325. *Bab.* 261. *Lind.* 205.

Fig. 941 to 960.

941   942   943   944
945   946   947   948
949   950   951   952
953   954   955   956
957   958   959   960

J. E. Sowerby, Fecit.

Genus 9. Leonurus.

L. Cardiaca. *Motherwort.* **Fig. 951.**
Leaves lanceolate, tapering to the petiole; lower ones 3-lobed, upper entire. Upper lip of corolla hairy. Hedge-banks. 1–3 ft. Perenn. July and Aug. White; lower lip purple. ($\frac{2}{3}$) *E. B.* 1. 286. *E. B.* 2. 826. *H. & Arn.* 325. *Bab.* 259. *Lind.* 204.

Genus 10. Galeopsis.

G. Ladanum. *Red Hemp-Nettle.* **Fig. 952.**
Stem not swollen beneath the nodes. Leaves lanceolate, hairy. Upper lip of corolla slightly notched. Dry fields. 6 in.–1 ft. Ann. Aug.–Oct. Purplish pink. ($\frac{2}{3}$) *E. B.* 1. 884. *E. B.* 2. 828. *H. & Arn.* 325. *Bab.* 260. *Lind.* 202.

G. villosa. *Dwarf Hemp-Nettle.* **Fig. 953.**
Stem not swollen beneath the nodes. Leaves ovate-lanceolate, very soft and downy. Upper lip of corolla deeply notched. Sandy fields. 1–2 ft. Ann. July and Aug. Pale yellow. ($\frac{2}{3}$) *E. B.* 1. 2353. *E. B.* 2. 829. *H. & Arn.* 326. *Bab.* 260. *Lind.* 203.

G. Tetrahit. *Hemp-Nettle.* **Fig. 954.**
Stem swollen beneath the nodes. Leaves ovate, bristly. Corolla twice as long as the calyx. Fields; common. 1–3 ft. Ann. Aug. Purplish or white. ($\frac{2}{3}$) *E. B.* 1. 207. *E. B.* 2. 830. *H. & Arn.* 326. *Bab.* 260. *Lind.* 203.

G. versicolor. *Bee-Nettle.* **Fig. 955.**
Stem swollen beneath the nodes. Corolla thrice as long as the calyx. Corn-fields. 2–3 ft. Ann. June–Aug. Yellow, with a purple spot on the lower lip. ($\frac{1}{2}$) *E. B.* 1. 667. *E. B.* 2. 831. *H. & Arn.* 326. *Bab.* 260. *Lind.* 203.

Genus 11. Galeobdolon.

G. luteum. *Weasel-snout.* **Fig. 956.**
Leaves ovate, pointed, bright green. Flowering stems erect, barren ones creeping. Hedges and thickets. 1 ft. Perenn. May and June. Yellow. ($\frac{1}{2}$) *E. B.* 1. 787. *E. B.* 2. 827. *H. & Arn.* 326. *Bab.* 259. *Lind.* 326.

Genus 12. Lamium.

L. album. *White Dead-Nettle.* **Fig. 957.**
Flowers about 20 in each whorl. Calyx-tube shorter than the teeth. Upper lip of corolla notched. Hedges and way-sides; abundant. 1–1½ ft. Perenn. April–Oct. White; anthers black. ($\frac{1}{2}$) *E. B.* 1. 768. *E. B.* 2. 832. *H. & Arn.* 327. *Bab.* 259. *Lind.* 203.

L. maculatum. *Spotted Dead-Nettle.* **Fig. 958.**
Lower leaves with a white spot. Flowers 8 or 10 in a whorl. Calyx-tube curved, as long as the teeth. Upper lip of corolla crenated. Hedge-banks; rare. 1 ft. Perenn. May–Oct. Reddish purple. ($\frac{1}{2}$) *E. B.* 1. 2550. *E. B.* 2. 833. *H. & Arn.* 327. *Bab.* 259. *Lind.* 202.

L. purpureum. *Red Dead-Nettle.* **Fig. 959.**
Stem leafless in the middle; upper leaves crowded. Tube of corolla bearded within. A common weed. 6–10 in. Ann. All the year. Purple or pink. ($\frac{2}{3}$) *E. B.* 1. 769. *E. B.* 2. 834. *H. & Arn.* 327. *Bab.* 258. *Lind.* 203.

L. incisum. *Cut-leaved Dead-Nettle.* **Fig. 960.**
Stem leafless in the middle. Leaves irregularly cut and serrated. Tube of corolla naked within. Fields. 6–10 in. Ann. May and June. Purplish red. ($\frac{2}{3}$) *E. B.* 1. 1933. *E. B.* 2. 835. *H. & Arn.* 327. *Bab.* 258. *Lind.* 204.

L. **AMPLEXICAULE.** *Henbit Dead-Nettle.* **Fig. 961.**
Leaves cordate ; upper ones stem-clasping. Calyx-teeth longer than the tube, linear. Corolla-tube very long. Waste places. 8 in. Ann. Feb.–June. Pink, with red spots. ($\frac{2}{3}$) *E. B.* 1. 770. *E. B.* 2. 836. *H. & Arn.* 328. *Bab.* 258. *Lind.* 204.

Genus 13. BETONICA.

B. **OFFICINALIS.** *Betony.* **Fig. 962.**
Root-leaves ovate-cordate, with long foot-stalks. Spike interrupted. Woods; common. 1–2 ft. Perenn. July and Aug. Purple-pink. ($\frac{2}{3}$) *E. B.* 1. 1142. *E. B.* 2. 837. *H. & Arn.* 328. *Bab.* 260. *Lind.* 205.

Genus 14. STACHYS.

S. **SYLVATICA.** *Hedge Woundwort.* **Fig. 963.**
Stem solid. Leaves ovate-cordate, with petioles. Flowers 6 in a whorl. Hedge-banks; common. 2–3 ft. Perenn. July and Aug. Deep purple, with streaks of white. ($\frac{2}{3}$) *E. B.* 1. 416. *E. B.* 2. 838. *H. & Arn.* 329. *Bab.* 261. *Lind.* 204.

S. **AMBIGUA.** **Fig. 964.**
Stem hollow. Leaves silky. A variety of *sylvatica.* Fields in Scotland. 2–3 ft. Perenn. Aug. and Sept. Reddish-purple. ($\frac{2}{3}$) *E. B.* 1. 2089. *E. B.* 2. 839. *H. & Arn.* 329. *Bab.* 261. *Lind.* 204.

S. **PALUSTRIS.** *Marsh Woundwort.* **Fig. 965.**
Root tuberous. Leaves linear-lanceolate, sessile. Flowers 6 in a whorl. Wet places. 2–3 ft. Perenn. Aug. Purple and white. ($\frac{2}{3}$) *E. B.* 1. 1675. *E. B.* 2. 840. *H. & Arn.* 329. *Bab.* 261. *Lind.* 205.

S. **GERMANICA.** *Downy Woundwort.* **Fig. 966.**
Stem erect, woolly. Leaves oblong, silky above, woolly beneath. Whorls many-flowered. Fields. 2–3 ft. Perenn. Aug. and Sept. Purple. ($\frac{2}{3}$) *E. B.* 1. 829. *E. B.* 2. 841. *H. & Arn.* 329. *Bab.* 261. *Lind.* 205.

S. **ARVENSIS.** *Corn Woundwort.* **Fig. 967.**
Stem weak, branched. Leaves cordate, slightly hairy. Whorls 6-flowered. Corn-fields; common. 6 in.–1 ft. Ann. July and Aug. Dull purple. ($\frac{2}{3}$) *E. B.* 1. 1154. *E. B.* 2. 842. *H. & Arn.* 329. *Bab.* 261. *Lind.* 205.

S. **ANNUA.** *Pale Woundwort.* **Fig. 968.**
Stem erect. Plant downy. Leaves oblong-lanceolate, the lower ones stalked. Calyx hairy. Fields; rare. 1 ft. Ann. Aug. and Sept. Pale yellow. ($\frac{2}{3}$) *E. B. Supp.* 2669. *E. B.* 2. 842*. *H. & Arn.* 330. *Bab.* 261. *Lind.* 204.

Genus 15. NEPETA.

N. **CATARIA.** *Cat-Mint.* **Fig. 969.**
Leaves downy, with foot-stalks. Whorls stalked, many-flowered. Hedge-banks. 2–3 ft. Perenn. July–Sept. Pale pink, with purple spots. ($\frac{2}{3}$) *E. B.* 1. 137. *E. B.* 2. 843. *H. & Arn.* 330. *Bab.* 257. *Lind.* 202.

Genus 16. GLECHOMA.

G. **HEDERACEA.** *Ground Ivy.* **Fig. 970.**
Stems procumbent, rooting. Leaves kidney-shaped, crenated. Flowers in axillary whorls, 3 or 4 together. Hedge-banks; abundant. 4–9 in. Perenn. April–Oct. Blue; sometimes white. ($\frac{2}{3}$) *E. B.* 1. 411. *E. B.* 2. 846. *H. & Arn.* 330. *Bab.* 257. *Lind.* 202.

Genus 17. MARRUBIUM.

M. VULGARE. *Horehound.*   **Fig. 971.**

Stem erect. Leaves roundish-ovate, wrinkled, covered with a dense white wool. Waste places. Aromatic. 1–2 ft. Perenn. Aug. and Sept. Whitish. ($\frac{2}{3}$) *E. B.* 1. 410. *E. B.* 2. 845. *H. & Arn.* 331. *Bab.* 262. *Lind.* 205.

Genus 18. ACINOS.

A. VULGARIS. *Basil Thyme.*   **Fig. 972.**

Stem ascending, branched. Leaves oblong, acute, serrated. Flowers about 6 in a whorl. Dry fields. 6–8 in. Ann. Aug. Purplish-blue, with a white spot on the lower lip. ($\frac{2}{3}$) *E. B.* 1. 411. *E. B.* 2. 846. *H. & Arn.* 330. *Bab.* 256. *Lind.* 201.

Genus 19. CALAMINTHA.

C. OFFICINALIS. *Calamint.*   **Fig. 973.**

Stem erect. Leaves with slight serratures. Flowers in unilateral cymes. Way-sides. 1½ ft. Perenn. July–Sept. Pale purple. ($\frac{2}{3}$) *E. B.* 1. 1676. *E. B.* 2. 847. *H. & Arn.* 332. *Bab.* 256. *Lind.* 201.

C. NEPETA. *Lesser Calamint.*   **Fig. 974.**

Leaves serrated. Hairs in the throat of the calyx prominent when in fruit. A variety of *officinalis.* Limestone hills and way-sides. 1 ft. Perenn. Aug. and Sept. Purple. ($\frac{2}{3}$) *E. B.* 1. 1414. *E. B.* 2. 848. *H. & Arn.* 331. *Bab.* 255. *Lind.* 202.

Genus 20. CLINOPODIUM.

C. VULGARE. *Wild Basil.*   **Fig. 975.**

Leaves ovate, hairy. Flowers in 2 or 3 close, hairy whorls. Limestone hills. 1–1½ ft. Perenn. Aug. Pinkish-purple. ($\frac{2}{3}$) *E. B.* 1. 1401. *E. B.* 2. 849. *H. & Arn.* 332. *Bab.* 256. *Lind.* 202.

Genus 21. MELITTIS.

M. MELISSOPHYLLUM. *Bastard Balm.*   **Fig. 976.**

Leaves oblong-ovate, serrated. Flowers large. Upper lip of the calyx with 2 or 3 teeth. Woods in the southern counties. 1 ft. Perenn. June. Reddish with crimson spots. ($\frac{1}{2}$) *E. B.* 1. 577. *E. B.* 2. 851. *H. & Arn.* 333. *Bab.* 258. *Lind.* 202.

M. GRANDIFLORA.   **Fig. 977.**

Calyx-lobes entire. A variety of *Melissophyllum.* Woods. 1 ft. Perenn. June. White, with a purple spot on the lower lip. ($\frac{1}{2}$) *E. B.* 1. 636. *E. B.* 2. 850. *H. & Arn.* 333. *Bab.* 258. *Lind.* 202.

Genus 22. PRUNELLA.

P. VULGARIS. *Self-heal.*   **Fig. 978.**

Leaves entire, with foot-stalks. Flowers in dense cylindrical spikes. Fields. 2 in.–1 ft. Perenn. June and July. Purplish-blue; sometimes pink or white. ($\frac{2}{3}$) *E. B.* 1. 961. *E. B.* 2. 852. *H. & Arn.* 333. *Bab.* 257. *Lind.* 206.

Genus 23. SCUTELLARIA.

S. GALERICULATA. *Skull-cap.*   **Fig. 979.**

Leaves lanceolate, cordate at the base, crenated. Wet places. 1 ft. Perenn. June–Aug. Purple or blue. ($\frac{2}{3}$) *E. B.* 1. 523. *E. B.* 2. 853. *H. & Arn.* 334. *Bab.* 257. *Lind.* 205.

S. MINOR. *Lesser Skull-cap.*   **Fig. 980.**

Leaves oblong-ovate, nearly entire, sometimes hastate at the base. Moist places; common. 4–6 in. Perenn. July and Aug. Pinkish. ($\frac{1}{2}$) *E. B.* 1. 524. *E. B.* 2. 854. *H. & Arn.* 334. *Bab.* 257. *Lind.* 205.

Fig. 961 to 980.

961 962 963 964

965 966 967 968

969 970 971 972

973 974 975 976

977 978 979 980

1 Octr 1859.

J. E. Sowerby, Fecit
49

Order LXIII. VERBENACEÆ.
Genus 1. Verbena.

V. officinalis. *Common Vervain.* **Fig. 981.**
Stem erect, hispid. Leaves lanceolate, deeply cut or serrated, sometimes trifid. Flowers in slender panicled spikes. Waste places; common. 1–2 ft. Perenn. July. Lilac. ($\frac{2}{3}$) *E. B.* 1. 767. *E. B.*
2. 883. *H. & Arn.* 335. *Bab.* 264. *Lind.* 196.

Order LXIV. LENTIBULARIACEÆ.
Genus 1. Pinguicula.

P. vulgaris. *Butterwort.* **Fig. 982.**
Leaves in a tuft at the root. Flowers solitary. Spur cylindrical, as
long as the petal. Segments of the calyx oblong. Bogs. 4–6 in.
Perenn. June and July. Purple-blue. ($\frac{2}{3}$) *E. B.* 1. 70. *E. B.* 2. 25.
H. & Arn. 335. *Bab.* 264. *Lind.* 186.

P. grandiflora. *Large-flowered Butterwort.* **Fig. 983.**
Spur cylindrical, as long as the nearly regular petal. Segments of
the calyx ovate. Marshes; rare. 6–8 in. Perenn. May. Blue. ($\frac{1}{2}$)
E. B. 1. 2184. *E. B.* 2. 26. *H. & Arn.* 336. *Bab.* 264. *Lind.* 186.

P. alpina. *Alpine Butterwort.* **Fig. 984.**
Spur conical, slightly curved, shorter than the petal. Flower-stalks
smooth. Alpine bogs. 4–6 in. Perenn. June. Pale yellow. ($\frac{2}{3}$)
E. B. Supp. 2747. *E. B.* 2. 24*. *H. & Arn.* 336. *Bab.* 264. *Lind.* 331.

P. lusitanica. *Pale Butterwort.* **Fig. 985.**
Spur blunt, shorter than the petal. Flower-stalks hairy. Flowers
nearly regular. Bogs; local. 4–6 in. Perenn. June. Pale blue.
($\frac{2}{3}$) *E. B.* 1. 145. *E. B.* 2. 24. *H. & Arn.* 336. *Bab.* 264. *Lind.* 186.

Genus 2. Utricularia.

U. vulgaris. *Bladderwort.* **Fig. 986.**
Stems submersed. Leaves pinnate, with numerous segments. Spur
conical. Upper lip of corolla as long as the palate. Stagnant water.
Perenn. July and Aug. Yellow. ($\frac{2}{3}$) *E. B.* 1. 253. *E. B.* 2. 27.
H. & Arn. 337. *Bab.* 265. *Lind.* 186.

U. intermedia. **Fig. 987.**
Spur conical. Spike 2- or 3-flowered. Upper lip twice as long as
the palate. Water; rare. Perenn. June–Sept. Yellow. ($\frac{2}{3}$) *E. B.*
1. 2489. *E. B.* 2. 28. *H. & Arn.* 337. *Bab.* 265. *Lind.* 186.

U. minor. *Small Bladderwort.* **Fig. 988.**
Spur keel-shaped. Spikes with several flowers. Pools on moors.
Perenn. June–Sept. Yellow. ($\frac{2}{3}$) *E. B.* 1. 254. *E. B.* 2. 29.
H. & Arn. 337. *Bab.* 265. *Lind.* 187.

Order LXV. PRIMULACEÆ.
Genus 1. Hottonia.

H. palustris. *Water Violet.* **Fig. 989.**
Stems submersed. Leaves pectinated. Flowers in whorls around an
upright stalk. Clear water. Perenn. June. Pale lilac. ($\frac{2}{3}$) *E. B.*
1. 364. *E. B.* 2. 282. *H. & Arn.* 338. *Bab.* 267. *Lind.* 185.

Genus 2. Primula.

P. vulgaris. *Primrose.* **Fig. 990.**
Leaves obovate, tapering to the base. Pedicels usually sessile, single-
flowered. Banks and thickets; abundant. 6–8 in. Perenn. March–
May. Pale yellow. ($\frac{1}{2}$) *E. B* 1. 4. *E. B.* 2. 275. *H. & Arn.* 339.
Bab. 266. *Lind.* 184.

Fig. 981 to 1000.

981   982   983   984

985   986   987   988

989   990   991   992

993   994   995   996

997   998   999   1000

J. E. Sowerby, fecit.

50

P. ELATIOR. *Oxlip.* **Fig. 991.**
Leaves ovate, contracted below the middle. Flowers in an umbel on a long stalk. Teeth of the calyx awl-shaped. Thickets. 6–9 in. Perenn. April. Pale yellow. ($\frac{1}{2}$) *E. B.* 1. 513. *E. B.* 2. 276. *H. & Arn.* 339. *Bab.* 267. *Lind.* 184.

P. VERIS. *Cowslip.* **Fig. 992.**
Leaves ovate, much contracted below the middle. Umbel on a long stalk. Limb of corolla shorter than the tube. Calyx-teeth short. Meadows and pastures; abundant. 6–10 in. Perenn. May. Deep yellow. ($\frac{1}{2}$) *E. B.* 1. 5. *E. B.* 2. 277. *H. & Arn.* 339. *Bab.* 266. *Lind.* 184.

P. FARINOSA. *Bird's-eye Primrose.* **Fig. 993.**
Leaves mealy beneath. Petals narrow. Moist places on mountains. 2–6 in. Perenn. June and July. Pale purple with a yellow eye. ($\frac{2}{3}$) *E. B.* 1. 6. *E. B.* 2. 278. *H. & Arn.* 340. *Bab.* 267. *Lind.* 184.

P. SCOTICA. *Scotch Primrose.* **Fig. 994.**
Leaves mealy. Petals broad. Northern Highlands. 1–4 in. Perenn. July. Bluish-purple with yellow eye. ($\frac{2}{3}$) *E. B. Supp.* 2608. *E. B.* 2. 278*. *H. & Arn.* 340. *Bab.* 267. *Lind.* 184.

Genus 3. CYCLAMEN.

C. HEDERIFOLIUM. *Sow-bread.* **Fig. 995.**
Leaves cordate, angular, with white blotches. Flowers solitary, on long stalks. Petals reflexed. Woods; local, scarcely wild. 6–8 in. Perenn. Aug. and Sept. Pink. ($\frac{1}{2}$) *E. B.* 1. 548. *E. B.* 2. 279. *H. & Arn.* 340. *Bab.* 267. *Lind.* 183.

Genus 4. GLAUX.

G. MARITIMA. *Sea Milkwort.* **Fig. 996.**
A small creeping plant with opposite, fleshy leaves. Flowers axillary. Sea-shores and salt marshes. 1–4 in. Perenn. June–Aug. Pink. ($\frac{2}{3}$) *E. B.* 1. 13. *E. B.* 2. 346. *H. & Arn.* 341. *Bab.* 269. *Lind.* 183.

Genus 5. TRIENTALIS.

T. EUROPÆA. *Chickweed Winter-green.* **Fig. 997.**
Stem erect, with a whorl of leaves at the apex beneath the flowers. Heaths; rare. 4–6 in. Perenn. June. White. ($\frac{1}{2}$) *E. B.* 1. 15. *E. B.* 2. 540. *H. & Arn.* 341. *Bab.* 269. *Lind.* 185.

Genus 6. LYSIMACHIA.

L. VULGARIS. *Loosestrife.* **Fig. 998.**
Stems erect. Flowers in terminal leafy clusters. Moist places. 3 ft. Perenn. July. Yellow. ($\frac{1}{2}$) *E. B.* 1. 761. *E. B.* 2. 283. *H. & Arn.* 342. *Bab.* 268. *Lind.* 184.

L. THYRSIFLORA. *Tufted Loosestrife.* **Fig. 999.**
Flowers in axillary stalked clusters. Leaves lanceolate. Borders of lakes; rare. 1½ ft. Perenn. July. Yellow. ($\frac{1}{2}$) *E. B.* 1. 176. *E. B.* 2. 284. *H. & Arn.* 342. *Bab.* 268. *Lind.* 184.

L. NEMORUM. *Wood Pimpernel.* **Fig. 1000.**
Stems procumbent, pinkish. Leaves ovate, acute. Sepals linear-lanceolate. Woods; common. 2–4 in. Perenn. May–Aug. Yellow. ($\frac{1}{2}$) *E. B.* 1. 527. *E. B.* 2. 285. *H. & Arn.* 342. *Bab.* 268. *Lind.* 184.

L. Nummularia. *Money-wort.*   Fig. 1001.
Stems creeping. Leaves ovate, somewhat heart-shaped. Sepals ovate, pointed. Ditch-banks and shady places; common. 1–3 in. Perenn. May–July. Yellow. ($\frac{1}{2}$) *E. B.* 1. 528. *E. B.* 2. 286. *H. & Arn.* 342. *Bab.* 268. *Lind.* 184.

Genus 7. Anagallis.

A. arvensis. *Scarlet Pimpernel.*   Fig. 1002.
Leaves ovate, sessile. Edges of corolla glandulose. A common weed. 2–5 in. Ann. May–Sept. Scarlet. ($\frac{2}{3}$) *E. B.* 1. 529. *E. B.* 2. 287. *H. & Arn.* 343. *Bab.* 268. *Lind.* 185.

A. cærulea. *Blue Pimpernel.*   Fig. 1003.
Edges of corolla toothed. Plant more erect. A variety of *arvensis.* 2–6 in. Ann. May–Sept. Blue, scarlet in the centre. ($\frac{2}{3}$) *E. B.* 1. 1823. *E. B.* 2. 287*. *H. & Arn.* 343. *Bab.* 185. *Lind.* 185.

A. tenella. *Bog Pimpernel.*   Fig. 1004.
Stem creeping. Leaves roundish. Bogs; common. 1–2 in. Perenn. July and Aug. Pink. ($\frac{2}{3}$) *E. B.* 1. 530. *E. B.* 2. 288. *H. & Arn.* 530. *Bab.* 269. *Lind.* 185.

Genus 8. Centunculus.

C. minimus. *Chaffweed.*   Fig. 1005.
Leaves alternate. Flowers axillary, sessile. Moist places. 1–2 in. Ann. June and July. Pink. *E. B.* 1. 531. *E. B.* 2. 225. *H. & Arn.* 333. *Bab.* 269. *Lind.* 183.

Genus 9. Samolus.

S. Valerandi. *Brook-weed.*   Fig. 1006.
Stem erect, rather succulent. Leaves alternate, blunt. Flowers in clusters, with a bract on each pedicel. Watery places. 1 ft. Perenn. June–Aug. White. ($\frac{2}{3}$) *E. B.* 1. 703. *E. B.* 2. 323. *H. & Arn.* 344. *Bab.* 269. *Lind.* 185.

Order LXVI. PLUMBAGINACEÆ.

Genus 1. Armeria.

A. maritima. *Sea Thrift.*   Fig. 1007.
Leaves linear. Flowers in a dense round head. Sea cliffs; common. 6–8 in. Perenn. June–Aug. Pink. ($\frac{1}{2}$) *E. B.* 1. 226. *E. B.* 2. 450. *H. & Arn.* 344. *Bab.* 271. *Lind.* 170.

Genus 2. Statice.

S. Limonium. *Sea Lavender.*   Fig. 1008.
Leaves elliptic-lanceolate, glaucous. Panicles corymbose. Sea-coast. 6 in.–1$\frac{1}{2}$ ft. Perenn. July and Aug. Purplish-blue. ($\frac{2}{3}$) *E. B.* 1. 102. *E. B.* 2. 451. *H. & Arn.* 345. *Bab.* 270. *Lind.* 170.

S. spathulata. *Narrow-leaved Sea Lavender.*   Fig. 1009.
Leaves spathulate, glaucous. Panicles distichous. Sea-coasts. 6–10 in. Perenn. Aug. Purplish-blue. ($\frac{2}{3}$) *E. B. Supp.* 2663. *E. B.* 2. 451*. *H. & Arn.* 346. *Bab.* 270. *Lind.* 330.

S. reticulata. *Matted Sea Lavender.*   Fig. 1010.
Leaves spathulate. Panicles much divided, the branches crossing each other. Stems prostrate. Coast of Norfolk. 6 in. Perenn. July and Aug. Purplish-blue. ($\frac{2}{3}$) *E. B.* 1. 328. *E. B.* 2 452. *H. & Arn.* 346. *Bab.* 271. *Lind.* 171.

ORDER LXVII. PLANTAGINACEÆ.

Genus 1. PLANTAGO.

P. MAJOR. *Greater Plantain.* **Fig. 1011.**
Leaves broadly ovate, with longish foot-stalks. A common weed.
2–10 in. Perenn. June–Aug. Pinkish. ($\frac{2}{3}$) E. B. 1. 1558.
E. B. 2. 220. H. & Arn. 347. Bab. 273. Lind. 169.

P. MEDIA. *Hoary Plantain.* **Fig. 1012.**
Leaves broadly ovate, nearly sessile, downy. Chalk hills. 4–6 in.
Perenn. June–Aug. Pinkish. ($\frac{2}{3}$) E. B. 1. 1559. E. B. 2. 221.
H. & Arn. 348. Bab. 273. Lind. 169.

P. LANCEOLATA. *Ribwort.* **Fig. 1013.**
Leaves lanceolate, long. Spike ovate. Stalks angular. A common
weed in pastures. 10 in.–1½ ft. Perenn. June. Pinkish. ($\frac{2}{3}$)
E. B. 1. 507. E. B. 2. 222. H. & Arn. 348. Bab. 272. Lind. 169.

P. MARITIMA. *Sea Plantain.* **Fig. 1014.**
Leaves linear, fleshy, channelled. Stalks round. Muddy sea-coasts.
4 in.–1 ft. Perenn. June–Aug. Pinkish. ($\frac{2}{3}$) E. B. 1. 175.
E. B. 2. 223. H. & Arn. 348. Bab. 272. Lind. 169.

P. CORONOPUS. *Buck's-horn Plantain.* **Fig. 1015.**
Leaves linear, pinnatifid. Dry places; common. 2–4 in. Ann.
June–Aug. Pinkish. ($\frac{2}{3}$) E. B. 1. 892. E. B. 2. 224. H. & Arn. 348.
Bab. 272. Lind. 169.

Genus 2. LITTORELLA.

L. LACUSTRIS. *Shore-weed.*
Leaves linear, fleshy, somewhat channelled. Flowers monœ us.
Margins of pools. 2–4 in. Perenn. June. Yellowish. ($\frac{2}{3}$) E. B.
1. 468. E. B. 2. 1304. H. & Arn. 349. Bab. 273. Lind. 170.

ORDER LXVIII. AMARANTHACEÆ.

Genus 1. AMARANTHUS.

A. BLITUM. *Wild Amaranth.* **Fig. 1017.**
Stem spreading. Leaves ovate, obtuse. Flowers 3-cleft, in small
lateral tufts. Waste places. 8 in.–1 ft. Ann. Aug. Green. ($\frac{2}{3}$)
E. B. 1. 2212. E. B. 2. 1311. H. & Arn. 352. Bab. 274. Lind. 213.

ORDER LXIX. CHENOPODIACEÆ.

Genus 1. BETA.

B. MARITIMA. *Beet.* **Fig. 1018.**
Stems procumbent. Flowers in pairs. Muddy sea-shores. The
origin of the Beet and Mangel Wurzel. 3–4 ft. Perenn.? June–Sept.
Green. ($\frac{2}{3}$) E. B. 1. 285. E. B. 2. 363. H. & Arn. 353. Bab. 277.
Lind. 216.

Genus 2. CHENOPODIUM.

C. FRUTICOSUM. *Shrubby Goosefoot.* **Fig. 1019.**
Erect, shrubby. Leaves semicylindrical, blunt. Bracts 3. Southern
coasts; rare. 3 ft. Perenn. July and Aug. Yellowish. ($\frac{2}{3}$)
E. B. 1. 635. E. B. 2. 349. H. & Arn. 361. Bab. 275. Lind. 216.

C. MARITIMUM. *Sea Goosefoot.* **Fig. 1020.**
Stem herbaceous, erect. Leaves semicylindrical, pointed. Bracts 2.
Sea-shores. 1 ft. Ann. July. Yellowish. ($\frac{2}{3}$) E. B. 1. 633.
E. B. 2. 350. H. & Arn. 361. Bab. 275. Lind. 216.

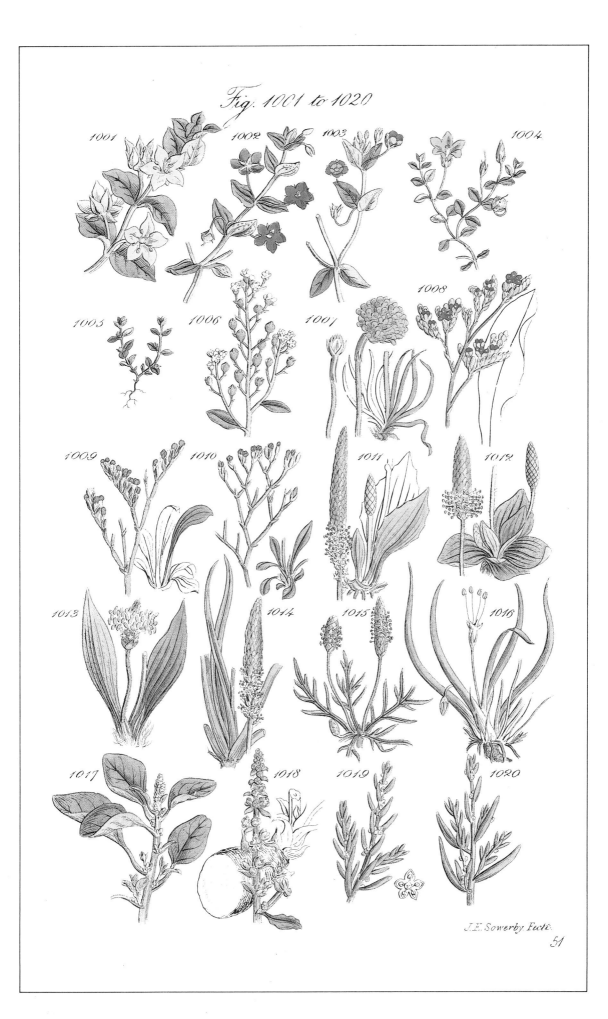

Fig. 1001 to 1020

1001 1002 1003 1004
1005 1006 1007 1008
1009 1010 1011 1012
1013 1014 1015 1016
1017 1018 1019 1020

J.E. Sowerby Fecit

C. OLIDUM. *Stinking Goosefoot.* **Fig. 1021.**
Leaves ovate, somewhat rhomboid, entire. Flowers in dense clustered
spikes. Waste places and sea-coast. 8–10 in. Ann. Aug. Green.
($\frac{2}{3}$) *E. B. 1. 1034. E. B. 2. 351. H. & Arn. 354. Bab. 275.
Lind. 216.*

C. POLYSPERMUM. *Round-leaved Goosefoot.* **Fig. 1022.**
Leaves ovate, obtuse, entire. Stem prostrate. Clusters cymose.
Waste ground. 6 in. Ann. Aug. Green. ($\frac{2}{3}$) *E. B. 1. 1480.
E. B. 2. 352. H. & Arn. 354. Bab. 276. Lind. 216.*

C. ACUTIFOLIUM. *Sharp-leaved Goosefoot.* **Fig. 1023.**
Leaves ovate, acute, entire. Stem erect. Clusters spiked, elongated.
Waste ground. 8 in.–1 ft. Ann. Aug. Green. ($\frac{2}{3}$) *E. B. 1. 1481.
E. B. 2. 353. H. & Arn. 354. Bab. 276. Lind. 216.*

C. BONUS-HENRICUS. *Wild Spinach.* **Fig. 1024.**
Leaves triangular, sagittate, entire. Spikes compound, leafless. Waste
places. 1 ft. Perenn. May–Aug. Green. ($\frac{2}{3}$) *E. B. 1. 1033.
E. B. 2. 354. H. & Arn. 356. Bab. 277. Lind. 215.*

C. URBICUM. *Upright Goosefoot.* **Fig. 1025.**
Leaves triangular, toothed. Spikes long, interrupted. Dunghills and
waste ground; common. 1 ft. Ann. Aug. and Sept. Green. ($\frac{2}{3}$)
E. B. 1. 717. E. B. 2. 355. H. & Arn. 354. Bab. 276. Lind. 215.

C. RUBRUM. *Red Goosefoot.* **Fig. 1026.**
Leaves triangular, deeply toothed and waved. Clusters upright,
leafy. Waste ground. 1–3 ft. Ann. Reddish. ($\frac{2}{3}$) *E. B. 1. 1721.
E. B. 2. 356. H. & Arn. 356. Bab. 277. Lind. 215.*

C. BOTRYOIDES. *Clustered Goosefoot.* **Fig. 1027.**
Leaves triangular, somewhat toothed. Spikes upright, clustered,
leafy. Sandy places; rare. 1 ft. Ann. Sept. Reddish. ($\frac{2}{3}$) *E. B.
1. 2247. E. B. 2. 357. H. & Arn. 356. Bab. 277. Lind. 215.*

C. MURALE. *Nettle-leaved Goosefoot.* **Fig. 1028.**
Leaves ovate, nearly rhomboidal, acute, toothed, shining. Clusters
cymose, leafless. Waste ground; very common. 1 ft. Ann. Aug.
and Sept. Green. ($\frac{2}{3}$) *E. B. 1. 1722. E. B. 2. 358. H. & Arn. 355.
Bab. 276. Lind. 215.*

C. HYBRIDUM. *Maple-leaved Goosefoot.* **Fig. 1029.**
Leaves heart-shaped, pointed, with angular teeth. Clusters cymose,
leafless, divaricated. Moist places; local. 1 ft. Ann. Aug. Green.
($\frac{2}{3}$) *E. B. 1. 1919. E. B. 2. 359. H. & Arn. 355. Bab. 276. Lind. 215.*

C. ALBUM. *White Goosefoot.* **Fig. 1030.**
Leaves ovate-rhomboid, sinuated, jagged, mealy; upper ones entire.
A common weed. 1 ft. Ann. May–Oct. Green. ($\frac{2}{3}$) *E. B. 1. 1723.
E. B. 2. 360. H. & Arn. 355. Bab. 276. Lind. 215.*

Fig. 1021 to 1040.

1021   1022   1023   1024

1025   1026   1027   1028

1029   1030   1031   1032

1033   1034   1035   1036

1037   1038   1039   1040

J. E. Sowerby, Fecit.

C. FICIFOLIUM. *Fig-leaved Goosefoot.* **Fig. 1031.**
Leaves sinuated, somewhat hastate, jagged; upper ones entire. Waste ground and fields. 1 ft. Ann. Aug. Green. ($\frac{2}{3}$) *E. B.* 1. 1724. *E. B.* 2. 361. *H. & Arn.* 355. *Bab.* 276. *Lind.* 215.

C. GLAUCUM. *Oak-leaved Goosefoot.* **Fig. 1032.**
Leaves all oblong, with a waved edge, glaucous. Sandy places. 6 in.–2 ft. Ann. Aug. Green. ($\frac{2}{3}$) *E. B.* 1. 1454. *E. B.* 2. 362. *H. & Arn.* 356. *Bab.* 277. *Lind.* 215.

Genus 3. ATRIPLEX.

A. PORTULACOIDES. *Shrubby Orache. Sea Purslane.* **Fig. 1033.**
Stem rather shrubby. Leaves obovate-lanceolate, silvery. Sea-shores. 1–2 ft. Perenn. July and Aug. Yellowish. ($\frac{2}{3}$) *E. B.* 1. 261. *E. B.* 2. 1401. *H. & Arn.* 357. *Bab.* 280. *Lind.* 216.

A. LACINIATA. *Frosted Sea Orache.* **Fig. 1034.**
Stem herbaceous, spreading. Leaves ovate, toothed and serrated, very mealy beneath. Sandy shores. 6–8 in. Ann. July. Greenish-yellow. ($\frac{2}{3}$) *E. B.* 1. 165. *E. B.* 2. 1402. *H. & Arn.* 357. *Bab.* 280. *Lind.* 217.

A. PATULA. *Spreading Orache.* **Fig. 1035.**
Leaves triangular, hastate, irregularly toothed and lobed. Dunghills and waste places. 1 ft. Ann. July. Reddish. ($\frac{2}{3}$) *E. B.* 1. 936. *E. B.* 2. 1403. *H. & Arn.* 358. *Bab.* 279. *Lind.* 217.

A. ANGUSTIFOLIA. *Narrow-leaved Orache.* **Fig. 1036.**
Stem herbaceous, spreading. Leaves lanceolate, entire; the lower ones 3-lobed. Waste ground. 1–3 ft. Ann. July. Green. ($\frac{2}{3}$) *E. B.* 1. 1774. *E. B.* 2. 1404. *H. & Arn.* 359. *Bab.* 278. *Lind.* 217.

A. ERECTA. *Spear-leaved Orache.* **Fig. 1037.**
Stem erect. Leaves ovate-lanceolate. Calyx of the fruit with sharp tubercles. Waste ground; rare. 1–2 ft. Ann. Aug. Green. ($\frac{2}{3}$) *E. B.* 1. 2223. *E. B.* 2. 1405. *H. & Arn.* 359. *Bab.* 279. *Lind.* 217.

A. LITTORALIS. *Grass-leaved Orache.* **Fig. 1038.**
Stem erect. Leaves linear, entire or toothed. Calyx sinuated. Salt-marshes. 2 ft. Ann. July–Sept. Green. ($\frac{2}{3}$) *E. B.* 1. 708. *E. B.* 2. 1406. *H. & Arn.* 359. *Bab.* 278. *Lind.* 217.

A. PEDUNCULATA. *Marsh Orache.* **Fig. 1039.**
Stem zigzag. Leaves ovate-lanceolate, entire. Seed-bearing flowers stalked. 6 in.–1 ft. Ann. July–Sept. Green. ($\frac{2}{3}$) *E. B.* 1. 232. *E. B.* 2. 1407. *H. & Arn.* 357. *Bab.* 280. *Lind.* 217.

A. DELTOIDEA. *Triangular-leaved Orache.* **Fig. 1040.**
Stems prostrate or ascending. Lower leaves triangular-hastate. Spikes in a branched many-flowered panicle. Waste ground. 1 ft. Ann. July–Oct. Reddish. ($\frac{2}{3}$) *E. B. Supp.* 2860. *H. & Arn.* 358. *Bab.* 279.

Genus 4. SALICORNIA.

S. HERBACEA. *Glasswort.* **Fig. 1041.**
Stem erect. Lower branches compound. Spikes cylindrical. Salt marshes and muddy shores. 6–10 in. Ann. Aug. Yellowish green. ($\frac{2}{3}$) *E. B.* 1. 415. *E. B.* 2. 1. *H. & Arn.* 360. *Bab.* 278. *Lind.* 214.

S. PROCUMBENS. *Procumbent Glasswort.* **Fig. 1042.**
Stem procumbent. Branches simple. Spikes tapering. A variety of *herbacea.* Salt marshes. 6 in. Ann. Aug. Yellowish green. ($\frac{2}{3}$) *E. B.* 1. 2475. *E. B.* 2. 1*. *H. & Arn.* 360. *Bab.* 278. *Lind.* 214.

S. RADICANS. *Creeping Glasswort.* **Fig. 1043.**
Stems woody, rooting at the base. Joints compressed. Spikes oblong. Muddy sea-shores. 1 ft. Perenn. Aug. Yellowish green. ($\frac{2}{3}$) *E. B.* 1. 1691. *E. B.* 2. 2. *H. & Arn.* 360. *Bab.* 278. *Lind.* 214.

S. FRUTICOSA. *Shrubby Glasswort.* **Fig. 1044.**
Stems woody. Joints cylindrical. Spikes cylindrical. A variety of *radicans.* 1 ft. Perenn. Aug. Yellowish green. ($\frac{2}{3}$) *E. B.* 1. 2467. *E. B.* 2. 2*. *H. & Arn.* 360. *Bab.* 278. *Lind.* 214.

Genus 5. SALSOLA.

S. KALI. *Saltwort.* **Fig. 1045.**
Stems procumbent. Leaves awl-shaped, spine-pointed. Calyx with a membranous expansion. Coasts. 1 ft. Ann. July. Pinkish. ($\frac{2}{5}$) *E. B.* 1. 634. *E. B.* 2. 364. *H. & Arn.* 362. *Bab.* 275. *Lind.* 214.

ORDER LXX. SCLERANTHACEÆ.

Genus 1. SCLERANTHUS.

S. ANNUUS. *Knawel.* **Fig. 1046.**
Stems many, procumbent. Calyx of fruit with erect or spreading segments. Corn-fields; common. 4–6 in. Ann. July. Green. ($\frac{2}{3}$) *E. B.* 1. 351. *E. B.* 2. 591. *H. & Arn.* 362. *Bab.* 125. *Lind.* 218.

S. PERENNIS. *Perennial Knawel.* **Fig. 1047.**
Calyx of fruit with incurved segments, edged with a white membrane. Sandy fields. 4 in. Perenn.? Aug.–Nov. Green. ($\frac{2}{3}$) *E. B.* 1. 352. *E. B.* 2. 590. *H. & Arn.* 363. *Bab.* 125. *Lind.* 218.

ORDER LXXI. POLYGONACEÆ.

Genus 1. POLYGONUM.

P. BISTORTA. *Bistort. Snakeweed.* **Fig. 1048.**
Stem simple, bearing one spike. Leaves ovate, waved; the lower ones with a winged foot-stalk. Moist meadows. Root very astringent. 1–1½ ft. Perenn. June–Sept. Pale pink. ($\frac{2}{3}$) *E. B.* 1. 509. *E. B.* 2. 571. *H. & Arn.* 363. *Bab.* 283. *Lind.* 212.

P. VIVIPARUM. *Alpine Bistort.* **Fig. 1049.**
Stem bearing one spike. Leaves linear-lanceolate, with revolute margins. Lower buds of the spike viviparous. Mountain pastures. 6 in. Perenn. July. Pale pink. ($\frac{2}{3}$) *E. B.* 1. 669. *E. B.* 2. 572. *H. & Arn.* 364. *Bab.* 283. *Lind.* 212.

P. AVICULARE. *Knot-grass.* **Fig. 1050.**
Stem procumbent. Leaves elliptic-lanceolate. Flowers axillary. Fruit rough and striated, covered by the calyx. A common weed. 1–6 in. Ann. April–Nov. Pinkish. ($\frac{2}{3}$) *E. B.* 1. 1253. *E. B.* 2. 573. *H. & Arn.* 364. *Bab.* 285. *Lind.* 212.

P. Rayii. *Ray's Knot-grass.* **Fig. 1051.**
Stem procumbent. Leaves lanceolate, flat. Flowers axillary. Fruit smooth and shining. A variety of *aviculare*? Sea-shores. 6–10 in. Ann. July–Nov. Pink. ($\frac{2}{3}$) *E. B. Supp.* 2805. *H. & Arn.* 364. *Bab.* 285. *Lind.* 232.

P. maritimum. *Sea Knot-grass.* **Fig. 1052.**
Stem procumbent, woody below. Joints very short. Leaves lanceolate, with revolute margins. Stipules as long as the joints. Sandy shores. 4–6 in. Perenn. July–Nov. Pinkish. ($\frac{2}{3}$) *E. B. Supp.* 2804. *H. & Arn.* 364. *Bab.* 286. *Lind.* 212.

P. Fagopyrum. *Buckwheat.* **Fig. 1053.**
Leaves cordate-sagittate. Stem nearly upright. Flowers in cymose panicles. Fields; naturalized. Seeds edible. 1 ft. Ann. July–Sept. Pink. ($\frac{2}{3}$) *E. B.* 1. 1044. *E. B.* 2. 574. *H. & Arn.* 365. *Bab.* 286. *Lind.* 212.

P. Convolvulus. *Black Bindweed. Climbing Buckwheat.* **Fig. 1054.**
Stem twining, angular. Leaves cordate-sagittate. Flowers in axillary leafy spikes. Fruit striated with minute points. A common weed. 1–6 ft. Ann. June–Sept. Greenish. ($\frac{2}{3}$) *E. B.* 1. 941. *E. B.* 2. 575. *H. & Arn.* 365. *Bab.* 286. *Lind.* 212.

P. dumetorum. *Copse Buckwheat.* **Fig. 1055.**
Leaves cordate-sagittate. Stems twining. Flowers in racemes. Fruit quite smooth, covered by the winged calyx. Woods. 4–6 ft. Ann. Aug.–Oct. Greenish. ($\frac{2}{3}$) *E. B. Supp.* 2811. *H. & Arn.* 365. *Bab.* 286. *Lind.* 212.

P. amphibium. *Water Persicaria. Water Bistort.* **Fig. 1056.**
Root creeping. Flowers in dense ovate spikes. Leaves, when floating, broad, ovate-oblong; when not in water, lanceolate, with short hairs. Ponds and wet places. Perenn. July and Aug. Rose-colour. ($\frac{2}{3}$) *E. B.* 1. 436. *E. B.* 2. 566. *H. & Arn.* 366. *Bab.* 284. *Lind.* 211.

P. Persicaria. *Spotted Persicaria.* **Fig. 1057.**
Leaves lanceolate, nearly sessile, often with a dark spot in the middle. Spikes oblong-cylindrical, on smooth stalks. Stipules fringed. Styles united to the middle. Moist ground; common. 1–2 ft. Ann. July–Oct. Pinkish. ($\frac{2}{3}$) *E. B.* 1. 756. *E. B.* 2. 567. *H. & Arn.* 366. *Bab.* 284. *Lind.* 211.

P. laxum. *Slender-headed Persicaria.* **Fig. 1058.**
Leaves lanceolate, with short stalks. Stipules fringed. Spikes on rough glandular stalks; sometimes very slender. A variety of *Persicaria*. 1–2 ft. Ann. July–Sept. Pinkish. ($\frac{2}{3}$) *E. B. Supp.* 2822. *H. & Arn.* 366. *Bab.* 284. *Lind.* 332.

P. lapathifolium. *Pale-flowered Persicaria.* **Fig. 1059.**
Leaves ovate-lanceolate, on short stalks. Stipules not fringed. Spikes on rough stalks. Styles distinct. Dunghills and waste ground; common. 1–2 ft. Ann. July and Aug. Greenish. ($\frac{2}{3}$) *E. B.* 1. 1382. *E. B.* 2. 568. *H. & Arn.* 366. *Bab.* 284. *Lind.* 212.

P. mite. *Lax-flowered Persicaria.* **Fig. 1060.**
Leaves lanceolate, with short stalks. Stipules hairy. Spikes very slender and interrupted. Styles united to the middle. Waste ground. 1–2 ft. Ann. Aug. Pink. ($\frac{2}{3}$) *E. B. Supp.* 2867. *H. & Arn.* 366. *Bab.* 285. *Lind.* 332.

Fig. 1041 to 1060.

1041 1042 1043 1044
1045 1046 1047 1048
1049 1050 1051 1052
1053 1054 1055 1056
1057 1058 1059 1060

J.E.Sov.

P. minus. *Small Creeping Persicaria.* **Fig. 1061.**
Procumbent. Leaves linear-lanceolate, nearly sessile. Spikes slender, upright. Style undivided. Wet places; common. 6–10 in. Ann. July–Sept. Pinkish. ($\frac{2}{3}$) *E. B.* 1. 1043. *E. B.* 2. 570. *H. & Arn.* 367. *Bab.* 285. *Lind.* 213.

P. Hydropiper. *Biting Persicaria.* **Fig. 1062.**
Leaves lanceolate, waved. Spikes slender, drooping. Stipules fringed. Watery places; common. 1–3 ft. Ann. Aug. and Sept. Pink. ($\frac{2}{3}$) *E. B.* 1. 989. *E. B.* 2. 569. *H. & Arn.* 367. *Bab.* 285. *Lind.* 212.

Genus 2. Rumex.

R. Hydrolapathum. *Great Water Dock.* **Fig. 1063.**
Leaves lanceolate, acute; lower ones rather cordate at the base. Clusters crowded. Enlarged sepals ovate-triangular, all tubercled. Ditches. 3–5 ft. Perenn. July and Aug. Green. ($\frac{2}{3}$) *E. B.* 1. 2104. *E. B.* 2. 528. *H. & Arn.* 367. *Bab.* 282. *Lind.* 211.

R. crispus. *Curled Dock.* **Fig. 1064.**
Leaves lanceolate, waved. Upper whorls leafless. Enlarged sepals cordate, acute; one tubercled. A common weed. 2–3 ft. Perenn. June–Aug. Greenish. ($\frac{2}{3}$) *E. B.* 1. 1998. *E. B.* 2. 523. *H. & Arn.* 367. *Bab.* 283. *Lind.* 211.

R. pratensis. *Meadow Dock.* **Fig. 1065.**
Leaves oblong-lanceolate, wavy. Enlarged sepals unequal, toothed at the base, with entire triangular point. Meadows; rare. 2–3 ft. Perenn. June and July. Pinkish. ($\frac{2}{3}$) *E. B. Supp.* 2757. *E. B.* 2. 523*. *H. & Arn.* 368. *Bab.* 282. *Lind.* 332.

R. obtusifolius. *Broad-leaved Dock.* **Fig. 1066.**
Root-leaves ovate-cordate, obtuse. Enlarged sepals oblong-ovate, toothed at the base, with an oblong point. A common weed. 1–2 ft. Perenn. July. Yellowish. ($\frac{2}{3}$) *E. B.* 1. 1999. *E. B.* 2. 524. *H. & Arn.* 368. *Bab.* 282. *Lind.* 210.

R. aquaticus. *Grainless Water Dock.* **Fig. 1067.**
Leaves lanceolate; lower ones cordate-oblong, crisped and waved. Enlarged sepals broadly cordate, without tubercles. Wet places. 2–3 ft. Perenn. July. Green. ($\frac{2}{3}$) *E. B. Supp.* 2698. *E. B.* 2. 523*. *H. & Arn.* 368. *Bab.* 282. *Lind.* 332.

R. alpinus. *Monk's Rhubarb.* **Fig. 1068.**
Leaves broadly cordate, very obtuse; upper ones ovate-lanceolate. Clusters rather crowded, leafless. Enlarged sepals cordate. 3–4 ft. Perenn. July. Green. ($\frac{2}{3}$) *E. B. Supp.* 2694. *E. B.* 2. 524. *H. & Arn.* 368. *Bab.* 283. *Lind.* 332.

R. sanguineus. *Red-veined Dock.* **Fig. 1069.**
Leaves ovate-lanceolate, generally with red veins. Enlarged sepals oblong, entire. Whorls distant, leafless. Woods and way-sides. 2–3 ft. Perenn. July. Yellowish. ($\frac{2}{3}$) *E. B.* 1. 1533. *E. B.* 2. 521. *H. & Arn.* 369. *Bab.* 281. *Lind.* 210.

R. acutus. *Sharp Dock.* **Fig. 1070.**
Lower leaves cordate-oblong, pointed; upper lanceolate. Enlarged sepals linear-oblong, obtuse. Whorls distant, leafy. Wet places; common. 1–3 ft. Perenn. July. Yellowish. ($\frac{2}{3}$) *E. B* 1 724. *E. B.* 2. 522. *H. & Arn.* 369. *Bab.* 281. *Lind.* 210.

Fig 1061 to 1080.

1061   1062   1063   1064

1065   1066   1067   1068

1069   1070   1071   1072

1073   1074   1075   1076

1077   1078   1079   1080

J. E. Sowerby. Fecit

R. PULCHER. *Fiddle Dock.* **Fig. 1071.**
Lower leaves fiddle-shaped. Whorls leafy. Enlarged sepals tri-
angular-ovate. Waste ground. 1–2 ft. Perenn. Aug. Yellow. ($\frac{2}{3}$)
E. B. 1. 1576. *E. B.* 2. 525. *H. & Arn.* 369. *Bab.* 281. *Lind.* 210.

R. MARITIMUS. *Golden Dock.* **Fig. 1072.**
Lower leaves ovate-lanceolate, not waved; upper linear-lanceolate.
Clusters very dense, axillary. Enlarged sepals with 4 bristly teeth.
Marshes. 2–3 ft. Perenn. July and Aug. Bright yellow. ($\frac{2}{3}$)
E. B. 1. 725. *E. B.* 2. 527. *H. & Arn.* 369. *Bab.* 281. *Lind.* 209.

R. PALUSTRIS. *Marsh Dock.* **Fig. 1073.**
Leaves linear-lanceolate. Clusters distant, axillary. Enlarged sepals
lanceolate, with 3 short teeth on each side. Marshes. 2 ft. Perenn.
July. Greenish. ($\frac{2}{3}$) *E. B.* 1. 1932. *E. B.* 2. 526. *H. & Arn.* 369.
Bab. 281. *Lind.* 210.

R. ACETOSA. *Sorrel.* **Fig. 1074.**
Leaves oblong sagittate. Flowers diœcious. Leaves acid. Meadows;
abundant. 1–2 ft. Perenn. May–July. Red. ($\frac{2}{3}$) *E. B.* 1. 127.
E. B. 2. 529. *H. & Arn.* 370. *Bab.* 283. *Lind.* 211.

R. ACETOSELLA. *Sheep's Sorrel.* **Fig. 1075.**
Lower leaves hastate. Flowers diœcious. Leaves acid. Heaths;
abundant. 6 in.–1 ft. Perenn. June–Aug. Red or yellowish. ($\frac{2}{3}$)
E. B. 1. 1674. *E. B.* 2. 530. *H. & Arn.* 370. *Bab.* 283. *Lind.* 211.

Genus 3. OXYRIA.

O. RENIFORMIS. *Mountain Sorrel.* **Fig. 1076.**
Stems nearly leafless. Leaves kidney-shaped. Mountains. Leaves
acid. 6–8 in. Perenn. June and July. Greenish; red when in fruit.
($\frac{2}{3}$) *E. B.* 1. 910. *E. B.* 2. 520. *H. & Arn.* 370. *Bab.* 283. *Lind.* 211.

ORDER LXXII. THYMELACEÆ.
Genus 1. DAPHNE.

D. MEZEREUM. *Mezereon.* **Fig. 1077.**
A shrub. Leaves lanceolate, deciduous. Flowers sessile, usually 3
together. Woods. 4–8 ft. March. Pink; berries scarlet. ($\frac{2}{3}$) *E. B.*
1. 1381. *E. B.* 2. 564. *H. & Arn.* 371. *Bab.* 287. *Lind.* 209.

D. LAUREOLA. *Spurge-Laurel.* **Fig. 1078.**
A shrub. Leaves broadly lanceolate, evergreen. Flowers in axillary
racemes. Woods. 2–8 ft. March. Yellowish green; berries black.
($\frac{2}{3}$) *E. B.* 1. 119. *E. B.* 2. 567. *H. & Arn.* 371. *Bab.* 287. *Lind.* 209.

ORDER LXXIII. SANTALACEÆ.
Genus 1. THESIUM.

T. LINOPHYLLUM. *Flax-leaved Toad-flax.* **Fig. 1079.**
Stems ascending. Leaves linear-lanceolate. Bracts in threes. Chalky
pastures. 6 in.–1 ft. Perenn. May–July. ($\frac{2}{3}$) *E. B.* 1. 247.
E. B. 2. 347. *H. & Arn.* 372. *Bab.* 288. *Lind.* 208.

ORDER LXXIV. ARISTOLOCHIACEÆ.
Genus 1. ARISTOLOCHIA.

A. CLEMATITIS. *Birthwort.* **Fig. 1080.**
Stems numerous, erect. Leaves cordate. Ruins and thickets;
naturalized. 2–4 ft. Perenn. July–Sept. Pale yellow. ($\frac{2}{3}$) *E. B.*
1. 398. *E. B.* 2. 1225. *H. & Arn.* 373. *Bab.* 288. *Lind.* 225.

Genus 2. ASARUM.

A. EUROPÆUM. *Asarabacca.* **Fig. 1081.**
Stems creeping and rooting. Leaves kidney-shaped, in pairs. Sepals recurved. Mountain woods. Emetic. 2–4 in. Perenn. May. Brown. ($\frac{2}{3}$) *E. B.* 1. 1083. *E. B.* 2. 681. *H. & Arn.* 374. *Bab.* 289. *Lind.* 225.

ORDER LXXV. EMPETRACEÆ.

Genus 1. EMPETRUM.

E. NIGRUM. *Crow-berry. Crake-berry.* **Fig. 1082.**
A trailing shrub. Leaves linear-oblong, the margins meeting beneath. Bogs. 4–6 in. Perenn. April–June. Purplish; berries black. ($\frac{2}{3}$) *E. B.* 1. 526. *E. B.* 2. 1384. *H. & Arn.* 375. *Bab.* 289. *Lind.* 224.

ORDER LXXVI. EUPHORBIACEÆ.

Genus 1. MERCURIALIS.

M. PERENNIS. *Mercury.* **Fig. 1083.**
Stem simple. Leaves rough. Fertile flowers on long stalks. Woods and thickets; common. 1–2 ft. Perenn. April and May. Green. ($\frac{2}{3}$) *E. B.* 1. 1872. *E. B.* 2. 1396. *H. & Arn.* 376. *Bab.* 292. *Lind.* 223.

M. ANNUA. *Annual Mercury.* **Fig. 1084.**
Stem branched. Leaves smooth and shining. Fertile flowers axillary, 2 together. Waste ground. 1 ft. Ann. Aug. Green. ($\frac{2}{3}$) *E. B.* 1. 559. *E. B.* 2. 1397. *H. & Arn.* 376. *Bab.* 292. *Lind.* 223.

M. AMBIGUA. **Fig. 1085.**
Stem branched. All the flowers in axillary whorls. A variety of *annua.* Waste ground. 1 ft. Ann. July. Green. ($\frac{2}{3}$) *E. B. Supp.* 2816. *E. B.* 2. 1397*. *H. & Arn.* 376. *Bab.* 292.

Genus 2. EUPHORBIA.

E. PEPLIS. *Purple Spurge.* **Fig. 1086.**
Stem procumbent, forked. Leaves oblong, semi-cordate at the base. Plant glaucous. Sandy shores. 2–6 in. Ann. July–Sept. Reddish. ($\frac{2}{3}$) *E. B.* 1. 2002. *E. B.* 2. 1226. *H. & Arn.* 376. *Bab.* 290. *Lind.* 220.

E. HELIOSCOPIA. *Sun-Spurge. Wart-weed.* **Fig. 1087.**
Umbel 5-cleft. Leaves bright green, obovate, somewhat cuneate, serrated towards the end. Capsules smooth. A common weed. 6–10 in. Ann. July and Aug. Yellowish green. ($\frac{1}{2}$) *E. B.* 1. 883. *E. B.* 2. 1227. *H. & Arn.* 377. *Bab.* 291. *Lind.* 221.

E. PLATYPHYLLA. *Broad-leaved Spurge.* **Fig. 1088.**
Leaves obovate-lanceolate. Umbel usually 5-cleft. Bracts cordate. Capsules warted. Fields. 1–2 ft. Ann. June–Oct. Glands yellow. ($\frac{1}{2}$) *E. B.* 1. 333. *E. B.* 2. 1229. *H. & Arn.* 377. *Bab.* 290. *Lind.* 221.

E. HIBERNA. *Irish Spurge.* **Fig. 1089.**
Leaves and bracts elliptical, hairy beneath. Umbel 5–6-cleft. Capsules warted. Thickets 1–2 ft. Perenn. May and June. Green; glands purple. ($\frac{1}{2}$) *E. B.* 1. 1337. *E. B.* 2. 1228. *H. & Arn.* 377. *Bab.* 290. *Lind.* 221.

E. PILOSA. *Hairy Spurge.* **Fig. 1090.**
Leaves ovate-lanceolate, hairy beneath. Bracts elliptical. Umbel 5-cleft. Capsules hairy. Woods near Bath; naturalized? 2 ft. Perenn. June. Yellowish green; glands yellow. ($\frac{1}{2}$) *E. B. Supp.* 2787. *E. B.* 2. 1229*. *H. & Arn.* 378. *Bab* 291. *Lind.* 333.

E. CORALLOIDES. *Coral Spurge.* **Fig. 1091.**
Leaves broadly lanceolate, downy. Bracts ovate-oblong or ovate, hairy. Umbel 5-cleft. Capsules nearly smooth, woolly. Hedges in Sussex. 1–2 ft. Bienn.? July. Greenish yellow; glands yellow. Capsules reddish. ($\frac{1}{2}$) *E. B. Supp.* 2837. *E. B.* 2. 1229*. *H. & Arn.* 378. *Bab.* 291.

E. ESULA. *Leafy-branched Spurge.* **Fig. 1092.**
Leaves oblong-lanceolate. Bracts cordate. Umbel many-cleft. Glands of involucrum with 2 horns. Shady woods. 8 in.–1 ft. Perenn. July. Greenish. ($\frac{2}{3}$) *E. B.* 1. 1399. *E. B.* 2. 1230. *H. & Arn.* 378. *Bab.* 291. *Lind.* 221.

E. CYPARISSIAS. *Cypress Spurge.* **Fig. 1093.**
Leaves linear, glaucous. Stems tufted, much branched. Umbel many-cleft. Thickets; local. 1–1$\frac{1}{2}$ ft. Perenn. June and July. Yellowish. ($\frac{1}{2}$) *E. B.* 1. 840. *E. B.* 2. 1231. *H. & Arn.* 378. *Bab.* 291. *Lind.* 221.

E. PARALIAS. *Sea Spurge.* **Fig. 1094.**
Leaves imbricated, glaucous; lower obovate-lanceolate, upper linear-lanceolate. Umbel 5-cleft. Capsules wrinkled. 1 ft. Perenn. Aug. and Sept. Greenish; glands orange. ($\frac{1}{2}$) *E. B.* 1. 195. *E. B.* 2. 1232. *H. & Arn.* 379. *Bab.* 291. *Lind.* 222.

E. PORTLANDICA. *Portland Spurge.* **Fig. 1095.**
Leaves very glaucous, obovate-lanceolate. Stems red. Umbel 5-cleft. Glands of involucrum with 2 long horns. Capsules rough at the angles. Southern coast. 6 in.–2 ft. Perenn. Aug. and Sept. Yellowish; glands deep orange. ($\frac{1}{2}$) *E. B.* 1. 441. *E. B.* 2. 1233. *H. & Arn.* 379. *Bab.* 292. *Lind.* 222.

E. PEPLUS. *Petty Spurge.* **Fig. 1096.**
Leaves broadly obovate, tapering to a petiole. Umbel 3-cleft. A common weed. 4 in.–1 ft. Ann. June–Nov. Greenish; glands yellow. ($\frac{2}{3}$) *E. B.* 1. 959. *E. B.* 2. 1235. *H. & Arn.* 379. *Bab.* 292. *Lind.* 222.

E. EXIGUA. *Dwarf Spurge.* **Fig. 1097.**
Leaves and bracts rather rigid, lanceolate, acute. Umbel 3-cleft. Glands with 2 long horns. Corn-fields. 5–6 in. Ann. July. Greenish. ($\frac{2}{3}$) *E. B.* 1. 1336. *E. B.* 2. 1234. *H. & Arn.* 379. *Bab.* 292. *Lind.* 222.

E. LATHYRIS. *Caper Spurge.* **Fig. 1098.**
Leaves oblong lanceolate, cordate at the base, glaucous. Bracts cordate. Umbel 4-cleft. Capsules smooth. Thickets. 1–2 ft. Bienn. July. Greenish. ($\frac{1}{2}$) *E. B.* 1. 2255. *E. B.* 2. 1236. *H. & Arn.* 379. *Bab.* 292. *Lind.* 222.

E. AMYGDALOIDES. *Wood Spurge.* **Fig. 1099.**
Leaves broadly lanceolate, tapering at the base, hairy beneath. Bracts perfoliate. Umbel about 6-cleft, with scattered peduncles below. Capsules dotted. Woods; common. 2–4 ft. Perenn. April–June. Yellowish; glands bright yellow. ($\frac{1}{2}$) *E. B.* 1. 256. *E. B.* 2. 1237. *H. & Arn.* 380. *Bab.* 291. *Lind.* 223.

E. CHARACIAS. *Shrubby Spurge.* **Fig. 1100.**
Plant shrubby. Leaves linear-lanceolate. Bracts connate. Umbel many-cleft. Capsules woolly when young. Bushy places; not native. 3–4 ft. Perenn. March. Greenish; glands purple. ($\frac{1}{2}$) *E. B.* 1. 442. *E. B.* 2. 1238. *H. & Arn.* 380. *Lind.* 223.

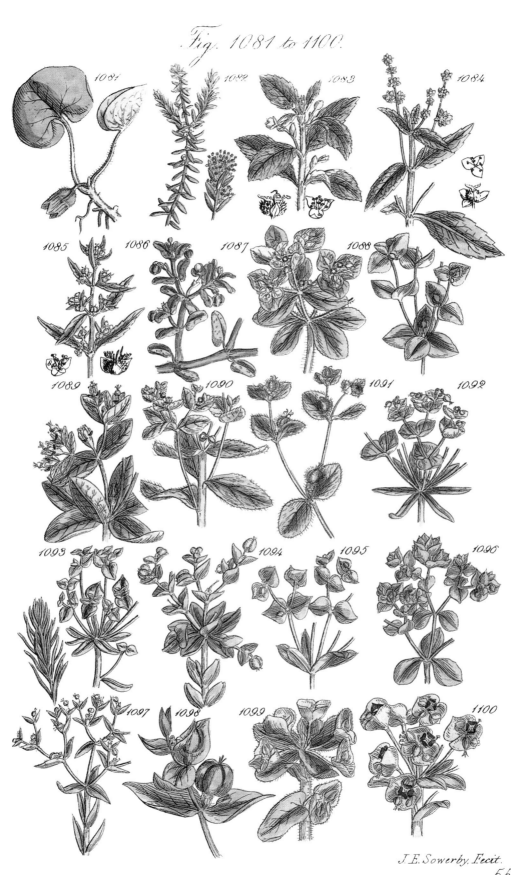

Fig. 1081 to 1100.

1081 1082 1083 1084

1085 1086 1087 1088

1089 1090 1091 1092

1093 1094 1095 1096

1097 1098 1099 1100

J.E. Sowerby, Fecit.

55.

Genus 3. Buxus.

B. SEMPERVIRENS. *Box.* **Fig. 1101.**
An evergreen shrub. Leaves oblong-ovate, convex, glossy. Chalk
hills; local. 3–15 ft. April. Yellowish. ($\frac{2}{3}$) *E. B.* 1. 1341.
E. B. 2. 1306. *H. & Arn.* 380. *Bab.* 290. *Lind.* 223.

ORDER LXXVII. CALLITRICHACEÆ.
Genus 1. CALLITRICHE.

C. VERNA. *Spring Water Starwort.* **Fig. 1102.**
Upper leaves floating in a star-like tuft, oval-lanceolate. Lobes of
capsule bluntly keeled. Ann. Pools; common. April–Oct. ($\frac{2}{3}$)
E. B. 1. 722. *E. B.* 2. 1239. *H. & Arn.* 381. *Bab.* 293. *Lind.* 243.

C. PLATYCARPA. **Fig. 1103.**
Fruit with the lobes slightly winged. A variety of *verna.* Pools
and ditches. Ann. April–Oct. ($\frac{2}{3}$) *E. B. Supp.* 2864. *H. &
Arn.* 381. *Bab.* 293. *Lind.* 243.

C. PEDUNCULATA. *Stalked Water Starwort.* **Fig. 1104.**
Leaves all submerged, linear. Fruit-bearing peduncles long. Lobes
of capsules bluntly keeled. Pools. Ann. June–Oct. ($\frac{2}{3}$) *E. B.
Supp.* 2606. *E. B.* 2. 1239*. *H. & Arn.* 381. *Bab.* 293. *Lind.* 243.

C. AUTUMNALIS. *Autumnal Water Starwort.* **Fig. 1105.**
Leaves all submerged, linear, notched at the apex. Lobes of fruit
broadly winged. Pools and ditches. Ann. June–Oct. ($\frac{2}{3}$) *E. B.
Supp.* 2732. *E. B.* 2. 1239**. *H. & Arn.* 381. *Bab.* 294. *Lind.* 243.

ORDER LXXVIII. CERATOPHYLLACEÆ.
Genus 1. CERATOPHYLLUM.

C. DEMERSUM. *Spiny-fruited Hornwort.* **Fig. 1106.**
Stems submerged. Leaves in narrow segments, densely whorled.
Fruit with 2 spines. Pools. Perenn. July and Aug. ($\frac{2}{3}$) *E. B.*
1. 947. *E. B.* 2. 1314. *H. & Arn.* 382. *Bab.* 293. *Lind.* 225.

C. SUBMERSUM. *Hornwort.* **Fig. 1107.**
Stems submerged. Leaves in more distant whorls. Sepals entire.
Fruit without spines. Pools. Perenn. Sept. ($\frac{2}{3}$) *E. B.* 1. 679. *E. B.*
2. 1315. *H. & Arn.* 382. *Bab.* 293. *Lind.* 225.

ORDER LXXIX. URTICACEÆ.
Genus 1. URTICA.

U. PILULIFERA. *Roman Nettle.* **Fig. 1108.**
Leaves opposite, ovate, serrated, with stinging hairs. Fertile flowers
in globular heads. Waste ground. 1–2 ft. Ann. June and July.
Green. ($\frac{2}{3}$) *E. B.* 1. 148. *E. B.* 2. 1307. *H. & Arn.* 384.
Bab. 295. *Lind.* 219.

U. URENS. *Small Nettle.* **Fig. 1109.**
Leaves elliptical, with stinging hairs. Flowers in loose racemes.
Waste ground; common. 8 in.–1 ft. Ann. June–Oct. Green. ($\frac{2}{3}$)
E. B. 1. 1236. *E. B.* 2. 1308. *H. & Arn.* 384. *Bab.* 295. *Lind.* 219.

U. DIOICA. *Common Nettle.* **Fig. 1110.**
Leaves cordate, with stinging hairs. Flowers in much-branched
axillary clusters; usually diœcious. Way-sides; abundant 2–4 ft.
Perenn. July and Aug. Green. ($\frac{2}{3}$) *E. B.* 1. 1750. *E. B.* 2 1309.
H. & Arn. 384. *Bab.* 295. *Lind.* 219.

Fig. 1101 to 1120.

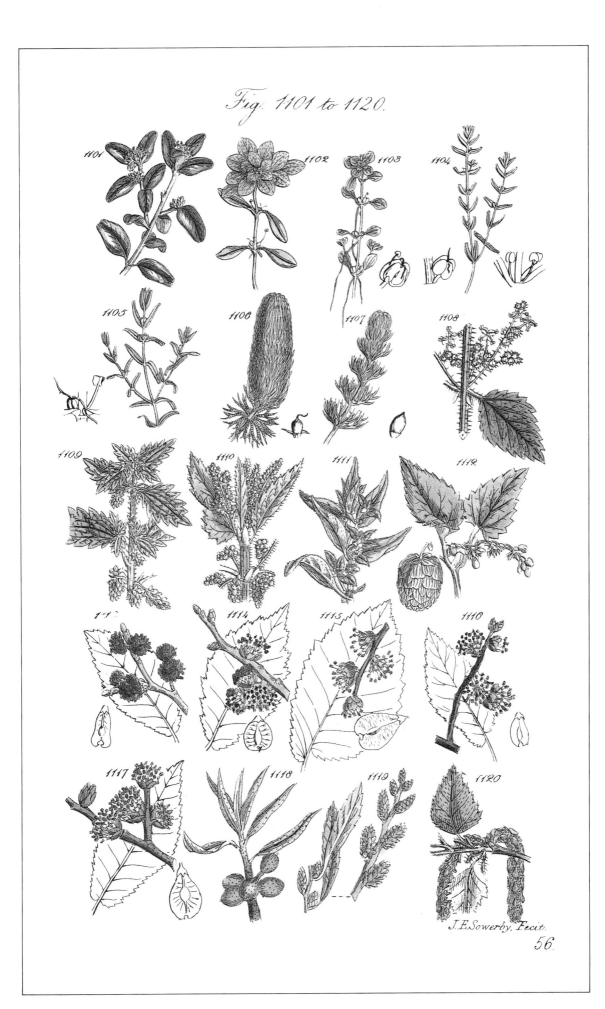

J.E. Sowerby, Fecit.

Genus 2. Parietaria.

P. officinalis. *Pellitory.* **Fig. 1111.**

Leaves ovate-lanceolate. Stems ascending. Involucrum 3-flowered. Old walls. 1–2 ft. Perenn. June–Nov. Pink. ($\frac{2}{3}$) *E. B.* 1. 879. *E. B.* 2. 229. *H. & Arn.* 384. *Bab.* 294. *Lind.* 218.

Genus 3. Humulus.

H. Lupulus. *Hop.* **Fig. 1112.**

A climbing diœcious plant. Barren flowers in panicles; fertile ones in axillary catkins. Hedges. Perenn. July. Greenish. ($\frac{1}{2}$) *E. B.* 1. 427. *E. B.* 2. 1389. *H. & Arn.* 386. *Bab.* 295. *Lind.* 219.

Order LXXX. ULMACEÆ.

Genus 1. Ulmus.

U. campestris. *Common Elm.* **Fig. 1113.**

Leaves rhomboid-ovate. Fruit oblong, deeply cloven. Woods and hedges. March and April. Purplish. ($\frac{2}{3}$) *E. B.* 1. 1886. *E. B.* 2. 365. *H. & Arn.* 386. *Bab.* 295. *Lind.* 226.

U. suberosa. *Cork-barked Elm.* **Fig. 1114.**

Leaves nearly orbicular. Flowers on short stalks. Fruit roundish, cloven. Branches corky. Hedges. March. Purplish. ($\frac{2}{3}$) *E. B.* 1. 2161. *E. B.* 2. 366. *H. & Arn.* 387. *Bab.* 295. *Lind.* 226.

U. major. *Dutch Elm.* **Fig. 1115.**

Leaves ovate. Flowers nearly sessile. Branches corky. A doubtful native. March. Yellowish. ($\frac{2}{3}$) *E. B.* 1. 2542. *E. B.* 2. 367. *H. & Arn.* 387. *Bab.* 296? *Lind.* 226.

U. glabra. *Smooth Elm.* **Fig. 1116.**

Branches smooth. Leaves ovate-lanceolate, very unequal at the base, smooth. Fruit slightly cloven. Woods. March. Purplish. ($\frac{2}{3}$) *E. B.* 1. 2248. *E. B.* 2. 369. *H. & Arn.* 387. *Bab.* 295. *Lind.* 226.

U. montana. *Wych Elm.* **Fig. 1117.**

Leaves large, obovate, nearly equal at the base, coarsely serrated. Branches drooping, smooth. Woods. March. Purplish. ($\frac{2}{3}$) *E. B.* 1. 1887. *E. B.* 2. 368. *H. & Arn.* 387. *Bab.* 296. *Lind.* 227.

Order LXXXI. ELÆAGNACEÆ.

Genus 1. Hippophaë.

H. rhamnoides. *Sallow Thorn.* **Fig. 1118.**

A diœcious shrub. Leaves linear-lanceolate, silvery white. Branches ending in thorns. Sea-coasts. 4–10 ft. May. Berries orange. ($\frac{2}{3}$) *E. B.* 1. 425. *E. B.* 2. 1387. *H. & Arn.* 388. *Bab.* 287. *Lind.* 208.

Order LXXXII. MYRICACEÆ.

Genus 1. Myrica.

✦M. Gale. *Sweet Gale.* **Fig. 1119.**

A low shrub. Leaves lanceolate. Plant covered with white resinous glands. Catkins with pointed scales. 2–4 ft. May. Yellowish red. ($\frac{2}{3}$) *E. B.* 1. 562. *E. B.* 2. 1388. *H. & Arn.* 389. *Bab.* 307. *Lind.* 242.

Order LXXXIII. BETULACEÆ.

Genus 1. Betula.

B. alba. *White Birch.* **Fig. 1120.**

Bark of trunk silvery white. Leaves ovate, acute. Flowers monœcious, in catkins. Woods. April and May. Greenish. ($\frac{1}{2}$) *E. B.* 1. 2198. *E. B.* 2. 1325. *H. & Arn.* 390. *Bab.* 307. *Lind.* 229.

B. NANA. *Dwarf Birch.* **Fig. 1121.**
A low shrub. Leaves orbicular. Catkins erect. Highland mountains.
1–5 ft. May. Greenish. ($\frac{1}{2}$) *E. B.* 1. 2326. *E. B.* 2. 1326.
H. & Arn. 390. *Bab.* 208. *Lind.* 229.

Genus 2. ALNUS.

A. GLUTINOSA. *Alder.* **Fig. 1122.**
A tree. Leaves roundish, somewhat wedge-shaped, slightly lobed;
sometimes deeply cut. Sterile catkins long; fertile ones ovate. Moist
ground. March and April. Sterile catkins reddish. ($\frac{1}{2}$) *E. B.* 1. 1508.
E. B. 2. 1305. *H. & Arn.* 390. *Bab.* 308. *Lind.* 229.

Order LXXXIV. SALICACEÆ.
Genus 1. SALIX.

S. PURPUREA. *Purple Willow.* **Fig. 1123.**
Branches decumbent, purple. Leaves lanceolate, broadest above.
Stamen 1. Stigmas very short, nearly sessile. 4–6 ft. Moist meadows.
March and April. Scales purplish. ($\frac{1}{2}$) *E. B.* 1. 1388. *E. B.* 2. 1330.
H. & Arn. 392. *Bab.* 299. *Lind.* 232.

S. LAMBERTIANA. **Fig. 1124.**
Branches erect, purplish. Stamen 1. Stigmas short, ovate, notched.
A variety of *Helix?* Meadows. 4–18 ft. April. Scales purplish. ($\frac{1}{2}$)
E. B. 1. 1359. *E. B.* 2. 1332. *H. & Arn.* 392. *Bab.* 299. *Lind.* 232.

S. WOOLGARIANA. **Fig. 1125.**
Branches erect, yellowish. Leaves cuneate-lanceolate. Stamen 1.
Stigmas short, obtuse, nearly sessile. A variety of *Helix?* Moist
ground. 6–20 ft. April. Scales purplish. ($\frac{1}{2}$) *E. B. Supp.* 2651.
E. B. 2. 1332*. *H. & Arn.* 392. *Bab.* 299. *Lind.* 232.

S. HELIX. *Rose Willow.* **Fig. 1126.**
Branches erect, yellowish. Leaves lanceolate, broadest above. Stamen 1. Style as long as stigmas. Moist ground. 8–20 ft. March.
Scales yellowish. ($\frac{1}{2}$) *E. B.* 1. 1343. *E. B.* 2. 1331. *H. & Arn.* 393.
Bab. 299. *Lind.* 232.

S. FORBYANA. **Fig. 1127.**
Branches erect, yellowish. Leaves oblong-lanceolate, glaucous beneath, with small, downy stipules. Stamen 1. Stigmas linear; style
equal in length. Meadows. 6–20 ft. April. Scales purple. ($\frac{1}{2}$)
E. B. 1. 1344. *E. B.* 2. 1333. *H. & Arn.* 393. *Bab.* 300. *Lind.* 232.

S. RUBRA. *Green-leaved Osier.* **Fig. 1128.**
Branches slender, purplish. Leaves linear-lanceolate, grass-green.
Stamens 2, united. Meadows and osier-beds. 8–15 ft. April.
Scales purple. ($\frac{1}{2}$) *E. B.* 1. 1145. *E. B.* 2. 1334. *H. & Arn.* 393.
Bab. 300. *Lind.* 232.

S. TRIANDRA. *Smooth Willow.* **Fig. 1129.**
A tree with deciduous bark. Leaves oblong-lanceolate, smooth.
Stipules rounded. Stamens 3. Stigmas cloven, sessile. Wet woods
and osier-beds. 10–30 ft. May–July. Yellow. ($\frac{1}{2}$) *E. B.* 1. 1435.
E. B. 2. 1336. *H. & Arn.* 394. *Bab.* 299. *Lind.* 231.

S. HOFFMANNIANA. **Fig. 1130.**
Leaves short, lanceolate. Stipules large, ear-shaped. Stamens 3.
Stigmas nearly sessile. A variety of *triandra?* Moist ground. 6–
12 ft. May. Yellow ($\frac{1}{2}$) *E. B. Supp.* 2620. *E. B.* 2. 1336.
H. & Arn. 394. *Bab.* 299. *Lind.* 231.

S. AMYGDALINA. *Almond Willow.* **Fig. 1131.**
Young branches furrowed. Leaves oblong-ovate. Stipules large. Stamens 3. Stigmas sessile, notched. River-sides. 12–30 ft. May. Yellowish. ($\frac{1}{2}$) *E. B.* 1. 1936. *E. B.* 2. 1337. *H. & Arn.* 394. *Bab.* 299. *Lind.* 231.

S. UNDULATA. **Fig. 1132.**
Leaves lanceolate, very long; petioles decurrent. Stipules pointed. Stamens 3. Stigmas linear, cloven; style equal in length. A variety of *triandra?* Meadows. 8–12 ft. April. Yellow. ($\frac{1}{2}$) *E. B.* 1. 1436. *E. B.* 2. 1335. *H. & Arn.* 394. *Bab.* 298. *Lind.* 231.

S. PENTANDRA. *Sweet Willow.* **Fig. 1133.**
Leaves ovate-lanceolate, with glandular serratures, fragrant. Stamens 5 or more. Capsule smooth. Stigmas nearly sessile. Banks of rivers. 10–20 ft. May and June. Yellow. ($\frac{1}{2}$) *E. B.* 1. 1805. *E. B.* 2. 1338. *H. & Arn.* 394. *Bab.* 297. *Lind.* 231.

S. FRAGILIS. *Crack Willow.* **Fig. 1134.**
A large tree. Young branches brittle at the joints. Leaves ovate-lanceolate, serrated; with glandular petioles. Stamens 2. Style shorter than the stigmas. Marshy ground. April and May. Yellowish. ($\frac{1}{2}$) *E. B.* 1. 1807. *E. B.* 2. 1340. *H. & Arn.* 395. *Bab.* 298. *Lind.* 230.

S. RUSSELLIANA. *Bedford Willow.* **Fig. 1135.**
A large tree. Leaves lanceolate, deeply and unequally serrated; the petioles glandular, sometimes leafy. Stamens 2. Style as long as the divided stigmas. Marshy woods. April and May. Yellowish. ($\frac{1}{2}$) *E. B.* 1. 1808. *E. B.* 2. 1341. *H. & Arn.* 396. *Bab.* 298. *Lind.* 231.

S. DECIPIENS. *Varnished Willow.* **Fig. 1136.**
Branches very smooth and glossy, brown. Leaves lanceolate, serrated. Petioles glandular. Style longer than the stigmas. A variety of *fragilis?* Moist woods. 15–20 ft. April. Yellowish. ($\frac{1}{2}$) *E. B.* 1. 1937. *E. B.* 2. 1339. *H. & Arn.* 396. *Bab.* 298. *Lind.* 230.

S. ALBA. *White Willow.* **Fig. 1137.**
A large tree. Leaves elliptic-lanceolate, grey and silky on both sides. Stamens 2. Scales of catkins short, rounded, downy. Stigmas nearly sessile, recurved, bifid. Woods and wet places. May. Yellowish. ($\frac{1}{2}$) *E. B.* 1. 2430. *E. B.* 2. 1342. *H. & Arn.* 396. *Bab.* 298. *Lind.* 231.

S. CÆRULEA. *Blue Willow.* **Fig. 1138.**
A slight variety of *alba.* Leaves less silky, sometimes nearly smooth. Moist woods and river-sides. ($\frac{1}{2}$) *E. B.* 1. 2431. *E. B.* 2. 1342*. *H. & Arn.* 396. *Bab.* 298. *Lind.* 231.

S. VITELLINA. *Yellow Willow. Golden Osier.* **Fig. 1139.**
Branches bright yellow, somewhat pendent. Leaves lanceolate, silky beneath, yellow-green. A variety of *alba?* Moist woods and meadows. 10–30 ft. May. Yellowish. ($\frac{1}{2}$) *E. B.* 1. 1389. *E. B.* 2. 1343. *H. & Arn.* 397. *Bab.* 298. *Lind.* 231.

S. PETIOLARIS. **Fig. 1140.**
Leaves lanceolate, glaucous beneath. Catkins lax. Capsules stalked. Stamens 2. Stigmas divided, nearly sessile. Not native. 6–12 ft. April. Green. ($\frac{1}{2}$) *E. B.* 1. 1147. *E. B.* 2. 1344. *H. & Arn.* 397. *Bab.* 299.

Fig. 1121 to 1140

1121 1122 1123 1124 1125 1126 1127 1128 1129 1130 1131 1132 1133 1134 1135 1136 1137 1138 1139 1140

J. E. Sowerby, Fecit.

S. ROSMARINIFOLIA. *Rosemary-leaved Willow.* **Fig. 1141.**
Leaves entire, linear-lanceolate, silky. Catkins recurved, lax, short,
hairy. Stamens 2. Stigmas linear, divided. Moist ground. 3 ft.
April. Scales black. ($\frac{1}{2}$) *E. B.* 1. 1365. *E. B.* 2. 1345. *H. &
Arn.* 397. *Bab.* 303. *Lind.* 236.

S. ANGUSTIFOLIA. *Little Tree Willow.* **Fig. 1142.**
Leaves linear-lanceolate, slightly toothed, glaucous beneath. Catkins
ovate, erect. Scales very hairy, as long as the capsule. Stamens 2.
Stigmas broad, entire. Highlands. 1–2 ft. April. Scales purple.
($\frac{1}{2}$) *E. B.* 1. 1366. *E. B.* 2. 1346. *H. & Arn.* 398. *Bab.* 303.
Lind. 236.

S. DONIANA. **Fig. 1143.**
Branches erect. Leaves obovate-lanceolate, slightly serrated, glaucous
beneath. Catkins erect, cylindrical. Stamens 2. A variety of *purpurea?* Scotland. 2–6 ft. May. Scales blackish. ($\frac{1}{2}$) *E. B.
Supp.* 2599. *E. B.* 2. 1346*. *H. & Arn.* 398. *Bab.* 303. *Lind.* 232.

S. FUSCA. *Creeping Willow.* **Fig. 1144.**
Stems procumbent. Leaves elliptical, somewhat downy, silky beneath.
Stamens 2. Stigmas bifid. Capsule silky, the pedicel very long. Heaths;
common. 6 in.–2 ft. April and May. Brownish. ($\frac{1}{2}$) *E. B.* 1. 1960.
E. B. 2. 1347. *H. & Arn.* 399. *Bab.* 303. *Lind.* 236.

S. REPENS. **Fig. 1145.**
Stem depressed, with short upright branches. Leaves elliptic-lanceolate.
A variety of *fusca.* Heaths. 6 in.–1 ft. April. Scales brownish.
($\frac{1}{2}$) *E. B.* 1. 183. *E. B.* 2. 1348. *H. & Arn.* 399. *Bab.* 303.
Lind. 236.

S. PROSTRATA. **Fig. 1146.**
Stem prostrate, with straight, elongated branches. Leaves elliptic-
oblong. A variety of *fusca.* Heaths. 6 in. April and May.
Brownish. ($\frac{1}{2}$) *E. B.* 1. 1959. *E. B.* 2. 1349. *H. & Arn.* 399.
Bab. 303. *Lind.* 236.

S. ASCENDENS. **Fig. 1147.**
Stem recumbent. Leaves elliptical. A variety of *fusca.* Heaths.
6 in.–1 ft. April and May. Scales purplish. ($\frac{1}{2}$) *E. B.* 1. 1962.
E. B. 2. 1350. *H. & Arn.* 399. *Bab.* 303. *Lind.* 236.

S. PARVIFOLIA. **Fig. 1148.**
Stem recumbent. Leaves very small, elliptical. A variety of *fusca.*
6–8 in. April and May. Scales reddish. ($\frac{1}{2}$) *E. B.* 1. 1961.
E. B. 2. 1350*. *H. & Arn.* 399. *Bab.* 303. *Lind.* 236.

S. INCUBACEA. **Fig. 1149.**
Stem procumbent. Leaves elliptic-lanceolate. A variety of *fusca.*
6 in.–1 ft. April and May. Scales greenish or brown. ($\frac{1}{2}$) *E. B.
Supp.* 2600. *E. B.* 2. 1350**. *H. & Arn.* 399. *Bab.* 304. *Lind.* 236.

S. ARGENTEA. **Fig. 1150.**
Stem erect or spreading. Leaves elliptical, with a recurved point,
very silvery beneath. A variety of *fusca?* Sandy sea-shores. 4 in.–
1 ft. April and May. Scales brown. ($\frac{1}{2}$) *E. B.* 1. 1364. *E. B.*
2. 1351. *H. & Arn.* 399. *Bab.* 304. *Lind.* 236.

Fig. 1141 to 1160.

1141 1142 1143 1144
1145 1146 1147 1148
1149 1150 1151 1152
1153 1154 1155 1156
1157 1158 1159 1160

J. E. Sowerby. Fecit

58

S. AMBIGUA.   **Fig. 1151.**

Leaves obovate, oval, or lanceolate, with a recurved point. Catkins erect, cylindrical. Stamens 2. Capsules on long hairy pedicels. Heaths. 2–4 ft. May. Brownish. ($\frac{1}{2}$) *E. B. Supp.* 2733. *E. B.* 2. 1351*. *H. & Arn.* 400. *Bab.* 304. *Lind.* 236.

S. RETICULATA. *Net-leaved Willow.*   **Fig. 1152.**

Stems very short, tufted. Leaves orbicular or elliptical, reticulated with veins, glaucous beneath. Catkins terminal. 1–4 in. June and July. Reddish. ($\frac{1}{2}$) *E. B.* 1. 1908. *E. B.* 2. 1352. *H. & Arn.* 400. *Bab.* 305. *Lind.* 238.

S. GLAUCA. *Downy Willow.*   **Fig. 1153.**

Leaves ovate-lanceolate, entire, downy; snow-white and cottony beneath. Capsules sessile, ovate, downy. Stigmas sessile. Stamens 2. Highlands. 1–3 ft. July. Scales black. ($\frac{1}{2}$) *E. B.* 1. 1809. *E. B.* 2. 1354. *H. & Arn.* 401. *Bab.* 304. *Lind.* 237.

S. ARENARIA.   **Fig. 1154.**

Leaves oblong-lanceolate, cottony beneath. Style as long as the capsule. Stigmas linear. A variety of *glauca*. Highlands. 2–3 ft. June. Scales blackish. ($\frac{1}{2}$) *E. B.* 1. 1809. *E. B.* 2. 1354. *H. & Arn.* 401. *Bab.* 304. *Lind.* 237.

S. STUARTIANA.   **Fig. 1155.**

Leaves ovate-lanceolate, shaggy. Style as long as the capsule. Stigmas hair-like, deeply divided. A variety of *glauca*. Highlands. 1–3 ft. July. Scales black. ($\frac{1}{2}$) *E. B.* 1. 2586. *E. B.* 2. 1355. *H. & Arn.* 401. *Bab.* 304. *Lind.* 237.

S. VIMINALIS. *Common Osier.*   **Fig. 1156.**

Branches straight, slender. Leaves linear-lanceolate, elongated, white beneath, revolute, with small stipules. Capsules nearly sessile. Style elongated. Stigmas linear, nearly entire. Stamens 2. Marshes. 10–20 ft. April and May. Scales brownish. ($\frac{1}{2}$) *E. B.* 1. 1898. *E. B.* 2. 1356. *H. & Arn.* 402. *Bab.* 300. *Lind.* 232.

S. STIPULARIS.   **Fig. 1157.**

Leaves lanceolate, downy beneath, with large semicordate stipules. Capsules with short pedicels. A variety of *viminalis*. Marshes. 10–20 ft. March. Scales brown. ($\frac{1}{2}$) *E. B.* 1. 1214. *E. B.* 2. 1357. *H. & Arn.* 402. *Bab.* 300. *Lind.* 233.

S. SMITHIANA.   **Fig. 1158.**

Leaves lanceolate, whitish beneath; with minute crescent-shaped stipules. Style short. Stigmas deeply cleft, linear. A variety of *viminalis?* 6–10 ft. April and May. Scales brown. ($\frac{1}{2}$) *E. B.* 1. 1509. *E. B.* 2. 1358. *H. & Arn.* 402. *Bab.* 300. *Lind.* 233.

S. FERRUGINEA.   **Fig. 1159.**

Leaves thin, lanceolate, slightly hairy, brownish when young. Stipules small, semiovate. Capsule stalked. Style as long as the oblong stigmas. A variety of *acuminata?* Marshes. 6–12 ft. April. Scales brown. ($\frac{1}{2}$) *E. B. Supp.* 2665. *E. B.* 2. 1358*. *H. & Arn.* 403. *Bab.* 301. *Lind.* 233.

S. ACUMINATA. *Long-leaved Willow.*   **Fig. 1160.**

Leaves oblong-lanceolate, wavy, glaucous and downy beneath; stipules kidney-shaped. Capsules stalked. Style as long as the blunt undivided stigmas. Stamens 2. Woods. 10–20 ft. April. Scales purplish. ($\frac{1}{2}$) *E. B.* 1. 1434. *E. B.* 2. 1359. *H. & Arn.* 402. *Bab.* 301. *Lind.* 233.

S. CINEREA. *Grey Sallow.* **Fig. 1161.**
Leaves obovate-lanceolate, glaucous above, downy and reticulated beneath. Stipules large, semicordate. Style short. Stigmas entire. Woods; common. 10–30 ft. April. Scales brown. ($\frac{1}{2}$) *E. B.* 1. 1897. *E. B.* 2. 1360. *H. & Arn.* 403. *Bab.* 301. *Lind.* 233.

S. AQUATICA. *Water Sallow.* **Fig. 1162.**
Leaves obovate-elliptical, rather downy. Stipules rounded, toothed. Stigmas nearly sessile. A variety of *cinerea.* Wet woods. 10–30 ft. April. Scales brown. ($\frac{1}{2}$) *E. B.* 1. 1437. *E. B.* 2. 1361. *H. & Arn.* 403. *Bab.* 301. *Lind.* 233.

S. OLEIFOLIA. **Fig. 1163.**
Leaves obovate-lanceolate, glaucous and reticulated beneath. Stipules small, rounded. Catkins oval. A variety of *cinerea.* 10–20 ft. March. Scales brown. ($\frac{1}{2}$) *E. B.* 1. 1402. *E. B.* 2. 1362. *H. & Arn.* 403. *Bab.* 301. *Lind.* 233.

S. AURITA. *Round-eared Sallow.* **Fig. 1164.**
Leaves obovate, wrinkled with veins, downy beneath, curved at the point. Stipules large, rounded. Style short. Stigmas ovate. Thickets; common. 4–12 ft. May. Scales brownish. ($\frac{1}{2}$) *E. B.* 1. 1487. *E. B.* 2. 1363. *H. & Arn.* 403. *Bab.* 301. *Lind.* 234.

S. CAPREA. *Great Sallow.* **Fig. 1165.**
Leaves very broad, roundish ovate, downy beneath. Stipules semicordate. Stigmas nearly sessile, entire. Hedges and thickets; common. 10–30 ft. April and May. Scales blackish. ($\frac{1}{2}$) *E. B.* 1. 1488. *E. B.* 2. 1364. *H. & Arn.* 404. *Bab.* 301. *Lind.* 234.

S. SPHACELATA. **Fig. 1166.**
Leaves obovate, downy, discoloured at the point. Stipules semicordate. Stigmas notched, longer than the style. A variety of *caprea.* Scotland. 6–10 ft. April and May. Scales brown. ($\frac{1}{2}$) *E. B.* 1. 2333. *E. B.* 2. 1365. *H. & Arn.* 404. *Bab.* 301. *Lind.* 234.

S. COTINIFOLIA. *Sumach-leaved Willow.* **Fig. 1167.**
Branches downy. Leaves broadly elliptical, nearly orbicular, glaucous. Style bifid. Stigmas notched. A variety of *nigricans?* Woods. 2–6 ft. April and May. Scales brown. ($\frac{1}{2}$) *E. B.* 1. 1403. *E. B.* 2. 1366. *H. & Arn.* 404. *Bab.* 302. *Lind.* 235.

S. HIRTA. *Hairy-branched Willow.* **Fig. 1168.**
Branches densely hairy. Leaves elliptical, somewhat heart-shaped, downy. Stipules semicordate. A variety of *nigricans.* 6–12 ft. April. Scales brown. ($\frac{1}{2}$) *E. B.* 1. 1404. *E. B.* 2. 1367. *H. & Arn.* 404. *Bab.* 302. *Lind.* 235.

S. NIGRICANS. *Dark-leaved Willow.* **Fig. 1169.**
Leaves elliptic-lanceolate, acute, smooth, with a downy rib above, glaucous beneath. Capsules downy. Woods. 10–12 ft. April. Scales brown. ($\frac{1}{2}$) *E. B.* 1. 1213. *E. B.* 2. 1368. *H. & Arn.* 404. *Bab.* 302. *Lind.* 234.

S. ANDERSONIANA. *Green Mountain Sallow.* **Fig. 1170.**
Branches minutely downy. Leaves elliptical, pale beneath. Stipules semiovate. Capsules smooth. Style bifid at the extremity. Stigmas cloven. 6–10 ft. May and June. Scales black. ($\frac{1}{2}$) *E. B.* 1. 2343. *E. B.* 2. 1369. *H. & Arn.* 405. *Bab.* 301. *Lind.* 234.

S. DAMASCENA. *Damson-leaved Willow.*   **Fig. 1171.**
Young shoots densely hairy. Leaves ovate, nearly smooth, green on both sides. Stipules semicordate. Capsules smooth. Scotland. 10–12 ft. April. Scales purplish. ($\frac{1}{2}$) *E. B. Supp.* 2709. *E. B.* 2. 1369*. *H. & Arn.* 405. *Bab.* 302. *Lind.* 234.

S. FORSTERIANA. *Glaucous Mountain Sallow.*   **Fig. 1172.**
Branches rather downy. Leaves elliptic-obovate, glaucous beneath. Stipules convex. Stigmas notched. A variety of *damascena.* 6–12 ft. May and June. Scales brownish. ($\frac{1}{2}$) *E. B.* 1. 2344. *E. B.* 2. 1370. *H. & Arn.* 404. *Bab.* 302. *Lind.* 234.

S. RUPESTRIS. *Rock Willow.*   **Fig. 1173.**
Stems trailing; branches slightly downy. Leaves obovate, silky. Capsule silky, stalked. Style as long as the entire stigmas. A variety of *nigricans?* 2–4 ft. May. Scales purplish. ($\frac{1}{2}$) *E. B.* 1. 2342. *E. B.* 2. 1371. *H. & Arn.* 405. *Bab.* 302. *Lind.* 234.

S. PETRÆA. *Dark Rock Willow.*   **Fig. 1174.**
Stems erect; branches hairy. Leaves oblong, reticulated with veins, glaucous beneath. Stipules large, semicordate. Style divided. Stigmas cloven. Scotland. 4–10 ft. May. Scales purplish. ($\frac{1}{2}$) *E. B. Supp.* 2729. *E. B.* 2. 1371*. *H. & Arn.* 404. *Lind.* 235.

S. PROPINQUA.   **Fig. 1175.**
Stems erect; shoots downy. Leaves elliptical. Stipules small, convex. Stigmas notched. A variety of *petræa?* 4–8 ft. May. Scales purplish. ($\frac{1}{2}$) *E. B. Supp.* 2729. *E. B.* 2. 1371**. *H. & Arn.* 404. *Bab.* 302, *Lind.* 235.

S. TENUIOR.   **Fig. 1176.**
Leaves obovate-lanceolate, glaucous beneath, on slender petioles. Stipules small-pointed. Catkins slender, lax. Style longer than the stigmas. Scotland. 4–8 ft. May. Scales purplish. ($\frac{1}{2}$) *E. B. Supp.* 2650. *E. B.* 2. 1371***. *H. & Arn.* 405. *Bab.* 302. *Lind.* 235.

S. LAURINA. *Laurel-leaved Willow.*   **Fig. 1177.**
Leaves elliptic-oblong, waved, dark shining green, glaucous beneath. Petioles dilated at the base. Stipules pointed. Capsules very downy. Woods. 6–16 ft. April and May. Scales purplish. ($\frac{1}{2}$) *E. B.* 1. 1806. *E. B.* 2. 1372. *H. & Arn.* 405. *Bab.* 302. *Lind.* 235.

S. LAXIFLORA. *Loose-flowered Willow.*   **Fig. 1178.**
Stems erect. Leaves broadly obovate, narrowed below. Stipules small, concave. Catkins loose. Stigmas divided, segments linear. A variety of *radicans?* 6–10 ft. April. Scales purplish. ($\frac{1}{2}$) *E. B. Supp.* 2749. *E. B.* 2. 1372*. *H. & Arn.* 406. *Bab.* 302. *Lind.* 235.

S. RADICANS. *Tea-leaved Willow.*   **Fig. 1179.**
Branches decumbent, rooting. Leaves obovate or elliptic-lanceolate, smooth, glaucous beneath. Stipules lunate, glandular. Capsules very silky. Style elongated. Stigmas entire or bifid. Scotland. 2–4 ft. May. Scales purplish. ($\frac{1}{2}$) *E. B.* 1. 1958. *E. B.* 2. 1373. *H. & Arn.* 406. *Bab.* 302. *Lind.* 235.

S. BORRERIANA.   **Fig. 1180.**
Branches erect. Leaves broadly lanceolate. Stipules small, lanceolate. A variety of *radicans.* Scotland. 2–6 ft. April. Scales purplish. ($\frac{1}{2}$) *E. B. Supp.* 2619. *E. B.* 2. 1373*. *H. & Arn.* 406. *Bab.* 303. *Lind.* 235.

Fig 1161 to 1180

J. E. Sowerby. 1

S, DAVALLIANA. Fig. 1181.
Branches erect; shoots downy. Leaves obovate-lanceolate, glaucous beneath. Stipules minute. A variety of *radicans*. Scotland. 2–4 ft. May. Scales brown. ($\frac{1}{2}$) *E. B. Supp.* 2701. *E. B.* 2. 1373**. *H. &* *Arn.* 406. *Bab.* 302. *Lind.* 235.

S. TETRAPLA. Fig. 1182.
Upright. Shoots downy. Leaves lanceolate, twisted, acutely pointed. Stipules small, semicordate. Style longer than the stigmas. A variety of *radicans*. Scotland. 4–10 ft. May. Scales blackish. ($\frac{1}{2}$) *E. B. Supp.* 2702. *E. B.* 2. 2137***. *H. & Arn.* 406. *Bab.* 303. *Lind.* 235.

S. WEIGELIANA. Fig. 1183.
Leaves elliptical, or nearly round, with a short point. Stipules small. Style longer than the stigmas. A variety of *radicans*. Mountains. 4–10 ft. April and May. Scales brown. ($\frac{1}{2}$) *E. B. Supp.* 2656. *E. B.* 2. 1373*, 4. *H. & Arn.* 406. *Bab.* 303. *Lind.* 235.

S. TENUIFOLIA. Fig. 1184.
Upright. Young shoots densely downy. Leaves elliptical or oblong, with a recurved point, glaucous beneath. Capsule smooth. A variety of *radicans*. Westmoreland. 4–6 ft. May. Scales brown. ($\frac{1}{2}$) *E. B. Supp.* 2795. *E. B.* 2. 1373*, 5. *H. & Arn.* 406. *Bab.* 302? *Lind.* 235.

S. NITENS. Fig. 1185.
Branches shining brown. Leaves ovate or elliptical; dark green above, whitish below. Capsule densely silky. A variety of *radicans*. 4–8 ft. April. Scales brown. ($\frac{1}{2}$) *E. B. Supp.* 2655. *E. B.* 2. 1373*, 6. *H. & Arn.* 406. *Bab.* 302. *Lind.* 235.

S. CROWEANA. Fig. 1186.
Leaves elliptical, smooth, bright green, glaucous beneath. Filaments of the stamens united. A variety of *radicans*. May. Scales brownish. ($\frac{1}{2}$) *E. B.* 1. 1146. *E. B.* 2. 1374. *H. & Arn.* 406. *Bab.* 302. *Lind.* 235.

S. BICOLOR. Fig. 1187.
Leaves elliptical, shining, glaucous beneath. Filaments of stamens bearded at the base. A variety of *radicans*. Scotland. 4–8 ft. April. Scales green. ($\frac{1}{2}$) *E. B.* 1. 2186. *E. B.* 2. 1375. *H. & Arn.* 406. *Bab.* 302. *Lind.* 235.

S. PHILLYREIFOLIA. Fig. 1188.
Young shoots downy. Leaves elliptic-lanceolate, acute at each end, glaucous beneath. Style as long as the stigma. A variety of *radicans*. 4–8 ft. April. Scales brownish. ($\frac{1}{2}$) *E. B. Supp.* 2660. *E. B.* 2. 1375*. *H. & Arn.* 406. *Bab.* 303. *Lind.* 235.

S. DICKSONIANA. Fig. 1189.
Young shoots smooth. Leaves elliptical, acute, glaucous below. Stigmas nearly sessile. A variety of *radicans*. Highlands. 2–3 ft. April. Scales reddish brown. ($\frac{1}{2}$) *E. B.* 1. 1390. *E. B.* 2. 1376. *H. & Arn.* 406. *Bab.* 302. *Lind.* 235.

S. VACCINIFOLIA. *Bilberry-leaved Willow.* Fig. 1190.
Stems decumbent. Leaves ovate-lanceolate, glaucous below. Capsules ovate, silky. Highlands. 1–2 ft. June. Scales brown. ($\frac{1}{2}$) *E. B.* 1. 2341. *E. B.* 2. 1377. *H. & Arn.* 407. *Bab.* 304. *Lind.* 237.

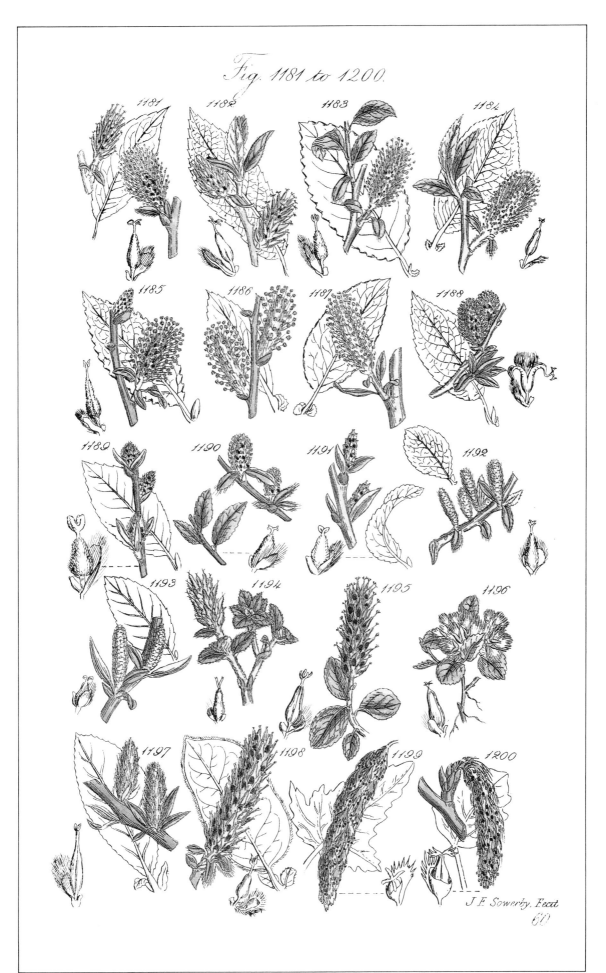

Fig. 1181 to 1200.

J. E. Sowerby, Fecit

60

S. CARINATA.   Fig. 1191.

Leaves ovate, sometimes folded. Capsule oblong-ovate. A variety of *vaccinifolia*. 4–6 ft. June. Scales brown. ($\frac{1}{2}$) *E. B.* 1. 1363. *E. B.* 2. 1378. *H. & Arn.* 407. *Bab.* 304. *Lind.* 237.

S. PRUNIFOLIA. *Plum-leaved Willow.*   Fig. 1192.

Stems erect. Leaves broadly ovate, glaucous beneath. Capsule oblong-ovate. A variety of *vaccinifolia*. Highlands. 2–3 ft. June. Scales brownish. ($\frac{1}{2}$) *E. B.* 1. 1361. *E. B.* 2. 1379. *H. & Arn.* 407. *Bab.* 304. *Lind.* 237.

S. VENULOSA.   Fig. 1193.

Stems erect. Leaves ovate, reticulated with prominent veins, glaucous beneath. Highlands. 2–4 ft. June. Scales reddish. ($\frac{1}{2}$) *E. B.* 1. 1362. *E. B.* 2. 1380. *H. & Arn.* 407. *Bab.* 304. *Lind.* 237.

S. MYRSINITES. *Whortle-leaved Willow.*   Fig. 1194.

Erect. Leaves elliptical, waved, glossy on both sides. Catkins short, lax. Style half as long as the capsule, bifid. Stigmas bifid, linear. Highlands. 1–2 ft. June. Scales blackish. ($\frac{1}{2}$) *E. B.* 1. 1360. *E. B.* 2. 1381. *H. & Arn.* 408. *Bab.* 305. *Lind.* 237.

S. PROCUMBENS.   Fig. 1195.

Leaves oval, green on both sides. Catkins elongated. Style very short, deeply cleft. Highlands. A variety of *myrsinites*. 1–4 ft. June. Scales blackish. ($\frac{1}{2}$) *E. B. Supp.* 2753. *E. B.* 2. 1381*. *H. & Arn.* 408. *Bab.* 304. *Lind.* 237.

S. HERBACEA. *Dwarf Willow.*   Fig. 1196.

A minute shrub. Leaves orbicular, reticulated with veins, very smooth. Catkins few-flowered. Mountains. 1–3 in. June. Scales yellowish. ($\frac{1}{2}$) *E. B.* 1. 1907. *E. B.* 2. 1382. *H. & Arn.* 409. *Bab.* 306. *Lind.* 238.

S. HASTATA. *Apple-leaved Willow.*   Fig. 1197.

Stems spreading. Leaves elliptical, very broad. Stipules heart-shaped, large. Stigmas cloven. 3–5 ft. May. Scales green. ($\frac{1}{2}$) *E. B.* 1. 1617. *E. B.* 2. 1383. *H. & Arn.* 410. *Bab.* 305. *Lind.* 235.

S. LANATA. *Woolly Willow.*   Fig. 1198.

Stems straggling. Leaves large, broadly oval, pointed, very shaggy. Catkins shaggy, with yellow hairs. Stigmas undivided. Highlands. 2–4 ft. April. Scales brown. ($\frac{1}{2}$) *E. B. Supp.* 2624. *E. B.* 2. 1383*. *H. & Arn.* 410. *Bab.* 305. *Lind.* 236.

Genus 2. POPULUS.

P. ALBA. *White Poplar.*   Fig. 1199.

A tree. Bark smooth. Leaves triangular, heart-shaped, lobed and toothed, very white beneath. Stigmas 4. Moist woods. March and April. Scales brown. ($\frac{1}{2}$) *E. B.* 1. 1618. *E. B.* 2. 1391. *H. & Arn.* 411. *Bab.* 306. *Lind.* 238.

P. CANESCENS. *Hoary Poplar.*   Fig. 1200.

A tree. Leaves roundish, deeply waved and toothed, hoary beneath. Stigmas 8. Meadows. March. Scales brown. ($\frac{1}{2}$) *E. B.* 1. 1619. *E. B.* 2. 1392. *H. & Arn.* 411. *Bab.* 307. *Lind.* 238.

P. TREMULA. *Aspen.*   **Fig. 1201.**
Leaves nearly orbicular, pointed; petioles much compressed. Stigmas 4. Moist woods. March and April. Stigmas purple. ($\frac{1}{2}$) *E. B.* 1. 1909. *E. B.* 2. 1393. *H. & Arn.* 412. *Bab.* 307. *Lind.* 238.

P. NIGRA. *Black Poplar.*   **Fig. 1202.**
Leaves triangular, rounded, pointed. Catkins very lax. Stigmas 4. Moist ground. April. Scales brown. ($\frac{1}{2}$) *E. B.* 1. 1910. *E. B.* 2. 1394. *H. & Arn.* 307. *Bab.* 412. *Lind.* 238.

ORDER LXXXV. CUPULIFERÆ.
Genus 1. FAGUS.

F. SYLVATICA. *Beech.*   **Fig. 1203.**
Leaves ovate, glossy, ciliated on the margin. Woods. A timber tree. April and May. Brownish. ($\frac{1}{2}$) *E. B.* 1. 1846. *E. B.* 2. 1323. *H. & Arn.* 413. *Bab.* 308. *Lind.* 239.

Genus 2. CASTANEA.

C. VULGARIS. *Spanish Chestnut.*   **Fig. 1204.**
Leaves large, oblong-lanceolate, pointed. Fertile and barren flowers on long pendulous stalks. Woods. Fruit edible. May. Yellowish. ($\frac{1}{2}$) *E. B.* 1. 886. *E. B.* 2. 1324. *H. & Arn.* 413. *Bab.* 308. *Lind.* 239.

Genus 3. QUERCUS.

Q. PEDUNCULATA. *Oak.*   **Fig. 1205.**
Leaves deeply sinuated, nearly sessile. Acorns 2 or 3 together, sessile upon long peduncles. A well-known timber tree. Woods and hedge-rows. April and May. Yellowish. ($\frac{1}{2}$) *E. B.* 1. 1342. *E. B.* 2. 1321. *H. & Arn.* 414. *Bab.* 308. *Lind.* 240.

Q. SESSILIFLORA. *Durmast Oak.*   **Fig. 1206.**
Leaves on foot-stalks. Acorns sessile or on short thick peduncles. A variety of *pedunculata?* Woods. May. Yellowish. ($\frac{1}{2}$) *E. B.* 1. 1845. *E. B.* 2. 1322. *H. & Arn.* 414. *Bab.* 308. *Lind.* 240.

Genus 4. CORYLUS.

C. AVELLANA. *Hazel.*   **Fig. 1207.**
A large shrub. Leaves roundish, cordate. Involucrum of the fruit bell-shaped, torn at the margin. Woods and thickets. Nuts edible. Feb.–April. Catkins yellowish. Stigmas crimson. ($\frac{1}{2}$) *E. B.* 1. 723. *E. B.* 2. 1328. *H. & Arn.* 415. *Bab.* 309. *Lind.* 240.

Genus 5. CARPINUS.

C. BETULUS. *Hornbeam.*   **Fig. 1208.**
A tree. Leaves ovate, pointed, with straight parallel veins, plaited when young. Woods. April and May. Brownish green. ($\frac{1}{2}$) *E. B.* 1. 2032. *E. B.* 2. 1327. *H. & Arn.* 416. *Bab.* 309. *Lind.* 240.

ORDER LXXXVI. CONIFERÆ.
Genus 1. PINUS.

P. SYLVESTRIS. *Scotch Fir. Pine.*   **Fig. 1209.**
Leaves in pairs, rigid, bluish green. Cones ovate-conical, recurved, usually in pairs. Northern forests. May and June. Catkins yellow. ($\frac{1}{2}$) *E. B.* 1. 2460. *E. B.* 2. 1329. *H. & Arn.* 418. *Bab.* 310. *Lind.* 310.

Genus 2. JUNIPERUS.

J. COMMUNIS. *Juniper.*   **Fig. 1210.**
An evergreen shrub. Leaves linear, spine-pointed, 3 in a whorl. Berries globular. Downs. 2–10 ft. May. Catkins brownish. ($\frac{1}{2}$) *E. B.* 1. 1100. *E. B.* 2. 1399. *H. & Arn.* 418. *Bab.* 310. *Lind.* 241.

J. NANA. *Dwarf Juniper.* **Fig. 1211.**
Procumbent. Fruit oval. Mountains. 6 in.–2 ft. June. Brownish; berries black, with a glaucous bloom. ($\frac{1}{2}$) *E. B. Supp.* 2743. *E. B.* 2. 1399. *H. & Arn.* 418. *Bab.* 310. *Lind.* 241.

Genus 3. TAXUS.

T. BACCATA. *Yew.* **Fig. 1212.**
An evergreen tree. Leaves linear, in 2 rows, crowded. Woods on chalk. Leaves poisonous. March and April. Yellowish. ($\frac{1}{2}$) *E. B.* 1. 746. *E. B.* 2. 1400. *H. & Arn.* 419. *Bab.* 310. *Lind.* 241.

ORDER LXXXVII. DIOSCOREACEÆ.
Genus 1. TAMUS.

T. COMMUNIS. *Black Briony.* **Fig. 1213.**
A climbing plant with heart-shaped, net-veined, glossy leaves. Thickets. Poisonous. Perenn. · June. Green; berries red. ($\frac{1}{2}$) *E. B.* 1. 91. *E. B.* 2. 1390. *H. & Arn.* 443. *Bab.* 312. *Lind.* 271.

ORDER LXXXVIII. TRILLIACEÆ.
Genus 1. PARIS.

P. QUADRIFOLIA. *Herb Paris.* **Fig. 1214.**
Leaves ovate, 4 in a whorl below the flower, dark green. Woods. Poisonous. 1 ft. Perenn. May and June. Green; berry black. ($\frac{1}{2}$) *E. B.* 1. 7. *E. B.* 2. 576. *H. & Arn.* 444. *Bab.* 311. *Lind.* 271.

ORDER LXXXIX. HYDROCHARIDACEÆ.
Genus 1. ANACHARIS.

A. ALSINASTRUM. *Water Thyme.* **Fig. 1215.**
Stems submersed. Leaves 3 or 4 in a whorl, oval-oblong, whorls close together. Flowers very small, in a leaf-like bract. Canals; naturalized? May–Oct. Green. ($\frac{1}{2}$) *H. & Arn.* 423. *Bab.* 313.

Genus 2. HYDROCHARIS.

H. MORSUS-RANÆ. *Frog-bit.* **Fig. 1216.**
Stems submersed. Leaves floating, on long petioles, kidney-shaped. Flowers large. Ponds and streams. Perenn. July–Aug. White. ($\frac{1}{2}$) *E. B.* 1. 808. *E. B.* 2. 1398. *H. & Arn.* 423. *Bab.* 312. *Lind.* 256.

Genus 3. STRATIOTES.

S. ALOIDES. *Water Soldier. Water Aloe.* **Fig. 1217.**
Leaves submersed, rising from the root, sword-shaped, with marginal prickles. Pools. Perenn. July. White. ($\frac{1}{2}$) *E. B.* 1. 379. *E. B.* 2. 771. *H. & Arn.* 424. *Bab.* 313. *Lind.* 254.

ORDER XC. ORCHIDACEÆ.
Genus 1. ORCHIS.

O. PYRAMIDALIS. *Pyramidal Orchis.* **Fig. 1218.**
Sepals spreading. Lip with 3 equal entire lobes and 2 tubercles at the base above. Pastures. 6 in.–1 ft. Perenn. July. Purple or white. ($\frac{1}{2}$) *E. B.* 1. 110. *E. B.* 2. 1193. *H. & Arn.* 435. *Bab.* 318. *Lind.* 261.

O. MORIO. *Green-winged Orchis.* **Fig. 1219.**
Sepals ascending, many-ribbed, converging. Meadows. 4 in.–1 ft. Perenn. May and June. Deep purple with green ribs. ($\frac{1}{2}$) *E. B.* 1. 2059. *E. B.* 2. 1194. *H. & Arn.* 432. *Bab.* 316. *Lind.* 260.

O. MASCULA. *Early Orchis.* **Fig. 1220**
Leaves usually spotted. Sepals 3-ribbed, the lateral ones reflexed. Lip 3-lobed. Spur obtuse. Pastures. 4–10 in. Perenn. May and June. Purple or white, lip spotted. ($\frac{1}{2}$) *E. B.* 1. 631. *E. B.* 2. 1195. *H. & Arn.* 432. *Bab.* 316. *Lind.* 260.

Fig. 1201 to 1220

1201 1202 1203 1204
1205 1206 1207 1208
1209 1210 1211 1212
1213 1214 1215 1216
1217 1218 1219 1220

J. E. Sowerby. Fecit.

61

O. USTULATA. *Dwarf Dark-winged Orchis.* **Fig. 1221.**
Bracts as long as the capsule. Sepals converging. Lobes of lip linear-oblong. Spur very short. Chalky pastures. 3–5 in. Perenn. June. Purplish-brown, lip white and spotted. ($\frac{1}{2}$) *E. B.* l. 18. *E. B.* 2. 1196. *H. & Arn.* 432. *Bab.* 317. *Lind.* 260.

O. FUSCA. *Brown-winged Orchis.* **Fig. 1222.**
Sepals obtuse, converging. Lip deeply 3-lobed; lateral lobes linear-oblong, middle one broad, obcordate, with a point in the cleft. Chalk hills. 1–2 ft. Perenn. May. Calyx greenish purple, lip pink with dark spots. ($\frac{1}{2}$) *E. B.* 1. 16. *E. B.* 2. 1197. *H. & Arn.* 432. *Bab.* 316. *Lind.* 260.

O. MILITARIS. *Man Orchis.* **Fig. 1223.**
Sepals converging, pointed. Lip deeply 4-lobed, with an intermediate point. Chalk hills. 8 in.–1 ft. Perenn. May. Calyx pale purplish, lip purple with darker spots. ($\frac{1}{2}$) *E. B. Supp.* 2675. *E. B.* 2. 1197*. *H. & Arn.* 316. *Bab.* 433. *Lind.* 260.

O. TEPHROSANTHOS. *Monkey Orchis.* **Fig. 1224.**
Sepals converging, pointed. Lip with 4 nearly equal linear lobes. Chalk hills. 8 in.–1 ft. Perenn. May. Purple. ($\frac{1}{2}$) *E. B.* l. 1873. *E. B.* 2. 1198. *H. & Arn.* 433. *Bab.* 317. *Lind.* 260.

O. HIRCINA. *Lizard Orchis.* **Fig. 1225.**
Sepals concave. Lip downy, with 3 linear segments; the middle one very long and twisted, bifid at the end. Spur very short. Chalky thickets. 1–3 ft. Perenn. July and Aug. Purplish green; lip purple with dark spots. ($\frac{1}{2}$) *E. B.* 1. 34. *E. B.* 2. 1199. *H. & Arn.* 434. *Bab.* 318. *Lind.* 260.

O. LAXIFLORA. *Loose-flowered Marsh Orchis.* **Fig. 1226.**
Lateral sepals reflexed. Upper petals converging; lip 3-lobed, lateral lobes rounded and crenulated, middle one very small and truncated. Channel Islands. 1–2 ft. Perenn. June. Purple-red. ($\frac{1}{2}$) *E. B. Supp.* 2828. *E. B.* 2. 1199*. *H. & Arn.* 433. *Bab.* 317.

O. LATIFOLIA. *Marsh Orchis.* **Fig. 1227.**
Bracts longer than the flowers. Sepals spreading. Upper petals converging. Lip convex, nearly entire, crenated. Spur conical. Marshes. 1–1½ ft. Perenn. May–July. Purple or pink, with spots. ($\frac{1}{2}$) *E. B.* 1. 2308. *E. B.* 2. 1200. *H. & Arn.* 433. *Bab.* 317. *Lind.* 260.

O. MACULATA. *Spotted Orchis.* **Fig. 1228.**
Leaves spotted. Bracts shorter than the flowers. Sepals spreading; lip flat, usually deeply 3-lobed, crenated. Spur cylindrical. Heaths. 1–1½ ft. Perenn. June and July. Pink or white, spotted. ($\frac{1}{2}$) *E. B.* 1. 632. *E. B.* 2. 1201. *H. & Arn.* 434. *Bab.* 317. *Lind.* 317.

Genus 2. GYMNADENIA.

G. CONOPSEA. *Fragrant Orchis.* **Fig. 1229.**
Lateral sepals widely spreading. Spur very slender, filiform. Chalk hills. 1 ft. Perenn. June–Aug. Purple. ($\frac{1}{2}$) *E. B.* 1. 10. *E. B.* 2. 1202. *H. & Arn.* 435. *Bab.* 318. *Lind.* 261.

Genus 3. HABENARIA.

H. VIRIDIS. *Frog Orchis.* **Fig. 1230.**
Bracts longer than the flowers. Sepals and upper petals converging. Lip linear, bifid, with an intermediate tooth. Spur short, slightly cloven. Hill pastures. 6–9 in. Perenn. June and July. Green, lip yellowish red at the margin. ($\frac{1}{2}$) *E. B* 1. 94. *E. B.* 2. 1203. *H. & Arn.* 435. *Bab* 319. *Lind.* 261.

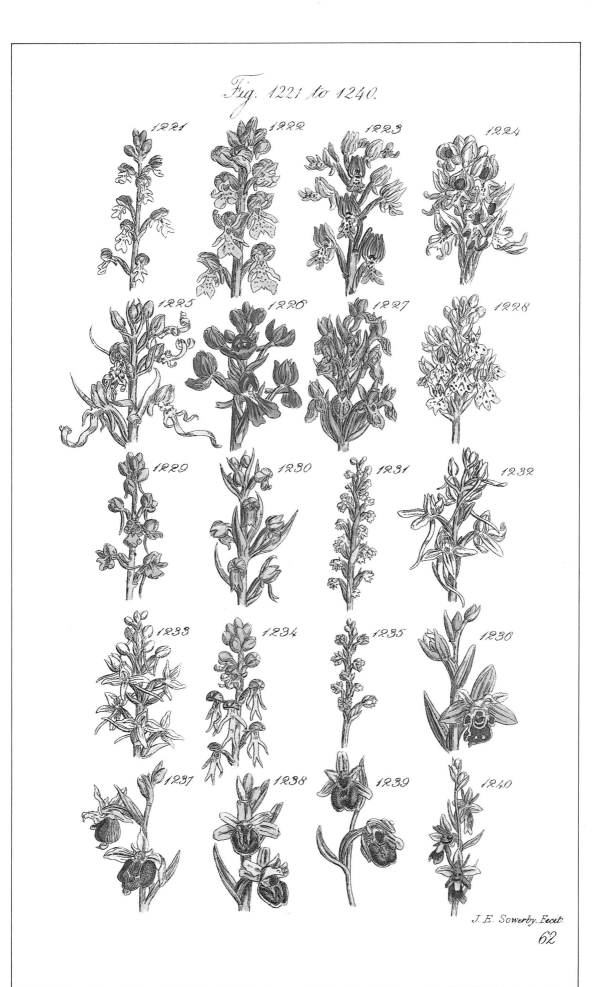

Fig. 1221 to 1240.

1221 1222 1223 1224
1225 1226 1227 1228
1229 1230 1231 1232
1233 1234 1235 1236
1237 1238 1239 1240

J. E. Sowerby, Fecit.

62

H. ALBIDA. *Small White Orchis.* **Fig. 1231.**
Sepals and lateral petals nearly equal, concave. Lips 3-cleft, the middle segment longest, pointed. Spur short. Mountains. 6–9 in. Perenn. June and July. Greenish white. ($\frac{1}{2}$) *E. B.* 1. 505. *E. B.* 2. 1204. *H. & Arn.* 435. *Bab.* 318. *Lind.* 261.

H. CHLORANTHA. *Butterfly Orchis.* **Fig. 1232.**
Lateral sepals spreading downwards. Lip lanceolate, entire. Spur long, filiform. Anther with diverging cells. Moist meadows. 1 ft. Perenn. June. Greenish white. ($\frac{1}{2}$) *E. B.* 1. 22. *E. B.* 2. 1205. *H. & Arn.* 436. *Bab.* 319. *Lind.* 335.

H. BIFOLIA. *Smaller Butterfly Orchis.* **Fig. 1233.**
Lip linear, entire. Anther-cells parallel. A variety of *chlorantha?* Heaths. 9 in.–1 ft. Perenn. June and July. Greenish white. ($\frac{1}{2}$) *E. B. Supp.* 2806. *E. B.* 2. 1205*. *H. & Arn.* 436. *Bab.* 319. *Lind.* 335.

Genus 4. ACERAS.

A. ANTHROPOPHORA. *Green Man Orchis.* **Fig. 1234.**
Calyx-leaves meeting like a helmet. Lip deeply 4-cleft, the segments linear. Chalk hills. 1–1$\frac{1}{2}$ ft. Perenn. June. Calyx green, lip yellow. ($\frac{1}{2}$) *E. B.* 1. 29. *E. B.* 2. 1206. *H. & Arn.* 436. *Bab.* 319. *Lind.* 262.

Genus 5. HERMINIUM.

H. MONORCHIS. *Green Musk Orchis.* **Fig. 1235.**
Petals 3-lobed, nearly equal. Stem with one leaf in the middle. Chalky pastures. 3–6 in. Perenn. July. Green. ($\frac{2}{3}$) *E. B.* 1. 71. *E. B.* 2. 1207. *H. & Arn.* 436. *Bab.* 262. *Lind.* 263.

Genus 6. OPHRYS.

O. APIFERA. *Bee Orchis.* **Fig. 1236.**
Calyx coloured. Lip as long as the calyx, velvety, convex, with 5 marginal lobes, the terminal one reflexed. Chalk hills. 6–10 in. Perenn. June. Calyx purplish, lip purplish brown, with yellow lines. ($\frac{1}{2}$) *E. B.* 1. 383. *E. B.* 2. 1208. *H. & Arn.* 437. *Bab.* 320. *Lind.* 262.

O. ARACHNITES. *Late Spider Orchis.* **Fig. 1237.**
Calyx coloured. Lip longer than the calyx, convex, velvety, terminal lobe projecting. Chalk hills. 6–10 in. Perenn. May and June. Calyx purplish, lip brown, with yellowish green lines. ($\frac{1}{2}$) *E. B. Supp.* 2596. *E. B.* 2. 1208*. *H. & Arn.* 437. *Bab.* 320. *Lind.* 262.

O. ARANIFERA. *Spider Orchis.* **Fig. 1238.**
Calyx green. Petals linear. Lip as long as the calyx, velvety, convex, 3-lobed, the middle lobe large, emarginate. Chalk hills. 6–10 in. Perenn. April and May. Petals green; lip brown, with pale lines. ($\frac{1}{2}$) *E. B.* 1. 65. *E. B.* 2. 1209. *H. & Arn.* 437. *Bab.* 320. *Lind.* 262.

O. FUCIFERA. *Drone Orchis.* **Fig. 1239.**
Lip longer than the calyx, undivided. A variety of *aranifera.* Chalk hills. 6–10 in. Perenn. May and June. Petals green, lip brown with pale lines. ($\frac{1}{2}$) *E. B. Supp.* 2649. *E. B.* 2. 1209*. *H. & Arn.* 437. *Bab.* 320. *Lind.* 262.

O. MUSCIFERA. *Fly Orchis.* **Fig. 1240.**
Calyx green. Petals linear, smooth. Lip flat, 3-lobed; the middle lobe bifid. Chalk hills. 6–10 in. Perenn. May and June. Purple-brown, with a blue spot on the lip. ($\frac{1}{2}$) *E. B.* 1. 64. *E. B.* 2. 1210. *H. & Arn.* 438. *Bab.* 320. *Lind.* 262.

Genus 7. GOODYERA.

G. REPENS.   **Fig. 1241.**

Plant creeping at the base. Root fibrous, lower leaves ovate-lanceolate, with petioles. Spike rather spiral, downy. Highland forests.
6–10 in. Perenn. Aug. Pinkish. ($\frac{2}{3}$) *E. B.* 1. 289. *E. B.* 2. 1211.
H. & Arn. 430. *Bab.* 320. *Lind.* 257.

Genus 8. NEOTTIA.

N. SPIRALIS. *Lady's Tresses.*   **Fig. 1242.**

Root-leaves spreading, ovate. Spike twisted spirally, one-sided.
Chalk hills and pastures. 4–6 in. Perenn. Aug. and Sept. Greenish
white. ($\frac{2}{3}$) *E. B.* 1. 541. *E. B.* 2. 1212. *H. & Arn.* 430. *Bab.* 321.
Lind. 257.

N. ÆSTIVALIS. *Summer Lady's Tresses.*   **Fig. 1243.**

Root-leaves oblong-lanceolate. Spike lax, twisted. Jersey. 3 in.–
1 ft. Perenn. July and Aug. Whitish. ($\frac{2}{3}$) *E. B. Supp.* 2817.
E. B. 2. 1212*. *H. & Arn.* 430. *Bab.* 321. *Lind.* 334.

N. GEMMIPARA. *Proliferous Lady's Tresses.*   **Fig. 1244.**

Leaves lanceolate, with buds at the base, as tall as the stalk. Spike
dense, 3-ranked. Ireland. 3–6 in. Perenn. Oct. Whitish. ($\frac{2}{3}$)
E. B. Supp. 2786. *E. B.* 2. 1212**. *H. & Arn.* 430. *Bab.* 321.
Lind. 334.

Genus 9. LISTERA.

L. OVATA. *Tway-blade.*   **Fig. 1245.**

Stem with two opposite oval leaves. Lip bifid. Column crested
with a hood. Woods. 1–1½ ft. Perenn. June. Yellowish green.
($\frac{1}{2}$) *E. B.* 1. 1548. *E. B.* 2. 1213. *H. & Arn.* 429. *Bab.* 321.
Lind. 258.

L. CORDATA. *Mountain Tway-blade.*   **Fig. 1246.**

Leaves cordate. Lip with a lobe on each side the base. Column
not crested. Mountains. 3–6 in. Perenn. July and Aug. Green.
($\frac{2}{3}$) *E. B.* 1. 358. *E. B.* 2. 1214. *H. & Arn.* 429. *Bab.* 321.
Lind. 258.

L. NIDUS-AVIS. *Bird's-nest.*   **Fig. 1247.**

Without leaves. Stem covered with brown scales. Lip with 2
spreading lobes. Epiphytic on the roots of Beech-trees. 8 in.–1 ft.
Perenn. May and June. Brown. ($\frac{1}{2}$) *E. B.* 1. 48. *E. B.* 2. 1215.
H. & Arn. 429. *Bab.* 321. *Lind.* 258.

Genus 10. EPIPACTIS.

E. LATIFOLIA. *Helleborine.*   **Fig. 1248.**

Leaves broadly ovate, stem-clasping. Lower bracts longer than the
flowers. Lip shorter than the sepals, entire. Woods. 1–2 ft. Perenn.
July and Aug. Reddish green, lip purple. ($\frac{1}{2}$) *E. B.* 1. 269. *E. B.* 2.
1216. *H. & Arn.* 427. *Bab.* 322. *Lind.* 258.

E. PURPURATA. *Purple-leaved Heleborine.*   **Fig. 1249.**

Leaves ovate-lanceolate, purplish. Bracts linear, twice as long as
the flowers. Lip shorter than the calyx, entire. Woods. 1–2 ft.
Perenn. Aug. Greenish purple. ($\frac{1}{2}$) *E. B. Supp.* 2775. *B. E.* 2.
1216*. *H. & Arn.* 427. *Bab.* 322. *Lind.* 259.

E. PALUSTRIS. *Marsh Helleborine.*   **Fig. 1250.**

Leaves lanceolate, stem-clasping. Bracts shorter than the flowers.
Lip 3-lobed. Marshy pastures. 1–1½ ft. Perenn. July. ($\frac{1}{2}$)
E. B. 1. 270. *E. B.* 2. 1217. *H. & Arn.* 428. *Bab.* 322. *Lind.* 259

E. GRANDIFLORA. *White Helleborine.* **Fig. 1251.**
Leaves elliptic-lanceolate, sessile. Bracts longer than the flowers.
Flowers sessile, erect. Woods on the chalk. 1–2 ft. Perenn. June
and July, Yellowish white. ($\frac{1}{2}$) *E. B.* 1. 271. *E. B.* 2. 1218.
H. & Arn. 428. *Bab.* 322. *Lind.* 259.

E. ENSIFOLIA. *Narrow-leaved Helleborine.* **Fig. 1252.**
Leaves narrow lanceolate. Bracts minute. Flowers sessile, erect.
Woods; rare. 1 ft. Perenn. May and June. White. ($\frac{1}{2}$) *E. B.* 1.
494. *E. B.* 2. 1229. *H. & Arn.* 428. *Bab.* 323. *Lind.* 259.

E. RUBRA. *Red Helleborine.* **Fig. 1253.**
Leaves lanceolate. Bracts longer than the capsule. Flowers sessile,
erect. Mountain woods; rare. 1 ft. Perenn. May and June.
Purple, lip whitish. ($\frac{1}{2}$) *E. B.* 1. 437. *E. B.* 2. 1220. *H. & Arn.*
428. *Bab.* 323. *Lind.* 259.

Genus 11. MALAXIS.

M. PALUDOSA. *Bog Orchis.* **Fig. 1254.**
Leaves oval, concave, with minute bulbs at the end. Flowers re-
versed, the lip pointing upwards. Peat bogs 2–4 in. Perenn.
Aug. and Sept. Greenish. ($\frac{1}{3}$) *E. B.* 1. 72. *E. B.* 2. 1221.
H. & Arn. 425. *Bab.* 323. *Lind.* 263.

Genus 12. LIPARIS.

L. LOESSELII. *Two-leaved Bog Orchis.* **Fig. 1255.**
Stem triangular. Leaves two, broadly lanceolate. Lip recurved,
longer than the perianth. 6–8 in. Perenn. July. Yellow. ($\frac{2}{3}$)
E. B. 1. 47. *E. B.* 2. 1222. *H. & Arn.* 426. *Bab.* 324. *Lind.* 263.

Genus 13. CORALLORRHIZA.

C. INNATA. *Coral-root.* **Fig. 1256.**
Leaves sheath-like. Spur very short. Scotland. 6–8 in. Perenn.
July. Yellowish green. ($\frac{2}{3}$) *E. B.* 1. 1546. *E. B.* 2. 1223.
H. & Arn. 426. *Bab.* 323. *Lind.* 258.

Genus 14. CYPRIPEDIUM.

C. CALCEOLUS. *Lady's Slipper.* **Fig. 1257.**
Stem leafy. Leaves ovate, pointed. Flower solitary. Terminal
lobe of corolla elliptical, channeled. Northern woods; very rare.
1–1½ ft. Perenn. July. Purple, lip yellow. ($\frac{1}{2}$) *E. B.* 1. 1. *E. B.* 2.
1224. *H. & Arn.* 438. *Bab.* 324. *Lind.* 263.

ORDER XCI. IRIDACEÆ.
Genus 1. IRIS.

I. PSEUD-ACORUS. *Yellow Iris.* **Fig. 1258.**
Inner segments of perianth smaller than the petaloid stigmas, the
outer very broad. Seeds angular. Watery places; common. 3–4 ft.
Perenn. July. Yellow. ($\frac{1}{3}$) *E. B.* 1. 578. *E. B.* 2. 47. *H. & Arn.* 439.
Bab. 325. *Lind.* 255.

I. FŒTIDISSIMA. *Stinking Iris.* **Fig. 1259.**
Inner segments of perianth spreading, outer narrow. Seeds rounded.
Fœtid. Pastures and thickets. 1–2 ft. Perenn. June–Aug. Purple,
sometimes yellow; seeds orange. ($\frac{1}{2}$) *E. B.* 1. 596. *E. B.* 2. 48.
H. & Arn. 439. *Bab.* 325. *Lind.* 255.

I. TUBEROSA. *Snake-head Iris.* **Fig. 1260.**
Leaves 4-angled. Segments of perianth acute. Not native. 1 ft.
Perenn. March and April. Purple, inner petals green. ($\frac{1}{2}$) *E. B.*
Supp. 2818. *Bab.* 325.

Fig. 1241 to 1260.

J. E. Sowerby.

Genus 2. TRICHONEMA.

T. BULBOCODIUM.   **Fig. 1261.**
Leaves linear, channeled, longer than the recurved stem.   Guernsey.
6 in.   Perenn.   March and April.   Purplish, white, or yellow.   ($\frac{1}{2}$)
E. B. 1. 2549.   *E. B.* 2. 46.   *H. & Arn.* 440.   *Bab.* 325.   *Lind.*
255.

Genus 3. CROCUS.

C. VERNUS.   *Spring Crocus.*   **Fig. 1262.**
Stigma within the flower, in 3 wedge-shaped lobes.   Tube hairy at
the mouth.   Meadows.   4–6 in.   Perenn.   March.   Purple.   ($\frac{1}{2}$)
E. B. 1. 344.   *E. B.* 2. 44.   *H. & Arn.* 440.   *Bab.* 325.   *Lind.* 255.

C. PRÆCOX.   *Small Purple Crocus.*   **Fig. 1263.**
Stigmas deeply trifid, longer than the stamens, within the flower,
divisions slightly notched at the end.   Suffolk ; not native.   4–6 in.
Perenn.   March.   Pale lilac with yellow and purple stripes.   ($\frac{1}{2}$)
E. B. Supp. 2645.   *E. B.* 2. 44**.   *H. & Arn.* 440.   *Bab.* 326.
Lind. 334.

C. AUREUS.   *Golden Crocus.*   **Fig. 1264.**
Stamens longer than the stigma.   Stigma small, shortly trifid.
Meadows.   4–6 in.   Perenn.   March.   Yellow.   ($\frac{1}{2}$)   *E. B. Supp.*
2646.   *E. B.* 2. 44*.   *H. & Arn.* 440.   *Bab.* 326.   *Lind.* 334.

C. SATIVUS.   *Saffron Crocus.*   **Fig. 1265.**
Stigma hanging out of the flower in 3 deep linear segments.   Na-
turalized.   The stamens are the saffron of commerce.   6–9 in.   Perenn.
Sept.   Purple.   ($\frac{1}{2}$)   *E. B.* 1. 343.   *E. B.* 2. 43.   *H. & Arn.* 441.
Bab. 326.   *Lind.* 255.

C. NUDIFLORUS.   *Naked-flowering Crocus.*   **Fig. 1266.**
Leaves appearing after the flowers.   Stigma within the flower, in 3
deeply fringed segments.   Meadows.   6–8 in.   Perenn.   Sept.–Nov.
Purple.   ($\frac{1}{2}$)   *E. B.* 1. 491.   *E. B.* 2. 45.   *H. & Arn.* 441.   *Bab.* 326.
Lind. 255.

C. SPECIOSUS.   *Large Purple Crocus.*   **Fig. 1267.**
Stigma much longer than the stamens.   A variety of *Nudiflorus.*
Meadows.   6–8 in.   Perenn.   Sept. and Oct.   Purple.   ($\frac{1}{2}$)   *E. B.*
Supp. 2752.   *H. & Arn.* 441.   *Bab.* 326.   *Lind.* 334.

ORDER XCII. AMARYLLIDACEÆ.

Genus 1. NARCISSUS.

N. PSEUDO-NARCISSUS.   *Daffodil.*   **Fig. 1268.**
Spathe single-flowered.   Nectary bell-shaped, erect, with 6 crisped
segments, equal to the perianth.   Moist woods.   1 ft.   Perenn.
March.   Yellow.   ($\frac{1}{2}$)   *E. B.* 1. 17.   *E. B.* 2. 468.   *H. & Arn.* 442.
Bab. 327.   *Lind.* 265.

N. POETICUS.   *Pheasant's-eye Narcissus.*   **Fig. 1269.**
Spathe single-flowered.   Nectary very short, depressed, crenated on
the margin.   Heaths and pastures.   1 ft.   Perenn.   May.   White,
nectary edged with crimson.   ($\frac{1}{2}$)   *E. B.* 1. 275.   *E. B.* 2. 469.
H. & Arn. 442.   *Bab.* 326.   *Lind.* 265.

N. BIFLORUS.   *Pale Narcissus.*   **Fig. 1270.**
Spathe 2-flowered.   Nectary very short, depressed.   Sandy fields.
1 ft.   Perenn.   May.   Pale yellow, nectary yellow.   ($\frac{1}{2}$)   *E. B.* 1. 276.
E. B. 2. 470.   *H. & Arn.* 442.   *Bab.* 326.   *Lind.* 265.

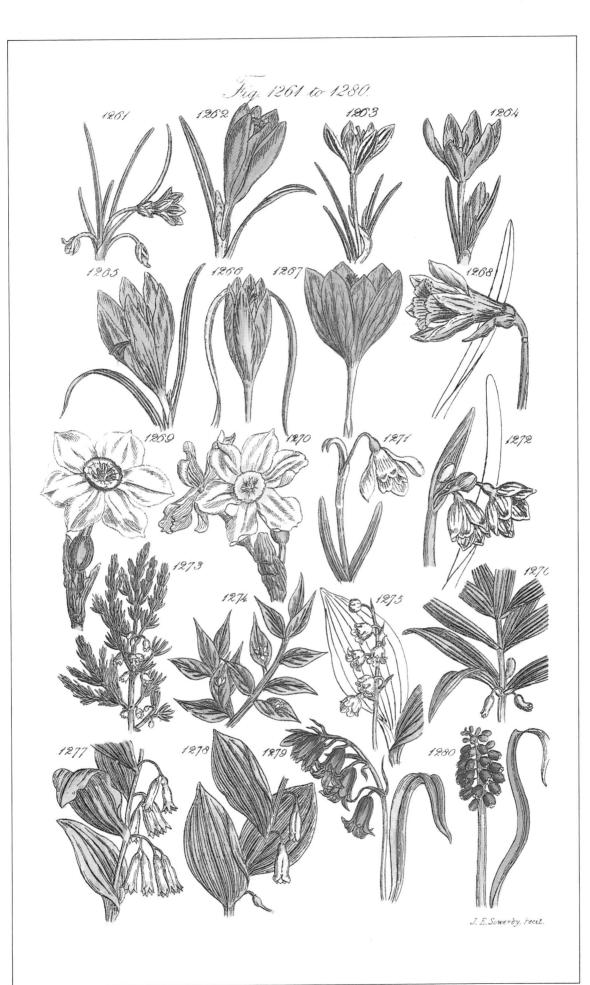

Fig. 1261 to 1280.

1261 1262 1263 1264

1265 1266 1267 1268

1269 1270 1271 1272

1273 1274 1275 1276

1277 1278 1279 1280

J. E. Sowerby, fecit.

Genus 2. GALANTHUS.

G. NIVALIS. *Snowdrop.* **Fig. 1271.**
Flowers solitary, pendant. Meadows and thickets. 4–8 in. Perenn.
Feb. and March. White, inner segments tipped with green. ($\frac{1}{2}$)
E. B. 1. 19. *E. B.* 2. 466. *H. & Arn.* 442. *Bab.* 327. *Lind.* 265.

Genus 3. LEUCOJUM.

L. ÆSTIVUM. *Summer Snowdrop.* **Fig. 1272.**
Spathe with several flowers. Stalk 2-edged. Marshes. 8 in.–1 ft.
Perenn. May. White. ($\frac{1}{2}$) *E. B.* 1. 621. *E. B.* 2. 467. *H. & Arn.* 443.
Bab. 327. *Lind.* 265.

ORDER XCIII. LILIACEÆ.
Genus 1. ASPARAGUS.

A. OFFICINALIS. *Asparagus.* **Fig. 1273.**
Stems usually erect, much branched. Leaves in tufts, bristle-shaped.
Sea-shores. 6–8 in. Perenn. Aug. Green; berries red. ($\frac{1}{2}$) *E. B.* 1.
339. *E. B.* 2. 490. *H. & Arn.* 446. *Bab.* 328. *Lind.* 270.

Genus 2. RUSCUS.

R. ACULEATUS. *Butcher's Broom.* **Fig. 1274.**
A small evergreen shrub. Leaves ovate, spine-pointed, bearing the
flower on the surface. Woods; common. 1–2 ft. Perenn. March
and April. Greenish; berries red. ($\frac{2}{3}$) *E. B.* 1. 560. *E. B.* 2. 1385.
H. & Arn. 446. *Bab.* 329. *Lind.* 270.

Genus 3. CONVALLARIA.

C. MAJALIS. *Lily of the Valley.* **Fig. 1275.**
Flowers in a drooping raceme. Leaves in pairs, ovate-lanceolate.
Hill woods; common. 6–9 in. Perenn. May. White, berries red.
($\frac{1}{2}$) *E. B.* 1. 1035. *E. B.* 2. 491. *H. & Arn.* 447. *Bab.* 328.
Lind. 270.

C. VERTICILLATA. *Narrow-leaved Solomon's Seal.* **Fig. 1276.**
Leaves whorled, linear-lanceolate. Flowers cylindrical. Scottish
woods. 2 ft. Perenn. June. White; berries blue. ($\frac{1}{2}$) *E. B.* 1.
128. *E. B.* 2. 492. *H. & Arn.* 447. *Bab.* 328. *Lind.* 270.

C. MULTIFLORA. *Solomon's Seal.* **Fig. 1277.**
Stem round, curved. Leaves alternate, stem-clasping. Pedicles
axillary, many-flowered. Woods. 1–2 ft. Perenn. June. White tipped
with green. ($\frac{1}{2}$) *E. B.* 1. 279. *E. B.* 2. 493. *H. & Arn.* 447. *Bab.*
329. *Lind.* 270.

C. POLYGONATUM. *Angular Solomon's Seal.* **Fig. 1278.**
Stem angular. Leaves stem-clasping, alternate. Peduncles axillary,
mostly single-flowered. Woods; rare. 1–2 ft. Perenn. June. White
and green; berries black. ($\frac{1}{2}$) *E. B.* 1. 280. *E. B.* 2. 494.
H. & Arn. 447. *Bab.* 329. *Lind.* 270.

Genus 4. HYACINTHUS.

H. NON-SCRIPTUS. *Wild Hyacinth. Hare-bell.* **Fig. 1279.**
Flowers in drooping racemes. Leaves linear, flaccid. Woods and
thickets; abundant. Poisonous. 6–10 in. Perenn. May and June.
Blue, sometimes pink. ($\frac{1}{2}$) *E. B.* 1. 377. *E. B.* 2. 487. *H. & Arn.*
449. *Bab.* 335. *Lind.* 270.

Genus 5. MUSCARI.

M. RACEMOSUM. *Grape-Hyacinth.* **Fig. 1280.**
Racemes crowded. Flowers ovate, furrowed; upper ones abortive.
Leaves linear, channeled. Naturalized. 6–8 in. Perenn. May.
Purple-blue. ($\frac{1}{2}$) *E. B.* 1. 1931. *E. B.* 2. 488. *H. & Arn.* 450.
Bab. 335. *Lind.* 269.

Genus 6. ALLIUM.

A. AMPELOPRASUM. *Great Round-headed Garlic.* **Fig. 1281.**
Umbel globose, without bulbs. Leaves linear, flat. Three alternate stamens deeply 3-cleft. Flat Holmes on the Severn. 4–5 ft. Perenn. Aug. White. ($\frac{1}{2}$) *E. B.* 1. 1657. *E. B.* 2. 473. *H. & Arn.* 450. *Bab.* 332. *Lind.* 267.

A. ARENARIUM. *Sand Garlic.* **Fig. 1282.**
Umbel globose, bearing bulbs. Leaves linear, with cylindrical sheaths. Alternate stamens 3-cleft. Leaves of spathe obtuse. Woods and pastures. 1$\frac{1}{2}$–2 ft. Perenn. July. Purple. ($\frac{1}{2}$) *E. B.* 1. 1358. *E. B.* 2. 475. *H. & Arn.* 451. *Bab.* 333. *Lind.* 267.

A. CARINATUM. *Mountain Garlic.* **Fig. 1283.**
Umbel lax, bulb-bearing. Leaves linear, keeled, flat. Stamens all simple. Leaves of spathe long, tapering, unequal. Pastures. 2–3 ft. Perenn. July. Pinkish. ($\frac{1}{2}$) *E. B.* 1. 1658. *E. B.* 2. 475. *H. & Arn.* 451. *Bab.* 333. *Lind.* 267.

A. OLERACEUM. *Wild Garlic.* **Fig. 1284.**
Umbels lax, bulb-bearing. Leaves semicylindrical, rough, channelled above. Stamens simple. Leaves of spathe concave below, with long points. Fields. Perenn. 2 ft. July. Pinkish. ($\frac{1}{2}$) *E. B.* 1. 488. *E. B.* 2. 476. *H. & Arn.* 451. *Bab.* 333. *Lind.* 267.

A. AMBIGUUM. *Rose-coloured Garlic.* **Fig. 1285.**
Umbels few-flowered, bulb-bearing. Leaves broadly linear. Spathe short, 3–4-leaved. Not native. 1–1$\frac{1}{2}$ ft. Perenn. June. Pink. ($\frac{1}{2}$) *E. B. Supp.* 2803. *Bab.* 335.

A. SPHÆROCEPHALUM. *Small Round-headed Garlic.* **Fig. 1286.**
Umbel spherical, dense, without bulbs. Three alternate stamens 3-cleft. Jersey. 1–3 ft. Perenn. June and July. Purple. ($\frac{1}{2}$) *E. B. Supp.* 2813. *H. & Arn.* 452. *Bab.* 333. *Lind.* 335.

A. VINEALE. *Crow Garlic.* **Fig. 1287.**
Umbel bulb-bearing. Leaves tubular. Three alternate stamens 3-cleft. Dry fields. 2 ft. Perenn. July. White. ($\frac{1}{2}$) *E. B.* 1. 1974. *E. B.* 2. 477. *H. & Arn.* 452. *Bab.* 333. *Lind.* 268.

A. URSINUM. *Ramsons.* **Fig. 1288.**
Umbel nearly flat. Leaves all radical, elliptic-lanceolate, on footstalks. Woods and hedge-banks; common. 1 ft. Perenn. May. White. ($\frac{1}{2}$) *E. B.* 1. 122. *E. B.* 2. 478. *H. & Arn.* 453. *Bab.* 335. *Lind.* 268.

A. SCHŒNOPRASUM. *Chives.* **Fig. 1289.**
Leaves all radical, tubular, pointed. Stamens simple. Meadows; rare. A culinary herb. 1 ft. Perenn. June. Purple. ($\frac{1}{2}$) *E. B.* 1. 2441. *E. B.* 2. 479. *H. & Arn.* 451. *Bab.* 334. *Lind.* 268.

Genus 7. SCILLA.

S. VERNA. *Spring Squill.* **Fig. 1290.**
Raceme few-flowered, corymbose. Bracts lanceolate, obtuse. Leaves many, linear. Sea-cliffs. 4–5 in. Perenn. April. Blue. ($\frac{2}{3}$) *E. B.* 1. 23. *E. B.* 2. 484. *H. & Arn.* 453. *Bab.* 332. *Lind.* 269.

S. BIFOLIA. *Two-leaved Squill.* **Fig. 1291.**
Raceme lax, without bracts. Leaves 2, lanceolate. A doubtful
native. 4–5 in. Perenn. March and April. Pale blue. ($\frac{2}{3}$) *E. B.*
1. 24. *E. B.* 2. 485. *H. & Arn.* 453. *Bab.* 332. *Lind.* 269.

S. AUTUMNALIS. *Autumnal Squill.* **Fig. 1292.**
Raceme without bracts. Leaves linear, numerous. Dry pastures.
2–5 in. Perenn. Sept. Blue. ($\frac{2}{3}$) *E. B.* 1. 78. *E. B.* 2. 486.
H. & Arn. 453. *Bab.* 332. *Lind.* 269.

Genus 8. ORNITHOGALUM.

O. PYRENAICUM. *Spiked Star of Bethlehem.* **Fig. 1293.**
Raceme very long. Filaments dilated. Peduncles equal, spreading;
erect when in fruit. Pastures; naturalized. 1½–2 ft. Perenn. July.
Greenish-white. ($\frac{1}{2}$) *E. B.* 1. 499. *E. B.* 2. 481. *H. & Arn.* 454.
Bab. 331. *Lind.* 268.

O. UMBELLATUM. *Star of Bethlehem.* **Fig. 1294.**
Flowers corymbose. Peduncles longer than the bracts. Naturalized.
1 ft. Perenn. April and May. White, greenish without. ($\frac{1}{2}$)
E. B. 1. 130. *E. B.* 2. 482. *H. & Arn.* 454. *Bab.* 331. *Lind.* 269.

O. NUTANS. *Drooping Star of Bethlehem.* **Fig. 1295.**
Flowers pendulous. Filaments dilated, cloven; 3 of them longer.
Naturalized. 1 ft. Perenn. May. White. ($\frac{1}{2}$) *E. B.* 1. 1997.
E. B. 2. 483. *H. & Arn.* 454. *Bab.* 331. *Lind.* 269.

Genus 9. GAGEA.

G. LUTEA. **Fig. 1296.**
Root-leaves 1 or 2, longer than the flower-stem. Bracts longer than
the umbel. Moist thickets and pastures; local. 4–8 in. Perenn.
March and April. Yellow. ($\frac{2}{3}$) *E. B.* 1. 21. *E. B.* 2. 480. *H. &
Arn.* 455. *Bab.* 332. *Lind.* 268.

Genus 10. ANTHERICUM.

A. SEROTINUM. *Mountain Spider-wort.* **Fig. 1297.**
Leaves semicylindrical; stem ones dilated at the base. Flowers mostly
solitary. Snowdon Mountains, Wales. 4–6 in. Perenn. June.
Pinkish. ($\frac{2}{3}$) *E. B.* 1. 793. *E. B.* 2. 489. *H. & Arn.* 455.
Bab. 331. *Lind.* 269.

Genus 11. TULIPA.

T. SYLVESTRIS. *Wild Tulip.* **Fig. 1298.**
Flowers solitary, somewhat drooping. Leaves lanceolate. Chalky
fields; local. 1 ft. Perenn. April. Yellow. ($\frac{1}{2}$) *E. B.* 1. 63.
E. B. 2. 472. *H. & Arn.* 456. *Bab.* 330. *Lind.* 266.

Genus 12. FRITILLARIA.

F. MELEAGRIS. *Fritillary. Snake's-head Lily.* **Fig. 1299.**
Stem 1-flowered. Leaves linear-lanceolate. Moist meadows. 1 ft.
Perenn. April. Purple, checkered with darker spots. ($\frac{1}{2}$) *E. B.*
1. 622. *E. B.* 2. 471. *H. & Arn.* 456. *Bab.* 330. *Lind.* 266.

Genus 13. LILIUM.

L. MARTAGON. *Turk's-cap Lily.* **Fig. 1300.**
Leaves whorled, ovate-lanceolate. Flowers reflexed. Woods; not
native. 2–3 ft. Perenn. June. Purple, with blackish spots. ($\frac{1}{2}$)
E. B. Supp. 2799. *Bab.* 331.

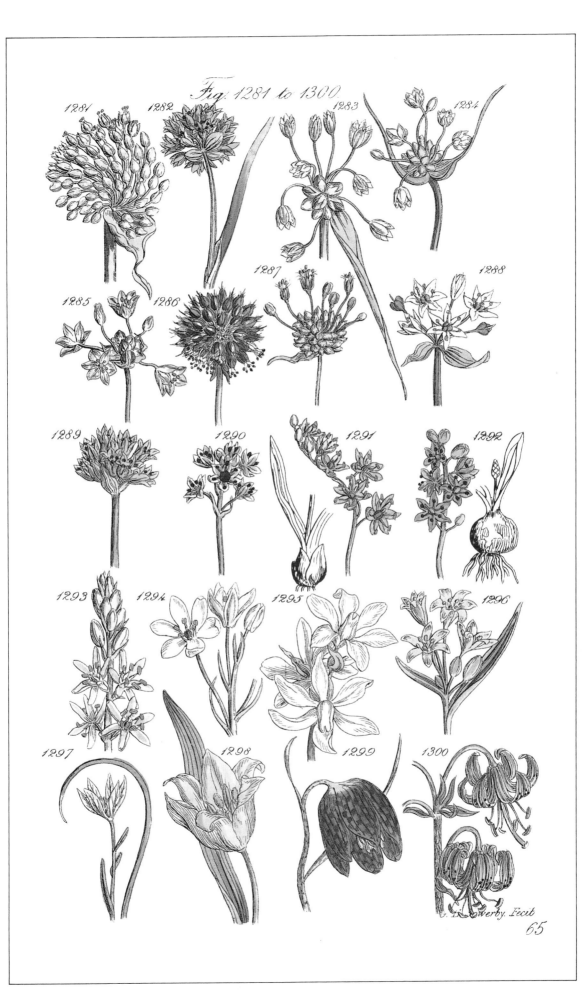

Fig. 1281 to 1300.

1281 1282 1283 1284

1285 1286 1287 1288

1289 1290 1291 1292

1293 1294 1295 1296

1297 1298 1299 1300

J. D. Sowerby, Fecit.

65

Order XCIV. MELANTHACEÆ.
Genus 1. Colchicum.

C. autumnale. *Meadow Saffron.*   Fig. **1301.**
Leaves erect, broadly lanceolate, withering in the summer. Meadows.
4–8 in. Perenn. Sept.–Nov. Purple. ($\frac{1}{2}$) *E. B.* 1. 133. *E. B.*
2. 535. *H. & Arn.* 457. *Bab.* 336. *Lind.* 264.

Genus 2. Tofieldia.

T. palustris. *Scottish Asphodel.*   Fig. **1302.**
Spike ovate. Stem nearly leafless. Leaves sword-shaped. Boggy
mountains. 4–6 in. Perenn. July and Aug. Yellowish. ($\frac{2}{3}$) *E. B.*
1. 536. *E. B.* 2. 534. *H. & Arn.* 457. *Bab.* 336. *Lind.* 264.

Order XCV. RESTIACEÆ.
Genus 1. Eriocaulon.

E. septangulare. *Pipewort.*   Fig. **1303.**
Leaves subulate, compressed, pellucid. Stem angular. Alpine lakes ;
rare. 6–10 in. Perenn. Aug. Purplish-white. ($\frac{2}{3}$) *E. B.* 1. 733.
E. B. 2. 1313. *H. & Arn.* 458. *Bab.* 337. *Lind.* 272.

Order XCVI. JUNCACEÆ.
Genus 1. Narthecium.

N. ossifragum. *Bog Asphodel.*   Fig. **1304.**
Leaves linear, equitant. Flowers in erect racemes. Bogs ; common.
6–8 in. Perenn. July and Aug. Bright yellow. ($\frac{2}{3}$) *E. B.* 1. 535.
E. B. 2. 519. *H. & Arn.* 468. *Bab.* 337. *Lind.* 277.

Genus 2. Juncus.

J. maritimus. *Small Sea-Rush.*   Fig. **1305.**
Leafless. Stems rigid, spine-pointed. Panicle terminal, proliferous.
Bracts spinous. Capsules oblong. Salt marshes. 2 ft. Perenn.
Aug. Brownish. ($\frac{2}{3}$) *E. B.* 1. 1725. *E. B.* 2. 496. *H. & Arn.* 461.
Bab. 338. *Lind.* 273.

J. acutus. *Great Sea-Rush.*   Fig. **1306.**
Leafless. Stems rigid, spine-pointed. Panicle terminal, rather dense.
Bracts spinous. Capsules roundish. Sandy shores. 2–6 ft. Perenn.
July. Brownish. ($\frac{2}{3}$) *E. B.* 1. 1614. *E. B.* 2. 497. *H. & Arn.* 461.
Bab. 338. *Lind.* 273.

J. conglomeratus. *Common Rush.*   Fig. **1307.**
Leafless. Stems soft. Panicle lateral, dense, globose. Stamens 3.
Moist ground ; abundant. 2–3 ft. Perenn. July. Brownish. ($\frac{2}{3}$)
E. B. 1. 835. *E. B.* 2. 498. *H. & Arn.* 459. *Bab.* 338. *Lind.* 273.

J. effusus. *Soft Rush.*   Fig. **1308.**
Leafless. Stems soft. Panicle lateral, loose, much branched.
Moist ground ; abundant. 2–4 ft. Perenn. July. Yellowish. ($\frac{2}{3}$)
E. B. 1. 836. *E. B.* 2. 499. *H. & Arn.* 459. *Bab.* 338. *Lind.* 273.

J. glaucus. *Hard Rush.*   Fig. **1309.**
Leafless. Stems rigid, glaucous, deeply striated. Panicle lateral,
spreading. Moist ground. 1–3 ft. Perenn. July. Brownish. ($\frac{2}{3}$)
E. B. 1. 665. *E. B.* 2. 500. *H. & Arn.* 460. *Bab.* 338. *Lind.* 273.

J. filiformis. *Thread Rush.*   Fig. **1310.**
Leafless. Stems very slender. Panicle below the middle of the
stem. Sepals longer than the capsule. Lake shores in the North.
1 ft. Perenn. July. Green. ($\frac{2}{3}$) *E. B.* 1. 1175. *E. B.* 2. 501.
H. & Arn. 460. *Bab.* 339. *Lind.* 273.

Fig. 1301 to 1320

1301   1302   1303   1304

1305   1306   1307   1308

1309   1310   1311   1312

1313   1314   1315   1316

1317   1318   1319   1320

J. E. Sowerby, Fe

J. BALTICUS. *Baltic Rush.*   Fig. **1311.**
Leafless. Stems rigid. Panicle lateral, erect. Sepals as long as
the capsule. Sandy shores. 1 ft. Perenn. July. Brown. ($\frac{2}{3}$)
E. B. Supp. 2621. *E. B.* 2. 501*. *H. & Arn.* 460. *Bab.* 339. *Lind.* 274.

J. ACUTIFLORUS. *Sharp-flowered Rush.*   Fig. **1312.**
Leaves compressed, jointed within. Stems leafy. Panicle branched
dichotomously. Sepals bristle-pointed. Moist ground; common.
1–2 ft. Perenn. June and July. Greenish-brown. ($\frac{2}{3}$) *E. B.*
1. 238. *E. B.* 2. 502. *H. & Arn.* 461. *Bab.* 340. *Lind.* 275.

J. LAMPROCARPUS. *Jointed Rush.*   Fig. **1313.**
Leaves with internal divisions. Stems leafy, compressed. Panicle
spreading. Sepals bordered, pointed, shorter than the capsule. Wet
places. 1–1$\frac{1}{2}$ ft. Perenn. July. Brown. ($\frac{2}{3}$) *E. B.* 1. 2143.
E. B. 2. 503. *H. & Arn.* 462. *Bab.* 340. *Lind.* 275.

J. NIGRITELLUS. *Black-headed Jointed Rush.*   Fig. **1314.**
Stems leafy. Leaves with internal divisions, cylindrical. Clusters
many-flowered. Sepals shorter than the capsule. Wet places in Scotland. 1 ft. Perenn. Aug. Brown. ($\frac{2}{3}$) *E. B. Supp.* 2643. *E. B.*
2. 503*. *H. & Arn.* 461. *Bab.* 341. *Lind.* 276.

J. OBTUSIFLORUS. *Blunt-flowered Jointed Rush.* Fig. **1315.**
Stem and leaves cylindrical, with internal partitions. Panicles much
branched, the branches reflexed. Sepals as long as the capsule. Marshes.
1–2 ft. Perenn. Aug. Brown. ($\frac{2}{3}$) *E. B.* 1. 2144. *E. B.* 2. 504.
H. & Arn. 462. *Bab.* 340. *Lind.* 276.

J. ULIGINOSUS. *Small Jointed Rush.*   Fig. **1316.**
Stem leafy, swollen at the base. Leaves channelled. Moist heaths.
3–6 in. Perenn. June and July. Brown. ($\frac{2}{3}$) *E. B.* 1. 801.
E. B. 2. 505. *H. & Arn.* 462. *Bab.* 341. *Lind.* 275.

J. COMPRESSUS. *Round-fruited Rush.*   Fig. **1317.**
Stem erect, compressed, leafy below. Leaves linear, incurved at the
edges. Marshes. 1 ft. Perenn. July and Aug. Greenish. ($\frac{2}{3}$)
E. B. 1. 934. *E. B.* 2. 506. *H. & Arn.* 463. *Bab.* 341. *Lind.* 274.

J. GESNERI. *Slender Spreading Rush.*   Fig. **1318.**
Stem leafless. Leaves slightly channelled. Panicle dichotomous,
shorter than the bracts. Highlands. 1 ft. Perenn. July. Brownish.
($\frac{2}{3}$) *E. B.* 1. 2174. *E. B.* 2. 507. *H. & Arn.* 464. *Bab.* 342. *Lind.* 274.

J. BUFONIUS. *Toad Rush.*   Fig. **1319.**
Stem leafy. Leaves angular, filiform, channelled. Panicle forked.
Flowers solitary. Moist heaths; common. 4–8 in. Ann. July and
Aug. Greenish. ($\frac{2}{3}$) *E. B.* 1. 802. *E. B.* 2. 508. *H. & Arn.* 464.
Bab. 342. *Lind.* 274.

J. TRIFIDUS. *Three-leaved Rush.*   Fig. **1320.**
Stem naked. Leaves few. Bracts 3, terminal, channelled. Flowers
1 to 3. Alpine bogs. 4–6 in. Perenn. July. Brown. ($\frac{2}{3}$) *E. B.*
1. 1482. *E. B.* 2. 509. *H. & Arn.* 463. *Bab.* 340. *Lind.* 274.

J. CASTANEUS. *Clustered Rush.* **Fig. 1321.**
Stem leafy, solitary, rounded. Leaves folded. Flowers in 1 to 3 terminal heads. Mountain bogs; rare. 6 in.–1 ft. Perenn. July. Brown. ($\frac{2}{3}$) *E. B.* 1. 900. *E. B.* 2. 510. *H. & Arn.* 463. *Bab.* 339. *Lind.* 275.

J. SQUARROSUS. *Moss Rush.* **Fig. 1322.**
Stems leafless. Leaves numerous, rigid, grooved. Panicle terminal, compound. Hill bogs; abundant. 6 in.–1 ft. Perenn. June and July. Brown; bracts light brown. ($\frac{2}{3}$) *E. B.* 1. 933. *E. B.* 2. 511. *H. & Arn.* 464. *Bab.* 341. *Lind.* 274.

J. CAPITATUS. *Dense-headed Rush.* **Fig. 1323.**
Stems erect, leafy at the base. Leaves channelled. Flowers in 1 or 2 heads. Jersey. 6 in. Ann. May–July. Brown. ($\frac{2}{3}$) *E. B. Supp.* 2644. *E. B.* 2. 511*. *H. & Arn.* 464. *Bab.* 340. *Lind.* 275.

J. BIGLUMIS. *Two-flowered Rush.* **Fig. 1324.**
Stem erect, leafy at the base. Leaves linear, with sheathing bases. Flowers 2, terminal, surmounted by a leafy bract. Alpine rills. 2–4 in. Perenn. Aug. Brownish. ($\frac{2}{3}$) *E. B.* 1. 898. *E. B.* 2. 512. *H. & Arn.* 465. *Bab.* 339. *Lind.* 275.

J. TRIGLUMIS. *Three-flowered Rush.* **Fig. 1325.**
Stem erect, leafy below. Leaves linear, channelled. Head solitary, of 1 to 3 flowers as long as the bracts. Mountain rills. 6–8 in. Perenn. July and Aug. Brownish. ($\frac{2}{3}$) *E. B.* 1. 899. *E. B.* 2. 513. *H. & Arn.* 465. *Bab.* 339. *Lind.* 275.

Genus 3. LUZULA.

L. SYLVATICA. *Great Hairy-Rush.* **Fig. 1326.**
Panicle cymose; peduncles elongated, about 3-flowered. Woods and hills. 1½–2 ft. Perenn. May and June. Brown. ($\frac{2}{3}$) *E. B.* 1. 737. *E. B.* 2. 514. *H. & Arn.* 466. *Bab.* 342. *Lind.* 276.

L. PILOSA. *Wood Hairy-Rush.* **Fig. 1327.**
Panicle cymose, reflexed; peduncles 1-flowered, reflexed. Sepals shorter than the capsule. Seed with a curved crest. Woods; common. 6 in.–1 ft. Perenn. March–May. Brown. ($\frac{2}{3}$) *E. B.* 1. 736. *E. B.* 2. 515. *H. & Arn.* 466. *Bab.* 343. *Lind.* 276.

L. FOSTERI. *Narrow-leaved Hairy-Rush.* **Fig. 1328.**
Panicle cymose, erect; peduncles 1-flowered, upright. Sepals longer than the capsule. Seeds with a straight crest. Woods. 6–8 in. Perenn. May and June. Brown. ($\frac{2}{3}$) *E. B.* 1. 1293. *E. B.* 2. 516. *H. & Arn.* 466. *Bab.* 342. *Lind.* 276.

L. CAMPESTRIS. *Field Hairy-Rush.* **Fig. 1329.**
Panicle of 3 or 4 sessile or pedunculated clusters. Sepals longer than the capsule. Heaths and dry pastures; common. 4–8 in. Perenn. April and May. Dark brown; anthers yellow. ($\frac{2}{3}$) *E. B.* 1. 672. *E. B.* 2. 517. *H. & Arn.* 467. *Bab.* 343. *Lind.* 276.

L. ARCUATA. *Curved Hairy-Rush.* **Fig. 1330.**
Leaves channelled, hairy. Panicle nearly umbellate, drooping. Summits of Highland mountains. 2–6 in. Perenn. July. Brown. ($\frac{2}{3}$) *E. B. Supp.* 2688. *E. B.* 2. 518*. *H. & Arn.* 467. *Bab.* 343. *Lind.* 277.

L. SPICATA. *Spiked Hairy-Rush.*   **Fig. 1331.**
Leaves recurved, somewhat channelled. Panicle spike-like, drooping. High mountains. 6–8 in. Perenn. July. Brown. ($\frac{2}{3}$) *E. B.* 1. 1176. *E. B.* 2. 518. *H. & Arn.* 343. *Lind.* 277.

ORDER XCVII. BUTOMACEÆ.
Genus 1. BUTOMUS.

B. UMBELLATUS. *Flowering Rush.*   **Fig. 1332.**
Leaves linear, three-sided. Flowers in a large umbel. Ponds and slow streams. 2–4 ft. Perenn. June and July. Pink or white. ($\frac{2}{3}$) *E. B.* 1. 651. *E. B.* 2. 579. *H. & Arn.* 469. *Bab.* 346. *Lind.* 272.

ORDER XCVIII. ALISMACEÆ.
Genus 1. ACTINOCARPUS.

A. DAMASONIUM. *Star-fruit.*   **Fig. 1333.**
Leaves floating, oblong-cordate. Capsules 6, in a star-like cluster. Pools. 6–8 in. Perenn. June and July. White. ($\frac{2}{3}$) *E. B.* 1. 1615. *E. B.* 2. 536. *H. & Arn.* 345. *Bab.* 345. *Lind.* 253.

Genus 2. ALISMA.

A. PLANTAGO. *Water-Plantain.*   **Fig. 1334.**
Leaves ovate or lanceolate, on long stalks. Flower-stalks in whorled panicles. Ditches. 1–2 ft. Perenn. July. Pale purple. ($\frac{2}{3}$) *E. B.* 1. 837. *E. B.* 2. 537. *H. & Arn.* 470. *Bab.* 345. *Lind.* 253.

A. NATANS. *Floating Water-Plantain.*   **Fig. 1335.**
Leaves elliptical, floating; those at the rooting base linear, tapering. Flowers single, on long peduncles. Lakes; local. 4–5 in. Perenn. July and Aug. White, with a yellow spot. ($\frac{2}{3}$) *E. B.* 1. 775. *E. B.* 2. 539. *H. & Arn.* 470. *Bab.* 345. *Lind.* 253.

A. RANUNCULOIDES. *Lesser Water-Plantain.*   **Fig. 1336.**
Leaves linear-lanceolate, sometimes floating. Flowers in umbels. Bogs and pools. 6 in.–1 ft. Perenn. Aug. and Sept. Pale purple. ($\frac{2}{3}$) *E. B.* 1. 326. *E. B.* 2. 538. *H. & Arn.* 470. *Bab.* 345. *Lind.* 253.

A. REPENS. *Creeping Water-Plantain.*   **Fig. 1337.**
Procumbent. Leaves lanceolate, sometimes floating. Flowers on solitary peduncles. Pools in Wales. 6 in. Perenn. Aug. and Sept. Pale purple or white. ($\frac{2}{3}$) *E. B. Supp.* 2722. *E. B.* 2. 538*. *H. & Arn.* 470. *Bab.* 345. *Lind.* 253.

Genus 3. SAGITTARIA.

S. SAGITTIFOLIA. *Arrow-head.*   **Fig. 1338.**
Leaves arrow-shaped. Stalks triangular. Ditches and pools. 1–2 ft. Perenn. July and Aug. White, with a purple spot. ($\frac{2}{3}$) *E. B.* 1. 84. *E. B.* 2. 1318. *H. & Arn.* 345. *Bab.* 471. *Lind.* 253.

ORDER XCIX. JUNCAGINACEÆ.
Genus 1. TRIGLOCHIN.

T. PALUSTRE. *Arrow-grass.*   **Fig. 1339.**
Leaves linear, fleshy. Fruit linear, 3-celled. Boggy meadows. 6–10 in. Perenn. Aug. Green. ($\frac{2}{3}$) *E. B.* 1. 366. *E. B.* 2. 532. *H. & Arn.* 472. *Bab.* 346. *Lind.* 252.

T. MARITIMUM. *Sea-side Arrow-grass.*   **Fig. 1340.**
Leaves linear, fleshy. Fruit ovate, 6-celled. Salt marshes and muddy shores. 6–10 in. Perenn. May–Aug. Green. ($\frac{2}{3}$) *E. B.* 1. 255. *E. B.* 2. 533. *H. & Arn.* 472. *Bab.* 346. *Lind.* 252.

Fig 1321 to 1340.

1321 1322 1323 1324
1325 1326 1327 1328
1329 1330 1331 1332
1333 1334 1335 1336
1337 1338 1339 1340

J. E. Sowerby, Fecit

Genus 2. SCHEUCHZERIA.

S. PALUSTRIS.   **Fig. 1341.**

Leaves semicylindrical.   Flowers in a terminal raceme.   Bogs; rare.
6 in.   Perenn.   July.   Green.   ($\frac{2}{3}$)   *E. B.* 1. 1801.   *E. B.* 2. 531.
H. & Arn. 472.   *Bab.* 346.   *Lind.* 252.

ORDER C. TYPHACEÆ.
Genus 1. TYPHA.

T. LATIFOLIA.   *Bull-rush. Cat's-tail.*   **Fig. 1342.**

Leaves broad, linear.   Flowers in a continuous spike.   Pools.   4–6 ft.
Perenn.   July and Aug.   Brown; sterile, yellow.   ($\frac{1}{3}$)   *E. B.* 1. 1455.
E. B. 2. 1241.   *H. & Arn.* 473.   *Bab.* 347.   *Lind.* 247.

T. ANGUSTIFOLIA.   *Lesser Bull-rush.*   **Fig. 1343.**

Leaves linear, narrow.   Sterile and fertile catkins rather distant.
Pools.   3–4 ft.   Perenn.   July.   Brown; sterile, yellow.   ($\frac{1}{3}$)   *E. B.*
1. 1456.   *E. B.* 2. 1242.   *H. & Arn.* 473.   *Bab.* 347.   *Lind.* 247.

T. MINOR.   *Dwarf Bull-rush.*   **Fig. 1344.**

Leaves linear-setaceous, convex beneath.   A doubtful native.   1–1$\frac{1}{2}$ ft.
Perenn.   July.   Brown; sterile, yellow.   ($\frac{2}{3}$)   *E. B.* 1. 1457.   *E. B.* 2.
1243.   *H. & Arn.* 473.   *Bab.* 346.   *Lind.* 247.

Genus 2. SPARGANIUM.

S. RAMOSUM.   *Branched Bur-Reed.*   **Fig. 1345.**

Leaves long, linear, concave at the sides.   Stem branched.   Stigma
linear.   Ditches.   2–3 ft.   Perenn.   July.   Stamens yellow. ($\frac{2}{3}$)   *E. B.*
1. 744.   *E. B.* 2. 1244.   *H. & Arn.* 474.   *Bab.* 347.   *Lind.* 247.

S. SIMPLEX.   *Upright Bur-Reed.*   **Fig. 1346.**

Leaves flat at the sides.   Stem simple.   Stigma linear.   Ditches.
1–2 ft.   Perenn.   July.   Stamens pale yellow.   ($\frac{2}{3}$)   *E. B.* 1. 745.
E. B. 2. 1245.   *H. & Arn.* 474.   *Bab.* 347.   *Lind.* 247.

S. NATANS.   *Floating Bur-Reed.*   **Fig. 1347.**

Leaves floating, flat.   Stem simple.   Stigma ovate.   Lakes.   6–10 in.
Perenn.   July and Aug.   Stamens yellow.   ($\frac{2}{3}$)   *E. B.* 1. 273.   *E. B.*
2. 1246.   *H. & Arn.* 474.   *Bab.* 348.   *Lind.* 248.

ORDER CI. ARACEÆ.
Genus 1. ARUM.

A. MACULATUM.   *Cuckow-pint. Lords-and-Ladies.*   **Fig. 1348.**

Leaves halberd-shaped, glossy, usually spotted.   Spadix club-shaped.
Hedges, banks, and thickets.   Poisonous.   6–10 in.   Perenn.   May.
Spathe greenish; spadix purple.   ($\frac{1}{2}$)   *E. B.* 1. 1298.   *E. B.* 2. 1319.
H. & Arn. 475.   *Bab.* 348.   *Lind.* 246.

ORDER CII. ORONTIACEÆ.
Genus 1. ACORUS.

A. CALAMUS.   *Sweet-Flag.*   **Fig. 1349.**

Leaves sword-shaped.   Stem leaf-like.   Flowers in a sessile spadix.
River-sides.   2–3 ft.   Perenn.   July.   Green.   ($\frac{1}{2}$)   *E. B.* 1. 356.
E. B. 2. 495.   *H. & Arn.* 476.   *Bab.* 348.   *Lind.* 246.

ORDER CIII. PISTIACEÆ.
Genus 1. LEMNA.

L. TRISULCA.   *Ivy-leaved Duckweed.*   **Fig. 1350.**

Fronds elliptic-lanceolate, linear at the base.   Ditches and ponds.
Ann.   June and July.   *E. B.* 1. 926.   *E. B.* 2. 33.   *H. & Arn.* 477.
Bab. 349.   *Lind.* 251.

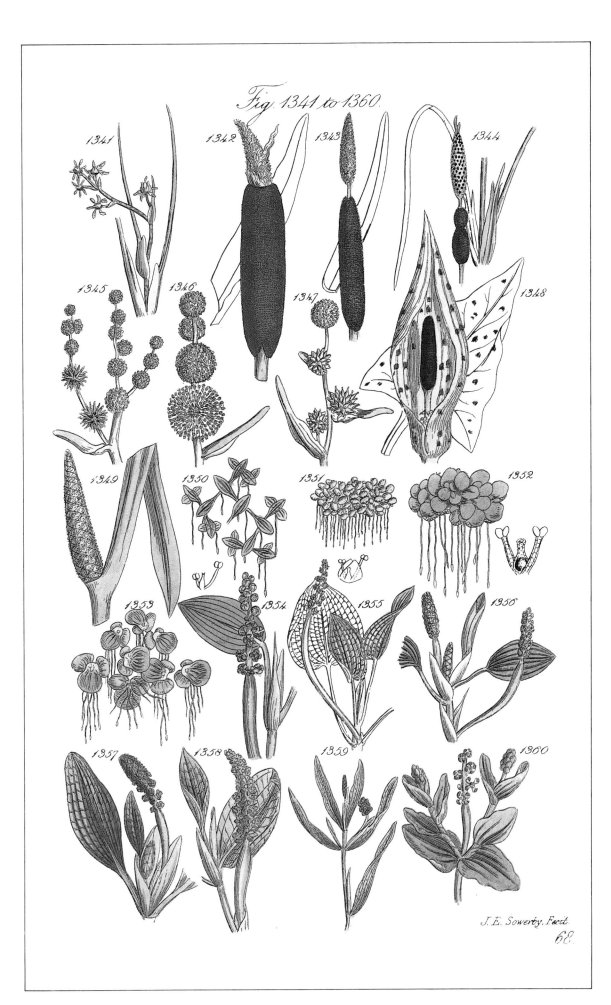

Fig. 1341 to 1360.

1341   1342   1343   1344

1345   1346   1347   1348

1349   1350   1351   1352

1353   1354   1355   1356

1357   1358   1359   1360

J. E. Sowerby, Fecit.

68.

L. MINOR. *Small Duckweed.* **Fig. 1351.**
Frond ovate, nearly flat. Root a single fibre. Ditches and ponds. Ann. June. *E. B. 1.* 1095. *E. B. 2.* 34. *H. & Arn.* 477. *Bab.* 349. *Lind.* 251.

L. GIBBA. *Thick-leaved Duckweed.* **Fig. 1352.**
Frond obovate, hemispherical beneath. Root of several fibres. Ponds and ditches. Ann. June. *E. B. 1.* 1233. *E. B. 2.* 35. *H. & Arn.* 477. *Bab.* 349. *Lind.* 252.

L. POLYRHIZA. *Great Duckweed.* **Fig. 1353.**
Frond roundish-ovate, furrowed. Root with numerous fibres. Ponds. Ann. June. *E. B. 1.* 2458. *E. B. 2.* 36. *H. & Arn.* 477. *Bab.* 349. *Lind.* 251.

ORDER CIV. NAIADACEÆ.

Genus 1. POTAMOGETON.

P. NATANS. *Broad-leaved Pond-weed.* **Fig. 1354.**
Upper leaves oblong-ovate, stalked, floating; lower linear, sessile. Stipules large, free. Pools and streams. Perenn. July. Green. ($\frac{2}{3}$) *E. B. 1.* 1822. *E. B. 2.* 236. *H. & Arn.* 484. *Bab.* 350. *Lind.* 250.

P. PLANTAGINEUS. *Plantain-leaved Pond-weed.* **Fig. 1355.**
Leaves membranous, reticulated, stalked; upper ones elliptical; lower oblong. Spike slender. Pools. Perenn. July. Green. ($\frac{2}{3}$) *E. B. Supp.* 2848. *H. & Arn.* 484. *Bab.* 350.

P. HETEROPHYLLUS. *Various-leaved Pond-weed.* **Fig. 1356.**
Upper leaves on footstalks, floating, elliptical; lower linear-lanceolate, sessile. Stipules small. Flower-stalks swelling upwards. Pools. Perenn. July. Green. ($\frac{2}{3}$) *E. B. 1.* 1285. *E. B. 2.* 237. *H. & Arn.* 482. *Bab.* 351. *Lind.* 250.

P. RUFESCENS. *Red Pond-weed.* **Fig. 1357.**
Upper leaves elliptic-lanceolate, on footstalks, floating; lower lanceolate, nearly sessile. Stipules small. Plant reddish. Pools. Perenn. Aug. Brownish. ($\frac{2}{3}$). *E. B. 1.* 1286. *E. B. 2.* 238. *H. & Arn.* 483. *Bab.* 351. *Lind.* 250.

P. LUCENS. *Shining Pond-weed.* **Fig. 1358.**
Leaves elliptic-lanceolate, submersed. Stipules large. Pools. Perenn. Aug. Green. ($\frac{2}{3}$) *E. B. 1.* 376. *E. B. 2.* 239. *H. & Arn.* 482. *Bab.* 352. *Lind.* 250.

P. LANCEOLATUS. *Lanceolate Pond-weed.* **Fig. 1359.**
Leaves lanceolate; upper ones sometimes floating. Spike ovate, dense, with few flowers. Stipules acute. Lakes. Perenn. Aug. Brown. ($\frac{2}{3}$) *E. B. 1.* 1985. *E. B. 2.* 240. *H. & Arn.* 483. *Bab.* 351. *Lind.* 250.

P. PERFOLIATUS. *Perfoliate Pond-weed.* **Fig. 1360.**
Leaves submersed, ovate, heart-shaped, stem-clasping. Stipules small. Ponds. Perenn. July and Aug. Brownish. ($\frac{2}{3}$) *E. B. 1.* 168. *E. B. 2.* 241. *H. & Arn.* 481. *Bab.* 352. *Lind.* 249.

P. CRISPUS. *Curled Pond-weed.* **Fig. 1361.**
Leaves submersed, lanceolate, serrated, waved at the margins. Pools and ditches. June and July. Greenish. ($\frac{2}{3}$) *E. B.* 1. 1012. *E. B.* 2. 242. *H. & Arn.* 481. *Bab.* 352. *Lind.* 249.

P. OBLONGUS. *Oblong-leaved Pond-weed.* **Fig. 1362.**
Leaves all stalked; upper ones floating, oblong-elliptical; lower linear-lanceolate. Spike cylindrical, on a cylindrical stalk. Ditches and pools. Perenn. July. Brown. ($\frac{2}{3}$) *E. B. Supp.* 2849. *H. & Arn.* 484. *Bab.* 350. *Lind.* 250.

P. PRÆLONGUS. *Long-stalked Pond-weed.* **Fig. 1363.**
Leaves narrow-oblong, stem-clasping, obtuse and hooded at the end. Peduncles very long, cylindrical. Pools. Perenn. July. Brown. ($\frac{2}{3}$) *E. B. Supp.* 2858. *H. & Arn.* 481. *Bab.* 352. *Lind.* 334.

P. COMPRESSUS. *Flat-stalked Pond-weed.* **Fig. 1364.**
Leaves linear, obtuse, 5-ribbed. Stem compressed. Ditches. Perenn. June and July. Brown. ($\frac{2}{3}$) *E. B.* 1. 418. *E. B.* 2. 243. *H. & Arn.* 480. *Bab.* 352. *Lind.* 249.

P. GRAMINEUS. *Grassy Pond-weed.* **Fig. 1365.**
Leaves linear-lanceolate, obtuse, 3-ribbed. Stalk shorter than the stipules. Ditches. Perenn. July. Brownish. ($\frac{2}{3}$) *E. B.* 1. 2253. *E. B.* 2. 244. *H. & Arn.* 480. *Bab.* 353. *Lind.* 249.

P. PUSILLUS. *Small Pond-weed.* **Fig. 1366.**
Leaves linear, obtuse, 3-ribbed. Stalks much longer than the stipules. Ponds and ditches. Perenn. July. Brown. ($\frac{2}{3}$) *E. B.* 1. 215. *E. B.* 2. 245. *H. & Arn.* 480. *Bab.* 353. *Lind.* 249.

P. ACUTIFOLIUS. *Sharp-leaved Pond-weed.* **Fig. 1367.**
Leaves linear, 3-ribbed, with many parallel veins. Stem flat. Ditches. Perenn. July. Brown. ($\frac{2}{3}$) *E. B. Supp.* 2609. *E. B.* 2. 245*. *H. & Arn.* 481. *Bab.* 353. *Lind.* 333.

P. ZOSTERÆFOLIUS. *Grass-wrack Pond-weed.* **Fig. 1368.**
Leaves broadly linear, 3-ribbed, with many parallel veins. Stalks swelling upward. Stem flat. Ponds and lakes. Perenn. July. Brown. ($\frac{2}{3}$) *E. B. Supp.* 2685. *E. B.* 2. 245**. *H. & Arn.* 481. *Bab.* 352. *Lind.* 249.

P. PECTINATUS. *Fennel-leaved Pond-weed.* **Fig. 1369.**
Leaves bristle-shaped, sheathing. Stipules adnate. Spike interrupted. Green. ($\frac{2}{3}$) *E. B.* 1. 323. *E. B.* 2. 246. *H. & Arn.* 479. *Bab.* 354. *Lind.* 248.

P. DENSUS. *Close-leaved Pond-weed.* **Fig. 1370.**
Leaves ovate, opposite, crowded. Stipules wanting. Ditches and pools. June. Brown. ($\frac{2}{3}$) *E. B.* 1. 397. *E. B.* 2. 247. *H. & Arn.* 479. *Bab.* 354. *Lind.* 248.

P. LONGIFOLIUS. *Long-leaved Pond-weed.* **Fig. 1371.**
Leaves elongate-lanceolate, narrowing below. Stipules winged. Peduncle very long, thickened upwards. Lakes. Perenn. Aug. Brown. ($\frac{2}{3}$) *E. B. Supp.* 2847. *H. & Arn.* 352. *Bab.* 482.

Genus 2. RUPPIA.

R. MARITIMA. **Fig. 1372.**
Leaves submersed, long, linear; sheaths inflated. Salt ditches. Flower-stalks long, often spiral. Perenn. June and July. Green. ($\frac{2}{3}$) *E. B.* 1. 136. *E. B.* 2. 248. *H. & Arn.* 485. *Bab.* 355. *Lind.* 251.

Genus 3. ZANNICHELLIA.

Z. PALUSTRIS. *Horned Pond-weed.* **Fig. 1373.**
Leaves grass-like. Flowers axillary, monœcious. Ditches. Ann. Aug. Greenish. ($\frac{2}{3}$) *E. B.* 1. 1844. *E. B.* 2. 1240. *H. & Arn.* 486. *Bab.* 355. *Lind.* 251.

Genus 4. ZOSTERA.

Z. MARINA. *Grass-wrack.* **Fig. 1374.**
Plant submersed. Leaves grass-like. Shallow bays and salt ditches. Perenn. Aug. ($\frac{2}{3}$) *E. B.* 1. 467. *E. B.* 2. 4. *H. & Arn.* 487. *Bab.* 356. *Lind.* 251.

ORDER CV. CYPERACEÆ.

Genus 1. CYPERUS.

C. LONGUS. *Sweet Cyperus.* **Fig. 1375.**
Stem triangular. Umbel leafy, twice compound. Bogs; rare. 2–3 ft. Perenn. July and Aug. Brown. ($\frac{1}{2}$) *E. B.* 1. 1309. *E. B.* 2. 55. *H. & Arn.* 489. *Bab.* 357. *Lind.* 279.

C. FUSCUS. *Brown Cyperus.* **Fig. 1376.**
Stem triangular. Umbel compound. Involucrum of three leaves. Bogs; rare. 4–6 in. Ann. July. ($\frac{2}{3}$) *E. B. Supp.* 2626. *E. B.* 2. 55*. *H. & Arn.* 489. *Bab.* 357. *Lind.* 279.

Genus 2. SCHŒNUS.

S. NIGRICANS. *Black Bog-rush.* **Fig. 1377.**
Stem round, naked. Flowers in roundish heads between two leaves. Leaves setaceous. Bogs. 8 in. Perenn. July. Brown. ($\frac{2}{3}$) *E. B.* 1. 1121. *E. B.* 2. 50. *H. & Arn.* 490. *Bab.* 358. *Lind.* 280.

S. COMPRESSUS. *Compressed Bog-rush.* **Fig. 1378.**
Stem roundish. Spikes 2-ranked, many-flowered. Leaves flat, rough. 1 ft. Perenn. July. Brown. ($\frac{2}{3}$) *E. B.* 1. 791. *E. B.* 2. 51. *H. & Arn.* 491. *Bab.* 362. *Lind.* 280.

S. RUFUS. *Brown Bog-rush.* **Fig. 1379.**
Stem round. Spikes 2-ranked, few-flowered. Leaves channelled, smooth. 8–10 in. Perenn. July. Brown. ($\frac{2}{3}$) *E. B.* 1. 1010. *E. B.* 2. 52. *H. & Arn.* 362. *Bab.* 491. *Lind.* 280.

Genus 3. CLADIUM.

C. MARISCUS. *Twig-rush.* **Fig. 1380.**
Panicle repeatedly compound, leafy. Stem round, leafy. Leaves prickly on the edges and keel. Bogs. 3–4 ft. Perenn. July and Aug. Brown. ($\frac{1}{2}$) *E. B.* 1. 950. *E. B.* 2. 49. *H. & Arn.* 490. *Bab.* 358. *Lind.* 283.

Fig. 1361 to 1380.

1361 1362 1363 1364

1365 1366 1367 1368

1369 1370 1371 1372

1373 1374 1375 1376

1377 1378 1379 1380

John E. Sowerby. Fecit.

69

Genus 4. RHYNCHOSPORA.

R. ALBA. *White Beak-rush.* **Fig. 1381.**
Flower-heads equal to the floral leaves. Leaves tapering. Bogs; rare. 6–10 in. Perenn. July. Pale brown. ($\frac{2}{3}$) *E. B.* 1. 985. *E. B.* 2. 53. *H. & Arn.* 490. *Bab.* 358. *Lind.* 279.

R. FUSCA. *Brown Beak-rush.* **Fig. 1382.**
Floral leaves longer than the spikes. Leaves thread-shaped. Bogs; rare. 6–8 in. Perenn. July. Brown. ($\frac{2}{3}$) *E. B.* 1. 1575. *E. B.* 2. 54. *H. & Arn.* 491. *Bab.* 358. *Lind.* 279.

Genus 5. ELEOCHARIS.

E. PALUSTRIS. *Creeping Spike-rush.* **Fig. 1383.**
Stem round. Root creeping. Stigmas 2. Fruit lenticular. Ditches and bogs. 4–8 in. Perenn. June and July. Brown. ($\frac{2}{3}$) *E. B.* 1. 131. *E. B.* 2. 56. *H. & Arn.* 492. *Bab.* 358. *Lind.* 280.

E. MULTICAULIS. *Many-stalked Spike-rush.* **Fig. 1384.**
Stem round. Stigmas 3. Fruit acutely triangular. 6–8 in. Perenn. June. Brown. ($\frac{2}{3}$) *E. B.* 1. 1187. *E. B.* 2. 57. *H. & Arn.* 492. *Bab.* 359. *Lind.* 280.

E. CÆSPITOSA. *Scaly Spike-rush.* **Fig. 1385.**
Stem round, sheathed and scaly at the base. Outer glumes as long as the spike. Mountains and heaths. 2–5 in. Perenn. July. Brown. ($\frac{2}{3}$) *E. B.* 1. 1029. *E. B.* 2. 58. *H. & Arn.* 497. *Bab.* 359. *Lind.* 281.

E. PAUCIFLORA. *Chocolate Spike-rush.* **Fig. 1386.**
Stem round. Spike few-flowered, longer than its outer glumes. Moors. 6–8 in. Perenn. July and Aug. Brown. ($\frac{2}{3}$) *E. B.* 1. 1122. *E. B.* 2. 59. *H. & Arn.* 496. *Bab.* 359. *Lind.* 281.

E. ACICULARIS. *Least Spike-rush.* **Fig. 1387.**
Stems very slender, 4-angled, sheathed at the base. Wet places. 2–5 in. Perenn. Aug. Brown. ($\frac{2}{3}$) *E. B.* 1. 749. *E. B.* 2. 60. *H. & Arn.* 493. *Bab.* 359. *Lind.* 280.

Genus 6. ELEOGITON.

E. FLUITANS. *Floating Water-rush.* **Fig. 1388.**
Flowering stalks alternate, round, naked. Stem branched, leafy. Leaves partly floating. Pools. Perenn. June and July. Brownish-green. ($\frac{2}{3}$) *E. B.* 1. 216. *E. B.* 2. 61. *H. & Arn.* 493. *Bab.* 361. *Lind.* 283.

Genus 7. SCIRPUS.

S. LACUSTRIS. *Bull-rush. Great Club-rush.* **Fig. 1389.**
Stem round. Panicle cymose, twice compound, terminal; spikes ovate. Ditches and pools. 6–8 ft. Perenn. July and Aug. Brown. ($\frac{2}{3}$) *E. B.* 1. 666. *E. B.* 2. 62. *H. & Arn.* 494. *Bab.* 360. *Lind.* 281.

S. GLAUCUS. *Glaucous Club-rush.* **Fig. 1390.**
Panicle rather dense. Bracts long. Leaves glaucous. A variety of *lacustris.* Pools. 2–4 ft. Perenn. July. Brown. ($\frac{2}{3}$) *E. B.* 1. 2321. *E. B.* 2. 62*. *H. & Arn.* 495. *Bab.* 361. *Lind.* 281.

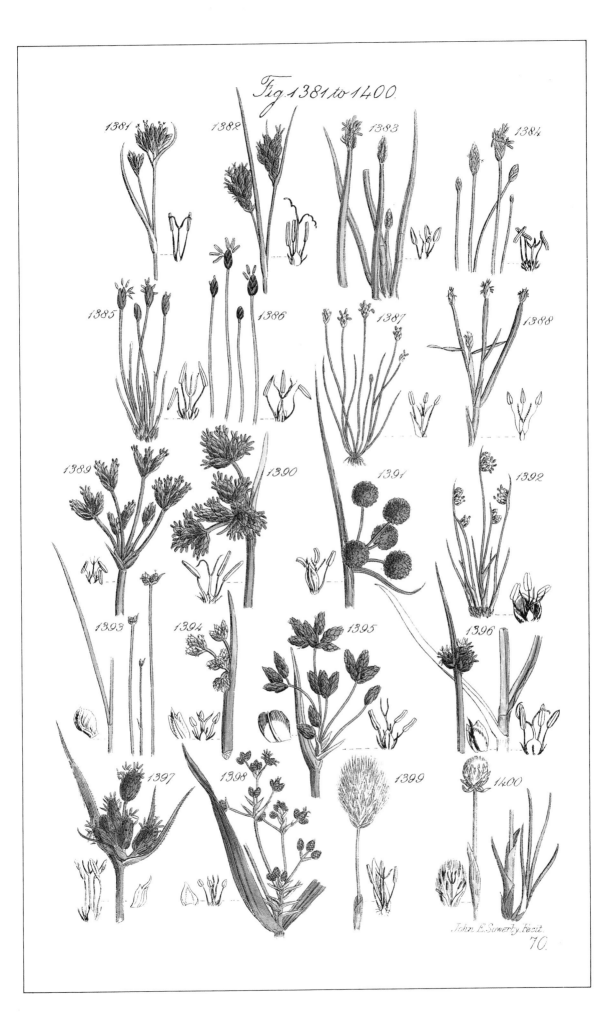

Fig. 1381 to 1400.

1381 1382 1383 1384
1385 1386 1387 1388
1389 1390 1391 1392
1393 1394 1395 1396
1397 1398 1399 1400

John E. Sowerby, fecit.

70.

140

S. Holoschœnus. *Round-headed Club-rush.* **Fig. 1391.**
Stem round, naked. Flowers in globular heads. Sea-shores. 2–3 ft. Perenn. Oct. Brown. ($\frac{2}{3}$) *E. B.* 1. 1612. *E. B.* 2. 63. *H. & Arn.* 494. *Bab.* 362. *Lind.* 283.

S. setaceus. *Least Club-rush.* **Fig. 1392.**
Stem bristle-shaped. Spikes about 2, sessile, terminal, shorter than the bracts. Watery places. 6 in. Perenn. July–Sept. Brown. ($\frac{2}{3}$) *E. B.* 1. 1693. *E. B.* 2. 64. *H. & Arn.* 494. *Bab.* 362. *Lind.* 283.

S. Savii. *Savi's Club-rush.* **Fig. 1393.**
Stem round, leafy below. Spikes terminal, 1–3, shorter than the bracts. Bogs. 6 in. Perenn. July. Brown. ($\frac{2}{3}$) *E. B. Supp.* 2782. *H. & Arn.* 494. *Bab.* 362.

S. triqueter. *Triangular Club-rush.* **Fig. 1394.**
Stem triangular, naked, sharp-pointed. Spikes lateral. Stigmas 2. River-banks. 3 ft. Perenn. Aug. Brown. ($\frac{2}{3}$) *E. B.* 1. 1694. *E. B.* 2. 65. *H. & Arn.* 495. *Bab.* 360. *Lind.* 281.

S. carinatus. *Blunt Club-rush.* **Fig. 1395.**
Stem bluntly triangular, round at the base. Leaves absent. Panicle cymose, terminal. Stigmas 2. River-banks. 3 ft. Perenn. Aug. Brown. ($\frac{2}{3}$) *E. B.* 1. 1983. *E. B.* 2. 66. *H. & Arn.* 495. *Bab.* 360. *Lind.* 281.

S. pungens. *Sharp Club-rush.* **Fig. 1396.**
Stem sharply triangular. Spikes sessile, lateral. Glumes with pointed lobes. Ponds; Jersey. 6 in.–1 ft. Perenn. June and July. Brown. ($\frac{2}{3}$) *E. B. Supp.* 2819. *H. & Arn.* 495. *Bab.* 360. *Lind.* 337.

S. maritimus. *Sea Club-rush.* **Fig. 1397.**
Stem triangular. Panicle leafy, terminal. Glumes pointed, in 3 segments. Sea-shores. 1–3 ft. Perenn. July and Aug. Brown. ($\frac{2}{3}$) *E. B.* 1. 542. *E. B.* 2. 67. *H. & Arn.* 496. *Bab.* 359. *Lind.* 281.

S. sylvaticus. *Wood Club-rush.* **Fig. 1398.**
Stem triangular, leafy. Cyme leafy, terminal, much divided. Spikes clustered. Glumes entire. Woods. 3 ft. Perenn. July. Brown. ($\frac{2}{3}$) *E. B.* 1. 919. *E. B.* 2. 68. *H. & Arn.* 496. *Bab.* 360. *Lind.* 281.

Genus 8. Eriophorum.

E. vaginatum. *Hare's-tail Cotton-grass.* **Fig. 1399.**
Spike solitary, ovate. Stem triangular above, with a swelling sheath below. Glumes membranous. Moors. 6–8 in. Perenn. May. Brownish; hairs white. ($\frac{2}{3}$) *E. B.* 1. 873. *E. B.* 2. 69. *H. & Arn.* 497. *Bab.* 363. *Lind.* 282.

E. capitatum. *Round-headed Cotton-grass.* **Fig. 1400.**
Spike solitary, roundish. Stem round, with a swelling sheath. Glumes membranous. Mountains. 6–8 in. Perenn. June. Greenish; hairs white. ($\frac{2}{3}$) *E. B.* 1. 2387. *E. B.* 2. 70. *H. & Arn.* 498. *Bab.* 363. *Lind.* 282.

E. ALPINUM. *Alpine Cotton-grass.*   **Fig. 1401.**
Spike solitary, oblong-ovate. Stem slender, naked, angular. Leaves short. Glumes strongly keeled. Mountain bogs; rare. 6 in. Perenn. May. Brownish; hairs white. ($\frac{2}{3}$) *E. B.* 1. 311. *E. B.* 2. 71. *H. & Arn.* 497. *Bab.* 363. *Lind.* 282.

E. POLYSTACHION. *Broad-leaved Cotton-grass.*   **Fig. 1402.**
Spikes several. Stems round. Leaves flat, with a triangular point. Bogs. 8 in. Perenn. May. ($\frac{2}{3}$) Brown; hairs white. *E. B.* 1. 563. *E. B.* 2. 72. *H. & Arn.* 498. *Bab.* 363.

E. ANGUSTIFOLIUM. *Common Cotton-grass.*   **Fig. 1403.**
Spikes many. Stem nearly round. Leaves linear, channelled. Bogs; abundant. 8–9 in. Perenn. May. Brown; hairs white. ($\frac{2}{3}$) *E. B.* 1. 364. *E. B.* 2. 73. *H. & Arn.* 498. *Bab.* 363. *Lind.* 282.

E. GRACILE. *Slender Cotton-grass.*   **Fig. 1404.**
Spikes many. Leaves triangular. A variety of *angustifolium.* Mountains. 6–8 in. Perenn. May–July. Brown; hairs white. ($\frac{2}{3}$) *E. B.* 1. 2402. *E. B.* 2. 74. *H. & Arn.* 498. *Bab.* 363. *Lind.* 282.

Genus 9. ELYNA.

E. CARICINA.   **Fig. 1405.**
Spikes crowded. Leaves slender, shorter than the stem. Moors. 6–8 in. Perenn. Aug. Brown. ($\frac{2}{3}$) *E. B.* 1. 1410. *E. B.* 2. 1303. *H. & Arn.* 499. *Bab.* 364. *Lind.* 284.

Genus 10. CAREX.

C. DIOICA. *Creeping Sedge.*   **Fig. 1406.**
Base creeping. Stem and leaves nearly smooth. Spike simple, diœcious. Fruit ovate, rough at the margin. Bogs. 5–6 in. Perenn. May. Brown. ($\frac{2}{3}$) *E. B.* 1. 543. *E. B.* 2. 1247. *H. & Arn.* 500. *Bab.* 364. *Lind.* 284.

C. DAVALLIANA. *Prickly Sedge.*   **Fig. 1407.**
Root tufted. Stem and leaves rough. Spike simple, diœcious. Fruit ovate-lanceolate. Bogs; rare. 6 in.–1 ft. Perenn. June. Brown. ($\frac{2}{3}$) *E. B.* 1. 2123. *E. B.* 2. 1248. *H. & Arn.* 500. *Bab.* 364. *Lind.* 284.

C. PULICARIS. *Flea Sedge.*   **Fig. 1408,**
Spike simple; upper half with barren, the lower with fertile flowers. Fruit smooth and polished. Bogs. 6 in.–1 ft. Perenn. May and June. Brown. ($\frac{2}{3}$) *E. B.* 1. 1051. *E. B.* 2. 1249. *H. & Arn.* 500. *Bab.* 364. *Lind.* 284.

C. INCURVA. *Curved Sedge.*   **Fig. 1409.**
Stem smooth, bluntly angular. Leaves channelled. Spikelets in a roundish head, sterile at the end. Fruit broadly ovate. Sea-shores. 3–4 in. Perenn. June. Brown. ($\frac{2}{3}$) *E. B.* 1. 927. *E. B.* 2. 1250. *H. & Arn.* 501. *Bab.* 365. *Lind.* 285.

C. ARENARIA. *Sea Sedge.*   **Fig. 1410.**
Roots creeping. Stem triangular. Leaves flat. Spikelets crowded; the lower fertile, upper barren. Fruit with a membranaceous wing. Sandy shores. 6 in.–1 ft. Perenn. June. Fertile green; barren brown. ($\frac{2}{3}$) *E. B.* 1. 928. *E. B.* 2. 1251. *H. & Arn.* 505. *Bab.* 366. *Lind.* 285.

C. INTERMEDIA. *Soft Brown Sedge.* **Fig. 1411.**
Stem triangular. Leaves flat. Spikelets in an oblong dense head.
Fruit acutely margined, longer than the scale. Marshes. 1–1½ ft.
Perenn. June. Brownish. ($\frac{2}{3}$) *E. B.* 1. 2042. *E. B.* 2. 1252.
H. & Arn. 506. *Bab.* 365. *Lind.* 286.

C. DIVISA. *Marsh Sedge.* **Fig. 1412.**
Base creeping. Spikelets few, chiefly in a dense head; the lowest
solitary, with a bract at its base; barren at the end. Marshes. 1 ft.
Perenn. May. Brownish. ($\frac{2}{3}$) *E. B.* 1. 1096. *E. B.* 2. 1253.
H. & Arn. 506. *Bab.* 365. *Lind.* 286.

C. MURICATA. *Greater Prickly Sedge.* **Fig. 1413.**
Spike oblong, of 4–6 spikelets. Fruit ovate, pointed, spreading.
Moist pastures. 1–2 ft. Perenn. May. Brownish. ($\frac{2}{3}$) *E. B.* 1.
1097. *E. B.* 2. 1254. *H. & Arn.* 505. *Bab.* 366. *Lind.* 286.

C. DIVULSA. *Grey Sedge.* **Fig. 1414.**
Spike elongated, lax. Spikelets 5 or 6, the lower somewhat distant.
Fruit ovate, rough at the point. 1 ft. Perenn. May. Greenish.
($\frac{2}{3}$) *E. B.* 1. 629. *E. B.* 2. 1255. *H. & Arn.* 505. *Bab.* 366. *Lind.* 286.

C. VULPINA. *Great Rough Sedge.* **Fig. 1415.**
Stem acutely triangular. Leaves broad. Spike crowded, cylindrical.
Fruit ovate, pointed, spreading. Meadows. 2 feet. Perenn. June.
Greenish. ($\frac{2}{3}$) *E. B.* 1. 307. *E. B.* 2. 1256. *H. & Arn.* 505. *Bab.*
366. *Lind.* 286.

C. TERETIUSCULA. *Smaller Panicled Sedge.* **Fig. 1416.**
Stem roundish. Leaves narrow. Spike dense, oblong. Fruit with
a notched, serrated beak. 2 ft. Perenn. May and June. Brown.
($\frac{2}{3}$) *E. B.* 1. 1065. *E. B.* 2. 1257. *H. & Arn.* 504. *Bab.* 367.
Lind. 286.

C. PANICULATA. *Greater Panicled Sedge.* **Fig. 1417.**
Stem acutely triangular. Leaves broad. Spikelets forming a panicle.
Fruit with a slightly cloven beak. 3–5 ft. Perenn. June. Brown.
($\frac{2}{3}$) *E. B.* 1. 1064. *E. B.* 2. 1258. *H. & Arn.* 503. *Bab.* 367.
Lind. 286.

C. STELLULATA. *Star-headed Sedge.* **Fig. 1418.**
Spikelets few, rather distant, sterile at the base. Fruit ovate, acute,
much attenuated, spreading. Marshes. 6 in.–1 ft. Perenn. May
and June. Yellowish. ($\frac{2}{3}$) *E. B.* 1. 806. *E. B.* 2. 1259. *H. & Arn.*
501. *Bab.* 368. *Lind.* 284.

C. LEPORINA. *Hare's-foot Sedge.* **Fig. 1419.**
Spikelets ovate, 3 or 4 together. Fruit elliptical, beaked, scarcely
longer than the scale. Highlands. 4–8 in. Perenn. July. Brown.
($\frac{2}{3}$) *E. B. Supp.* 2815. *E. B.* 2. 1259*. *H. & Arn.* 502. *Bab.* 369.
Lind. 338.

C. CURTA. *White Sedge.* **Fig. 1420.**
Spikelets 5–7, rather distant. Involucral bracts minute. Fruit
broadly ovate, smooth, as long as the scale. Bogs. 1 ft. Perenn.
June. ($\frac{2}{3}$) *E. B.* 1. 1386. *E. B.* 2. 1260. *H. & Arn.* 501. *Bab.*
369. *Lind.* 285.

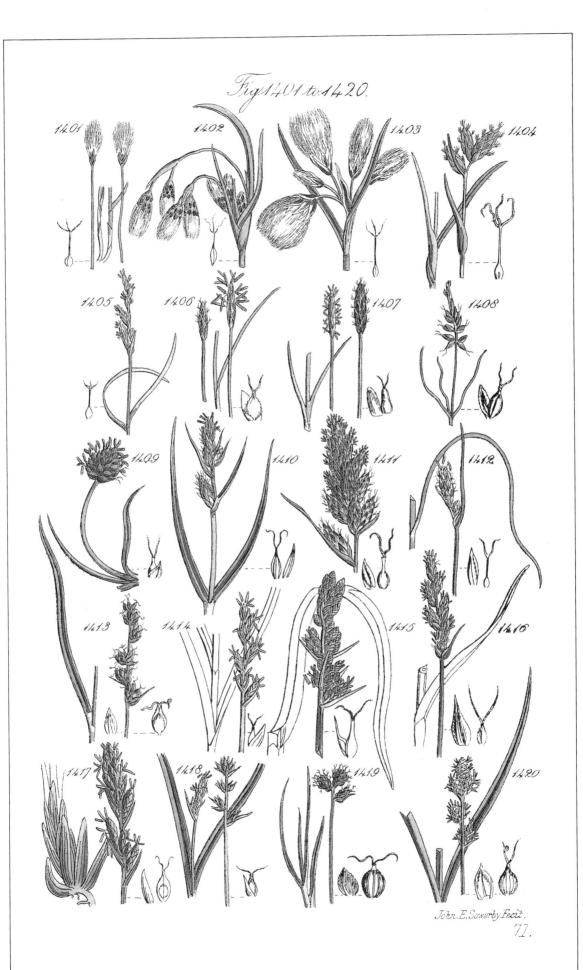

Fig.1401 to 1420.

1401 1402 1403 1404
1405 1406 1407 1408
1409 1410 1411 1412
1413 1414 1415 1416
1417 1418 1419 1420

John E. Sowerby Fecit.

77.

C. ELONGATA. *Elongated Sedge.* **Fig. 1421.**
Spikelets numerous, oblong, lax, rather distant. Involucral bracts minute. Fruit ovate-oblong, longer than the scales. Marshes. 1–1½ ft. Perenn. June. Brownish. ($\frac{2}{3}$) *E. B.* 1. 1920. *E. B.* 2. 1261. *H. & Arn.* 502. *Bab.* 369. *Lind.* 285.

C. OVALIS. *Oval Sedge.* **Fig. 1422.**
Spikelets in an oval head. Fruit ovate, pointed, with a broad membranous margin. Marshes. 1 ft. Perenn. June. Greenish. ($\frac{2}{3}$) *E. B.* 1. 306. *E. B.* 2. 1262. *H. & Arn.* 501. *Bab.* 369. *Lind.* 285.

C. REMOTA. *Remote-flowered Sedge.* **Fig. 1423.**
Spikelets nearly sessile, solitary, very distant. Bracts leafy, higher than the stem. Fruit oblong-ovate, longer than the scale. Moist woods. 1–1½ ft. Perenn. June. Green. ($\frac{2}{3}$) *E. B.* 1. 832. *E. B.* 2. 1263. *H. & Arn.* 502. *Bab.* 368. *Lind.* 285.

C. AXILLARIS. *Axillary-clustered Sedge.* **Fig. 1424.**
Lower spikelets in distant clusters. Bracts leafy ; the lowermost as long as the spike. Marshes. 1–2 ft. Perenn. June. Green. ($\frac{2}{3}$) *E. B.* 1. 993. *E. B.* 2. 1264. *H. & Arn.* 503. *Bab.* 368. *Lind.* 285.

C. PULLA. *Russet Sedge.* **Fig. 1425.**
Spikes ovate, obtuse, the lower fertile one stalked. Bracts leafy, not sheathing. Fruit elliptical, inflated, spreading. Mountain bogs. 1–2 ft. Perenn. June. Brown. ($\frac{2}{3}$) *E. B.* 1. 2045. *E. B.* 2. 1265. *H. & Arn.* 510. *Bab.* 379. *Lind.* 289.

C. CÆSPITOSA. *Bog Sedge.* **Fig. 1426.**
Leaves erect, linear. Bracts leafy, auricled at the base. Fertile spikes sessile, cylindrical, obtuse. Marshes. 6 in.–1 ft. Perenn. May and June. Dark purple. ($\frac{2}{3}$) *E. B.* 1. 1507. *E. B.* 2. 1266. *H. & Arn.* 509. *Bab.* 370. *Lind.* 291.

C. RIGIDA. *Rigid Sedge.* **Fig. 1427.**
Leaves rigid, broadly linear. Bracts leafy, auricled at the base. Fertile spikes subcylindrical, obtuse, the lowest stalked. Mountains. 3–6 in. Perenn. June and July. Brown. ($\frac{2}{3}$) *E. B.* 1. 2047. *E. B.* 2. 1267. *H. & Arn.* 508. *Bab.* 371. *Lind.* 290.

C. STRICTA. *Glaucous Sedge.* **Fig. 1428.**
Leaves erect, glaucous, reticulated with filaments at the base. Fertile spikes nearly sessile, erect, cylindrical, elongated. Marshes. 2 ft. Perenn. April and May. Dark brown. ($\frac{2}{3}$) *E. B.* 1. 914. *E. B.* 2. 1268. *H. & Arn.* 509. *Bab.* 370. *Lind.* 291.

C. AQUATILIS. *Straight-leaved Mountain Sedge.* **Fig. 1429.**
Stem smooth, obtusely triangular. Bracteal leaves very long. Fertile spikes nearly sessile, linear, elongated, attenuated below. Marshes in Scotland. 1–2 ft. Perenn. July and Aug. Dark brown. ($\frac{2}{3}$) *E. B. Supp.* 2758. *E. B.* 2. 1268*. *H. & Arn.* 508. *Bab.* 371. *Lind.* 339.

C. ACUTA. *Slender-spiked Sedge.* **Fig. 1430.**
Stem sharply triangular. Bracts very long. Spikes cylindrical, acuminate, slender, drooping when in flower. Marshes. 2–3 ft. Perenn. May. Purplish. ($\frac{2}{3}$) *E. B.* 1. 580. *E. B.* 2. 1269. *H. & Arn.* 509. *Bab.* 370. *Lind.* 291.

Fig 1421 to 1440.

1421 1422 1423 1424
1425 1426 1427 1428
1429 1430 1431 1432
1433 1434 1435 1436
1437 1438 1439 1440

J.E.Sowerby. Fecit.

72

144

C. PAUCIFLORA. *Few-flowered Sedge.* **Fig. 1431.**
Spike simple, of few flowers; the uppermost barren. Fruit rather longer than the scale. Peaty moors. 3–6 in. Perenn. June. Brownish. ($\frac{2}{3}$) *E. B.* 1. 2041. *E. B.* 2. 1270. *H. & Arn.* 500. *Bab.* 365. *Lind.* 284.

C. RUPESTRIS. *Rock Sedge.* **Fig. 1432.**
Spike linear, with a few lax fertile flowers at the base. Fruit obovate, triquetrous. Rocks in Scotland. 3–9 in. Perenn. Aug. Brown. ($\frac{2}{3}$) *E. B. Supp.* 2814. *E. B.* 2. 1270*. *H. & Arn.* 500. *Bab.* 365. *Lind.* 338.

C. DIGITATA. *Fingered Sedge.* **Fig. 1433.**
Leaves plane. Bracts membranaceous, sheathing. Spikes linear, lax, erect, approximated; fertile ones 2 or 3, longer than the barren. Woods. 6–8 in. Perenn. May. Brownish. ($\frac{2}{3}$) *E. B.* 1. 615. *E. B.* 2. 1271. *H. & Arn.* 517. *Bab.* 374. *Lind.* 287.

C. CLANDESTINA. *Dwarf Silvery Sedge.* **Fig. 1434.**
Leaves channelled. Bracts membranaceous, sheathing. Fertile spikes distant, few-flowered, nearly covered by the sheaths. Near Bristol. 1–2 in. Perenn. May. Brown. ($\frac{2}{3}$) *E. B.* 1. 2124. *E. B.* 2. 1272. *H. & Arn.* 517. *Bab.* 374. *Lind.* 287.

C. PENDULA. *Pendulous Sedge.* **Fig. 1435.**
Sheaths nearly equal to the flower-stalks. Spikes very long, cylindrical, drooping. Moist woods. 3–6 ft. Perenn. May and June. Fertile greenish; barren brown. ($\frac{1}{2}$) *E. B.* 1. 2315. *E. B.* 2. 1273. *H. & Arn.* 516. *Bab.* 374. *Lind.* 287.

C. STRIGOSA. *Loose Pendulous Sedge.* **Fig. 1436.**
Sheaths nearly as long as the stalks. Spikes very slender, nearly erect. Woods. 1–2 ft. Perenn. May and June. Green. ($\frac{2}{3}$) *E. B.* 1. 994. *E. B.* 2. 1274. *H. & Arn.* 516. *Bab.* 374. *Lind.* 287.

C. SYLVATICA. *Pendulous Wood Sedge.* **Fig. 1437.**
Sheaths not half the length of the stalks. Spikes slender, lax, drooping. Moist woods; common. 1–2 ft. Perenn. May and June. Brownish. ($\frac{2}{3}$) *E. B.* 1. 995. *E. B.* 2. 1275. *H. & Arn.* 516. *Bab.* 378. *Lind.* 287.

C. DEPAUPERATA. *Starved Sedge.* **Fig. 1438.**
Sheaths much shorter than the stalks. Spikes erect; fertile ones distant, few-flowered. Dry woods. 1–1½ ft. Perenn. May and June. Brown. ($\frac{2}{3}$) *E. B.* 1. 1098. *E. B.* 2. 1276. *H. & Arn.* 513. *Bab.* 378. *Lind.* 287.

C. MIELICHOFERI. *Loose-spiked Rock Sedge.* **Fig. 1439.**
Sheaths not half as long as the stalks. Fertile spikes few-flowered, lax, drooping. Mountains. 2–6 in. Perenn. June and July. Brown. ($\frac{2}{3}$) *E. B.* 1. 2293. *E. B.* 2. 1277. *H. & Arn.* 513. *Bab.* 373. *Lind.* 287.

C. CAPILLARIS. *Dwarf Sedge.* **Fig. 1440.**
Sheath shorter than the stalks. Fertile spikes lax, drooping, few-flowered. Mountains. 2–6 in. Perenn. June and July. Brown; fruit dark brown. ($\frac{2}{3}$) *E. B.* 1. 2069. *E. B.* 2. 1278. *H. & Arn.* 514. *Bab.* 374. *Lind.* 288.

C. LIMOSA. *Mud Sedge.*   **Fig. 1441.**
Sheaths very short. Fertile spikes oblong-ovate, dense, pendulous. Scales as long as the fruit. Muddy bogs. 8–10 in. Perenn. June. Brown. (⅔) *E. B.* 1. 2043. *E. B.* 2. 1279. *H. & Arn.* 514. *Bab.* 373. *Lind.* 288.

C. RARIFLORA. *Loose-flowered Sedge.*   **Fig. 1442.**
Sheaths nearly wanting. Fertile spikes narrow-oblong, few-flowered, pendulous. Scales longer than the fruit. 5–6 in. Perenn. June. Dark brown. (⅔) *E. B.* 1. 2516. *E. B.* 2. 1280. *H. & Arn.* 514. *Bab.* 373. *Lind.* 288.

C. PSEUDO-CYPERUS. *Cyperus Sedge.*   **Fig. 1443.**
Sheaths nearly absent. Fertile spikes dense, cylindrical, pendulous, on very long stalks. Scales setaceous. Moist places. 2–3 ft. Perenn. June. Fertile green; barren brown. (½) *E. B.* 1. 242. *E. B.* 2. 1281. *H. & Arn.* 516. *Bab.* 379. *Lind.* 288.

C. USTULATA. *Scorched Sedge.*   **Fig. 1444.**
Sheaths shorter than the stalks. Fertile spikes oval, pendulous. Fruit elliptical, compressed. Highlands. 8 in. Perenn. July. Dark brown. (⅔) *E. B.* 1. 2404. *E. B.* 2. 1282. *H. & Arn.* 515. *Bab.* 376. *Lind.* 288.

C. ATRATA. *Black Sedge.*   **Fig. 1445.**
Sheaths nearly absent. Spikes ovate, rather pendulous; the terminal one sterile at the base. Mountains. 1 ft. Perenn. June and July. Dark purple. (⅔) *E. B.* 1. 2044. *E. B.* 2. 1283. *H. & Arn.* 507. *Bab.* 372. *Lind.* 289.

C. VAHLII. *Close-headed Mountain Sedge.*   **Fig. 1446.**
Sheath nearly absent. Spikes three or four, roundish or oblong, close together; the terminal barren at the base. Rocks. 6 in.–1 ft. Perenn. Aug. and Sept. Dark brown. (⅔) *E. B. Supp.* 2666. *E. B.* 2. 1283*. *H. & Arn.* 506. *Bab.* 372. *Lind.* 338.

C. PALLESCENS. *Pale Sedge.*   **Fig. 1447.**
Sheaths very short. Fertile spikes pedunculated, oblong-cylindrical, pendulous in fruit. Marshes. 1–1½ ft. Perenn. June. Fertile green; barren brown. (⅔) *E. B.* 1. 2185. *E. B.* 2. 1284. *H. & Arn.* 514. *Bab.* 372. *Lind.* 289.

C. FLAVA. *Yellow Sedge.*   **Fig. 1448.**
Sheaths short, about equal to the stalks. Fertile spikes roundish-oval. Beak of fruit curved. Turfy bogs. 4 in.–1 ft. Perenn. June. Brownish. (⅔) *E. B.* 1. 1294. *E. B.* 2. 1285. *H. & Arn.* 511. *Bab.* 376. *Lind.* 289.

C. ŒDERI.   **Fig. 1449.**
Sheaths short. Beak of the fruit straight. A variety of *flava.* Moist heaths. 4 in.–1 ft. Perenn. June. Brownish. (⅔) *E. B.* 1. 1773. *E. B.* 2. 1286. *H. & Arn.* 511. *Bab.* 54. *Lind.* 289.

C. FULVA. *Tawny Sedge.*   **Fig. 1450.**
Sheaths shorter than the stalks. Fertile spikes ovate, distant, erect. Boggy meadows. 1 ft. Perenn. June. Tawny brown. (⅔) *E. B.* 1. 1295. *E. B.* 2. 1287. *H. & Arn.* 511. *Bab.* 377. *Lind.* 289.

C. SPEIROSTACHYA. *Short-spiked Sedge.* **Fig. 1451.**
Sheaths about half as long as the stalks. Fertile spikes mostly three, erect, ovate, distant. Bogs. 1 ft. Perenn. July and Aug. Brown. ($\frac{2}{3}$) *E. B. Supp.* 2770. *E. B.* 2. 1287*. *H. & Arn.* 511. *Bab.* 377. *Lind.* 288.

C. EXTENSA. *Long-bracteated Sedge.* **Fig. 1452.**
Sheaths as long as the stalks. Bracts leafy, very long and spreading. Fertile spikes roundish-ovate, nearly sessile, erect. Marshes. 4 in.-1 ft. Perenn. June. Fertile greenish; barren brown. ($\frac{2}{3}$) *E. B.* 1. 833. *E. B.* 2. 1288. *H. & Arn.* 510. *Bab.* 377. *Lind.* 289.

C. DISTANS. *Distant-spiked Sedge.* **Fig. 1453.**
Stems smooth. Sheaths very long, nearly equal to the stalks. Fertile spikes oblong, very remote. Marshes. 1-2 ft. Perenn. June. Brown. ($\frac{2}{3}$) *E. B.* 1. 1234. *E. B.* 2. 1289. *H. & Arn.* 511. *Bab.* 377. *Lind.* 289.

C. BINERVIS. *Green-ribbed Sedge.* **Fig. 1454.**
Stem smooth. Sheaths elongated, shorter than the stalks. Fertile spikes cylindrical, remote; sometimes compound. Dry heaths. 2-3 ft. Perenn. June. Brown. ($\frac{2}{3}$) *E. B.* 1. 1235. *E. B.* 2. 1290. *H. & Arn.* 512. *Bab.* 378. *Lind.* 289.

C. PRÆCOX. *Vernal Sedge.* **Fig. 1455.**
Stalks very short; sheaths equal in length. Spikes oval-oblong. Dry heaths and pastures. 3 in.-1 ft. Perenn. April and May. Pale brown. ($\frac{2}{3}$) *E. B.* 1. 1099. *E. B.* 2. 1291. *H. & Arn.* 518. *Bab.* 375. *Lind.* 290.

C. PILULIFERA. *Round-headed Sedge.* **Fig. 1456.**
Sheaths absent. Fertile spikes sessile, clustered, roundish. Heaths and moors. 6 in.-1 ft. Perenn. June. Brown. ($\frac{2}{3}$) *E. B.* 1. 885. *E. B.* 2. 1292. *H. & Arn.* 518. *Bab.* 375. *Lind.* 290.

C. TOMENTOSA. *Downy-fruited Sedge.* **Fig. 1457.**
Sheaths minute. Fertile spikes nearly sessile, cylindrical, obtuse. Fruit globose, densely downy. Meadows; rare. 1 ft. Perenn. June. Brown. ($\frac{2}{3}$) *E. B.* 1. 2046. *E. B.* 2. 1293. *H. & Arn.* 518. *Bab.* 375. *Lind.* 290.

C. PANICEA. *Pink-leaved Sedge.* **Fig. 1458.**
Base creeping. Sheaths about half as long as the stalks. Fertile spikes subcylindrical; the flowers rather distant. Bogs and meadows. 1-1½ ft. Perenn. June. Greenish-brown. ($\frac{2}{3}$) *E. B.* 1. 1505. *E. B.* 2. 1294. *H. & Arn.* 513. *Bab.* 372. *Lind.* 290.

C. PHÆOSTACHYA. *Short Brown-spiked Sedge.* **Fig. 1459.**
Sheaths shorter than the stalks. Fertile spikes two, distant, erect, oval. Scales of barren spike pointed, of the fertile obtuse. Mountains. 5-6 in. Perenn. July. Brownish. ($\frac{2}{3}$) *E. B. Supp.* 2731. *E. B.* 2. 1294*. *H. & Arn.* 513. *Bab.* 373.

C. RECURVA. *Glaucous Heath Sedge.* **Fig. 1460.**
Creeping at the base. Sheaths very short. Fertile spikes cylindrical, dense, slightly drooping, on long slender stalks. Leaves short, glaucous. Woods and pastures. 6 in.-1 ft. Perenn. June. Blackish-green. ($\frac{2}{3}$) *E. B.* 1. 1506. *E. B.* 2. 1295. *H. & Arn.* 517. *Bab.* 376. *Lind.* 290.

Fig. 1441 to 1460.

J. E. Sowerby, Fecit

73

C. STICTOCARPA. *Dotted-fruited Sedge.* **Fig. 1461.**
Fertile spikes subovate. Fruit with minute brown spots. A variety of *recurva*. 1 ft. Perenn. June. Brown. ($\frac{2}{3}$) *E. B. Supp.* 2772. *E. B.* 2. 1295**. *H. & Arn.* 517. *Bab.* 376. *Lind.* 339.

C. PALUDOSA. *River Sedge.* **Fig. 1462.**
Sheaths absent. Spikes cylindrical, obtuse, erect. Fruit oblong-ovate. Leaves broad, rough, strongly keeled. River-sides. 2–3 ft. Perenn. May. Dark brown. ($\frac{2}{3}$) *E. B.* 1. 807. *E. B.* 2. 1296. *H. & Arn.* 520. *Bab.* 380. *Lind.* 291.

C. RIPARIA. *Great River Sedge.* **Fig. 1463.**
Stem sharply triangular, rough. Sheaths absent. Spikes broadly cylindrical, acute, erect. River-sides and ditches. 2–3 ft. Perenn. May. Fertile greenish; barren brown. ($\frac{2}{3}$) *E. B.* 1. 579. *E. B.* 2. 1297. *H. & Arn.* 521. *Bab.* 380. *Lind.* 291.

C. LÆVIGATA. *Smooth-beaked Sedge.* **Fig. 1464.**
Sheaths elongated, shorter than the stalks. Spikes cylindrical; the fertile ones drooping. Beak of fruit very long. Boggy woods. 2–3 ft. Perenn. June. Fertile greenish; barren brown. ($\frac{2}{3}$) *E. B.* 1. 1387. *E. B.* 2. 1298. *H. & Arn.* 513. *Bab.* 378. *Lind.* 291.

C. VESICARIA. *Short-spiked Bladder Sedge.* **Fig. 1465.**
Sheaths none. Fertile spikes cylindrical, slightly drooping, on very short stalks. Marshes. 1–2 ft. Perenn. May and June. Brown. ($\frac{2}{3}$) *E. B.* 1. 779. *E. B.* 2. 1299. *H. & Arn.* 520. *Bab.* 380. *Lind.* 291.

C. AMPULLACEA. *Slender-beaked Bladder Sedge.* **Fig. 1466.**
Sheaths none. Fertile spikes cylindrical, erect, nearly sessile, long. Fruit inflated. Marshes. 1–2 ft. Perenn. June. Brown. ($\frac{2}{3}$) *E. B.* 1. 780. *E. B.* 2. 1300. *H. & Arn.* 520. *Bab.* 380. *Lind.* 292.

C. HIRTA. *Hairy Sedge.* **Fig. 1467.**
Hairy. Leaves flat. Sheaths nearly equal to the stalks. Fertile spikes short, cylindrical, remote. Scales awned. Moist places. 1–2 ft. Perenn. May and June. Brown. ($\frac{2}{3}$) *E. B.* 1. 685. *E. B.* 2. 1301. *H. & Arn.* 519. *Bab.* 378. *Lind.* 292.

C. FILIFORMIS. *Slender-leaved Sedge.* **Fig. 1468.**
Smooth. Sheaths very short. Fertile spikes nearly sessile. Fruit hairy, ovate. Boggy meadows. 1–2 ft. ($\frac{2}{3}$) *E. B.* 1. 904. *E. B.* 2. 1302. *H. & Arn.* 519. *Bab.* 379. *Lind.* 292.

ORDER CVI. GRAMINEÆ.

Genus 1. ANTHOXANTHUM.

A. ODORATUM. *Sweet Vernal-grass.* **Fig. 1469.**
Panicle spike-like, ovate-oblong. Flowers longer than their awns, upon short stalks. Pastures; abundant. 1–1½ ft. Perenn. May and June. Anthers purple. ($\frac{2}{3}$) *E. B.* 1. 647. *E. B.* 2. 114. *H. & Arn.* 528. *Bab.* 390. *Lind.* 306.

Genus 2. NARDUS.

N. STRICTA. *Mat-grass.* **Fig. 1470.**
Spike slender, erect, the flowers all pointing one way. Leaves hard, setaceous. 8–10 in. Perenn. June. Purplish. ($\frac{2}{3}$) *E. B.* 1. 290. *E. B.* 2. 75. *H. & Arn.* 529. *Bab.* 393. *Lind.* 296.

Fig. 1461 to 1480.

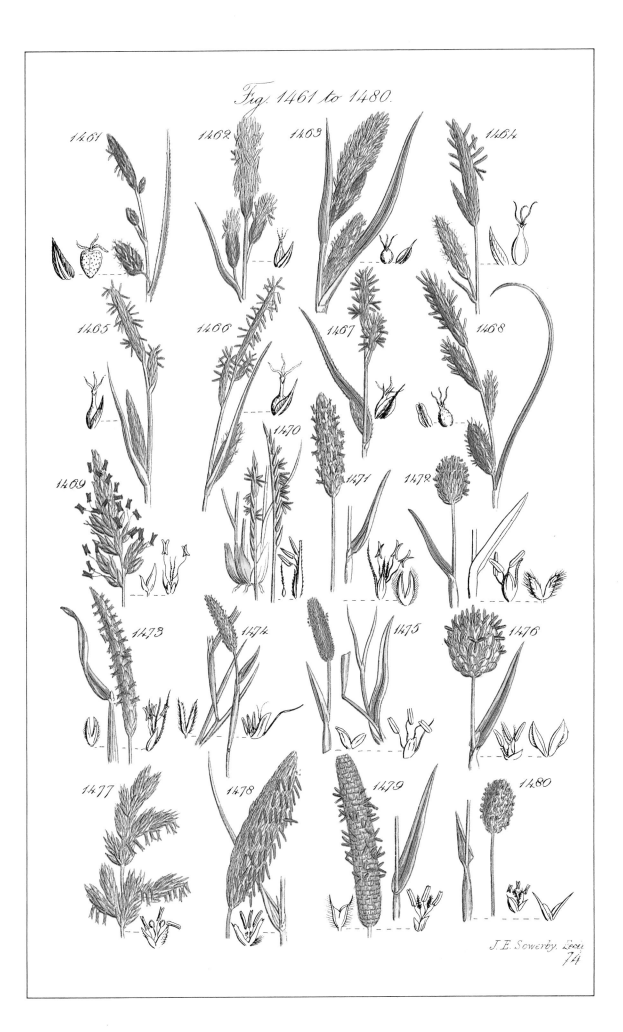

1461   1462   1463   1464

1465   1466   1467   1468

1469   1470   1471   1472

1473   1474   1475   1476

1477   1478   1479   1480

74

Genus 3. ALOPECURUS.

A. PRATENSIS. *Fox-tail-grass.* **Fig. 1471.**
Stem erect, smooth. Panicle nearly cylindrical. Calyx-valves hairy, united at their base. Pastures; abundant. 1–2½ ft. Perenn. April–June. (⅔) *E. B.* 1. 759. *E. B.* 2. 85. *H. & Arn.* 530. *Bab.* 391. *Lind.* 299.

A. ALPINUS. *Alpine Fox-tail-grass.* **Fig. 1472.**
Stem erect, smooth. Panicle ovate. Glumes downy, united at their base. Awn little longer than the paleæ. Mountains; rare. 1 ft. Perenn. July. (⅔) *E. B.* 1. 1126. *E. B.* 2. 86. *H. & Arn.* 530. *Bab.* 391. *Lind.* 299.

A. AGRESTIS. *Slender Fox-tail-grass. Black Bent.* **Fig. 1473.**
Stem erect, roughish. Panicle rather cylindrical, tapering. Glumes nearly naked, united at the base. Awn very long. Waste ground. 2 ft. Ann. July–Oct. (⅔) *E. B.* 1. 848. *E. B.* 2. 87. *H. & Arn.* 530. *Bab.* 392. *Lind.* 299.

A. BULBOSUS. *Bulbous Fox-tail-grass.* **Fig. 1474.**
Stem erect. Panicle rather cylindrical, tapering. Glumes distinct, linear, downy. Root bulbous. Salt marshes. 1 ft. Perenn. July. (⅔) *E. B.* 1. 1249. *E. B.* 2. 88. *H. & Arn.* 530. *Bab.* 392. *Lind.* 299.

A. GENICULATUS. *Floating Fox-tail-grass.* **Fig. 1475.**
Stem bent at the joints. Panicle cylindrical, obtuse. Glumes united at the base; hairy. Leaves often floating. Wet places. 6 in.–1 ft. Perenn. May–Aug. (⅔) *E. B.* 1. 1250. *E. B.* 2. 89. *H. & Arn.* 531. *Bab.* 392. *Lind.* 300.

Genus 4. PHALARIS.

P. CANARIENSIS. *Canary-grass.* **Fig. 1476.**
Panicle ovate, spike-like. Glumes with broad keels. Naturalized. 2 ft. Ann. June–Aug. (⅔) *E. B.* 1. 1310. *E. B.* 2. 76. *H. & Arn.* 531. *Bab.* 389. *Lind.* 300.

P. ARUNDINACEA. *Reed Canary-grass.* **Fig. 1477.**
Panicle upright, with spreading branches. Flowers crowded. Pools and ditches; common. 2–5 ft. Perenn. July. Purplish-green. (½) *E. B.* 1. 402. *E. B.* 2. 77. *H. & Arn.* 531. *Bab.* 390. *Lind.* 300.

Genus 5. AMMOPHILA.

A. ARUNDINACEA. *Sea-reed. Marram.* **Fig. 1478.**
Panicle cylindrical, acuminate. Glumes acute. Sandy sea-shores. 3 ft. Perenn. July. Anthers purple. (⅔) *E. B.* 1. 520. *E. B.* 2. 78. *H. & Arn.* 532. *Bab.* 394. *Lind.* 303.

Genus 6. PHLEUM.

P. PRATENSE. *Cat's-tail-grass.* **Fig. 1479.**
Panicle cylindrical, very long. Glumes truncated, twice as long as the awn. Pastures. 2–3 ft. Perenn. June and July. (½) *E. B.* 1. 1076. *E. B.* 2. 79. *H. & Arn.* 532. *Bab.* 391. *Lind.* 300.

P. ALPINUM. *Mountain Cat's-tail-grass.* **Fig. 1480.**
Panicle ovate-oblong. Glumes truncated, as long as the awn. Lower palea jagged at the summit. Mountains. 1–2 ft. Perenn. July. (⅔) *E. B.* 1. 519. *E. B.* 2. 80. *H. & Arn.* 533. *Bab.* 391. *Lind.* 300.

P. asperum. *Rough Cat's-tail-grass.* **Fig. 1481.**
Panicle cylindrical. Glumes wedge-shaped, truncate, swelling upwards. Stem branched. 1 ft. Ann. July. ($\frac{2}{3}$) *E. B.* 1. 1077. *E. B.* 2. 81. *H. & Arn.* 532. *Bab.* 391. *Lind.* 301.

P. Bœhmeri. *Purple-stalked Cat's-tail-grass.* **Fig. 1482.**
Panicle long, cylindrical. Glumes linear-lanceolate, acuminate, twice as long as the paleæ. Pastures. 1–2 ft. Perenn. July. ($\frac{2}{3}$) *E. B.* 1. 459. *E. B.* 2. 82. *H. & Arn.* 533. *Bab.* 390. *Lind.* 301.

P. Michelii. **Fig. 1483.**
Panicle nearly cylindrical. Glumes lanceolate, acuminate. Paleæ nearly equal in length to the glumes. A doubtful native ; mountains. 2 ft. Perenn. July. ($\frac{2}{3}$) *E. B.* 1. 2265. *E. B.* 2. 83. *H. & Arn.* 533. *Bab.* 390. *Lind.* 301.

P. arenarium. *Sea Cat's-tail-grass.* **Fig. 1484.**
Panicle ovate, elongated. Glumes lanceolate, thrice as long as the paleæ. Sandy shores. 6 in.–1 ft. Ann. June. ($\frac{2}{3}$) *E. B.* 1. 222. *E. B.* 2. 84. *H. & Arn.* 533. *Bab.* 391. *Lind.* 300.

Genus 7. Lagurus.

L. ovatus. *Hare's-tail-grass.* **Fig. 1485.**
Panicle obovate. Glumes with a long subulate point, fringed with long hairs. Sandy shores ; Guernsey. 1 ft. Ann. June. White. ($\frac{2}{3}$) *E. B.* 1. 1334. *E. B.* 2. 90. *H. & Arn.* 534. *Bab.* 396. *Lind.* 299.

Genus 8. Milium.

M. effusum. *Millet-grass.* **Fig. 1486.**
Panicle loose and spreading. Seed covered with the hardened paleæ. Damp woods. 2 ft. Perenn. June. ($\frac{2}{3}$) *E. B.* 1. 1106. *E. B.* 2. 93. *H. & Arn.* 534. *Bab.* 393. *Lind.* 301.

Genus 9. Gastridium.

G. lendigerum. *Nit-grass.* **Fig. 1487.**
Panicle contracted. Glumes lanceolate-acuminate. Awns twice as long as the calyx. Fields near the sea. 1 ft. Ann. Aug. ($\frac{2}{3}$) *E. B.* 1. 1107. *E. B.* 2. 94. *H. & Arn.* 534. *Bab.* 396. *Lind.* 302.

Genus 10. Stipa.

S. pinnata. *Feather-grass.* **Fig. 1488.**
Leaves rigid, setaceous. Awns very long, feathered. A doubtful native. 1 ft. Perenn. June. ($\frac{1}{2}$) *E. B.* 1. 1356. *H. & Arn.* 535. *Bab.* 393. *Lind.* 302.

Genus 11. Polypogon.

P. monspeliensis. *Annual Beard-grass.* **Fig. 1489.**
Panicle dense, lobed. Glumes rough, the awns thrice as long. 2 ft. Ann. June–Aug. Pinkish. ($\frac{2}{3}$) *E. B.* 1. 1704. *E. B.* 2. 91. *H. & Arn.* 535. *Bab.* 396. *Lind.* 302.

P. littoralis. *Perennial Beard-grass.* **Fig. 1490.**
Panicle lobed. Glumes nearly smooth ; awns about equal in length. Salt marshes. 1–2 ft. Perenn. July. Pinkish. ($\frac{2}{3}$) *E. B.* 1. 1251. *E. B.* 2. 92. *H. & Arn.* 535. *Bab.* 396. *Lind.* 302.

Genus 12. CALAMAGROSTIS.

C. EPIGEJOS. *Wood-reed.* **Fig. 1491.**
Panicle erect, close. Spikelets crowded, unilateral. Outer palea with an awn from the middle. Moist places. 3–5 ft. Perenn. June. ($\frac{1}{2}$) *E. B.* 1. 403. *E. B.* 2. 168. *H. & Arn.* 536. *Bab.* 394. *Lind.* 304.

C. LANCEOLATA. *Small-reed.* **Fig. 1492.**
Panicle erect, loose; spikelets spreading. Outer palea with a short terminal awn. Moist places. 3–4 ft. Perenn. June. Purplish. ($\frac{1}{2}$) *E. B.* 1. 2159. *E. B.* 2. 169. *H. & Arn.* 536. *Bab.* 394. *Lind.* 304.

C. STRICTA. *Close-reed.* **Fig. 1493.**
Panicle erect, close. Lower palea deeply notched, with an awn from below the middle. Bogs; rare. $1\frac{1}{2}$–3 ft. Perenn. June and July. Purplish. ($\frac{2}{3}$) *E. B.* 1. 2160. *E. B.* 2. 170. *H. & Arn.* 536. *Bab.* 394. *Lind.* 304.

Genus 13. AGROSTIS.

A. SPICA-VENTI. *Silky Bent-grass.* **Fig. 1494.**
Panicle spreading. Glumes smaller than the paleæ. Outer palea with a long straight awn. Sandy fields. 2–3 ft. Ann. July. Pinkish. ($\frac{2}{3}$) *E. B.* 1. 951. *E. B.* 2. 95. *H. & Arn.* 538. *Bab.* 394. *Lind.* 304.

A. CANINA. *Brown Bent-grass.* **Fig. 1495.**
Panicle spreading, elongated. Awn short, bent. Inner palea minute. Damp fields. 1–2 ft. Perenn. June and July. Purplish. ($\frac{2}{3}$) *E. B.* 1. 1856. *E. B.* 2. 96. *H. & Arn.* 538. *Bab.* 395. *Lind.* 303.

A. SETACEA. *Bristle-leaved Bent-grass.* **Fig. 1496.**
Branches of the panicle short, few-flowered. Outer palea with a long bent awn from the base. Leaves setaceous. Turfy heaths. 1–2 ft. Perenn. July and Aug. Pinkish. ($\frac{2}{3}$) *E. B.* 1. 1188. *E. B.* 2. 92. *H. & Arn.* 537. *Bab.* 395. *Lind.* 303.

A. VULGARIS. *Fine Bent-grass.* **Fig. 1497.**
Branches of the panicle spreading. Glumes nearly equal. Ligule very short. Pastures. 1–$1\frac{1}{2}$ ft. Perenn. Aug. Pinkish. ($\frac{2}{3}$) *E. B.* 1. 1671. *E. B.* 2. 98. *H. & Arn.* 538. *Bab.* 395. *Lind.* 303.

A. ALBA. *Marsh Bent-grass.* **Fig. 1498.**
Branches of the panicle crowded, rough. Glumes bristly on the keel, nearly equal. Ligule long, acute. 1–2 ft. Perenn. July. Pinkish. ($\frac{2}{3}$) *E. B.* 1. 1189. *E. B.* 2. 99. *H. & Arn.* 538. *Bab.* 395. *Lind.* 303.

A. STOLONIFERA. *Fiorin-grass.* **Fig. 1499.**
A variety of *alba.* Stems with long prostrate scions. Pastures. 2 ft. Perenn. July. Light green. ($\frac{2}{3}$) *E. B.* 1. 1532. *E. B.* 2. 99*. *H. & Arn.* 539. *Bab.* 395. *Lind.* 304.

Genus 14. CATABROSA.

C. AQUATICA. *Water Whorl-grass.* **Fig. 1500.**
Panicle with whorled branches. Paleæ longer than the glumes. Leaves linear, flat, sometimes floating. Wet places. 3 in.–2 ft. Perenn. May and June. Purplish. ($\frac{2}{3}$) *E. B.* 1. 1557. *E. B.* 2. 110. *H. & Arn.* 539. *Bab.* 405. *Lind.* 306.

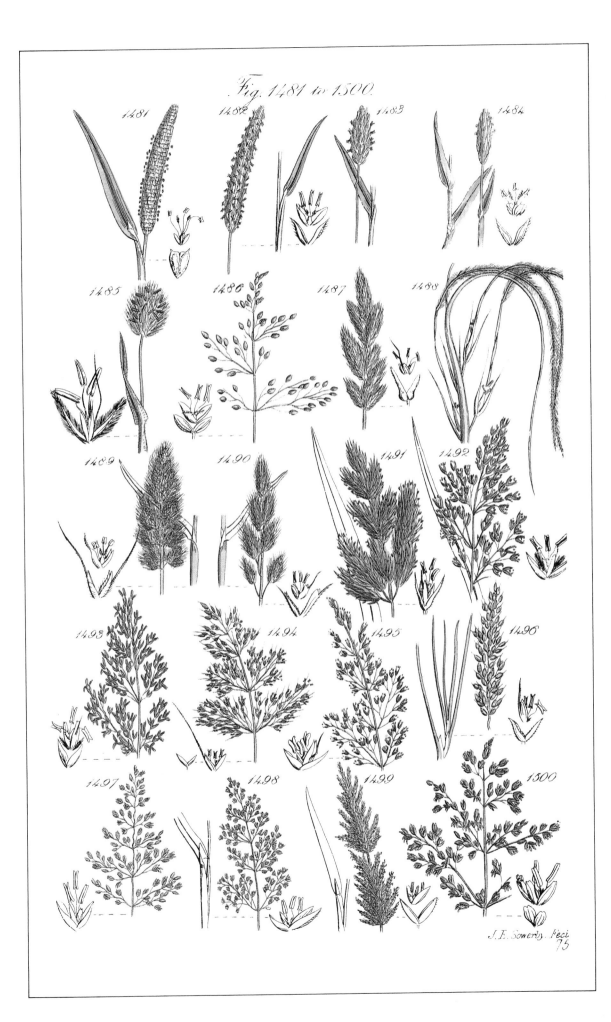

Fig. 1481 to 1500.

1481 1482 1483 1484

1485 1486 1487 1488

1489 1490 1491 1492

1493 1494 1495 1496

1497 1498 1499 1500

J. E. Sowerby, feci.
75

Genus 15. Aira.

A. cæspitosa. *Turfy Hair-grass.* **Fig. 1501.**
Panicle spreading. Paleæ as long as the glumes, hairy at the base. Awn short, from the bottom of the outer palea. Leaves flat. Pastures. 1–3 ft. Perenn. July. Purple. ($\frac{2}{3}$) *E. B.* 1. 1453. *E. B.* 2. 104. *H. & Arn.* 540. *Bab.* 397. *Lind.* 308.

A. alpina. *Smooth Alpine Hair-grass.* **Fig. 1502.**
Panicle rather close, smooth. Paleæ nearly as long as the glumes, hairy at the base. Awn short, from the top of the outer palea. Mountains. 1 ft. Perenn. June and July. Green. ($\frac{2}{3}$) *E. B.* 1. 2102. *E. B.* 2. 105. *H. & Arn.* 541. *Bab.* 397. *Lind.* 308.

A. flexuosa. *Waved Hair-grass.* **Fig. 1503.**
Panicle spreading, 3-forked, the branches wavy. Paleæ the length of the glumes, acute. Awn from the middle of the outer palea. Leaves bristle-shaped. Heaths. 1–2 ft. Perenn. July. Pinkish. ($\frac{2}{3}$) *E. B.* 1. 1519. *E. B.* 2. 106. *H. & Arn.* 541. *Bab.* 397. *Lind.* 308.

A. canescens. *Grey Hair-grass.* **Fig. 1504.**
Panicle rather dense. Paleæ shorter than the glumes. Awn club-shaped. Leaves bristle-shaped. Sandy fields near the sea. 1–2 ft. Perenn. July and Aug. Green; anthers purple. ($\frac{2}{3}$) *E. B.* 1. 1190. *E. B.* 2. 107. *H. & Arn.* 541. *Bab.* 397. *Lind.* 308.

A. præcox. *Early Hair-grass.* **Fig. 1505.**
Panicle close, oblong, few-flowered. Awn long, from near the base of the palea. Dry ground. 1–4 in. Ann. June. Pale green. ($\frac{2}{3}$) *E. B.* 1. 1296. *E. B.* 2. 108. *H. & Arn.* 542. *Bab.* 398. *Lind.* 308.

A. caryophyllea. *Silver Hair-grass.* **Fig. 1506.**
Panicle rather spreading, its branches ternate. Paleæ shorter than the glumes. Awn very long, from the middle of the palea. Leaves bristle-shaped. Hill-pastures. 6–9 in. Perenn. June. Silvery-grey. ($\frac{2}{3}$) *E. B.* 1. 812. *E. B.* 2. 109. *H. & Arn.* 541. *Bab.* 398. *Lind.* 308.

Genus 16. Melica.

M. cærulea. *Purple Melic-grass.* **Fig. 1507.**
Paleæ acute, awnless. Panicle close, erect, compound. Stems rigid. Heaths. 6 in.–2 ft. Perenn. Aug. Purplish. ($\frac{2}{3}$) *E. B.* 1. 750. *E. B.* 2. 117. *H. & Arn.* 542. *Bab.* 400. *Lind.* 307.

M. uniflora. *Wood Melic-grass.* **Fig. 1508.**
Panicle close, drooping to one side, its branches very slender. Spikelets 1-flowered. Shady woods. 1–2 ft. Perenn. May–July. Purple. ($\frac{2}{3}$) *E. B.* 1. 1058. *E. B.* 2. 115. *H. & Arn.* 543. *Bab.* 400. *Lind.* 307.

M. nutans. *Mountain Melic-grass.* **Fig. 1509.**
Panicle close, leaning to one side. Spikelets 2-flowered. Mountain woods; rare. 1–2 feet. Perenn. May and June. Purple. ($\frac{2}{3}$) *E. B.* 1. 1059. *E. B.* 2. 116. *Bab.* 400. *Lind.* 307.

Genus 17. Holcus.

H. lanatus. *Soft-grass.* **Fig. 1510.**
Glumes woolly, rather blunt. Root tufted. Leaves soft and woolly. Meadows; common. 1–1½ ft. Perenn. June. Pinkish. ($\frac{2}{3}$) *E. B.* 1. 1169. *E. B.* 2. 111. *H. & Arn.* 543. *Bab.* 396. *Lind.* 305.

Fig. 1501 to 1520.

J. E. Sowerby Fecit.

H. MOLLIS. *Creeping Soft-grass.* **Fig. 1511.**
Glumes partly naked, acuminated. Root creeping. Leaves woolly.
Pastures; common. 6 in.–1 ft. Perenn. July. Pinkish. ($\frac{2}{3}$) *E. B.* 1.
1170. *E. B.* 2. 112. *H. & Arn.* 543. *Bab.* 396. *Lind.* 305.

Genus 18. ARRHENATHERUM.

A. AVENACEUM. *Oat-grass.* **Fig. 1512.**
Panicle long. Leaves flat. Hedges and way-sides; frequent. 3 ft.
Perenn. June. Pinkish or green. ($\frac{2}{3}$) *E. B.* 1. 813. *E. B.* 2. 113.
H. & Arn. 544. *Bab.* 399. *Lind.* 305.

Genus 19. HIEROCHLOE.

H. BOREALIS. *Holy-grass.* **Fig. 1513.**
Panicle erect, raceme-like. Paleæ shorter than the glumes, awnless.
Leaves flat. Root creeping. 1 ft. Perenn. May. Purplish. ($\frac{2}{3}$)
E. B. Supp. 2641. *E. B.* 2. 113*. *H. & Arn.* 544. *Bab.* 390. *Lind.*
306.

Genus 20. KŒLERIA.

K. CRISTATA. *Crested Hair-grass.* **Fig. 1514.**
Panicle spiked, interrupted below. Awn short, from the bottom of
the outer palea. Dry pastures. 8 in.–1 ft. Perenn. July and Aug.
Green. ($\frac{2}{3}$) *E. B.* 1. 648. *E. B.* 2. 103. *H. & Arn.* 545. *Bab.* 399.
Lind. 307.

Genus 21. SESLERIA.

S. CÆRULEA. *Blue Moor-grass.* **Fig. 1515.**
Panicle ovate-oblong, imbricated. Outer palea jagged with four
teeth. Plant glaucous. Mountains. 1 ft. Perenn. May and June.
Bluish. ($\frac{2}{3}$) *E. B.* 1. 1613. *E. B.* 2. 118. *H. & Arn.* 545. *Bab.*
392. *Lind.* 309.

Genus 22. PANICUM.

P. CRUS-GALLI. *Panick-grass.* **Fig. 1516.**
Panicle bristly. Leaves without ligules. Fields; naturalized?
2 ft. Ann. July. ($\frac{2}{3}$) *E. B.* 1. 876. *E. B.* 2. 102. *H. & Arn.*
546. *Bab.* 388. *Lind.* 305.

Genus 23. SETARIA.

S. VERTICILLATA. *Rough Panick-grass.* **Fig. 1517.**
Panicle spiked, lobed, with whorled branches. Bristles few, with
reversed teeth. Fields; naturalized? 2 ft. Ann. July. ($\frac{2}{3}$) *E. B.*
1. 874. *E. B.* 2. 100. *H. & Arn.* 547. *Bab.* 388. *Lind.* 309.

S. VIRIDIS. *Green Panick-grass.* **Fig. 1518.**
Panicle spiked, cylindrical. Bristles many, with erect teeth.
Fields; naturalized? 1 ft. Ann. July. ($\frac{2}{3}$) *E. B.* 1. 875. *E. B.*
2. 101. *H. & Arn.* 547. *Bab.* 388. *Lind.* 309.

Genus 24. POA.

P. AQUATICA. *Reed Meadow-grass.* **Fig. 1519.**
Panicle upright, much branched, spreading. Spikelets linear, with
5–10 florets. Ditches. 4–6 ft. Perenn. May–Aug. Green. ($\frac{1}{2}$)
E. B. 1. 1315. *E. B.* 2. 120. *H. & Arn.* 548. *Bab.* 403. *Lind.* 316.

P. DISTANS. *Reflexed Meadow-grass.* **Fig. 1520.**
Panicle branched, lax, the branches at length reflexed. Florets 5;
root not creeping. 2 ft. Perenn. July–Oct. Pinkish. ($\frac{2}{3}$) *E. B.*
1. 986. *E. B.* 2. 121. *H. & Arn.* 549. *Bab.* 404. *Lind.* 318.

153

P. MARITIMA. *Sea Meadow-grass.* **Fig. 1521.**
Panicle branched, rather close. Florets 5–10, cylindrical, 5-ribbed. Root creeping. Leaves involute. Salt marshes. 8 in.–1 ft. Perenn. July–Oct. ($\frac{2}{3}$) *E. B.* 1. 1140. *E. B.* 2. 122. *H. & Arn.* 549. *Bab.* 404. *Lind.* 315.

P. PROCUMBENS. *Procumbent Meadow-grass.* **Fig. 1522.**
Stem procumbent. Panicle lanceolate; the branches rough. Flowers close, pointing one way. Florets 4 or 5, 5-ribbed. Salt marshes. 6–8 in. Ann. July and Aug. ($\frac{2}{3}$) *E. B.* 1. 532. *E. B.* 2. 123. *H. & Arn.* 550. *Bab.* 405. *Lind.* 316.

P. RIGIDA. *Hard Meadow-grass.* **Fig. 1523.**
Stems very rigid. Panicle lanceolate; the branches smooth. Flowers dense, pointing one way. Florets about 7, without ribs. Walls and dry ground. 4–6 in. Ann. June. ($\frac{2}{3}$) *E. B.* 1. 1371. *E. B.* 2. 124. *H. & Arn.* 550. *Bab.* 405. *Lind.* 316.

P. COMPRESSA. *Flat-stalked Meadow-grass.* **Fig. 1524.**
Panicle condensed; the branches leaning one way. Florets in ovate spikelets. Stem flattened. Dry places. 6–8 in. Perenn. June–Sept. ($\frac{2}{3}$) *E. B.* 1. 365. *E. B.* 2. 125. *H. & Arn.* 551. *Bab.* 402. *Lind.* 316.

P. ALPINA. *Alpine Meadow-grass.* **Fig. 1525.**
Panicle loose. Florets ovate, 3- or 4-flowered. Upper sheath longer than its leaf; ligule long, pointed. Mountains. 6–8 in. Perenn. July and Aug. ($\frac{2}{3}$) *E. B.* 1. 1003. *E. B.* 2. 126. *H. & Arn.* 552. *Bab.* 401. *Lind.* 316.

P. LAXA. *Wavy Meadow-grass.* **Fig. 1526.**
Panicle zigzag, slightly drooping. Florets 3–4, connected by a web, in ovate spikelets. Grampians. 6–8 in. Perenn. July. ($\frac{2}{3}$) *E. B.* 1. 1123. *E. B.* 2. 127. *H. & Arn.* 553. *Bab.* 401. *Lind.* 316.

P. BULBOSA. *Bulbous Meadow-grass.* **Fig. 1527.**
Panicle slightly zigzag. Florets 4, connected by a web. Leaves finely serrated. Stems bulbous at the base. Sandy ground. 6–8 in. Perenn. April and May. ($\frac{2}{3}$) *E. B.* 1. 1071. *E. B.* 2. 128. *H. & Arn.* 552. *Bab.* 400. *Lind.* 317.

P. TRIVIALIS. *Rough Meadow-grass.* **Fig. 1528.**
Panicle spreading. Florets 3, connected by a web. Stem and leaves roughish. Ligules lanceolate. Root fibrous. Meadows; abundant. 1–2 ft. Perenn. June. ($\frac{2}{3}$) *E. B.* 1. 1072. *E. B.* 2. 129. *H. & Arn.* 552. *Bab.* 402. *Lind.* 317.

P. PRATENSIS. *Smooth Meadow-grass.* **Fig. 1529.**
Panicle spreading. Florets usually 4, connected by a web. Stem and leaves smooth. Ligules short and blunt. Root creeping. Plant sometimes glaucous. 1–2 ft. Meadows; abundant. Perenn. June. ($\frac{2}{3}$) *E. B.* 1. 1073. *E. B.* 2. 129*. *H. & Arn.* 551. *Bab.* 402. *Lind.* 317.

P. ANNUA. *Annual Meadow-grass.* **Fig. 1530.**
Panicle widely spreading. Spikelets ovate, 5-flowered. Stems oblique, compressed. Root fibrous. Waste ground; abundant. 2–10 in. Ann. March–Nov. ($\frac{2}{3}$) *E. B.* 1. 1141. *E. B.* 2. 131. *H. & Arn.* 554. *Bab.* 400. *Lind.* 317.

P. glauca. *Glaucous Meadow-grass.* **Fig. 1531.**
Panicle spreading. Spikelets ovate, 2–3-flowered, hairy at the base.
Ligules of the lower leaves very short and blunt. Mountains. 1–2 ft.
Perenn. June. ($\frac{2}{3}$) *E. B.* 1. 1720. *E. B.* 2. 132. *H. & Arn.* 553.
Lind. 317.

P. cæsia. **Fig. 1532.**
A variety of *glauca.* Leaves broad, blunt. Florets about 5. Mountain pastures. 1–2 ft. Perenn. June. ($\frac{2}{3}$) *E. B.* 1. 1719. *E. B.* 2.
133. *H. & Arn.* 552? *Bab.* 401. *Lind.* 317.

P. nemoralis. *Wood Meadow-grass.* **Fig. 1533.**
Panicle spreading; the branches waved, hair-like. Florets 3, in
lanceolate spikelets. Glumes 3-ribbed. Ligules short, notched. Woods.
1½–3 ft. Perenn. July and Aug. ($\frac{2}{3}$) *E. B.* 1. 1265. *E. B.* 2. 134.
H. & Arn. 553. *Bab.* 401. *Lind.* 317.

P. borreri. *Borrer's Meadow-grass.* **Fig. 1534.**
Panicle spreading, in fruit ascending. Outer palea with a minute
point formed of the midrib. Leaves flat. Salt marshes. 6–8 in.
Perenn.? July. ($\frac{2}{3}$) *E. B. Supp.* 2797. *H. & Arn.* 549. *Bab.* 404.

P. fluitans. *Sweet-grass.* **Fig. 1535.**
Panicle nearly erect, slightly branched. Spikelets linear-oblong, of
7–12 florets. Leaves folded on the midrib. Ditches and pool-margins.
1–2 ft. Perenn. June–Aug. ($\frac{2}{3}$) *E. B.* 1. 1520. *E. B.* 2. 119.
H. & Arn. 548. *Bab.* 403. *Lind.* 315.

P. loliacea. *Wheat Meadow-grass.* **Fig. 1536.**
Spikelets linear-oblong, of 8–12 florets, alternate, solitary; footstalks
very short. Lower palea with distinct marginal veins. Sandy shores.
6 in. Ann. June. ($\frac{2}{3}$) *E. B.* 1. 221. *E. B.* 2. 181. *H. & Arn.*
550. *Bab.* 405. *Lind.* 297.

Genus 25. Triodia.

T. decumbens. *Heath-grass.* **Fig. 1537.**
Panicle simple, condensed, erect. Florets 4, in an ovate spikelet the
length of the calyx. Plant rigid, decumbent. Moors. 8 in. Perenn.
July. Pinkish. ($\frac{2}{3}$) *E. B.* 1. 792. *E. B.* 2. 135. *H. & Arn.* 554.
Bab. 399. *Lind.* 311.

Genus 26. Briza.

B. media. *Quaking-grass.* **Fig. 1538.**
Spikelets broadly ovate, on slender pendent branches; glumes shorter
than the lower florets. Ligule short. Downs; common. 1 ft. Perenn.
June. Purplish. ($\frac{2}{3}$) *E. B.* 1. 340. *E. B.* 2. 137. *H. & Arn.* 555.
Bab. 405. *Lind.* 315.

B. minor. *Smaller Quaking-grass.* **Fig. 1539.**
Spikelets triangular; glumes longer than the florets. Ligule elongated, acute. Fields; rare. 1 ft. Ann. July. Green. ($\frac{2}{3}$) *E. B.* 1.
1316. *E. B.* 2. 136. *H. & Arn.* 555. *Bab.* 405. *Lind.* 315.

Genus 27. Dactylis.

D. glomerata. *Cock's-foot-grass.* **Fig. 1540.**
Panicle distantly branched. Spikelets in dense tufts, leaning one
way. Fields. 1–2 ft. Perenn. June–Aug. ($\frac{2}{3}$) *E. B.* 1. 335.
E. B. 2. 138. *H. & Arn.* 555. *Bab.* 406. *Lind.* 310.

Fig. 1521 to 1540.

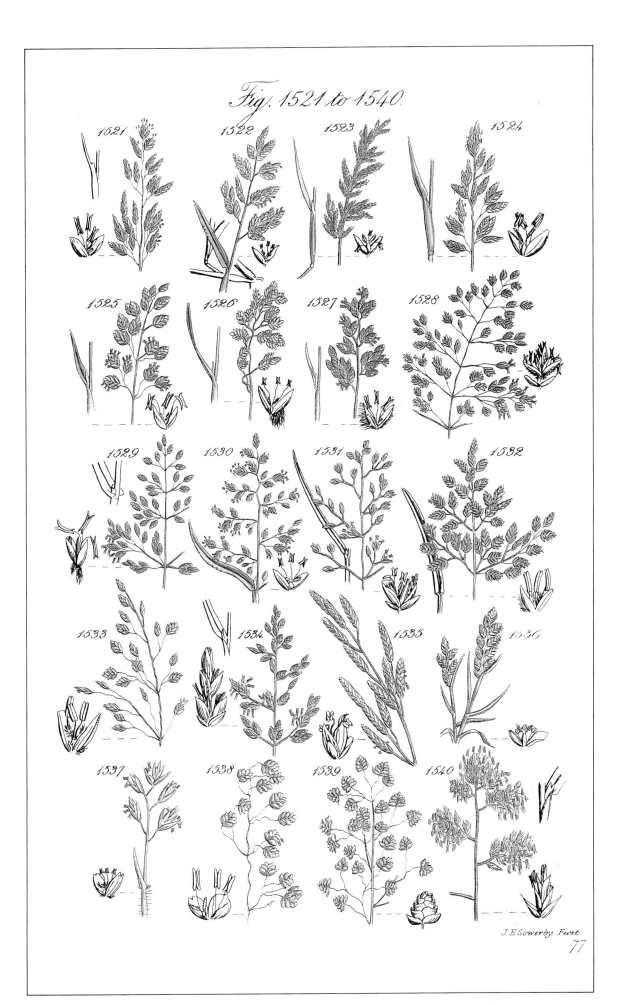

1521　1522　1523　1524
1525　1526　1527　1528
1529　1530　1531　1532
1533　1534　1535　1536
1537　1538　1539　1540

J.E Sowerby, Fecit.

Genus 28. CYNOSURUS.

C. CRISTATUS. *Dog's-tail-grass.* **Fig. 1541.**
Spike elongated, simple. Florets with a short awn. Pastures; common. 1–2 ft. Perenn. July. ($\frac{2}{3}$) *E. B.* 1. 316. *E. B.* 2. 139. *H. & Arn.* 556. *Bab.* 406. *Lind.* 306.

C. ECHINATUS. *Rough Dog's-tail-grass.* **Fig. 1542.**
Spike ovate. Florets with awns as long as the paleæ. Southern sea-shores. 6–10 in. Ann. July. ($\frac{2}{3}$) *E. B.* 1. 1333. *E. B.* 2. 140. *H. & Arn.* 556. *Bab.* 406. *Lind.* 306.

Genus 29. FESTUCA.

F. UNIGLUMIS. *Single-husked Fescue-grass.* **Fig. 1543.**
Panicle upright, nearly simple, pointing one way. Florets tapering, compressed, awned; lower glume minute. Sandy shores. 8 in.–1 ft. Bienn. June. Green. ($\frac{2}{3}$) *E. B.* 1. 1430. *E. B.* 2. 145. *H. & Arn.* 557. *Bab.* 406. *Lind.* 314.

F. BROMOIDES. *Barren Fescue-grass.* **Fig. 1544.**
Panicle upright, pointing one way. Florets shorter than their awns, rough at the top. Upper half of stem leafless. Leaves bristle-shaped. Dry ground. 6–8 in. Ann. July. ($\frac{2}{3}$) *E. B.* 1. 1411. *E. B.* 2. 144. *H. & Arn.* 557. *Bab.* 406. *Lind.* 315.

F. MYURUS. *Wall Fescue-grass.* **Fig. 1545.**
A variety of *bromoides.* Panicle drooping one way. Stem leafy to the summit. Walls and dry ground. 6–8 in. Ann. June and July. ($\frac{2}{3}$) *E. B.* 1. 1412. *E. B.* 2. 144*. *H. & Arn.* 557. *Bab.* 406. *Lind.* 314.

F. OVINA. *Sheep's Fescue-grass.* **Fig. 1546.**
Panicle close, pointing one way. Florets roundish, smooth at the base. Stem square. Leaves bristle-shaped, rough. Dry pastures; abundant. 6–8 in. Perenn. June. ($\frac{2}{3}$) *E. B.* 1. 585. *E. B.* 2. 141. *H. & Arn.* 557. *Bab.* 407. *Lind.* 313.

F. CÆSIA. **Fig. 1547.**
A variety of *ovina.* Stems many-angled, leaves glaucous. Pastures. 10 in.–1 ft. Perenn. June and July. ($\frac{2}{3}$) *E. B.* 1. 1917. *E. B.* 2. 141*. *H. & Arn.* 557. *Bab.* 407. *Lind.* 315.

F. VIVIPARA. **Fig. 1548.**
A variety of *ovina.* Flowers viviparous. Leaves smooth and long. Mountains. 6–8 in. Perenn. July. ($\frac{2}{3}$) *E. B.* 1. 1355. *E. B.* 2. 141**. *H. & Arn.* 557. *Bab.* 407. *Lind.* 313.

F. DURIUSCULA. *Hard Fescue-grass.* **Fig. 1549.**
Panicle spreading, pointing one way. Florets about 6, cylindrical, longer than their awns. Stem leaves flat. Pastures. 1 ft. Perenn. June and July. ($\frac{2}{3}$) *E. B.* 1. 470. *E. B.* 2. 142. *H. & Arn.* 557. *Bab.* 407. *Lind.* 314.

F. RUBRA. *Creeping Fescue-grass.* **Fig. 1550.**
A variety of *duriuscula.* Leaves downy. Root creeping. Sandy shores. 1 ft. Perenn. July. Reddish. ($\frac{2}{3}$) *E. B.* 1. 2056. *E. B.* 2. 143. *H. & Arn.* 558. *Bab.* 407. *Lind* 314.

Fig. 1541 to 1560.

J. E. Sowerby, F.

F. GIGANTEA. *Giant Fescue-grass.* **Fig. 1551.**
Panicle drooping, twice compound, spreading. Florets 3–6, ovate-lanceolate, shorter than the awns. Shady places. 3–4 ft. Perenn. July and Aug. ($\frac{1}{2}$) *E. B.* 1. 1820. *E. B.* 2. 146. *H. & Arn.* 559. *Bab.* 407. *Lind.* 314.

F. TRIFLORA. **Fig. 1552.**
A variety of *gigantea.* Florets about 3. Leaves narrower. Woods. 2 ft. Perenn. July and Aug. ($\frac{1}{2}$) *E. B.* 1. 1918. *E. B.* 2. 146*. *H. & Arn.* 560. *Bab.* 408. *Lind.* 314.

F. CALAMARIA. *Reed Fescue-grass.* **Fig. 1553.**
Panicle repeatedly branched, spreading, erect. Florets 2–5, oblong, cylindrical, pointed. Moist woods. 3 ft. Perenn. July. Purplish. ($\frac{2}{3}$) *E. B.* 1. 1005. *E. B.* 2. 147. *H. & Arn.* 558. *Bab.* 407. *Lind.* 313.

F. DECIDUA. **Fig. 1554.**
A variety of *calamaria.* Spikelets of 2–3 florets. Woods. 1–2 ft. Perenn. July. ($\frac{2}{3}$) *E. B.* 1. 2266. *E. B.* 2. 147*. *H. & Arn.* 558. *Bab.* 407. *Lind.* 313.

F. PRATENSIS. *Meadow Fescue-grass.* **Fig. 1555.**
Panicle nearly erect, loose, pointing to one side. Spikelets linear, compressed. Meadows. 2 ft. Perenn. June. ($\frac{2}{3}$) *E. B.* 1. 1592. *E. B.* 2. 148. *H. & Arn.* 559. *Bab.* 408. *Lind.* 312.

F. LOLIACEA. *Spiked Fescue-grass.* **Fig. 1556.**
Spike 2-ranked, drooping. Spikelets linear-oblong. Florets without awns. Pastures. 2 ft. Perenn. July. ($\frac{2}{3}$) *E. B.* 1. 1821. *E. B.* 2. 150. *H. & Arn.* 559. *Bab.* 408. *Lind.* 313.

F. ELATIOR. *Tall Fescue-grass.* **Fig. 1557.**
Panicle drooping, spreading, much branched. Florets cylindrical, awned. Moist pastures. 3–5 ft. Perenn. July. ($\frac{1}{2}$) *E. B.* 1. 1593. *E. B.* 2. 149. *H. & Arn.* 559. *Bab.* 408. *Lind.* 313.

Genus 30. BROMUS.

B. ERECTUS. *Upright Brome-grass.* **Fig. 1558.**
Panicle erect, little-branched. Spikelets linear-lanceolate. Florets numerous, remote, compressed. Awns shorter than the florets. Root-leaves very narrow. Sandy pastures. 2–3 ft. Perenn. July. ($\frac{1}{2}$) *E. B.* 1. 471. *E. B.* 2. 157. *H. & Arn.* 560. *Bab.* 408. *Lind.* 312.

B. ASPER. *Hairy Brome-grass.* **Fig. 1559.**
Panicle drooping, branched. Spikelets linear-oblong. Florets cylindrical, rather distant. Awns shorter than the florets. Lower leaves hairy. Woods. 4–6 ft. Ann. July and Aug. ($\frac{1}{2}$) *E. B.* 1. 1172. *E. B.* 2. 158. *H. & Arn.* 560. *Bab.* 409. *Lind.* 312.

B. STERILIS. *Barren Brome-grass.* **Fig. 1560.**
Panicle drooping, usually simple. Spikelets linear-lanceolate. Awns longer than the florets. Leaves downy. Fields. 2 ft. Ann. June and July. ($\frac{1}{2}$) *E. B.* 1. 1030. *E. B.* 2. 159. *H. & Arn.* 561. *Bab.* 409. *Lind.* 312.

B. DIANDRUS. *Upright Annual Brome-grass.*   **Fig. 1561.**
Panicle upright, spreading, slightly branched. Florets with only 2 stamens. Dry places. 1–2 ft. Ann. June. ($\frac{1}{2}$) *E. B.* 1. 1006. *E. B.* 2. 160. *H. & Arn.* 561. *Bab.* 409. *Lind.* 312.

B. MAXIMUS. *Great Brome-grass.*   **Fig. 1562.**
Panicle erect, lax, drooping. Spikelets lanceolate, downy. Awns two or three times the length of the glumes. Jersey. 6 in.–2 ft. Ann. June and July. ($\frac{1}{2}$) *E. B. Supp.* 2820. *H. & Arn.* 561. *Bab.* 409.

B. SECALINUS. *Rye Brome-grass.*   **Fig. 1563.**
Panicle spreading, little-branched. Spikelets ovate, compressed, with about 10 florets. Awns shorter than the florets. Fields. 2–3 ft. Ann. July–Sept. ($\frac{1}{2}$) *E. B.* 1. 1171. *E. B.* 2. 151. *H. & Arn.* 562. *Bab.* 409. *Lind.* 311.

B. VELUTINUS.   **Fig. 1564.**
A variety of *Secalinus.* Panicle nearly simple. Spikelets downy. Fields. 2 ft. Ann. July–Sept. ($\frac{1}{2}$) *E. B.* 1. 1884. *E. B.* 2. 152. *H. & Arn.* 562. *Bab.* 409. *Lind.* 311.

B. RACEMOSUS. *Smooth Brome-grass.*   **Fig. 1565.**
Panicle nearly erect, simple. Spikelets ovate-oblong, with 6–10 smooth florets. Awns as long as the florets. Pastures. 2 ft. Ann. June. ($\frac{1}{2}$) *E. B.* 1. 1079. *E. B.* 2. 154. *H. & Arn.* 563. *Bab.* 410. *Lind.* 311.

B. COMMUTATUS.   **Fig. 1566.**
Panicle loose, drooping in fruit; lower peduncles often branched. Awns as long as the floret. Fields. 1–2 ft. Ann. June and July. ($\frac{1}{2}$) *E. B.* 1. 920. *E. B.* 2. 154*. *H. & Arn.* 562. *Bab.* 410. *Lind.* 311.

B. MOLLIS. *Soft Brome-grass.*   **Fig. 1567.**
Panicle erect, close, compound. Spikelets ovate. Florets depressed, ribbed, downy. Leaves hairy. Pastures and road-sides; abundant. 1–2 ft. Ann. May and June. ($\frac{1}{2}$) *E. B.* 1. 1078. *E. B.* 2. 153. *H. & Arn.* 563. *Bab.* 410. *Lind.* 311.

B. ARVENSIS. *Field Brome-grass.*   **Fig. 1568.**
Panicle spreading, drooping, compound. Spikelets lanceolate, pointed, about 8-flowered. Florets elliptical. Leaves hairy. Sea-coast. 3 ft. Ann. July and Aug. ($\frac{1}{2}$) *E. B.* 1. 1984. *E. B.* 2. 156. *H. & Arn.* 563. *Bab.* 410. *Lind.* 312.

B. SQUARROSUS. *Corn Brome-grass.*   **Fig. 1569.**
Panicle drooping, simple. Spikelets ovate-oblong, with about 12 florets. Awns spreading. Leaves downy. Corn-fields; rare. 2 ft. Ann. June and July. ($\frac{2}{3}$) *E. B.* 1. 1885. *E. B.* 2. 155. *H. & Arn.* 564. *Bab.* 411. *Lind.* 311.

Genus 31. AVENA.

A. FATUA. *Wild Oat. Haver.*   **Fig. 1570.**
Panicle erect; flowers drooping. Spikelets of about 3 florets, with long hairs at the base. Corn-fields. 3 ft. Ann. July. ($\frac{1}{2}$) *E. B.* 1. 2221. *E. B.* 2. 161. *H. & Arn.* 565. *Bab.* 398. *Lind.* 310.

A. STRIGOSA. *Bristle Oat.* **Fig. 1571.**
Panicle oblong, pointing one way. Florets 2. Outer palea with 2 straight bristles. Corn-fields. 2–3 ft. Ann. July. ($\frac{1}{2}$) *E. B.* 1. 1266. *E. B.* 2. 162. *H. & Arn.* 565. *Bab.* 398. *Lind.* 310.

A. PUBESCENS. *Downy Oat-grass.* **Fig. 1572.**
Panicle erect, nearly simple. Florets 3, scarcely longer than the glumes. Leaves downy. Chalky pastures. 1–2 ft. Perenn. June. ($\frac{1}{2}$) *E. B.* 1. 1640. *E. B.* 2. 163. *H. & Arn.* 566. *Bab.* 399. *Lind.* 308.

A. PRATENSIS. *Narrow-leaved Oat-grass.* **Fig. 1573.**
Panicle erect, simple. Florets 3–5. Leaves narrow, involute. Dry pastures. 1–1$\frac{1}{2}$ ft. Perenn. July. ($\frac{1}{2}$) *E. B.* 1. 1204. *E. B.* 2. 164. *H. & Arn.* 565. *Bab.* 398. *Lind.* 310.

A. ALPINA. *Alpine Oat-grass.* **Fig. 1574.**
Panicle erect. Florets 5, tufted with hairs beneath. Leaves flat, finely serrated. Mountains. 2–3 ft. Perenn. July. ($\frac{1}{2}$) *E. B.* 1. 2141. *E. B.* 2. 165. *H. & Arn.* 565. *Bab.* 399. *Lind.* 310.

A. PLANICULMIS. *Flat-stemmed Oat-grass.* **Fig. 1575.**
Panicle erect, compound. Spikelets erect, linear-oblong. Florets 5–7, much longer than the glumes. Mountains. 3 ft. Perenn. July. ($\frac{1}{2}$) *E. B. Supp.* 2684. *E. B.* 2. 165*. *H. & Arn.* 566. *Bab.* 399. *Lind.* 339.

A. FLAVESCENS. *Yellow Oat-grass.* **Fig. 1576.**
Panicle much-branched, spreading, erect. Glumes very unequal; florets 3. Leaves flat. Chalky fields. 1 ft. Perenn. July. ($\frac{1}{2}$) *E. B.* 1. 952. *E. B.* 2. 166. *H. & Arn.* 566. *Bab.* 398. *Lind.* 309.

Genus 32. ARUNDO.

A. PHRAGMITES. *Reed.* **Fig. 1577.**
Flowers in a loose panicle. Spikelets 5-flowered. Florets with long silky hairs at the base. Ditches and river-sides. 6–12 ft. Perenn. July. Purple. ($\frac{1}{2}$) *E. B.* 1. 401. *E. B.* 2. 167. *H. & Arn.* 567. *Bab.* 393. *Lind.* 310.

Genus 33. ELYMUS.

E. ARENARIUS. *Lyme-grass.* **Fig. 1578.**
Spike upright, close. Florets as long as the glumes. Root creeping. Sandy shores. 3–4 ft. Perenn. July. ($\frac{1}{2}$) *E. B.* 1. 1672. *E. B.* 2. 171. *H. & Arn.* 567. *Bab.* 412. *Lind.* 296.

E. GENICULATUS. *Drooping Lyme-grass.* **Fig. 1579.**
Spike bent downwards, lax. Glumes longer than the florets. Salt marshes. 3 ft. Perenn. July. ($\frac{1}{2}$) *E. B.* 1. 1586. *E. B.* 2. 172. *H. & Arn.* 568. *Bab.* 412. *Lind.* 296.

Genus 34. HORDEUM.

H. SYLVATICUM. *Wood Barley.* **Fig. 1580.**
All the glumes bristle-shaped and rough; outer glume of each spikelet half as long as the awn. Woods. 2 ft. Perenn. July and Aug. ($\frac{2}{3}$) *E. B.* 1. 1317. *E. B.* 2. 173. *H. & Arn.* 568. *Bab.* 412. *Lind.* 297.

Fig. 1561 to 1580

1561   1562   1563   1564

1565   1566   1567   1568

1569   1570   1571   1572

1573   1574   1575   1576

1577   1578   1579   1580

John E. Sowerby fecit.

H. MURINUM. *Wall Barley.* **Fig. 1581.**
Lateral glumes bristle-shaped; intermediate ones lanceolate, ciliated.
Road-sides; common. 8 in.–1 ft. Ann. June and July. ($\frac{2}{3}$)
E. B. 1. 1971. *E. B.* 2. 174. *H. & Arn.* 568. *Bab.* 412. *Lind.* 296.

H. PRATENSE. *Meadow Barley.* **Fig. 1582.**
Glumes all bristle-shaped. Outer paleæ of the middle spikelets as
long as their awns, lateral ones shorter than the awns. Moist pastures.
1–2 ft. Ann. June and July. ($\frac{2}{3}$) *E. B.* 1. 409. *E. B.* 2. 175.
H. & Arn. 568. *Bab.* 412. *Lind.* 296.

H. MARITIMUM. *Sea Barley.* **Fig. 1583.**
Inner glumes of the outer spikelets semi-ovate, the rest bristle-shaped.
Sea-side pastures. 1 ft. Ann. June and July. ($\frac{2}{3}$) *E. B.* 1. 1205.
E. B. 2. 176. *H. & Arn.* 569. *Bab.* 413. *Lind.* 296.

Genus 35. TRITICUM.

T. CRISTATUM. *Crested Wheat-grass.* **Fig. 1584.**
Spikelets closely imbricated, depressed, straight. Florets 4, awned.
Glumes elliptical, with a long terminal awn. Sea-side. 6–10 in.
Perenn. July. ($\frac{2}{3}$) *E. B.* 1. 2267. *E. B.* 2. 180. *H. & Arn.* 569.
Bab. 412. *Lind.* 297.

T. JUNCEUM. *Rushy Wheat-grass.* **Fig. 1585.**
Glaucous. Spikelets distant, 4–6-flowered. Glumes obtuse, many-
ribbed. Leaves rolled inward. Sand-dunes. 2–3 ft. Perenn. July
and Aug. ($\frac{2}{3}$) *E. B.* 1. 814. *E. B.* 2. 177. *H. & Arn.* 569. *Bab.* 412.
Lind. 298.

T. REPENS. *Couch-grass. Dog-grass.* **Fig. 1586.**
Glumes awl-shaped, acute, many-ribbed. Florets 5, the outer palea
awned or sharp-pointed. Leaves flat. Root creeping. A common
weed. 2 ft. Perenn. June–Sept. ($\frac{2}{3}$) *E. B.* 1. 909. *E. B.* 2. 178.
H. & Arn. 571. *Bab.* 411. *Lind.* 298.

T. CANINUM. *Bearded Wheat-grass.* **Fig. 1587.**
Glumes pointed, 3–5-ribbed. Florets 4, with long rough awns.
Root fibrous. Woods. 2 ft. Perenn. July. ($\frac{2}{3}$) *E. B.* 1. 1372.
E. B. 2. 179. *H. & Arn.* 571. *Bab.* 411. *Lind.* 298.

Genus 36. BRACHYPODIUM.

B. SYLVATICUM. *False Brome-grass.* **Fig. 1588.**
Spike drooping, flowers leaning one way. Awns longer than the
florets. Copses and hedge-banks. 2 ft. Perenn. June and July.
($\frac{2}{3}$) *E. B.* 1. 729. *E. B.* 2. 182. *H. & Arn.* 572. *Bab.* 411. *Lind.* 297.

B. PINNATUM. *Heath Brome-grass.* **Fig. 1589.**
Spike erect. Awns shorter than the florets. Heaths. 2 ft. Perenn.
July. ($\frac{2}{3}$) *E. B.* 1. 730. *E. B.* 2. 183. *H. & Arn.* 572. *Bab.* 411.
Lind. 297.

Genus 37. LOLIUM.

L. PERENNE. *Darnel. Rye-grass.* **Fig. 1590.**
Spikelets longer than the glumes. Florets awnless. Pastures; com-
mon. 1–2 ft. Perenn. or bienn. June and July. ($\frac{2}{3}$) *E. B.* 1. 315.
E. B. 2. 184. *H. & Arn.* 573. *Bab.* 413. *Lind.* 295.

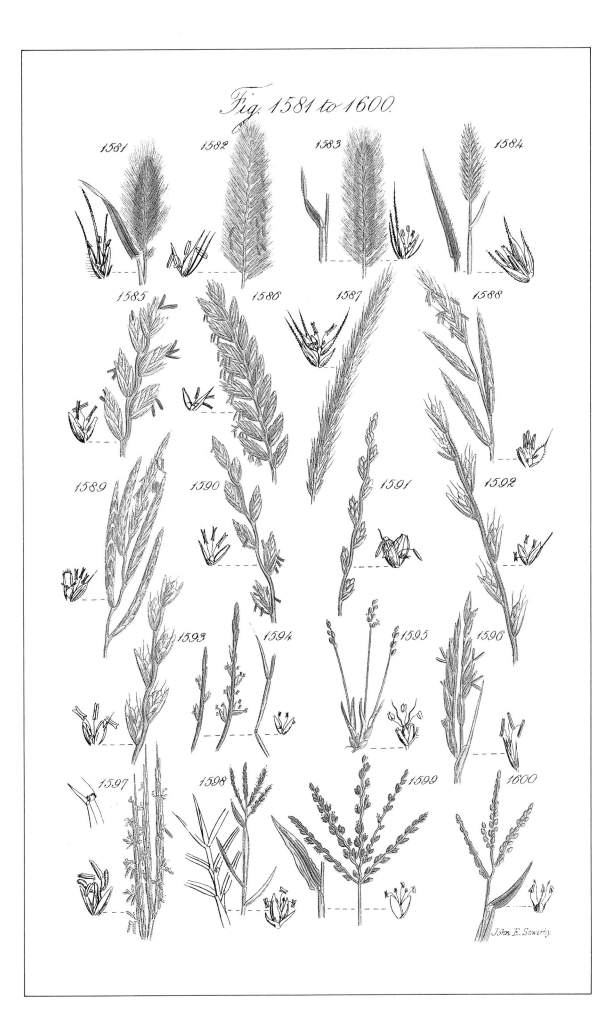

Fig. 1581 to 1600.

1581
1582
1583
1584
1585
1586
1587
1588
1589
1590
1591
1592
1593
1594
1595
1596
1597
1598
1599
1600

John E. Sowerby.

L. LINICOLA. *Annual Rye-grass.* **Fig. 1591.**
Spikelets about twice as long as the glumes. Fields; rare. Florets
slightly awned. 1–2 ft. Ann. July. ($\frac{2}{3}$) *E. B. Supp.* 2955.
H. & Arn. 573. *Bab.* 413.

L. TEMULENTUM. *Bearded Darnel.* **Fig. 1592.**
Spikelets shorter than the glumes. Florets awned. Fields. Seeds
poisonous. 2 ft. Ann. July. ($\frac{2}{3}$) *E. B.* 1. 1124. *E. B.* 2. 185.
H. & Arn. 574. *Bab.* 413. *Lind.* 295.

L. ARVENSE. **Fig. 1593.**
A variety of *temulentum.* Awns small and weak. Fields. 2 ft.
Ann. July. ($\frac{2}{3}$) *E. B.* 1. 1125. *E. B.* 2. 185*. *H. & Arn.* 573.
Bab. 413. *Lind.* 295.

Genus 38. LEPTURUS.

L. INCURVATUS. *Hard-grass.* **Fig. 1594.**
Spike round, awl-shaped. Glumes united below. Sea-coast. 4–8 in.
Ann. July–Sept. ($\frac{2}{3}$) *E. B.* 1. 760. *E. B.* 2. 186. *H. & Arn.* 574.
Bab. 413. *Lind.* 76.

Genus 39. KNAPPIA.

K. AGROSTIDEA. **Fig. 1595.**
Spikelets in 2 rows, each with a single floret. Leaves short, linear.
Sandy sea-side pastures. 2–4 in. Ann. March and April. ($\frac{2}{3}$)
E. B. 1. 1127. *E. B.* 2. 187. *H. & Arn.* 575. *Bab.* 389. *Lind.* 301.

Genus 40. SPARTINA.

S. STRICTA. *Cord-grass.* **Fig. 1596.**
Spikes 2 or 3, erect, smooth. Spikelets downy. Salt marshes. 1 ft.
Perenn. Aug. ($\frac{2}{3}$) *E. B.* 1. 380. *E. B.* 2. 190. *H. & Arn.* 575.
Bab. 389. *Lind.* 298.

S. ALTERNIFLORA. *Many-spiked Cord-grass.* **Fig. 1597.**
Spikes numerous. Stalk extending beyond the spikelets, with an
awn-like point. Salt marshes. 2 ft. Perenn. Aug. and Sept. ($\frac{2}{3}$)
E. B. Supp. 2812. *H. & Arn.* 576. *Bab.* 389. *Lind.* 339.

Genus 41. CYNODON.

C. DACTYLON. *Dog's-tooth-grass.* **Fig. 1598.**
Spikelets 3–5, digitate. Root creeping. Sandy shores. 4–8 in.
Perenn. July and Aug. ($\frac{2}{3}$) *E. B.* 1. 850. *E. B.* 2. 188. *H. & Arn.*
576. *Bab.* 389. *Lind.* 298.

Genus 42. DIGITARIA.

D. SANGUINALIS. *Hairy Finger-grass.* **Fig. 1599.**
Leaves hairy. Spikelets oblong. Stems ascending. Fields; rare.
1 ft. Ann. July and Aug. ($\frac{2}{3}$) *E. B.* 1. 849. *E. B.* 2. 189.
H. & Arn. 577. *Bab.* 388. *Lind.* 299.

D. HUMIFUSA. *Finger-grass.* **Fig. 1600.**
Leaves smooth. Spikelets ovate, downy. Stems procumbent. Fields.
6–8 in. Ann. July and Aug. ($\frac{2}{3}$) *E. B. Supp.* 2613. *E. B.* 2. 189*.
H. & Arn. 577. *Bab.* 388. *Lind.* 339.

INDEX OF LATIN NAMES.

Acer, 26.
Aceraceæ, 26.
Aceras, 124.
Achillæa, 76.
Acinos, 98.
Aconitum, 4.
Acorus, 135.
Actæa, 4.
Actinocarpus, 134.
Adonis, 1.
Adoxa, 58.
Ægopodium, 53.
Æthusa, 55.
Agrimonia, 40.
Agrostemma, 19.
Agrostis, 150.
Aira, 151.
Ajuga, 95.
Alchemilla, 40.
Alisma, 134.
Alismaceæ, 134.
Allium, 129.
Alnus, 113.
Alopecurus, 148.
Althæa, 24.
Alyssum, 10.
Amaranthaceæ, 102.
Amaranthus, 102.
Amaryllidaceæ. 127.
Ammophila, 148.
Anacharis, 122.
Anagallis, 101.
Anchusa, 85.
Andromeda, 80.
Anemone, 1.
Angelica, 55.
Antennaria, 71.
Anthemis, 75.
Anthericum, 130.
Anthoxanthum, 147.
Anthriscus, 57.
Anthyllis, 29.
Antirrhinum, 91.
Apargia, 65.
Apium, 52.
Apocynaceæ, 81.
Aquifoliaceæ, 81.
Aquilegia, 4.

Arabis, 10.
Araceæ, 135.
Araliaceæ, 58.
Arbutus, 80.
Arctium, 68.
Arctostaphylos, 80.
Arenaria, 21.
Aristolochia, 108.
Aristolochiaceæ, 108.
Armeria, 101.
Arrhenatherum, 152.
Artemisia, 70.
Arum, 135.
Arundo, 158.
Asarum, 109.
Asparagus, 128.
Asperugo, 86.
Asperula, 61.
Aster, 73.
Astragalus, 33.
Atriplex, 104.
Atropa, 86.
Avena, 157.
Azalea, 80.

Ballota, 95.
Balsaminaceæ, 28.
Barbarea, 11.
Bartsia, 89.
Bellis, 74.
Berberidaceæ, 4.
Berberis, 4.
Beta, 102.
Betonica, 97.
Betula, 112.
Betulaceæ, 112.
Bidens, 70.
Boraginaceæ, 83.
Borago, 86.
Borkhausia, 67.
Brachypodium, 160.
Brassica, 13.
Briza, 154.
Bromus, 156.
Bryonia, 46.
Buffonia, 19.
Bunium, 53.
Bupleurum, 54.

Butomaceæ, 134.
Butomus, 134.
Buxus, 111.

Cakile, 7.
Calamagrostis, 150.
Calamintha, 98.
Callitrichaceæ, 111.
Callitriche, 111.
Calluna, 79.
Caltha, 3.
Camelina, 9.
Campanula, 77.
Campanulaceæ, 77.
Caprifoliaceæ, 59.
Capsella, 7.
Cardamine, 10.
Carduus, 68.
Carex, 141.
Carlina, 70.
Carpinus, 121.
Carum, 53.
Caryophyllaceæ, 17.
Castanea, 121.
Catabrosa. 150.
Caucalis, 56.
Celastraceæ, 28.
Centaurea, 76.
Centranthus, 62.
Centunculus, 101.
Cerastium, 22.
Ceratophyllaceæ, 111.
Ceratophyllum, 111.
Chærophyllum, 57.
Cheiranthus, 12.
Chelidonium, 6.
Chenopodiaceæ, 102.
Chenopodium, 102.
Cherleria, 23.
Chlora, 82.
Chrysanthemum, 75.
Chrysocoma, 70.
Chrysosplenium, 51.
Cichorium, 68.
Cicuta, 52.
Cineraria, 74.
Circæa, 45.
Cistaceæ, 14.

162

Cladium, 138.
Clematis, 1.
Clinopodium, 98.
Cnicus, 69.
Cochlearia, 8.
Colchicum, 131.
Comarum, 39.
Compositæ, 63.
Coniferæ, 121.
Conium, 58.
Convallaria, 128.
Convolvulaceæ, 83.
Convolvulus, 83.
Conyza, 72.
Corallorhiza, 126.
Coriandrum, 58.
Cornaceæ, 58.
Cornus, 58.
Coronopus, 7.
Corrigiola, 46.
Corydalis, 6.
Corylus, 121.
Cotoneaster, 43.
Cotyledon, 47.
Crambe, 7.
Crassulaceæ, 47.
Cratægus, 43.
Crepis, 67.
Crithmum, 55.
Crocus, 127.
Cruciferæ, 7.
Cucubalus, 18.
Cucurbitaceæ, 46.
Cupuliferæ, 121.
Cuscuta, 83.
Cyclamen, 100.
Cynodon, 160.
Cynoglossum, 86.
Cynosurus, 155.
Cyperaceæ, 138.
Cyperus, 138.
Cypripedium, 126.
Cytisus, 29.

Dactylis, 154.
Daphne, 108.
Datura, 86.
Daucus, 56.
Delphinium, 4.
Dentaria, 10.
Dianthus, 17.
Digitalis, 91.
Digitaria, 160.
Dioscoreaceæ, 122.
Diotis, 70.
Dipsaceæ, 62.
Dipsacus, 62.
Doronicum, 74.
Draba, 9.
Drosera, 16.
Droseraceæ, 16.
Dryas, 37.

Echinophora, 58.

Echium, 83.
Elæagnaceæ, 112.
Elatine, 17.
Eleocharis, 139.
Eleogiton, 139.
Elymus, 158.
Elyna, 141.
Empetraceæ, 109.
Empetrum, 109.
Epilobium, 44.
Epimedium, 4.
Epipactis, 125.
Erica, 79.
Ericaceæ, 79.
Erigeron, 72.
Eriocaulon, 131.
Eriophorum, 140.
Erodium, 27.
Ervum, 34.
Eryngium, 52.
Erysimum, 12.
Erythræa, 81.
Euonymus, 28.
Eupatorium, 70.
Euphorbia, 109.
Euphorbiaceæ, 109.
Euphrasia, 90.
Exacum, 81.

Fagus, 121.
Fedia, 62.
Festuca, 155.
Fœniculum, 55.
Fragaria, 38.
Frankenia, 17.
Frankeniaceæ, 17.
Fraxinus, 81.
Fritillaria, 130.
Fumaria, 6.
Fumariaceæ, 6.

Gagea, 130.
Galanthus, 128.
Galeobdolon, 96.
Galeopsis, 96.
Galium, 60.
Gastridium, 149.
Genista, 29.
Gentiana, 82.
Gentianaceæ, 81.
Geraniaceæ, 26.
Geranium, 26.
Geum, 37.
Glaucium, 6.
Glaux, 100.
Glechoma, 97.
Gnaphalium, 71.
Goodyera, 125.
Gramineæ, 147.
Grossulariaceæ, 49.
Gymnadenia, 123.

Habenaria, 123.
Haloragaceæ, 45.

Hedera, 58.
Helianthemum, 14.
Helleborus, 4.
Helminthia, 63.
Helosciadium, 52.
Heracleum, 56.
Herminium, 124.
Herniaria, 47.
Hesperis, 13.
Hieracium, 65.
Hierochloe, 152.
Hippocrepis, 33.
Hippophaë, 112.
Hippuris, 45.
Holcus, 151.
Holosteum, 20.
Hordeum, 158.
Hottonia, 99.
Humulus, 112.
Hutchinsia, 8.
Hyacinthus, 128.
Hydrocharidaceæ, 122.
Hydrocharis, 122.
Hydrocotyle, 51.
Hyoscyamus, 86.
Hypericaceæ, 24.
Hypericum, 24.
Hypochœris, 67.

Iberis, 8.
Ilex, 81.
Illecebraceæ, 46.
Illecebrum, 47.
Impatiens, 28.
Inula, 74.
Iridaceæ, 126.
Iris, 126.
Isatis, 7.
Isnardia, 45.

Jasione, 78.
Juncaceæ, 131.
Juncaginaceæ, 134.
Juncus, 131.
Juniperus, 121.

Knappia, 160.
Kœleria, 152.
Koniga, 10.

Labiatæ, 93.
Lactuca, 64.
Lagurus, 149.
Lamium, 96.
Lapsana, 68.
Lathræa, 87.
Lathyrus, 35.
Lavatera, 24.
Leguminosæ, 28.
Lemna, 135.
Lentibulariaceæ, 99.
Leontodon, 64.
Leonurus, 96.
Lepidium, 8.
Lepturus, 160.

INDEX OF ENGLISH NAMES.

THE END.

GLOSSARY

OF

TECHNICAL TERMS EMPLOYED IN THE WORK.

Abortive.—Imperfectly developed, rudimentary.

Acuminate.—Tapering to a long point.

Acute.—Pointed.

Adnate (*Anthers*).—Continuous with the *filament*.

Alternate (*Leaves*).—Placed alternately on either side of the stem.

Amplexicaul (*Leaves*).—Embracing the stem at the base.

Articulated.—United by a joint.

Ascending (*Stem*).—Depressed towards the ground at the base and rising above.

Auricles (*Leaves*).—Ear-like lobes at the base.

Awn.—A terminal bristle.

Axil.—Place of attachment to the stem.

Axile (*Placenta*).—Attached to the centre of the seed-vessel.

Barren (*Flower*).—Producing stamens only : forming no seed.

Bifid.—Two-lobed.

Bilabiate (*Corolla*).—Two-lipped.

Bi-pinnate (*Leaves*).—Twice pinnately compound.

Bi-pinnatifid (*Leaves*).—Twice pinnately lobed.

Biternate (*Leaves*).—Twice ternately compound.

Campanulate.—Bell-shaped.

Canescent.—Covered with short whitish hairs.

Capillary.—Hair-like ; very slender.

Capitate (*Inflorescence*).—In a close head or cluster.

Ciliated.—Fringed at the margin with hairs.

Clavate.—Club-shaped.

Compound (*Leaves*).—Formed of several leaflets.

Convolute (*Leaves*).—Turned inwards at the edges.

Cordate (*Leaves*).—Heart-shaped, or with rounded lobes at the base.

Coriaceous (*Leaves*).—Tough and dry or leathery.

Corymbose (*Inflorescence*).—In a corymb, or flattened *panicle*.

Cottony.—Covered with white down.

Creeping (*Stem* or *Root*).—Running along or beneath the surface.

Crenated (*Leaves*).—Indented on the margin with rounded teeth.

Cuneate (*Leaves*).—Wedge-shaped, tapering towards the base.

Cymose (*Inflorescence*).—In a cyme. *See* Introduction.

Deciduous.—Falling when ripe or withered.

Decumbent (*Stem*).—Lying near the ground at the base. More depressed than when *Ascending*.

Decurrent (*Leaves*).—With the edges prolonged and running down the stem.

Dehiscent (*Fruit*).—Discharging its seeds.

Diadelphous (*Stamens*).—United by the filaments into two groups.

Dichotomous.—Forked, or dividing by twos.

Digitate (*Leaves*).—Leaflets radiating from the point of the stalk, as in the Horse-Chestnut.

Diœcious.—Barren and fertile flowers on separate plants.

Downy.—Covered with close soft hairs.

Elliptical.—Oval in general outline.

Emarginated.—Indented at the apex.

Entire.—Not lobed or divided.

Epigynous (*Stamens*).—Placed apparently upon the ovary.

Equitant (*Leaves*).—Flattened vertically and clasping the bud or stem in a slit at the base, as in Iris.

Fertile (*Flower*).—Producing seed ; containing perfect pistils.

Filiform.—Thread-like.

Fleshy (*Leaves*).—Thick and soft.

Fusiform (*Root*).—Spindle-shaped.

Glabrous.—Not quite smooth, but without hairs.

Glandular.—Bearing glands or small secreting organs.

Glaucous.—Whitish-green.

Hastate (*Leaves*).—With diverging horizontal lobes at the base, like a halbert blade.

Herbaceous (*Stem*).—Not woody.

Hirsute.—Densely hairy.

Hispid.—Covered with stiff hairs.

Hoary.—Covered with minute white down or hairs.

Hypogynous (*Stamens*).—Placed beneath the *ovary*.

Imbricated.—Overlapping like tiles.

Indehiscent (*Fruit*).—Not shedding its seed.

Lanceolate (*Leaves*).—Broadest below the middle and tapering towards the apex, like a Greek spear-head.

Ligulate (*Petals*).—Furnished with a limb or flattened portion.

Ligule.—A small stipule-like appendage at the base of the leaves of grasses.

Linear (*Leaves*).—Very narrow, but flat.

Linear-lanceolate.—Long and narrow, but tapering, and broadest below the middle.

Linear-oblong.—Somewhat broader than when *linear*.

Lyrate (*Leaves*).—With horizontal lobes, the terminal one largest.

Mealy.—Covered with minute white powdery down.

Membranous (*Leaves*).—Very thin and lax.

Monadelphous (*Stamens*).—United by the filaments into one group.

Monœcious.—Barren and fertile flowers distinct, but upon the same plant.

Mucronate (*Leaves*).—With the midrib projecting from the apex.

Obcordate.—Cordate, with the lobes upward.

Obovate (*Leaves*).—Egg-shaped, with the broadest part above.

Obsolete (*Calyx*.)—Rudimentary, a mere rim.

Obtuse (*Leaves*).—Blunt at the apex.

Opposite (*Leaves*).—Placed in pairs on opposite sides of the stem.

Orbicular (*Leaves*).—Circular in general outline. (*Root*).—Globular.

Oval (*Leaves*).—Oval in general outline.

Ovate (*Leaves*).—Egg-shaped, with the broadest part below.

Palmate (*Leaves*).—With finger-like lobes.

Papilionaceous (*Flowers*).—Like the Pea-flower. *See* Introduction.

Pappus.—The hairs or scales (rudimentary calyx) below the florets of Compositæ.

Parietal (*Placenta*).—Attached to the sides of the carpels.

Pectinated.—Toothed like a comb.

Pedate (*Leaves*).—Divided primarily into three, the two lateral branches forked or divided into leaflets on their inner margin only, as in Hellebore.

Pedatifid (*Leaves*).—With pedate lobes.

Pedicel.—The stalk supporting each flower on a branched flower-stem.

Peltate (*Leaves*).—With the stalk attached to the underside, as in Hydrocotyle.

Perfoliate (*Leaves*).—Base of the leaf surrounding the stem, as in Chlora.

Perigynous (*Stamens*).—Situated apparently upon the calyx.

Persistent.—Remaining attached, not deciduous.

Pilose.—Covered with long hairs.

Pinnate (*Leaves*).—Composed of a row of leaflets on each side of the stalk, as in the Rose.

Pinnatifid (*Leaves*).—Pinnately lobed.

Procumbent (*Stem*).—Lying on the ground for the greater part of its length.

Prostrate (*Stem*).—Lying close to the ground.

Pubescent.—Downy; covered with close soft hairs.

Quinate (*Leaves*).—With five diverging leaflets.

Radical.—Springing from the root.

Ray.—The outer ligulate flowers of some Compositæ.

Reniform (*Leaves*).—Kidney-shaped or very broadly cordate.

Retuse (*Leaves*).—Truncate and slightly indented at the apex.

Revolute (*Leaves*).—The margins rolled backwards.

Rotate (*Flowers*).—With the petals radiating horizontally.

Runcinate (*Leaves*).—With lateral lobes curving towards the stem.

Runners.—Creeping stems thrown out from the root.

Sagittate (*Leaves*).—With acute lobes at the base, like a barbed arrow-head.

Scape.—A flower-stalk rising from the root, without leaves.

Scions.—Runners.

Serrated (*Leaves*).—Indented on the margin with sharp teeth, like a saw.

Sessile.—Placed directly upon the stem, without stalks.

Setaceous (*Leaves*).—Very slender or bristle-like.

Setæ.—Bristly hairs.

Sinuated (*Leaves*).—With broad shallow rounded indentations on the margin.

Spatulate (*Leaves*).—Broadest at the apex, and long and tapering below.

Spinous.—Furnished with thorns or prickles.

Subulate (*Leaves*).—Awl-shaped, narrow-linear, as thick as broad.

Succulent.—Thick, soft and juicy.

Ternate (*Leaves*).—Composed of three leaflets.

Tomentose.—Cottony, or covered with thick down.

Toothed (*Leaves*).—Cut on the margin into deep teeth.

Trifid (*Leaves*).—Three-cleft.

Tri-pinnate (*Leaves*).—Thrice pinnately compound.

Tri-pinnatifid (*Leaves*).—Thrice pinnately lobed.

Urceolate (*Corolla*).—Cup-shaped, but contracted at the top.

Vittæ.—Channels filled with oil in the fruit of Umbelliferæ.

Whorled (*Leaves*).—Arranged in circles around the nodes, several together.